DATE DUE

DEMCO 128-5046

SOMETHING ABOUT THE AUTHOR

SOMETHING ABOUT THE AUTHOR

Facts and Pictures about Contemporary Authors

and Illustrators of Books for Young People

Anne Commire

VOLUME 12

GALE RESEARCH
BOOK TOWER
DETROIT, MICHIGAN
48226

Also Published by Gale

CONTEMPORARY AUTHORS:
A Bio-Bibliographical Guide to
Current Authors and Their Works
(Now Covers About 50,000 Authors)

Associate Editor: Agnes Garrett

Assistant Editor: Linda Shedd

Research Assistants: Cathy Coray,
Elisa Ann Sawchuk, Anna Deavere Smith

Library of Congress Catalog Card Number 72-27107

Copyright © 1977 by Gale Research Company. All rights reserved.

ISBN 0-8103-0072-9

GRATEFUL ACKNOWLEDGMENT

is made to the following publishers, authors, and artists, for their kind permission to reproduce copyrighted material. ■ **ABELARD-SCHUMAN.** Illustration by Charles Pickard from *Stories Told by the Aztecs* by Carleton Beals. Copyright © 1970 by Carleton Beals. Reprinted by permission of Abelard-Schuman. ■ **ABINGDON PRESS.** Illustration by Meg Wohlberg from *A Small Green Tree and a Square Brick Church* by Bernice Hogan. Copyright © 1967 by Abingdon Press./ Drawing by Jim Padgett from *Donkey Tales* by Jill Pelaez. Copyright © 1971 by Abingdon Press./ Illustration by Ati Forberg from *Josie's Handful of Quietness* by Nancy Covert Smith. Copyright © 1975 by Abingdon Press./ Drawing by Allan Eitzen from *Adventures of B.J., the Amateur Detective* by Toni Sorter. Copyright © 1975 by Abingdon Press./ Illustration by Jean Tamburine from *I Think I Will Go to the Hospital* by Jean Tamburine. Copyright © 1965 by Abingdon Press. All reprinted by permission of Abingdon Press. ■ **ADDISON-WESLEY.** Illustration by Ingrid Fetz from *Paddy's Preposterous Promises* by Julia Bristol Bischoff. Text © 1968 by Julia Bristol Bischoff. Illustration © 1968 by Ingrid Fetz./ Photo by Charles J. Belden from *Cowboys and the Songs They Sang* by S.J. Sackett. Text copyright © 1967 by Samuel J. Sackett. Musical accompaniments copyright © 1967 by Lionel Nowak./ Illustration by Victor Ambrus from *Living in a Castle* by R.J. Unstead. Copyright © 1971 by Addison-Wesley. All reprinted by Addison-Wesley Publishing Co. (Young Scott Books, W.R. Scott, Inc.) ■ **ATHENEUM PUBLISHERS.** Illustration by Ray Abel from *Cousins and Circuses* by Lucy Johnston Sypher. Copyright © 1974 by Lucy Johnston Sypher./ Illustration by Joseph Schindelman from *Unfinished Symphony* by Freda Pastor Berkowitz. Copyright © 1963 by Freda Pastor Berkowitz./ Illustration by Thomas Quirk from *The Ghost Garden* by Hila Feil. Copyright © 1976 by Hila Feil./ Illustration from *How to Make 19 Kinds of American Folk Art from Masks to TV Commercials* by Jean & Cle Kinney. Copyright © 1974 by Jean & Cle Kinney./ Illustration by Gail Owens from *Witch's Sister* by Phyllis Reynolds Naylor. Copyright © 1975 by Phyllis Reynolds Naylor./ Illustration by Douglas Tait from *Once More Upon a Totem* by Christie Harris. Text copyright © 1973 by Christie Harris. Pictures copyright © 1973 by Doug Tait. All reprinted by permission of Atheneum Publishers. ■ **BEHAVIORAL PUBLICATIONS.** Illustration by M. Jane Smyth from *Billy and Our New Baby* by Helene S. Arnstein. Copyright © 1973 by Behavioral Publications. Reprinted by permission of Human Sciences Press, a division of Behavioral Publications, Inc. ■ **A & C BLACK, LTD.** Illustration by Victor Ambrus from *Living in a Castle* by R.J. Unstead. Copyright © 1971 by A & C Black Ltd. Reprinted by permission of A & C Black, Ltd. ■ **BLACKIE & SON, LTD.** Illustration by Gervase from *Alison's Easter Adventure* by Sheila Stuart. Reprinted by permission of Blackie & Son, Ltd. ■ **THE BOBBS-MERRILL CO.** Illustrations by Laurie Anderson from *Certainly, Carrie, Cut the Cake* by Margaret and John Travers Moore. Illustrations copyright © 1971 by Laurie Anderson. Reprinted by permission of The Bobbs-Merrill Co., Inc. ■ **CURTIS BROWN, LTD.** Illustration by Victoria Chess from *Peacocks are Very Special* by Sue Alexander. Illustration copyright © 1976 by Victoria Chess. Reprinted by permission of Curtis Brown, Ltd. ■ **JONATHAN CAPE, LTD.** Illustration by Pascale Allamand from *The Pop Rooster* by Pascale Allamand. English version by Michael Bullock. Copyright © 1975 by Pascale Allamand. English version copyright © 1975 by Jonathan Cape, Ltd. Reprinted by permission of Jonathan Cape, Ltd. ■ **CAROLRHODA BOOKS, INC.** Illustration by Robert Sweetland from *Fit for a King* by Aure Sheldon. Copyright © 1974 by Carolrhoda Books, Inc. Reprinted by permission of Carolrhoda Books, Inc. ■ **CHILDRENS PRESS.** Illustration from *Botswana* by Allan Carpenter and Tom Balow. Copyright © 1973 Regensteiner Publishing Enterprises./ Illustration from *Christmas Kitten* by Janet Konkle. Copyright 1953 by Childrens Press./ Illustration from *Hubert Hippo's World* by Faith B. Lasher. Copyright © 1971 by Regensteiner Publishing Enterprises./ Illustration by Rob Sprattler from *Killer, the Outrageous Hawk* by

Illustration from *The Great Energy Search* by Elaine Israel. Reprinted by permission of American Petroleum Institute./ Cover by Bert Devito from *Kids Camping* by Aileen Paul. Reprinted by permission of Bert Devito./ Photo by Charles Philip Fox from *Come to the Circus* by Charles Philip Fox. Reprinted by permission of Charles Philip Fox./ Illustration from *The Sea Otter's Struggle* by Jane H. Bailey. Reprinted by permission of Karl W. Kenyon./ Photo from *Homes Beneath the Sea* by Boris Arnov, Jr. Reprinted by permission of Marineland of Florida.

PHOTOGRAPH CREDITS

Chester Jay Alkema: Van Dyke Studios (Grand Rapids, Mich); George Ancona: Helga Ancona; Michael J. Anton: C.S.S. Publishing Co.; Anna Rita Atene: G. Provenzano (Philadelphia, Pa.); Margaret J. Baker: B. Kingsley Tayler; Mary Gladys Baker: J. Dickie, "Tobarfuar"; Rona Beame: Pete Linzy, Ladder Co. 108; Theodore M. Bernstein: *The New York Times*; Algernon D. Black: Hugh J. Stern; Ronald G. Bliss: Mark Gale; Idella F. Bodie: H.M. Harvey; Louise Budde DeLaurentis: Bennett Studio; Dorothy Dowdell: Sirlin Studios; Dorothy Hamilton: Jerry Burney; Robert W. Hill: Fabian Bachrach; Bernhardt J. Hurwood: Wallace Driver; Helen Hull Jacobs: Dodd, Mead & Co.; Daniel Jacobson: Michigan State University Photographic Laboratory; Johanna Johnston: Dodd, Mead & Co.; James Kirkup: Daniel Kaufman; Julius Lester: David Gahr; Douglas Lord: J.A. Hewes Photographer; Rita Micklish: Reyman Photographers; Scott O'Dell : Robert C. Frampton; Victor Seroff: Joan Kennedy; Martin P. Simon: Orlin Kohli; Susan C. Smith: Walter E. Shackelford; Mary Stewart: Mark Gerson; Jean Tamburine: *Meriden Record-Journal.*

SOMETHING ABOUT THE AUTHOR

ABDUL, Raoul   1929-

PERSONAL: Born November 7, 1929, in Cleveland, Ohio; son of Hamid and Beatrice (Shreve) Abdul. *Education:* Vienna Academy of Music, Diploma, 1962; additional study at Harvard University, summer, 1966, New School for Social Research, and at music schools, including Cleveland Institute of Music, New York College of Music, and Mannes College of Music; vocal training with Alexander Kipnis, Lola Hayes, Yves Tinayre, Adolf Vogel, and others. *Home and office:* 360 West 22nd St., New York, N.Y. 10011.

CAREER: Concert and opera singer; organizer of Coffee Concerts, Harlem's first subscription series of chamber music concerts, 1958-59, and director, 1958-63; sang abroad in Marlboro Music Festival, 1956, and Vienna Music Festival, 1962; made his New York debut with John Wustman in a recital of German lieder at Carnegie Hall, 1967; has appeared in other concerts on tours in United States, Canada, Austria, Netherlands, Hungary, and Germany. Had operatic roles in first American stage productions of Karl Orff's "Die Kluge" and Darius Milhaud's "Les Malheures d'-Orphee" (title role); also appeared in seventeen performances of "Cosi fan Tutte" and twelve performances of "Amahl and the Night Visitors" at Clevelands' Karamu Theatre. At one time was editorial assistant to Langston Hughes. Member of various committees, Friends of Symphony of the New World.

WRITINGS: (Editor with Alan Lomax) *3000 Years of Black Poetry,* Dodd, 1970; (editor) *The Magic of Black Poetry,* Dodd, 1972; *Famous Black Entertainers of Today,*

RAOUL ABDUL

■ (From *The Magic of Black Poetry* by Raoul Abdul. Illustrated by Dane Burr.)

Dodd, 1974; *Blacks in Classical Music*, Dodd, 1977. Articles included in *Anthology of the American Negro in the Theatre* and *The Negro in Music and Art*. Writer of column, "The Cultural Scene," for Associated Negro Press. Cultural editor, *New York Age*; music critic, *The New York Amsterdam News*.

WORK IN PROGRESS: Writing a book about great Black performers in the theatre; researching a biography of Langston Hughes.

SIDELIGHTS: "Twenty-seven years ago, when I was graduated from John Hay High School in Cleveland, I re-ceived my first offer of a full-time job. Charles Loeb, city editor of the *Call and Post* invited me to join the staff of his newspaper doing rewrites, obituaries *and* musical reviews.

"My writing experience had only been on the *John Hay Ledger* under the guidance of Emma J. Wilson, out of whose classes had come novelist Jo Sinclair and one of the creators of Superman, Jerry Siegel. My columns won several awards from the National Scholastic Press Association.

"Music played an important part in my family life. My aunt and foster mother, Ada Harding, taught piano in North Buxton (Ontario) and my Uncle Ben played the violin. Their son, Buster, became a leading big band arranger. I studied piano with Leota Palmer, mother of Natalie Hinderas.

"Our home was a kind of informal salon where important musicians gathered from time to time. These included composer R. Nathaniel Dett, Count Basie, Cab Callaway, Billie Holiday, and Hale Smith. Melodies, both classical and popular, mingled harmoniously in our parlor.

"I cut my reviewing teeth on the orchestral concerts of the Cleveland Orchestra, opera productions of Benno D. Frank at Karamu Theatre, annual visits of the Metropolitan Opera and all of the musical events which took place in the middle class Black community of which our family was a part.

"Several years later when I moved to New York, I walked into the office of Al Duckett, executive editor of the *New York Age,* and told him that he needed a music critic. He said that he was not aware of the fact that he needed such an animal, but he hired me on the spot.

"When the *Age* went out of business, Al Duckett arranged for my column, 'The Cultural Scene,' to be syndicated by the Associated Negro Press. This enabled me to reach the readers of twenty Black newspapers throughout the United States and express my opinions on music.

"I am currently music critic of *The New York Amsterdam News,* the largest Black weekly in the country. It's executive editor, James Hicks, publisher John Procope and his assistant Lucia Robinson have stood behind my editorial opinions with fierce loyalty."

FOR MORE INFORMATION SEE: Library Journal, February 1, 1970, October 15, 1972; *New York Times,* September 27, 1970; *Publishers' Weekly,* October 2, 1972; *Boston Globe,* October 22, 1972; *Christian Science Monitor,* November 8, 1972; *San Francisco Examiner Chronicle,* November 5, 1972; *The Record,* June 6, 1974.

ABEL, Raymond   1911-

PERSONAL: Born September 19, 1911, in Chicago, Illinois; son of Harry (a businessman) and Etta (Bobinsky) Abel; married Ruth Herzman (a rehabilitation counselor for the blind), June 22, 1941; children: Helen, Peter. *Education:* Attended School of Art Institute of Chicago, 1930-31, 1937-39; University of Chicago, A.B., 1937; also attended Art Students' League of New York, 1941-43, 1946-48. *Politics:* Democrat. *Religion:* Jewish. *Home and Office:* 18 Vassar Place, Scarsdale, N.Y. 10583.

CAREER: Free-lance book and advertising artist. Newark Academy of Arts, Newark, N.J., instructor, 1947-50; Packer Institute, Brooklyn, N.Y., instructor, 1950-51; American Art School, New York, N.Y., instructor, 1955-58; New York City Community College, New York, N.Y., instructor, 1970-72; Art Students' League of New York, New York, N.Y., board of control, 1942-43, 1946-48; Eastchester Public Library, Eastchester, N.Y., president, board of directors, 1971-73. *Exhibitions:* Art Institute of Chicago, Artists of Chicago and Vicinity, group show, 1943; National Academy of Art Annual Exhibition, 1942; 92nd St. Young Mens Christian Association, group shows in the 1940's; Mint Museum, Charlotte, N.C.; Illinois State Museum; Gloucester Art Association Group; Society of Illustrators, 1972; United States Army Air Corps Exhibition, Greensboro, N.C. *Military service:* United States Army Air Corps, 1943-46. *Member:* Society of Illustrators, Art Students' League of New York. *Awards, honors:* Missouri State Annual, honorable mention; Mint Museum, honorable mention.

WRITINGS: (With wife, Ruth Abel; self-illustrated) *The New Sitter,* Walck, 1950.

Illustrator: Rene Prudhommeux, *The Extra Hand,* Viking, 1952; Lee Windham, *Binkie's Billions,* Knopf, 1954; Robb White, *Midshipman Lee of the Naval Academy,* Random House, 1954; Shields, *Chris Muldoon,* McKay, 1955; Mary C. Jane, *Mystery in Old Quebec,* Lippincott, 1955; Goodspeed, *Let's Take a Trip to Watch a Building Go Up,* Putnam, 1956; Mary C. Jane, *Ghost Rock Mystery,* Lippincott, 1956; Mary Adrian, *Refugee Hero,* Hastings House, 1957; Jeanne M. Goodspeed, *Let's Take a Trip to a Dairy,* Putnam, 1957; Mary C. Jane, *Mystery at Pemaquid Point,* Lippincott, 1957; Wright, *Andrew Jackson, Fighting Frontiersman,* Abingdon, 1958; Mary C. Jane, *Mystery at Shadow Pond,* Lippincott, 1958; Mary C. Jane, *Mystery at Echo Ridge,* Lippincott, 1959.

Mary C. Jane, *Mystery Back of the Mountain,* Lippincott, 1960; Mary C. Jane, *Mystery at Dead End Farm,* 1961; Mary C. Jane, *Mystery Behind Dark Windows,* Lippincott, 1962; Mary C. Jane, *Mystery by Moonlight,* Lippincott, 1963; Mary C. Jane, *Mystery at Longfellow Square,* Lippincott, 1964; Mary C. Jane, *Indian Island Mystery,* Lippincott, 1965; Mary C. Jane, *The Dark Tower Mystery,* Lippincott, 1966; Mary C. Jane, *Mystery on Nine Mule Marsh,* Lippincott, 1967; Mary C. Jane, *Mystery of the Red Carnations,* Lippincott, 1968; Emily Nathan, *I Know a Farmer,* Putnam, 1968; Priscilla Hagan, *The Mystery of the Secret Square,* World, 1969.

Lucy Johnston Sypher, *The Edge of Nowhere,* Atheneum, 1973; Gertrude Kerman, *Cabeza De Vaca,* Harvey House, 1974; L. D. Chaffin, *Coal and the Energy Crisis,* Harvey House, 1974; Lucy Johnston Sypher, *Cousins and Circuses,* Atheneum, 1974; Hilary Beckett, *Street Fair Summer,* Dodd. 1974; Lucy Johnston Sypher, *The Spell of the Northern Lights,* Atheneum, 1975; Ernst, *Escape King: The Story of Harry Houdini,* Prentice-Hall, 1975; Lucy Johnston Sypher, *The Turnabout Year,* Atheneum, 1976; W. G. Nicholson, *Pete Gray, One Armed Major Leaguer,* Prentice-Hall, 1976.

SIDELIGHTS: "From a quite respectable grammar school career I was thrust into a huge, overcrowded high school where it was sink or swim, and I nearly drowned. What

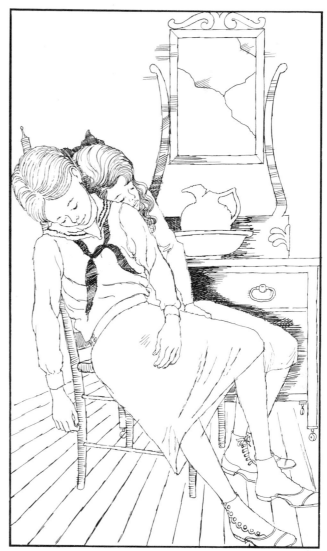

■ (From *Cousins and Circuses* by Lucy Johnston Sypher. Illustrated by Ray Abel.)

saved me were the art classes and a great teacher, Miss Nell Devine, through whose help I managed to graduate with my class and to go on to the School of the Art Institute of Chicago. After three years of art school and four years of college I looked for a job which would hopefully develop my main interest, drawing.

"These were depression years and the only job I could find was with a big Chicago mat house where for about a year I drew merchandise, clothing of all kinds and saw my work in print. At home I did book samples based on such classics as *The Cloister and the Hearth, The Idiot* and other books which appealed to me at that time. Through these I obtained a small amount of free-lance work from *Compton's Encyclopedia* and other Chicago based publishers.

"William Welsh, a prominent illustrator of the day, took me on as his assistant, and since he was very busy I was permitted to work on such parts of his illustrations which required not the master's hand. I painted on the side and shipped my work to annual exhibitions at the Art Institute of Chicago, the Illinois State Museum, and other shows around the country.

RAYMOND ABEL

"In 1939 I filled a portfolio with black and white illustration samples and went to New York. On the way I stopped off at the art editor's office of the *Christian Science Monitor* in Boston where they were in need of a political cartoonist. After glancing at my efforts, the lady editor earnestly suggested that I look into Christian Science. Obviously I needed help!

"In New York my first move was to enroll as a part-time student at The Art Students League. In time I found various free-lance jobs—a display house in New Jersey, small portrait commissions through a well-connected friend. One summer I worked for Wayman Adams at his portrait school in the Adirondacks. I also did adventure comic strips which were getting very popular at that time, and finally some textile design work for my father-in-law's business, for I married in 1941.

"In April, 1943, I was drafted into the Army Air Corps and assigned to Special Services. I did a variety of art chores such as silk-screened posters and post maps, murals at Mitchel Field, and finally the job of instructing soon-to-be-discharged men in arts and crafts. I was seldom without a sketch pad and an old Waterman's India Ink pen. An artist who influenced me at this time was the Pole, Feliks Topolski, whose work I had come across in a magazine. In the hope of seeing some Topolski originals, I visited the Fogg Museum at Cambridge, but the curator there had never heard of him.

"After the War I settled in Manhattan with my wife and infant daughter, enrolled part-time at The Art Students' League and taught art for the New York City Board of Edu-

cation veteran's training program, the Newark Academy of Arts and one year at Packer Institute.

"Encouraged when my wife and I sold a book, I did many more samples and started to get a few commissions from Viking, Putnam, Longmans and others. Since that time I have earned a living in commercial art and in teaching, but have never lost interest in the illustrated book and over the years have done jackets, spots and illustrations for many.

"Looking back I realize that my long interest in book illustration is less related to children, though I always have had their interests in mind when I drew pictures for them, than to a love of books. My ambition is to do a truly beautiful book, one which a bibliophile like myself would recognize as such. I'm still trying."

AIKEN, Clarissa (Lorenz) 1899-

PERSONAL: Born January 28, 1899, in Milwaukee, Wis.; daughter of Louis Robert (a manufacturer) and Mary (Mich) Lorenz; married Conrad Aiken (the poet and critic), February 27, 1930 (divorced, 1938). *Education:* Attended high school in Milwaukee, Wis., and New England Conservatory of Music. *Politics:* Democrat. *Home and office:* 290 Marlborough St., Boston, Mass. 02116. *Agent:* Bertha Case, 42 West 43rd St., New York, N.Y. 10019.

CAREER: Brookline Music School, Brookline, Mass., piano teacher, 1960-73.

WRITINGS: Junket to Japan (teen-age book illustrated with photographs by Peter Bell), Little, Brown, 1960. Also a wide range of magazine articles included in *The New Yorker, Redbook, Harpers' Bazaar, Atlantic Monthly.*

CLARISSA AIKEN

WORK IN PROGRESS: Memoirs pinpointing married life with a poet.

SIDELIGHTS: "*Junket to Japan* evolved out of letters and diaries of Peter Bell, a Gloucester, Massachusetts youth who spent a summer with a Buddhist family in Tokyo, the first year 'the Orient was opened to American Field Service scholarship winners. From his observations and impressions, I distilled the excitement of his experiences, the warm friendly contacts he made with the Japanese, the exuberance of his comradeship with other teenagers. My purpose in writing the book was to help inoculate young people against social prejudices. All messages aside, however, Japan was fun for Peter, and he managed to pass some of it on to me. I hope I have to you."

Clarissa Aiken lived for six years in Sussex, England.

HOBBIES AND OTHER INTERESTS: Music, sewing, cooking, tennis, swimming.

ALBRECHT, Lillie (Vanderveer) 1894-

PERSONAL: Born January 2, 1894, in Monroe, N.Y.; daughter of John Charles (a physician) and Charlotte (Baird) Vanderveer; married Ira Werner Albrecht (a teacher), June 28, 1924; children: Johanna Albrecht Betzl. *Education:* Syracuse University, graduated from Library School, 1916, graduate study in English and history, 1916-17. *Politics:* Republican. *Religion:* Episcopalian. *Home:* Shutesbury, Mass.

CAREER: Brooklyn Public Library, Brooklyn, N.Y., librarian, 1917-18; Baldwin School, Saranac Lake, N.Y., English teacher, 1918-24; Westfield Athenaeum, Westfield, Mass., museum curator and librarian, 1928-62. *Member:* Massachusetts Library Association, Western Massachusetts Library Association.

WRITINGS: Hannah's Hessian, Hastings, 1958; *Deborah Remembers,* Hastings, 1960; *The Grist Mill Secret,* Hastings, 1962; *The Spinning Wheel Secret,* Hastings, 1965; *Susannah's Candlestick,* Hastings, 1970. Writer of radio scripts, plays, and stories for children.

LILLIE ALBRECHT

"I love candlelight," mused Susanna as she tucked the silver candlestick lovingly between a pile of shifts... ▪ (From *Susanna's Candlestick* by Lillie V. Albrecht. Illustrated by Lois Woehr.)

SIDELIGHTS: Lillie Albrecht lives in Shutesbury with her granddaughter, Susanna. Her daughter, Johanna, is a singer in New York City.

ALEXANDER, Sue 1933-

PERSONAL: Born August 20, 1933, in Tucson, Ariz.; daughter of Jack M. (an electronic component manufacturer) and Edith (Pollock) Ratner; married second husband, Joel Alexander (a car agency sales manager), November 29, 1959; children: (first marriage) Glenn David; (second marriage) Marc Jeffry, Stacey Joy. *Education:* Attended Drake University, 1950-52, and Northwestern University, 1952-53. *Religion:* Jewish. *Home and office:* 6846 McLaren, Canoga Park, Calif. 91307. *Agent:* Marilyn Marlow, Curtis Brown Ltd., 575 Madison Ave., New York, N.Y. 10022.

CAREER: Writer, 1969—. *Member:* American Civil Liberties Union, Society of Children's Book Writers (member of board of directors, 1972—), Southern California Council on Literature for Children and Young People.

WRITINGS—Juvenile: Small Plays for You and a Friend, Scholastic Book Services, 1973, hardcover edition, Seabury, 1974; *Nadir of the Streets,* Macmillan, 1975; *Peacocks Are*

"All right, Peacock. In go the delicate spices. And in you will go!" ■ (From *Peacocks Are Very Special* by Sue Alexander. Illustrated by Victoria Chess.)

SUE ALEXANDER

I'm going to be very tired when I've finished making it!' I never did make the minestrone—instead I went to my desk and began a story in which a greedy jackal gets tired!

"I love writing stories! It's my work and my joy. It satisfies my sense of fun and my need to share. I wouldn't trade what I do for any other profession in the world. I write for young people because they have imaginations that soar, touched off by a word, a phrase, an image . . . a condition I share. To be able to provide the spark for this process gives me the greatest personal joy."

ALKEMA, Chester Jay   1932-

PERSONAL: Surname is accented on first syllable; born July 17, 1932, in Martin, Mich.; son of William (a clergyman) and Jennie (Vander Meer) Alkema. *Education:* Calvin College, A.B., 1954; Michigan State University, M.A., 1959, M.F.A., 1961. *Politics:* Republican. *Religion:* Christian Reformed. *Home:* 3365 Wildridge Dr. N.E., Grand Rapids, Mich. 49505. *Office:* College of Arts and Science, Grand Valley State Colleges, College Landing, Allendale, Mich. 49401.

CAREER: Elementary school teacher in Grand Rapids, Mich., 1954-59; art teacher in public schools in Wyoming, Mich., 1959-65; Grand Valley State Colleges, Allendale, Mich., lecturer, 1965, assistant professor, 1966-72, associate

Very Special, Doubleday, 1976; *Witch, Goblin and Sometimes Ghost,* Pantheon, 1976; *Small Plays for Special Days,* Seabury, 1977. Contributor of short stories to *Children's Playmate, Weekly Reader, Jack and Jill* and Walt Disney Productions; occasional contributor of book reviews to *Los Angeles Times.*

WORK IN PROGRESS: Tales of Amber; other stories as yet untitled.

SIDELIGHTS: "I began writing stories and telling them to my friends when I was about eight years old. At that time I was small for my age (I still am) and very clumsy. So clumsy, in fact, that none of my classmates wanted me on their teams at recess time. So I would sit on the school steps and watch them play. One day, one of the boys wasn't playing either and he sat down beside me. Looking for something to say, I said, 'I'll tell you a story.' And I did—making it up as I went along. Before the story was finished, all the rest of the class had come to listen. It made me feel very good! So I told stories almost every recess time that whole year. And I've been telling stories ever since.

"Most of the stories I write are fantasy; that is, they are about goblins and talking peacocks and ghosts instead of real people. But all of the stories I write begin the same way; with how I *feel* about something. *Peacocks Are Very Special* began when I looked in a cookbook at the recipe for minestrone soup and thought, 'So many things go into this soup.

CHESTER JAY ALKEMA

professor of art, 1972—. *Member:* National Art Education Association, Michigan Art Education Association, Michigan Education Association.

WRITINGS—Self-illustrated with photographs: *Creative Paper Crafts in Color,* Sterling, 1967; *The Complete Crayon Book in Color,* Sterling, 1969; *Alkema's Complete Guide to Creative Art for Young People,* Sterling, 1971; *Art for the Exceptional,* Pruett Press, 1971; *Masks,* Sterling, 1971; *Puppet Making,* Sterling, 1972; *Crafting with Nature's Materials,* Sterling, 1973; *Monster Masks,* Sterling, 1973; *Tissue Paper Creations,* Sterling, 1973; *Greeting Cards You Can Make,* Sterling, 1973; *Aluminum and Copper Tooling,* Sterling, 1974; *Beginning with Papier Mache,* Sterling, 1974; *Alkema's Scrap Magic,* Sterling, 1976.

Contributor to *Practical Encyclopedia of Crafts, Family Book of Crafts, Family Book of Hobbies, Giant Book of Crafts, Easy Crafts Book,* and *Metalcrafting Encyclopedia,* all published by Sterling. Contributor of more than sixty articles to art and education journals, including *Design, Instructor, Children's House, School Arts, Arts and Activities, Grade Teacher, Journal of Exceptional Children,* and the Spanish language journal, *Saber.*

SIDELIGHTS: "In 1961, I began photographing children's and adults' art work to illustrate my adult art education lectures offered at the college and university levels. The illustrative materials described for prospective teachers the possibilities and limitations of various art materials and techniques.

"In 1963, I submitted my first article, illustrated with photographs of children's art work, to the education journal, *Arts and Activities.* To my great amazement, the article was accepted for publication. The writing fever hit me and from that point on approximately sixty illustrated articles were published in national and international education journals.

"In 1966, I was commissioned to develop an eight-page feature for *The Instructor* on paper sculpture. Numerous photographs were taken for the article and the thought occurred to me that with the inclusion of additional material, a book might be in the offering. The material was submitted to the Sterling Publishing Company and they produced my first book, a beautiful, colorful volume entitled *Creative Paper Crafts in Color.* The book comprises 177 pages with 350 photographs, 150 of them in full color.

"In preparing journal articles and books, research is required. But the greatest contribution to my publications is made by my students—who are so creative. They take a suggested idea and move far beyond it, thereby suggesting new possibilities and insights into the use of familiar art techniques and media. The teacher teaches his students and vice versa. This intimate interaction is reflected in all of my publications.

"I continue to photograph student art work and my own art creations. My photographs, in black and white, and in color, now run into the thousands. One single lens reflex camera is always loaded with black and white film, and a second camera is reserved for color film—always in preparation for another journal article—another book."

Chester Alkema has had two books translated into French and one in Dutch.

ALLAMAND, Pascale 1942-

PERSONAL: Born September 22, 1942, in Montreux, Switzerland; daughter of Pierre (a travel agent) and Yvette (Milharoux) Allamand. *Education:* Studied privately in Germany, 1959-60; Ecole secondaire, Montreux, Switzerland, diploma, 1963. *Home and office:* Grand Rue 25, 1095 Lutry, Switzerland.

CAREER: Apprentice in photography, Montreux, Switzerland, 1960-63; assistant to publicity and fashion photographer, Lausanne, Switzerland, 1963-70; free-lance photographic reporter, Lutry, Switzerland, 1970—. *Member:* Swiss Association of Press Photographers.

WRITINGS—All self-illustrated: *The Boy and His Friend the Bear,* English version by Michael Bullock, J. Cape, 1974; *The Pop Rooster,* English version by Bullock, Scribner, 1975; *The Camel Who Left the Zoo,* J. Cape, 1976; *The Little Goat in the Alps,* J. Cape, 1977.

Illustrator with photographs: *A la Mode de Chez Nous,* Livre de Cuisine, 1976.

WORK IN PROGRESS: The Bear Who Wanted to Change Color, publication by J. Cape expected in 1978.

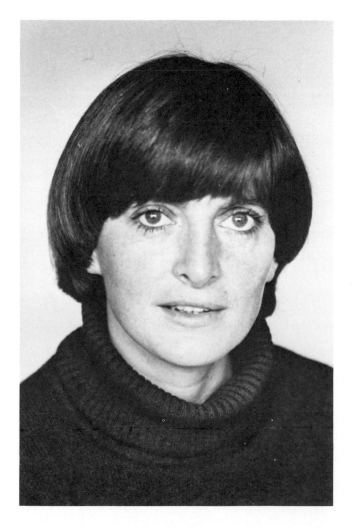

PASCALE ALLAMAND

Back on the island, people saw the rooster on television. They were very proud of him. They left the windows open so the chickens could watch as well. ■ (From *The Pop Rooster* by Pascale Allamand. English version by Michael Bullock. Illustrated by Pascale Allamand.)

SIDELIGHTS: "I love children and my aim is to show them, by way of a little story, the small realities of their future life as adults. For example, that one can have disappointments, but that one mustn't be discouraged in spite of them. I use my momories of travel for the settings of my little stories, and I adapt them to those little animals I love so well.

"I love my profession as photographer because I am greatly affected by everything visual. But one day I had a dream that I wanted to make permanent. And for that, photography, despite all its technical feats, was insufficient. So I tried to paint for the first time. This was about twelve years ago. Since then, I've done a whole series of paintings and I am still doing them. These are almost always dream images, or, sometimes, something that I see and prefer to depict in a painting than in a photograph. Thus, I began to paint regularly.

"Then one day, four years ago, I went to buy a bear in a toy shop for a little girl. There was only one in the whole store, and it had a funny kind of head, a little lopsided, so I didn't buy it, and I left to go to another store. On my way there I thought about that bear, who, because it had an odd head would perhaps never be bought, and I imagined a little story, and that gave me the idea to do a children's book. I wrote the story and illustrated it, and the book was published by Jonathan Cape in London who commissioned a series from me.

"When I first began to paint I used water color. But very quickly I began to use oils, and now I paint only in oils. First I do a pencil drawing on a sheet of paper, and when I'm satisfied with it, I paint it in oils on strips of cardboard, specially treated for this kind of work. I get enormous pleasure from doing these books."

ANCONA, George 1929-

PERSONAL: Born December 4, 1929, in New York; son of Efraim Jose Ancona and Emma Ancona Diaz; married Patricia Apatow (divorced); married Helga Von Sydow (a journalist), June 20, 1968; children: (first marriage) Lisa, Gina, Tom; (second marriage) Isabel, Marina. *Education:* Attended Academia San Carlos, 1949-50, Cooper Union, and Art Students League (all New York, N.Y.). *Home address:* Crickettown Rd., Stony Point, N.Y. 10980.

CAREER: Esquire (magazine), New York, N.Y., art director, 1951-54; Grey Advertising, New York, N.Y., art director, 1954-57; Daniel & Charles, New York, N.Y., art director, 1957-61; George Ancona, Inc., New York, N.Y., photographer and film maker, 1961—. Instructor at Rockland Community College and School of Visual Arts, New York; lecturer on film, design, photography, and books.

AWARDS, HONORS: Art Director's Show awards, 1959, 1960, 1967; Cine Golden Eagle Awards from Council on Non-Theatrical Events, 1967, for film, "Reflections," and 1972, for film, "Cities of the Web"; awards from American Institute of Graphic Arts, 1967, 1968, 1974; Cindy Award from Industry Film Producers Association, 1967.

WRITINGS: Monsters on Wheels, Dutton, 1974; (with Remy Charlip and Mary Beth; also illustrator) *Handtalk,* Parents Press, 1974; *And What Do You Do?,* Dutton, 1975.

Illustrator: Barbara Brenner, *A Snake-Lover's Diary,* Scott Young Books, 1970; Brenner, *Faces,* Dutton, 1970; Brenner, *Bodies,* Dutton, 1973.

Filmscripts: "Doctor" and "Dentist," two short films for "Sesame Street"; "Faces" and "The River," for children; "Getting It Together," a documentary film about the Children's Television Workshop and Neighborhood Youth Corps; "Cities of the Web," for Macmillan; "Looking for Pictures," "Looking for Color," "Seeing Rhythm," a series; "Reflections," for American Crafts Council.

WORK IN PROGRESS: "At present I'm at work on my next book and planning a film and another book along with some teaching aides for the deaf. I am also interested in doing some work in the bilingual area."

SIDELIGHTS: "Growing up in Coney Island, my world consisted of the contrast between the fantasies of the amusement rides and the limitless space of the sea. Summers were spent in a bathing suit running with a pack of boys through the streets to the beach, swimming out beyond the third barrel, straining the sands for coins and sneaking into the amusement parks.

"My parents had come from Yucatan in Mexico and I was raised a Mexican, learning to speak Spanish first. My father wanted me to grow up in the American way so we never lived in a Latin barrio. Instead, I grew up the only Latin in an Italian neighborhood. There I acquired my English, work skills, street wisdom and a godfather.

"My father's hobby was photography and it was my first introduction to the making of images. My mother worked as a seamstress and cooked fabulous Mexican dishes. It was at home that I began to draw by copying photographs.

"From the age of twelve I worked weekends and summers for a variety of craftsmen. An auto mechanic, a carpenter, and in the amusement parks. I would, also, make money with a friend by collecting junk and scrap paper in an old push cart. When loaded with newspaper it took both of us to raise it on its two big wheels and push it to the junk dealer. This way we always had money for the movies and a hot dog.

"It was in Mark Twain Junior High School that I began to take an active interest in drawing and design. It was the sign painting teacher who got me interested in lettering and painting the sets for the dramatic performances. When I graduated I was given the Sign Painting Medal.

"In Lincoln High School I had the good fortune of studying design with Mr. Leon Friend, who had organized an extracurricular group called the Art Squad. He made sure that the

Your cells,
your fingerprints,

your face. . .
The color of your eyes. . .

alumni would keep in touch with the students which gave us a sense of professionalism. We also competed in every contest we could find and won many prizes. The Art Squad alumni also organized a benefit performance by the New York Philharmonic in order to raise funds for scholarships. When I graduated I received one to the Art Students League.

"After graduating high school I went for the first time to Mexico. There, with the help of Rufino Tamayo, I studied in the Academy of San Carlos. I stayed for six months studying fresco painting until my money ran out and I returned to New York to begin my studies at the Art Students League. I stayed there for nine months and then began to work.

"My first jobs were with art studios where I did mechanicals and some designing. The first major job was in the bullpen of *Esquire* magazine. After a few months I was assigned to layout one of their magazines called 'Apparel Arts' which was the predecessor of *Gentleman's Quarterly*. I was there for two years. Then I wanted to try something else, so I took a job as head of the promotion department of *Seventeen* magazine. This gave me a taste of advertising. Two years later I went to my first agency art director job with Grey Advertising. For the next four years I designed ads for NBC Television and other consumer accounts. I then became interested in fashion so I joined the Daniel & Charles Advertising Agency. Another four years went by during which time my interest in photography and films increased. It was during this time that I shot my first film which got good reviews.

"In 1960 I opened my studio in New York where I did photographs for advertising and magazines. My work appeared in magazines such as *Vogue, Children, Parents, Harpers' Bazaar, Modern Photography, New York Magazine, Steelways* and others. I, also, did many record album covers. My photographs were for the most part illustrative. People and children in real situations was my main interest.

"The past three years I have become interested in food photography. Several times a year I will spend a week in Minneapolis photographing food for the *Betty Crocker Cookbook*

series. The weight I put on during these assignments are usually worked off on the next film job.

"During this time I was able to develop my interest in film. These include a documentary of the South Bronx called, 'Uptown' which was shown at the Lincoln Center Film Festival. Another documentary was shot for N.E.T. This was the story of the Menominee Indians. For the Children's Television Workshop, I shot a film about the work they did with the Neighborhood Youth Corp among the migrant farmers, the barrios of Dallas and Los Angeles. (It was on this assignment that I was told I'm really a Chicano.)

"It was because of all this travel that I decided to move my studio and combine it with my home in Stony Point. Today I shoot my pictures and edit my films in the studio next to the house. This enables me to spend more time with my family.

"My first experience with books was when my friend, Barbara Brenner, asked me to illustrate a manuscript she had written called *Faces*. After it was published I did a film of it. Two more books with Barbara were published, *Bodies* and *Snake Lovers Diary*. Then E. P. Dutton asked me to try my hand at writing. The result was *Monsters on Wheels* which was selected for the American Institute of Graphic Arts 'Children's Books Show, 1974' along with the book I did with Remy Charlip and Mary Beth called *Handtalk*.

"Curiosity is the biggest element in my work. Watching people at work gave me the idea for *And What Do You Do?* I think people are fascinating and I love to find myself in strange places, meeting people, getting to know them and learning about them. This helps me to learn about myself. Photographing, filming or writing about someone or someplace is my way of feeling alive and in touch with the world around me. I believe that work does this for many people. Whether it is baking bread, building a house, driving a truck or singing a song, people reach each other each in their own way. I think that's what living is all about."

FOR MORE INFORMATION SEE: Journal-News, Rockland County, N.Y., July 23, 1972; *Horn Book,* October, 1974.

They're yours alone.
■ (From *Bodies* by Barbara Brenner. Illustrated by George Ancona.)

GEORGE ANCONA

ANGIER, Bradford

PERSONAL: Born in Boston, Mass.; son of George Marvin and Bessie (Brison) Angier; married Vena Watt. *Home:* 38-900 Island Dr., Unit 601, Rancho Mirage, Calif. 92270; and Hudson Hope, British Columbia, Canada.

CAREER: Free-lance writer. *Member:* Authors Guild of Authors League of America, Outdoor Writers Association of America, Camp Fire Club of America.

WRITINGS: At Home in the Woods, Sheridan, 1951; *How to Build Your Home in the Woods,* Sheridan, 1952; *Living Off the Country,* Stackpole, 1956; (with Colonel Townsend Whelen) *On Your Own in the Wilderness,* Stackpole, 1958; *How to Go Live in the Woods on $10 a Week,* Stackpole, 1959.

Wilderness Cookery, Stackpole, 1961; *We Like It Wild,* Stackpole, 1963; (with Townsend Whelen) *Mister Rifleman,* Peterson, 1965; *Home in Your Pack,* Stackpole, 1965; *Free for the Eating,* Stackpole, 1966; *Skills for Taming the Wilds,* Stackpole, 1967; (with E. Russell Kodet) *How To Be Your Own Wilderness Doctor,* Stackpole, 1967; *Gourmet Cooking for Free,* Stackpole, 1968; (with Jeanne Dixon) *The Ghost of Spirit River,* Atheneum, 1968; *More Free-for-the-Eating Wild Foods,* Stackpole, 1969.

(With E. Russel Kodet) *Home Medical Handbook,* Association Press, 1970; (with Barbara Corcoran) *A Star to the North,* Nelson, 1970; (with C. B. Colby) *The Art and Science of Taking to the Woods,* Stackpole, 1970; *How to Live in the Woods on Pennies a Day,* Stackpole, 1971; *Feasting Free on Wild Edibles,* Stackpole, 1972; *One Acre and Security,* Stackpole, 1972; *Wilderness Gear You Can Make Yourself,* Macmillan, 1973; *Survival with Style,* National Wildlife Federation, 1972; (with Zack Taylor) *Introduction to Canoeing,* Stackpole, 1973; *Field Guide to Edible Wild Plants,* Stackpole, 1974; *The Freighter Travel Manual,* Chilton, 1974; *Looking for Gold,* Stackpole, 1975; *The Home Book of Cooking Venison and Other Natural Meats,* Stackpole, 1975; (with Vena Angier) *Wilderness Wife* (autobiographical), Chilton, 1976; *Color Field Guide to Common Wild Edibles,* Stackpole, 1976; (with Barbara Corcoran) *Ask for Love and They Give You Rice Pudding,* Houghton, 1977.

WORK IN PROGRESS: The Master Outdoorsman.

BRADFORD ANGIER

ANTICAGLIA, Elizabeth 1939-

PERSONAL: Surname pronounced without "g" sound; born September 14, 1939, in New York, N.Y.; daughter of Harold William (a construction rigger) and Hilma Elizabeth (Nevalainen) Ahlfors; married Joseph R. Anticaglia (a facial plastic surgeon and otolaryngologist), September 21, 1962; children: Jeannine, Jason. *Education:* New York University, B.A., 1961. *Politics:* Democrat. *Religion:* Unitarian-Universalist. *Home:* R.D. 2, Box 49A, Hockessin, Del. 19707.

CAREER: Living for Young Homemakers, New York, N.Y., assistant production editor, 1961; *Vogue,* New York, N.Y., assistant production editor, 1961-62; Speaker's Showcase (lecture bureau), Philadelphia, Pa., lecturer, 1973—. *Member:* Authors Guild, National Organization for Women.

WRITINGS: A Housewife's Guide to Women's Liberation, Nelson-Hall, 1972; *Twelve American Women,* Nelson-Hall, 1975; *Heroines of '76* (juvenile), Walker, 1975. Contributor to *Yankee, Coronet,* and other magazines. Author of two columns: "The Doctor's Bag" for *Companion,* 1971, and "Woman Today" for *Today's Post,* 1971-73.

WORK IN PROGRESS: Novels for children.

Other women joined the men in battle. Some nursed the wounded. Some ran through heavy fire lugging cool water or hot soup for the fighting soldiers. Still other women were fighting soldiers themselves. ■ (From *Heroines of '76* by Elizabeth Anticaglia.)

ELIZABETH ANTICAGLIA

ANTON, Michael J(ames) 1940-

PERSONAL: Born December 6, 1940, in Memphis, Tenn.; son of William H. (a mechanic) and Dorothy (Eken) Anton; married Charlotte Ann Kirsch, June 7, 1964; children: Mark, Philip, Matthew. *Education:* St. Paul's College, A.A., 1960; Concordia College, Fort Wayne, Ind., B.A., 1962; Concordia Theological Seminary, B.Div. and M.Div., 1966. *Politics:* Independent. *Home:* 2658 Quakezik, Hastings, Mich. 49058. *Office:* Grace Lutheran Church, 239 East North St., Hastings, Mich. 49058.

CAREER: Ordained Lutheran minister in 1966; pastor in Niagara Falls, Ontario, 1966-67; Niagara College of Applied Arts and Technology, Welland, Ontario, master teacher of English, philosophy, and social science, 1967-69; Grace Lutheran Church, Hastings, Mich., pastor, 1969—. President of Hastings Community Activities Center, 1971-72.

WRITINGS: From Humbug to Heaven (advent dialogue), C.S.S. Publishing, 1972; *What Are We Going to Do with the King?* (juvenile Christmas play), C.S.S. Publishing, 1972; *The Night That Was* (juvenile Christmas play), C.S.S. Publishing, 1972; *Evangelism in 3-D* chancel drama), C.S.S. Publishing, 1973; *Snoring through Sermons* (collection), C.S.S. Publishing, 1974; *Good News for Now* (sermon series for Advent/Christmas), C.S.S. Publishing Co., 1976.

WORK IN PROGRESS: A chancel drama for Lent.

SIDELIGHTS: "A long-held dream of my life is to be a full-time author. I have maintained a strong fascination with words and the way words can be used to communicate ideas, images, feelings and moods. So far I have not moved that close to making that dream a reality, but the vision remains.

MICHAEL J. ANTON

All my published writings to date have had a pragmatic beginning. I wrote each of them for use in my present parish. Only after their use here did I submit them for publication."

ARNOV, Boris, Jr.   1926-

PERSONAL: Born October 17, 1926, in Los Angeles, Calif.; son of Boris and Helen (Mindlin) Arnov; married 1955. *Education:* Chicaco Medical School, student, 1944-45; Rollins College, B.S., 1948; University of Miami, Coral Gables, Fla., graduate student, 1950-52, M.Ed., 1967; University of California, graduate student, 1958-59. *Office:* Florida Atlantic University, Boca Raton, Fla. *Agent:* Anita Diament, 51 East 42nd St., New York, N.Y.

CAREER: Florida Atlantic University, Boca Raton, Fla., associate professor of education.

WRITINGS: Wonders of the Ocean Zoo, Dodd, 1957; *Wonders of the Deep Sea,* Dodd, 1959; *Inside Our Earth,* Bobbs, 1961; *Oceans of the World,* Bobbs, 1962; *Bally, the Blue Whale,* Criterion, 1964; *Secrets of Inland Waters,* Little, Brown, 1965; *Homes Beneath the Sea,* Little, Brown, 1969; *Fishing for Everyone,* Hawthorn, 1971. Contributor of articles to fishing magazines and to newspapers.

WORK IN PROGRESS: Two books, articles, and fiction.

SIDELIGHTS: "I love the ocean to live near it and write about it. Fishing used to be my main hobby, but now it is sailing.

A sargassum fish from the Sargasso Sea. The fish is well camouflaged, blending in with the weeds that make up its environment. ■ (From *Homes Beneath the Sea* by Boris Arnov, Jr.)

"I write when the mood inspires me, sometimes for many days and weeks until I have completed the work at hand. Often I do not write for many months, not until I am certain about what I want to get down on paper. I consider writing very hard work, but a way in which one can sometimes manage to live without confining himself to a routine schedule, and that is reward enough."

BORIS ARNOV, JR.

HELENE S. ARNSTEIN

ARNSTEIN, Helene S(olomon)   1915-

PERSONAL: Name is pronounced Hel-*lane Arn*-steen; born April 23, 1915, in New York, N.Y.; daughter of Meyer (in real estate) and Rose (Born) Solomon; married William E. Arnstein (a management consultant), June 16, 1937; children: Nancy (Mrs. Peter G. Wilson), Lawrence. *Education:* Sarah Lawrence College, A.A., 1932. *Home:* 1095 Park Ave., New York, N.Y. 10028. *Agent:* Carl Brandt, Brandt & Brandt, 101 Park Ave., New York, N.Y. 10017.

CAREER: Former piano teacher; free-lance writer on mental health, family relations, and parent-child relations. *Member:* Authors Guild, Authors League of America, Child Study Association of America (member of board of directors).

WRITINGS: What to Tell Your Child About Birth, Illness, Death, Divorce, and Other Family Crises, Bobbs-Merrill, 1962; *Your Growing Child and Sex,* Bobbs-Merrill, 1965; *Getting Along with Your Grown-Up Children,* M. Evans, 1970; *What Every Woman Needs to Know About Abortion,* Scribner, 1973; *Billy and Our New Baby* (juvenile), Behavioral Publications, 1973; *The Roots of Love: Helping Your Child Learn to Love in the First Three Years of Life,* Bobbs-Merrill, 1975. Contributor to popular magazines, including *Ladies' Home Journal, Parents' Magazine, Today's Health, Girl Talk, Family Circle,* and New York *Times Sunday Magazine.*

SIDELIGHTS: Helene Arnstein takes care of her three grandchildren one day a week. "They and my children have been my best 'laboratory' for observing children's emotional needs, growth, and development—even though I've spent years in research, backing up my beliefs with data . . . I believe the first years are vital in producing caring, lovable, and loving human beings who can make this world a better one." Her books have been published in Spanish, Italian, and Japanese.

HOBBIES AND OTHER INTERESTS: Cooking, playing piano, travel.

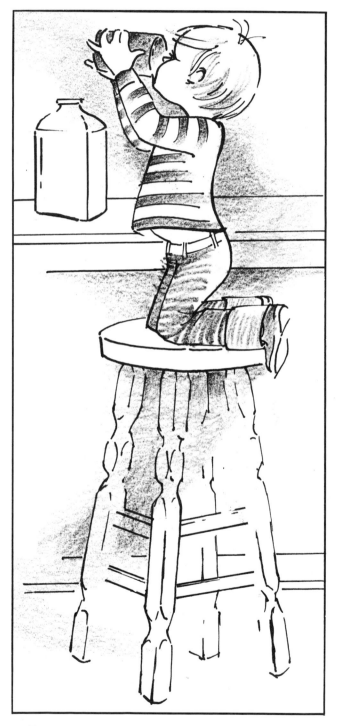

But you can get more out of a cup when you're hungry and thirsty. ■ (From *Billy and Our New Baby* by Helene S. Arnstein. Illustrated by M. Jane Smyth.)

HERBERT E. ARNTSON

ARNTSON, Herbert E(dward) 1911-

PERSONAL: Born April 8, 1911, in Tacoma, Wash.; son of Anthony M. and Sigrid (Wingard) Arntson; married Dorothy Horine (a writer, teacher, and now potter), November 8, 1946; children: Paul R., Helen, Laura. *Education:* University of Puget Sound, B.A., 1937, M.A., 1940; several years of graduate study at University of Washington, Seattle. *Religion:* Congregational. *Home:* Lives on an island in Puget Sound; P.O. Box 132, Grapeview, Wash. 98546. *Agent:* McIntosh & Otis, Inc., 18 East 41st St., New York, N.Y. 10017.

CAREER: Worked on ships out of Seattle and San Francisco, 1933-34; grade and high school teacher in Waterville, Wash., 1941-42; Cunningham Steel Foundry, Seattle, Wash., purchasing agent, 1942-43; Washington State University, Pullman, instructor, 1946-50, assistant professor, 1950-58, associate professor of English, 1958-65, professor and member of graduate faculty, 1965-74, now professor emeritus. *Member:* Modern Language Association of America (life emeritus), and various societies. *Awards, honors:* Franklin Watts Juvenile Ficton Award for distinguished contribution to children's literature, for *Adam Gray: Stowaway,* 1961; governor's citation, State of Washington, 1966.

WRITINGS: Caravan to Oregon, Binfords, 1957; *Adam Gray: Stowaway,* Watts, 1961; *Two Guns in Old Oregon,* Watts, 1964; *Frontier Boy,* Washburn, 1967; *Mountain Boy,* Washburn, 1968; *River Boy,* Washburn, 1969. Also author of scholarly articles, essays, poems, short stories.

WORK IN PROGRESS: Experimental short stories.

SIDELIGHTS: "Spent my summers as a boy on a ranch in the mountains, close to Mount Rainier. We lived in a log cabin, carried water from Big Creek, fished, climbed trees, climbed mountains, hiked through the woods, cleared land. There was an old trapper's trail and a moss-covered lean-to where we built the new cabin. We waged a losing war with the beavers when they diverted the creek with their dams. We found an antique automobile with carriage wheels, no engine, in an abandoned shed. There was a strange bog studded with mossy hummocks and delicate flowers. It bubbled mysteriously when we crossed on our floating walkway. Later, there were summers on Puget Sound, spent mostly in a catboat. Trips to Dead Man's Island, where people had found ancient skulls. In 1933 and 1934, worked on ships to Alaska, Japan, China and around the world. All these experiences, and not just the spectacular events or exotic places, were fodder for stories.

"Much later, I became interested in the early history of Washington, which led to writing historical fiction for young people. How does a book of this sort evolve? For me, it begins with a piece of history, something with a bite to it, something concerned with this region. It's nice to put together an episode that really happened, visit the place where it occurred, reconstruct the details and the feel of the times. This is, also, a matter of research, digging out facts and putting them together, looking through old records, talking to people, learning how old guns worked, what tools were like, and so on. Maybe the next thing is finding a central character, and a theme, or meaning to the story development.

"In *River Boy,* for instance, there was the initial idea from an article in *Oregon Historical Quarterly* about early bridges in Oregon and their development. The idea of a bridge has good implications, and it brought many things together. The central character and a friend for him to talk to emerged naturally, since this was to be written for young people. Central theme? Growing up. The idea that there comes a time when a person assumes responsibility. Up to a certain point, we are accountable to someone for what we do, but we aren't mature enough to make the decisions. But, one day, something happens.

"The important thing about a story is that it is not an essay about an idea. It is an experience, a series of linked incidents where people do things, act and talk. It happens to the reader. He lives through the experiences, feels that this is happening to him. Putting everything together to bring this about usually doesn't happen easily. The whole thing grows. You write down what you have, maybe outline it, think about it as changing and developing from the original situation, evolving with greater tension all the time, until the course of events is clear, and the central idea is borne out by what takes place. By what happens to the central character, and therefore to the reader.

"There are two unexpected aspects to this procedure. The incidents, which are after all the most interesting part of the story, creep in by themselves. The yarn suddenly comes to life and the right things happen, things you hadn't planned. The wind howls down the chimney, someone pounds on the cabin door in the middle of the night, and you become almost a spectator at your own story.

"The other surprise is that the last rewriting is the most enjoyable part. Everything is set down in order, all the facts, the details, the development, and you can think about the effect of your sentences, how to say your words for just the right feeling. And that, if you like to write, is the frosting on the cake.

"We now live on Stretch Island, in the southern part of Puget Sound, close to the water. About twenty feet from it, when the tide is in. And there's a bridge to the island. . . . A good place to work."

ARTIS, Vicki Kimmel 1945-

PERSONAL: Born December 14, 1945, in Milwaukee, Wis.; daughter of Robert Alden and Clara (Manes) Kimmel; married Paul Gregory Artis (a medical student), May 17, 1965; children: Tad Barrett, Shane Gregory. *Education:* University of Wisconsin, B.A., 1970. *Home:* 4710 C.T.B., Oregon, Wis. 53575.

VICKI KIMMEL ARTIS

She found a shady spot. Then she built her trap.
■ (From *Gray Duck Catches a Friend* by Vicki Kimmel Artis. Illustrated by Giulio Maestro.)

CAREER: Writer and artist. *Member:* Wisconsin Council for the Gifted and Talented, Council for Wisconsin Writers, Wisconsin Regional Writers Association, International Platform Association.

WRITINGS—Juvenile: *Gray Duck Catches a Friend,* Putnam, 1974; *Brown Mouse and Vole,* Putnam, 1975. Contributor of stories to juvenile magazines.

SIDELIGHTS: "While living on an island off the coast of British Columbia, my interest in writing developed. Many dark nights were spent near the fireplace reading books to my young children, Tad and Shane, and my dissatisfaction with much of the material prompted me to begin my own manuscripts. Although I had always enjoyed writing since my childhood in Milwaukee, Wisconsin, I did not consider it seriously and instead pursued philosophy at the University of Wisconsin-Madison where I graduated with a bachelor of science degree in 1970. My husband, Gregory, my two children, and I then moved to the islands where I became a pie-maker and artist, with sculptural exhibitions in Vancouver, British Columbia. We returned to the United States so that my husband could become a medical student at the university.

"Today my family and I live in an old farmhouse outside of Madison, surrounded by wild parsnip and mustard and my African geese. I have taught and lectured on the writing of juvenile fiction but consider myself a full-time writer. Many people wish to know where my ideas come from and I can only say from the hard facts of physical existence and the soft facts of mind-produced phantasy. When I write, my characters often bend my conscious plot-line, for writing is very nearly an extension of the dream phase into the conscious state with exhausting combinations of past episodes, unconscious emotions, irrationality, fantasy, and reality. Writing is a rearranged recording of one individual's mental and physical existence on earth. I enjoy it."

ANN ATENE

ATENE, (Rita) Anna   1922-
(Ann Atene)

PERSONAL: Born April 24, 1922, in Philadelphia, Pa.; daughter of Oliviero and Amleta (Marasco) Atene. *Education:* Graduate of Moore Institute (now known as Moore College of Art), Philadelphia, Pa., 1943. *Home:* Philadelphia, Pa. 19145.

CAREER: The Philadelphia Inquirer, Philadelphia, Pa., artist, 1944-53; free-lance designer-illustrator, 1953—; J. B. Lippincott Company, Philadelphia, Pa., artist (part-time), 1966-76. *Member:* Philadelphia Children's Reading Round Table. *Awards, honors:* The cover of *Civic for Citizens* received the Gold Award from Neographics (Delaware Valley Printers Association) and the Graphic Arts Competition Printing Industries of America award, 1974.

WRITINGS—Self-illustrated: *The Golden Guitar,* Little, Brown, 1967.

Illustrator: Francoise de Saint Andre, *The Messenger of Fair Island,* Winston, 1956; Elizabeth Foreman Lewis, *To Beat A Tiger* (book jacket), Winston, 1956; "Alexandre Dumas" Series (book jackets), Chilton, 1959-64; Lee Cooper, *Fun With Spanish,* Little, Brown, 1960; *Bringing Up Babies,* Harper, 1962; Lee Cooper and Clifton McIntosh, *Fun With French,* Little, Brown, 1963; Cooper,

Greene, and Beretta, *Fun With Italian,* Little, Brown, 1964; Allen and Briggs, *Mind Your Manners,* Lippincott, 1964, 1971; Lee Cooper, *More Fun With Spanish,* Little, Brown, 1967; Hazel Thompson Craig, *Clothing, A Comprehensive Study,* Lippincott, 1968, 1973; Dimond and Pflieger, *Civics of Citizens* (cover), Lippincott, 1970; Louise Bates Ames, *Child Care and Development,* Lippincott, 1970; Burns and Bishop, "Super Sewing" Series (four paperbacks), Lippincott, 1976. Has also illustrated many religious books and story papers for Philadelphia area publishers.

SIDELIGHTS: "Art and books captivated me from childhood. I looked forward to working in commercial art but aspired only to reading books. Bookmaking was a mystery I enjoyed without question, but the answer eventually became my occupation. After beginnings in advertising, I turned to books with increasing involvement.

"The impact of typographic design and the value of printing restrictions were early discoveries of my newspaper days and shaped my claim to be a designer-illustrator. My philosophy as an illustrator has probably been influenced by my early concept of the book as a stimulus for creative thought. The right to conjure belongs to the reader as well as to the illustrator who seeks self expression. I try not to monopolize the pages by telling all in a picture.

"I welcome a variety of assignments which dictates a variety of styles ranging from a free pen line to richly shaded pastels and pencil drawings. Whether it be whimsy or realism, I express it best in charcoal pencil. For the *Fun With Language* series, I worked directly with ink for my roughs, refining them in the final rendering on tracing paper to maintain spontaneity. For *The Golden Guitar,* I made separated pencil tone drawings (four drawings on vellum overlays for each picture) to simulate full-color reproduction.

"In subject, the fanciful, the foreign, and the past engross me. I am curious about origins. Unearthing roots adds another dimension to the present. Our surname my father used to say, hinted of Greek origin because it is the Italian for Athens. Italian parentage led me to write *The Golden Guitar* inspired by an old family story told by my father decades ago and to write 'Buon Natale,' an article about my

Pedro es un muchacho. ■ (From *More Fun with Spanish* by Lee Cooper. Illustrated by Ann Atene.)

mother's childhood memories, to appear in a future issue of *Christmas*, the Augsburg annual.

"I have traveled in many directions throughout the United States, Canada, Mexico, the Caribbean, and Europe, but have always come back to Mom's tiny brick row house which has always been home. Models, especially children in action, fill the streets and yards around me. The city's museums and galleries are minutes away.

"I have an older sister whose children have given me great pleasure and inspiration. It was my sister who showed me how to draw as soon as I could hold the penci!, as my father had shown her and as his father had shown him, though none pursued art.

"To pursue art—to sculpt, to paint and draw—is a joy in itself. Seeing my art put to purpose in books, intensifies that joy."

BACHMAN, Fred 1949-

PERSONAL: Born January 24, 1949, in Niles, Mich.; son of Edmund Leroy and June (Waldorf) Bachman; married Nina Jones (a substitute teacher), June 27, 1970; children: Angela, Troy. *Education:* Michigan State University, B.A., 1971. *Home:* 1214 Walsh, Lansing, Mich. 48912. *Office:* Willow Street School, Lansing, Mich. 48906.

CAREER: Willow Street School, Lansing, Mich., first grade teacher, 1972—. *Member:* National Education Association, Michigan Education Association, Lansing Schools Education Association, Conservation Club (Lansing).

WRITINGS: Hang in at the Plate (juvenile), Walck, 1974.

WORK IN PROGRESS: The Making of an Elementary Teacher: One Man's Experience, an autobiography; *Bitter-*

FRED BACHMAN

I was six batters away from pitching a perfect game.
■ (From *Hang In at the Plate* by Fred Bachman. Illustrated by Harold Berson.)

sweet Basketball, for young people; *Rock Singer,* for young people.

SIDELIGHTS: "All of the books mentioned in my bibliography have been written from deep personal experiences. I know what I'm talking about in these books, and anyone else who has had my experiences should delight in reading them.

"When I write a book, I usually go into a world of my own, as if a time machine put me back to the time I played baseball or basketball. Memory, I guess, is the key to writing about past experiences.

"When I write, I must have a certain feeling about what I'm putting on the paper. I can't just sit down at eight o'clock in the morning and finish at 11:30 in time for lunch. Somedays, I can't put my pen down, while other days I can't pick it up.

"The most important thing about writing? The best story or book you've ever read may be the worst story someone else has ever read. This is why there are very few books that everyone says are great. The same goes for music, food, and everything else in life.

"Writing makes me feel good because it helps me to remember the good times and the bad times. I like the idea of leaving a kind of record or diary behind for my children and their children. They will know me and everything I thought was important in life.

"I have been fortunate to have the time to write in the summer when I am not teaching. Not many people have this opportunity. I live a simple kind of life—easy going and one day at a time. I think positively and try to see the good in life. And there's a lot of good to be found."

HOBBIES AND OTHER INTERESTS: Music (composing).

BAERG, Harry J(ohn)   1909-

PERSONAL: Surname is pronounced Berg; born May 17, 1909, in Waldheim, Saskatchewan, Canada, became naturalized American citizen, July, 1965; son of John George (a farmer) and Helena (Nickel) Baerg; married Ida May Wentworth (an elementary teacher), February 29, 1944; children: Coral Anne, Willard Wentworth, Nadene Lenore. *Education:* Walla Walla College, B.A., 1947. *Religion:* Seventh-day Adventist. *Home:* 11009 Lombardy Rd., Silver Spring, Md. 20901.

CAREER: Free-lance writer and illustrator, 1947-56; Review & Herald Publishing Association, Washington, D.C., book and periodical illustrator, 1956—. Illustrator of sixty-five books besides his own. Columbia Union College, evening school instructor. *Military service:* U.S. Army, Saddler in Veterinary Corps and artist in headquarters unit, 1942-45.

WRITINGS—All self-illustrated: *Bright Eyes, the Story of a Wild Duckling,* Southern Publishing, 1952; *Gray Ghosts,* Southern Publishing, 1952; *How to Know the Western Trees* (adult), W. C. Brown, 1955; *Chipmunk Willie,* Review & Herald, 1958; *Tico the Coyote,* Review & Herald, 1959; *Kari the Elephant,* Review & Herald, 1960; *Humpy the Moose,* Review & Herald, 1963; *Benny the Beaver,* Review & Herald, 1964; *Billy the Buck,* Review & Herald, 1964; *Molly Cottontail,* Review & Herald, 1971; *Bill the Whooping Crane,* Review & Herald, 1971; *Winnie the White Heron,* Review & Herald, 1971; *Creation and Catastrophe* (adult), Review & Herald, 1972; *Coco, the Story of a Range Pony,* Review & Herald, 1973. Author and illustrator of some fifty articles, mainly on natural history subjects, for youth and farm magazines, several coloring books and three nature card games. Wrote and drew weekly animal biography series for youth papers, 1950-60.

Illustrator—All published by Review & Herald unless indicated: Ruth Wheeler, *His Messenger,* 1939; Ernest S. Booth, *Birds of the West,* Outdoor Pictures, 1950, re-illustrated, 1971; Ernest S. Booth, *Biology, the Story of Life,* Pacific Press, 1950; Ernest S. Booth, *How to Know the Mammals,* Brown & Co., 1950; Ernest S. Booth, *Spring Wild Flowers,* Walla Walla College Press, 1953; Roma Dent, *Caw, Caw, the Crow,* Southern Publication Association, 1953; W. H. Lowe, *African Animal Stories,* Southern Publication Association, 1954; Floyd Bralliar, *Zip the Coon,* Southern Publishing Association, 1955; Opal Dick, *Pep, the Collie,* Southern Publication Association, 1955; May Lemon, *Hacky, Teacher's Pet,* Southern Publishing Association, 1955; Howard Munson, *Perky the Partridge,* 1956; Tillman, *Jo, Jo, the Monkey,* 1956; Dorothy Christianson,

Pretty Boy, 1956; Fern Row Casebeer, *Wagon Wheels to Oregon,* 1957; Irene Engelbert, *Listen to Me, Children,* 1957; Herta Glanzer, *Pep and Pepper,* 1957; George Graham, *Log Booms and Mountain Trails,* 1957; Marjorie L. Loyd, *Song of the Leaves,* 1957; Howard Munson, *Smudgie,* 1957; Norma Norris, *Gems From Storyland,* Southern Publication Association, 1957; Tom Tucker, *Hi, Mark,* 1958; Lois Parker, *Brave Heart,* 1958; Pearl Hall, *Valiant Mother,* Southern Publication Association, 1959; Bruce Hallstead, *Poisonous Marine Animals,* United States Navy, 1959; Lois Parker, *Yellow Cat,* 1959; Beatrice Peterson, *Bullet,* 1959; Virgil Robinson, *Those Adventurous Years,* Southern Publication Association, 1959.

Virgil Robinson, *Cabin Boy to Crusader,* Southern Publishing Association, 1960; Kali Paw, *Jungle Flower,* 1960; Josephine Edwards, *I Saw Thee, Philip,* Southern Publication Association, 1960; H. E. Jacques, *How to Know the Water Birds,* Brown & Co., 1960; Evangeline Carr, *Montana Flash,* Southern Publishing Association, 1961; Louise Price Bell, *Pedro,* 1961; Harry M. Tippett, *People of the Book,* 1961; Eunice Soper, *Red Wagons and Billy Goats,* 1962; Bert Rhodes, *Bickie's Cow College,* 1962; Elsie L. Rawson, *Nicku,* 1962; Frank Peterson, *Climbing High Mountains,* 1962; Beatrice Peterson, *Farm Life with Danny,* 1962; Ernest S. Booth, *Birds of the East,* Outdoor Pictures, 1962; Ivy Daugherty, *My Magic Carpet Never Wears Out,* 1963; William Loveless, *Beating Wings,* 1964; Alma McKibbon, *Step by Step,* 1964; (illustrated with others) Arthur S. Maxwell, *Bedtime Stories,* 20 volumes, 1964-68; Harold Clark, *Creation & Flood Film,* 1965; Curtis Barger, *Tomorrow in Your Head,* 1966; Ernie Holyer, *A Cow for Hansel,* 1967; Inez Storie Carr, *Here Comes Willie,* Southern Publication Association, 1968; Ernest S. Booth, *Mammals of Southern California,* University of California Press, 1968; Carolyn Styvesant, *Storytime in Africa,* 1968.

Elsie L. Rawson, *Cuddles and Chuckles,* 1970; George Taggart, *Wonderful World of Trees,* 1970; Alvin M. Bartlett, *K-9 Guard,* 1971; Ella M. Robinson, *Stars in Her Heart,* 1971; George Taggart, *Wonderful World of Animals,* 1971; George Taggart, *Wonderful World of Flowers,* 1971; Kathryn Wilhelm, *Old Joe, the Surprise Horse,* 1973; Ernest S. Booth, *Eastern Bird Guide,* Country Beautiful, 1975; Ruth Conard, *Across the Plains and Back;* Bertha Crow, *Hootlet Home;* Merlin Neff, *Faith of our Fathers,* Faith For Today Press; Harry M. Tippett, *Songs for Children.* Also illustrator of a series of science texts by Ruth Wheeler for Pacific Press Publishers, 1970—.

SIDELIGHTS: "I was fortunate to have been raised on a farm near the small village of Waldheim in a Mennonite community in central Saskatchewan. There I lived as a youngster and I became intimately acquainted with all the details of farm life before farms became so highly mechanized as they are now. I came to love and appreciate the world of nature not only through contact with it, but through the writings of William J. Long in his Wood Folk series of books, and later the fascinating animal stories of Ernest Thompson Seton.

"I thought then as a boy that I would like nothing better when I grew up than to write and illustrate books like those of author-artist-naturalist Seton, but I did not see how this could happen to a shy little farm boy such as I was then, in such an unknown spot as Waldheim. However, I copied many of the little line drawings from Seton's *Animal Heroes* and bound them in a leather cover made from the uppers of a pair of worn out boots. The paper I used was from the blank end papers of books. I still have this little booklet.

"When I was seventeen our family moved to the Okanagan Valley of British Columbia. I was then part way through grade eleven and I dropped out of school for about ten years. During that time I worked in the orchards and truck gardens. I also spent a lot of my spare time on the cattle ranges and forested mountains surrounding our valley. It was for me a time of rich and varied experiences as I discovered a very different world from the one I grew up in, and many of the things I learned then have since found a place in my stories.

"During this time I also did a lot of reading and took a number of correspondence courses. One in taxidermy revived my interest in art and I took several courses in illustration, cartooning, lettering and scene painting. Then I decided that it was time I at least finished high school, and I did this through a government correspondence course. One of the subjects was English composition and literature. Fortunately I had an instructor who encouraged me to write. I got an old Empire typewriter, that did not even have a standard keyboard, and using it, I wrote about everything I could think of that would make a story. It was fun, but I did not try to sell the stories and I am sure they would not have been accepted, still it was good training.

"About this time, during the Depression, I got the idea of taking a trip back to the prairies. I planned to hike over the mountains, then to build a raft on the Saskatchewan river and float down near my home town and on to the great forests of the northland. The actual trip was quite different from what I had planned, but it was packed with experiences. When I got back I wrote them all down, making a book and illustrating it with drawings and paintings. I let the family and friends read it, but that was as far as I went with it then. I knew that it was very immature writing, but it gave me a lot of experience, especially since I rewrote it twice in the years following. By then I realized that it was not the type of manuscript that would impress publishers.

"After that I decided I also needed to get to college, so one fall I went to Canadian Junior College, at Lacombe, Alberta. Here I had a wonderful experience widening my horizons, and while there I had my first article published after winning a prize in a contest. That started me writing for publication. I went on to Walla Walla College, and after a three year stretch in the army returned and graduated in 1947.

"While I was in the army I got married and I also started writing nature articles, before that mine had been inspirational. This I enjoyed and I found a market for all I wrote. Most of my time in the army was spent in Texas and Kansas, the latter part in an art department. This gave me additional background and helped me see where I stood among artists. I returned to school just too late to finish in one year so I filled in another year with additional subjects in biology. I also started illustrating a mammal book and a bird book for one of my professors.

"After that my wife and I moved up into a wilderness area in British Columbia where we lived for a while storing up more

HARRY J. BAERG

experiences while free-lancing in illustrating and writing. Art work was slow coming and I taught school for a year. By then work had picked up and I free-lanced until the children became older and we realized that we needed a more steady income, then we came to the Washington, D.C. area.

"My animal stories are mostly composites that grew out of real animals that I knew. *Gray Ghosts* has in it the stories of three different coyotes in widely separated places where I had lived. *Coco* is the story of a horse I knew and briefly owned while in the Okanagan. I changed names and places, and filled in with things that could have happened. *Benny the Beaver* is based on the locale and the experiences I had with beavers on Mission Creek where I used to herd the farmer's cattle when we first moved to British Columbia. Six of my books are compilations of animal nature biographies that I did over a period of ten years. They are still re-running serially in a children's paper."

Much of Harry Baerg's illustrating (also for books written by others) has been in the natural history field, on subjects pursued and researched over a large part of North America. His work includes about one-hundred full-color paintings for bird, fish, and mammal guides.

ALICE COOPER BAILEY

BAILEY, Alice Cooper   1890-

PERSONAL: Born December 9, 1890, in San Diego, Calif.; daughter of Henry Ernest (a judge and first secretary of Territory of Hawaii) and Mary Ellen (Porter) Cooper; married George William Bailey (member of advisory board, Electrical & Electronics Engineers, Inc.), June 16, 1913; children: Mary Alice (Mrs. Luke Hamilton Montgomery), George William, Jr., Richard Briggs. *Education:* Wellesley College, student, one year (taken at Oahu College); Oahu College, graduate; College of Hawaii (now University of Hawaii), special student, one year; Honolulu Normal School, life diploma in teaching; also attended Boston Conservatory of Music. *Politics:* Republican. *Religion:* Episcopalian. *Home:* 255 Lexington Rd., Concord, Mass. 01742.

CAREER: Author; lecturer on Hawaii and Robert Louis Stevenson. Weston School Committee, member, 1931-39, chairman, 1939-40. *Member:* Women's National Book Association, National League of American Pen Women (state president for Massachusetts, 1946-50, Hawaii, 1954-56; president of Honolulu branch, 1952-54), New England Woman's Press Club (past vice-president), Hawaiian Historical Society, Friends of Iolani Palace (Honolulu), Boston Authors Club (president, 1941-43), Weston Community League (life member), Weston Historical Association, Concord Antiquarian Museum, Concord Woman's Club, Friends of the Concord Public Library. *Awards, honors:* Second prize, National League of Pen Women, for *Footprints in the Dust.*

WRITINGS: Katrina and Jan, P. F. Volland, 1923, reprinted by Wise; *The Skating Gander,* P. F. Volland, 1926, reprinted by Wise; *Kimo, the Whistling Boy of Hawaii,* P. F. Volland, 1927, reprinted by Wise; *Sun Gold,* Houghton, 1930: *Footprints in the Dust,* Longmans, Green, 1936; *The*

Hawaiian Box Mystery, Longmans, Green, 1960; *To Remember Robert Louis Stevenson,* McKay, 1966. Contributor to *Travel, American Girl, Child Life,* and *Story Parade.*

WORK IN PROGRESS: A book, tentatively titled *Rainbow over Manoa,* on the life of her father during the monarchial, provisional, and annexation periods in Hawaii.

SIDELIGHTS: "William Castle of the United States State Department carried copies of *Katrina and Jan* and *The Skating Gander* to Queen Wilhelmina who then commanded her secretary to convey in writing her thanks to me. I still have her letter somewhere. When I wrote about Holland I got some of my information by going to call on the Dutch consul in Boston. When I told him I was writing about his country but had never been there, I think he thought ! was a bit crazy. He read my manuscript before I sent it to Vollands, and gave me a few of the Dutch words I used in the book. When the book was featured in the window of The Corner Bookstore in Boston, the consul and his wife gave a lovely tea for me, inviting all the people of his country living in Boston to it.

"I think I'm probably the exception that proves the rule . . . I never knew what the next page in my books would have on it. . . . I never planned a story, never wrote a synopsis. I was more like a detective following along behind—eager, myself, to find out what my characters would do next. I think that is why I considered writing a great adventure."

Alice Bailey was taken to Honolulu at the age of six weeks, and lived there until 1913. At one time her father owned fifty-two coral atolls in the South Pacific; she inherited title to one-sixth of two islands she has never seen. Her father's office was in Iolani Palace and she has donated all her Hawaiian possessions, including bronze seals, candelabra, etc., to the committee restoring that landmark. Her present home is a pre-revolutionary house on Concord's famous Historic Mile, within walking distance of the homes of Ralph Waldo Emerson, Louisa May Alcott, and Nathaniel Hawthorne.

All Alice Bailey's galley proofs are part of the de Grummond Collection in the library of the University of Southern Mississippi; one book and all her magazine stories for teenagers have been transcribed into Braille.

BAILEY, Jane H(orton)   1916-

PERSONAL: Born May 14, 1916, in Chicago, Ill.; daughter of Ralph (a businessman) and Frances (Chadwick) Horton; married Donald W. Bailey, September 29, 1941; children: David Alan, Phyllis (Mrs. Michael Fisher), Christopher. *Education:* University of California, Berkeley, A.B., 1938. *Home:* 545 Bernardo Ave., Morro Bay, Calif. 93442. *Agent:* Lenniger Literary Agency, Inc., 11 West 42nd St., New York, N.Y. 10036.

CAREER: California State Relief Administration, caseworker in San Luis Obispo and Riverside counties, 1938-39; Padua Hills Institute, Claremont, Calif., employed in public relations, 1940-41; Sacramento Country Day School, Sacramento, Calif., teacher of Spanish, 1964-66. *Member:* International House Association, American Association of University Women, Sierra Club, Audubon Society, Common

Cause, California Writers Club, Morro Bay Tomorrow, Morro Bay Environmental Association.

WRITINGS: The Sea Otter's Struggle, Follett, 1973.

WORK IN PROGRESS: A juvenile novel on the sea otter; plays, skits, monologs, and dialogs in Spanish for students; research on our violent language, on war, and on peace.

SIDELIGHTS: "Natural history (nature) intrigues me, perhaps, because I was reared for the most part in the country. Brought up in a California Mission town may, also, have led me into the Spanish language and a love for Mexico, and history of the southwest. I find that most of my scribblings of the past fifteen years is for young people and concerns wild animals—especially the ones calling the sea their home. Spiny urchins, sea otters, seastars, abalones, for example. The book on the sea otter materialized because I

thought that almost everyone would like to know about a sea mammal which *did not leave the sea* and yet seldom wet its skin! "And, about an animal which mother nature has not yet prepared for life in the sea, yet which fled perhaps one hundred years ago from land to sea just to escape hunters of his unbelievable soft and dense fur (800,000,000 hairs!).

"How could we be unaware of the behavior of any wild animal on our globe? Especially one which is visible, which spends an entire year training its offspring to make its way in its watery world? One which uses a tool (only three other animals do this), and one which can play 'catch' with a hubcap?

"The reason for our ignorance is that the animal was nearly extinct, and only in recent years have there been enough of them for man to observe them and learn from the very fine marine scientists who have studied them. I collected photos

Because the otter sometimes demonstrates responsibility, affection, and humor, it is easy to consider him a notch above most creatures. ■ (From *The Sea Otter's Struggle* by Jane H. Bailey.)

JANE H. BAILEY

and information until I had enough for newspaper and magazine articles, and finally, a book: *The Sea Otter's Struggle*.

"My other writing preferences are skits, plays, jokes, and stories in Spanish, for students of Spanish. Not a *born* writer, surely, I wonder if I do not write because I want to share curious information. I heartily endorse the writing craft, not merely because one can learn to know oneself this way, and to learn to know others, and what makes us tick. But, also, once one's 'children' are published, having gone forth to 'seek their fortune' in the world, the mail can bring surprises beyond one's dreams. What's more, an encounter with a reader can pop up anywhere, anytime and 'warm the cockles of the writer's heart' by saying only 'I read your book.'"

BAILEY, Maralyn Collins (Harrison) 1941-

PERSONAL: Born April 24, 1941, in Nottingham, England; married Maurice Charles Bailey (a printer's clerk), December 21, 1963. *Education:* Educated in Derby, England. *Politics:* None. *Religion:* None. *Home:* 18 La Petite Rue, St. Annes, Ile d'Aurigny, Channel Islands. *Agent:* John Farquharson Ltd., 8 Bell Yard, London W.C.2, England.

CAREER: Government tax officer. Director of Maulyn Ltd. of Jersey. *Awards, honors:* Named Southern Yachtsman of the Year, 1973; Uffa Fox trophy from Southern Newspapers, 1973, for outstanding seamanship.

WRITINGS: (With husband, Maurice Charles Bailey) *Staying Alive,* McKay, 1974; *Maralyn Bailey's Cook Book,* Nautical Publishing, 1977. Contributor to *Bookseller*.

WORK IN PROGRESS: Aftermath of Staying Alive and *Voyage to Patagonia*.

SIDELIGHTS: "We both grew up in the centre of England, far from the sea. We pursued various outdoor activities including camping, climbing and gliding. Gradually our activities turned to the sea and our love of sailing predominated. We had begun our married life in a new house ruled over by an aristocratic Siamese cat. Journeys to and from the office became increasingly frustrating and we exchanged the house and its contents for a yacht. Our disdainful cat refused to move south and remained with the house to become the lord and master of its new owners.

"We lived aboard our yacht for a few years accepting philosophically the snow and cold of the English winters. We eventually decided to make our dreams become reality and sailed away to begin a new life in New Zealand.

"The sinking of our yacht 'Auralyn,' by an injured sperm whale, shattered our dream. But by this time the sea had

MARALYN and MAURICE BAILEY

become our way of life and during the many weeks we lived in a liferaft in the Pacific Ocean, we made a vow. If by some chance we survived the ordeal we decided we would build another yacht and sail again across the oceans we found so fascinating.

"We did survive and built our dream ship. She is named 'Auralyn II.' On her maiden voyage she carried us almost 20,000 miles, spending enroute just over two months cruising the channels north of Cape Horn. It was a region of immense beauty, a blending of glaciers, icebergs, rocky channels, fierce winds and land-locked bays. It was desolate, wild and at times inhospitable, but it's over-awing beauty will remain with us always.

"'Auralyn II' is now provisioned and ready to leave America for England, her second Atlantic crossing within twelve months."

In 1973, the Bailey's twin-keel sloop was shipwrecked about four-hundred and fifty miles from the Galapagos Islands, enroute from England to New Zealand. They spent a hundred and seventeen days adrift on a covered rubber raft, sometimes passing near large ships which failed to see them. They were rescued by a Korean fishing boat about fifteen hundred miles from the spot where they had been shipwrecked, and *Staying Alive* is one result of their misadventure.

HOBBIES AND OTHER INTERESTS: Wildlife, conservation, travel, needlework, medieval history.

FOR MORE INFORMATION SEE: Time, June 3, 1974.

BAILEY, Maurice Charles   1932-

PERSONAL: Born December 27, 1932, in Derby, England; married Maralyn Collins Harrison, December 21, 1963. *Education:* Educated in Derby, England. *Politics:* Socialist. *Religion:* None. *Home:* 18 La Petite Rue, St. Annes, Ile d'Aurigny, Channel Islands. *Agent:* John Farquharson Ltd., 8 Bell Yard, London W.C.2, England.

CAREER: Printer's clerk. Managing director of Maulyn Ltd. of Jersey. *Military service:* British Army, 1951-54. *Member:* Ocean Cruising Club. *Awards, honors:* Named Southern Yachtsman of the Year, 1973; Uffa Fox trophy from Southern Newspapers, 1973, for outstanding seamanship.

WRITINGS: (With wife, Maralyn Collins Bailey) *Staying Alive,* McKay, 1974; *Second Chance,* McKay, 1977. Contributor to *Sail, Yachting Monthly.*

WORK IN PROGRESS: Aftermath of Staying Alive and *Voyage to Patagonia.*

SIDELIGHTS: See Bailey, Maralyn Collins (Harrison).

HOBBIES AND OTHER INTERESTS: Wildlife, conservation, travel, yachting, gliding, walking, navigation.

FOR MORE INFORMATION SEE: Time, June 3, 1974.

BAKER, Margaret J(oyce)   1918-

PERSONAL: Born May 21, 1918, in Reading, Berkshire, England; daughter of Alfred Cosier Slaney (a sales manager) and Irene Wentworth (Aveline) Baker. *Education:* Attended King's College, University of London, 1936-37. *Home and office:* Prickets, Old Cleeve, Minehead, Somerset, TA24 6HW, England. *Agent:* Curtis Brown Ltd., 1 Craven Hill, London W2 3EP, England; and Curtis Brown, 575 Madison Ave., New York, N.Y. 10022.

CAREER: Author of children's books, 1948—. Church Army, driver of mobile canteen, World War II. *Member:* Society of Authors. *Awards, honors:* Second prize for short story, *Child Life,* 1945; *Homer the Tortoise* was an honor book in *New York Herald Tribune* Children's Spring Book Festival, 1950; *Castaway Christmas* was a runner-up for Carnegie Medal of Library Association (British), 1963.

WRITINGS: Nonsense Said the Tortoise, Brockhampton Press, 1949, published as *Homer the Tortoise,* Whittlesey

"When the bus slows down, be ready to jump, and don't let go of my paws. Even if we do bump, it won't matter because we've nothing to break." ■ (From *The Shoe Shop Bears* by Margaret J. Baker. Illustrated by C. Walter Hodges.)

MARGARET J. BAKER

House, 1950; *Four Farthings and a Thimble*, Longmans, Green, 1950; *A Castle and Sixpence*, Longmans, Green, 1951; *Benbow and the Angels*, Longmans, Green, 1952; *The Family That Grew and Grew*, Whittlesey House, 1952; *Homer Sees the Queen*, Whittlesey House, 1953; *Lions in the Potting Shed*, Brockhampton Press, 1954, published as *Lions in the Woodshed*, Whittlesey House, 1955; *Anna Sewell and Black Beauty*, Harrap, 1956, Longmans, Green, 1957; *Acorns and Aerials*, Brockhampton Press, 1956; *The Bright High Flyer*, Longmans, Green, 1957; *Homer Goes to Stratford*, Prentice-Hall, 1958; *The Magic Seashell*, Harrap, 1959, Holt, 1960.

The Birds of the Thimblepins, Harrap, 1960; *Homer in Orbit*, Brockhampton Press, 1961; *The Cats of Honeytown*, Harrap, 1962; *Away Went Galloper*, Methuen, 1962, Encyclopaedia Britannica, 1964; *Castaway Christmas*, Methuen, 1963, Farrar, Straus, 1964; *Cut Off from Crumpets*, Methuen, 1964; *The Shoe Shop Bears*, Harrap, 1964, Farrar, Straus, 1965; *Homer Goes West*, Brockhampton Press, 1965; *Hannibal and the Bears*, Harrap, 1965, Farrar, Straus, 1966; *Porterhouse Major*, Prentice-Hall, 1967; *Bears Back in Business*, Farrar, Straus, 1967; *Hi-Jinks Joins the Bears*, Harrap, 1968, Farrar, Straus, 1969; *Home From the Hill*, Methuen, 1968, Farrar, Straus, 1969.

Teabag and the Bears, Harrap, 1970; *Snails' Pace*, Dent, 1970; *The Last Straw*, Methuen, 1971; *Boots and the Ginger Bears*, Harrap, 1972; *The Sand Bird*, Thomas Nelson, 1973; *Prickets Way*, Methuen, 1973; *Lock Stock & Barrel*, Methuen, 1974; *Sand in Our Shoes*, Methuen, in press.

Short story collections: *Treasure Trove*, 1952, *The Young Magicians*, 1954, *The Wonderful Wellington Boots*, 1955, *Into the Castle,* 1962 (all published by Brockhampton Press).

Contributor of short stories to *Christian Science Monitor, Story Parade, Jack and Jill,* and *Child Life.*

WORK IN PROGRESS: Don't Ask for Bubble and Squeak.

SIDELIGHTS: "My interests mostly centre round the countryside, particularly Somerset and North Devon. I used to live in a house which was once an inn close to Exmoor. Now I live in a bungalow near the sea. I am interested in gardening, motoring, antiques, the Brontes, the history of children's books, tortoises and Pekingese dogs who come into my books, walking, swimming, house decorating. I think humanism and realism are the two qualities I strive for when writing for children. I like to write two kinds of books—magic books for younger children and family adventure stories for children from 10 to 13."

Two of her books, *A Castle and Sixpence* and *Benbow and the Angels* were serialized on British Broadcasting Corp. television programs; ten of them have appeared in translations.

FOR MORE INFORMATION SEE: Margery Fisher, *Intent on Reading*, Brockhampton Press, 1961; *More Junior Authors*, edited by Muriel Fuller, H. W. Wilson, 1963; Naomi Lewis, *The Best Children's Books of 1963*, Hamish Hamilton, 1964.

Something about the Author

BAKER, Mary Gladys Steel   1892-1974
(Sheila Stuart)

PERSONAL: Born in 1892, in Johnstone, Renfrewshire, Scotland; daughter of William (a clergyman) and E. S. (Thomson) Westwood; married S. Howard Baker (deceased). *Education:* Attended High School for Girls, Glasgow, Scotland. *Religion:* Scottish Presbyterian. *Home:* Clarig, Crieff, Perthshire, Scotland.

CAREER: Author and journalist.

WRITINGS—All under pseudonym Sheila Stuart: *Kitty Comes to Stay,* J. Leng & Co., 1929; *The Morisons of Cleave,* J. Leng & Co., 1929; *Antiques on a Modest Income,* Chambers, 1939; *Dictionary of Antiques,* DeGraff, 1954; *Antiques for the Modern Home,* Chambers, 1962, A. S. Barnes, 1964; *A Home from Home,* Longmans, 1967; *Small Antiques for the Small Home,* A. S. Barnes, 1969. Contributor to *Scottish Field.*

"Alison" series of adventure stories for young people (all published by Blackie & Son): *Alison's Highland Holiday,* 1946; *More Adventures of Alison,* 1947; *Alison's Christmas*

MARY GLADYS STEEL BAKER

Adventure, 1948; *Well Done, Alison!,* 1949; *Alison's Easter Adventure,* 1950; *Alison's Poaching Adventure,* 1951; *Alison's Kidnapping Adventure,* 1952; *Alison's Pony Adventure,* 1953; *Alison's Island Adventure,* 1954; *Alison's Spy Adventure,* 1955; *Alison and the Witch's Cave,* 1956; *Alison's Yacht Adventure,* 1957; *Alison's Riding Adventure,* 1958; *Alison's Cliff Adventure,* 1959; *Riddle of Corran Lodge,* 1959; *Alison's Caravan Adventure,* 1960.

(Died January 29, 1974)

The rock was desperately hard and her kilt was sopping. ■ (From *Alison's Easter Adventure* by Sheila Stuart. Illustrated by Gervase.)

BAKER, Samm S(inclair)   1909-

PERSONAL: Born July 29, 1909, in Paterson, N.J.; son of Simon (a textile manufacturer) and Sara (Carlin) Baker; married June 12, 1937 (wife is a professional painter and teacher); children: Wendy (Mrs. Robert Cammer), Steven Jeffrey. *Education:* University of Pennsylvania, B.S. in Economics, 1929; special courses at Columbia University, New York University, New School for Social Research. *Home and office:* 1027 Constable Dr. S., Mamaroneck, N.Y. 10543.

SAMM SINCLAIR BAKER

How to be an Optimist, and Make It Pay, Doubleday, 1960; *How to be a Self-Starter,* Doubleday, 1960; *Miracle Gardening Encyclopedia,* Grosset, 1961; *Your Key to Creative Thinking,* Harper, 1962; *Samm Baker's Clear & Simple Gardening Handbook,* Grosset, 1964; *1001 Questions & Answers to Your Skin Problems,* Harper & Row, 1965; *Indoor & Outdoor Grow-It Book for Children,* Random, 1966; *The Doctor's Quick Weight Loss Diet,* Prentice-Hall, 1967; *Vigor for Men Over 30,* Macmillan, 1967; *The Permissible Lie,* World Publishing, 1968; *Introduction to Art,* Abrams, 1969; *The Doctor's Quick Inches-Off Diet,* Prentice-Hall, 1969.

How to Protect Yourself Today, Stein & Day, 1970; *Gardening Do's and Don'ts,* Funk & Wagnalls, 1970; *The Doctor's Quick Teenage Diet,* McKay, 1971; *The Doctor's Quick Weight Loss Diet Cookbook,* McKay, 1972; *"Doctor, Make Me Beautiful!",* McKay, 1973; *Dr. Stillman's 14-Day Shape-Up Program,* Delacorte, 1974; *Conscious Happiness,* Grosset, 1975; *Straight Talk to Parents About School,* Stein & Day, 1976. Articles for *McCall's, This Week, Reader's Digest, Popular Science, Ladies' Home Journal, Family Circle,* and other popular magazines; gardening series for King Features Syndicate; columnist for advertising publications and contributor of articles; radio and television scripts for "Famous Jury Trials," "Lives of Famous Artists," "Medical Horizons," other programs.

WORK IN PROGRESS: Another book for young people on great art and artists; another gardening book for children; a book on fitness for all ages; another creative thinking book; two suspense novels; other books and magazine articles.

SIDELIGHTS: "I began writing as soon as I could grip a pencil, and I have been writing ever since. Now I'm on my twenty-sixth book, and have numbers twenty-seven, twenty-eight and twenty-nine in the researching and writing. I can't stop, and never want to. Like Shakespeare's character, each night I can hardly wait for 'the fair adventure of tomorrow.' All my books follow my one writing aim: 'To help people live happier, more rewarding lives.' The best-selling success of my books proves that when you try to help others, you also help yourself. My heartblood book and therefore my favorite is *Conscious Happiness, How to Get the Most Out of Living.* The fan mail I have received on that alone makes all my writing efforts worthwhile. One wrote, 'I will have a happier, more fulfilling life because of reading your book!' For me, such rewards are what writing and living are all about.

"If you want to be a writer, I can assure you that I have never known anyone who has written enough who didn't get published. I'm asked, 'When is enough?' My answer: 'When you get published.' That's not a puzzle, it means that to write you have to write—you won't get there if you just *talk* about writing. Starting now, keep a journal, write notes on subjects that excite you, put all such material into a file for future use. Write! Write! Write! That way you *are* a writer, and eventually you will be a published writer. And, from my experience, you will be one of the happiest people in the world because you are expressing yourself creatively, and doing what you want to do as a caring, striving individual.

"I have taught writing to many students in grade school, high school, and college courses. Their accomplishments are proof that you too can gain success and happiness as a writer—*if you will make it so.*"

CAREER: Part-time and summer work in textile factories, retail stores, and on newspapers prior to 1930; worked with Rauch Associates, Inc. (advertising agency), New York, N.Y.; Kiesewetter, Baker, Hagedorn & Smith, Inc., from copy writer to president, 1937-55; Donahue and Coe, Inc. (advertising agency), New York, N.Y., vice-president and member of executive staff, 1955-63; self-employed writer and personal business consultant, 1963—. Consultant to firms in advertising, promotion, merchandising, marketing and mystery story writing. New York University, teacher in advanced retail copy writing. Gardening writer and lecturer for "Flair," American Broadcasting Co. daily network program. *Member:* Mystery Writers of America, Garden Writers of America, Authors League of America. *Awards, honors:* Awards from U.S. Coast Guard and U.S. Treasury Department for war-time writing activities.

WRITINGS: One Touch of Blood, Graphic, 1955; *Murder, Very Dry,* Graphic, 1956; (contributor) *The Mystery Writer's Handbook,* Harper, 1956; *Miracle Gardening,* Bantam, 1958; *Casebook of Successful Ideas for Advertising and Selling,* Doubleday, 1959.

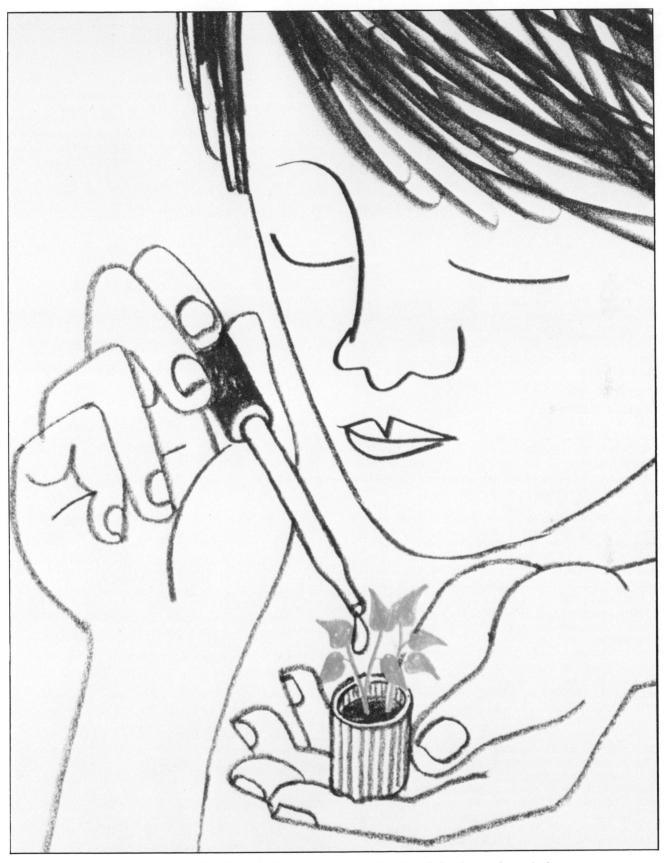

It takes a lot of care, but if you try hard you can grow tiny plants in bottle caps instead of pots.
■ (From *The Indoor and Outdoor Grow-it Book* by Samm Sinclair Baker. Illustrated by Eric Carle.)

GORDON C. BALDWIN

BALDWIN, Gordon C.   1908-
(Gordo Baldwin, Lew Gordon)

PERSONAL: Born June 5, 1908, in Portland, Ore.; son of John A. and Pearl E. (Gibbs) Baldwin; married Pauline Fariss (high school teacher), May 25, 1935; children: Mrs. Patricia Jane Hutchings, Mrs. Marjorie Louise Clarkson. *Education:* University of Arizona, B.A., 1933, M.A., 1934; University of Southern California, Ph.D., 1941. *Politics:* Republican. *Religion:* Baptist. *Home:* 2920 East Mabel, Tucson, Ariz. 85716. *Agent:* Malcolm Reiss, Paul R. Reynolds & Son, 12 East 41st, New York, N.Y. 10017.

CAREER: University of Arizona, Tucson, instructor in archaeology, 1934-37; Arizona State Museum, Tucson, assistant curator, 1937-40; National Park Service, Boulder City, Nev., archaeologist, 1940-48; National Park Service, Omaha, Neb., archaeologist, 1948-53; University of Omaha (Neb.), instructor in anthropology, 1953-54. Board of directors, Westerners International, 1971—, first vice-president, 1974-75. *Member:* Tucson Corral of the Westerners (sheriff, 1973), Western Writers of America (member, board of directors, 1962-63, 1968-70; president, 1968-69), Society for American Archaeology.

WRITINGS: Trail North, Arcadia, 1957; *Trouble Range,* Arcadia, 1959; *Sundown Country,* Arcadia, 1959; *Roundup at Wagonmound,* Arcadia, 1960; *Ambush Basin,* Avalon, 1960; *Brand of Yuma,* Avalon, 1960; *Powdersmoke Justice,* Avalon, 1961; *Wyoming Rawhide,* Avalon, 1961; *America's Buried Past,* Putnam, 1962; *The Ancient Ones,* Norton, 1963; *The World of Prehistory,* Putnam, 1963; *Stone Age Peoples Today,* Norton, 1964; *The Riddle of the Past,* Norton, 1965; *The Warrior Apaches,* Dale Stuart King, 1965.

Race Against Time, Putnam, 1966; *Strange People and Stranger Customs,* Norton, 1967; *Calendars to the Past,* Norton, 1967; *How the Indians Really Lived,* Putnam, 1967;

Games of the American Indian, Norton, 1969; *Talking Drums to Written Word,* Norton, 1970; *Indians of the Southwest,* Putnam, 1970; *Schemers, Dreamers, and Medicine Men,* Four Winds, 1970; *Pyramids of the New World,* Putnam, 1971; *Inventors and Inventions of the Ancient World,* Four Winds, 1973; *The Apache Indians,* Four Winds, 1977. Contributor of articles on anthropology to professional journals. Editor, *The Round-up,* 1962-66.

HOBBIES AND OTHER INTERESTS: Reading westerns, mysteries and spy stories; volunteer work at University of Arizona Hospital; exercising at Tucson Athletic Club; walking.

BALLARD, Lowell Clyne   1904-

PERSONAL: Born December 29, 1904, in Bisbee, Ariz.; son of George Philip (a farmer) and Margaret Delight (Winsor) Ballard; married Margaret Marion Holt, October 25, 1939; children: Roger Lowell, Robert Holt. *Education:* Arizona State University, student; San Diego State College (now California State University), B.A., 1939; Claremont College, M.A., 1943. *Politics:* Democrat. *Religion:* Church of Jesus Christ of Latter-day Saints (Mormon). *Home:* 4533 Highland Ave., San Diego, Calif. 92115. *Office:* John F. Kennedy Elementary School, 447 South 47th St., San Diego, Calif. 92113.

LOWELL CLYNE BALLARD

CAREER: Elementary school principal in Safford, Ariz., 1929-39, and in San Diego, Calif., 1941—. *Member:* National Education Association, Phi Delta Kappa.

WRITINGS—With Frank L. Beals; all juveniles: "American Heroes" Series, published jointly by San Diego City Schools and Stanford Press, 1951; *Real Adventure with the Discoverers of America,* Harr Wagner, 1954; *Real Adventure with the Pilgrim Settlers,* Harr Wagner, 1954; *Real Adventure with American Pathfinders: Daniel Boone, Lewis and Clark, Zebulon Pike, David Crockett,* Harr Wagner, 1954; *Real Adventure with American Plainsmen,* Harr Wagner, 1954; *Real Adventure with American Patriots,* Harr Wagner, 1954; *Spanish Adventure Trails,* Naylor, 1960. Contributor to *The Caravan of Verse,* 1938, and *Winston Basic Reader,* fourth grade. Contributor to scholastic and curriculum periodicals and to yearbooks; also poems to *National History Bulletin* and other magazines. Publisher of several educational history and arithmetic games for young people.

SIDELIGHTS: Lowell Ballard has travelled to the British Isles, Europe, Greece, Turkey, Syria, Lebanon, Israel, Hungary, Yugoslavia, Morocco, Sahara, West Africa, Canary Islands, Canada, Alaska, United States, Mexico, Peru, Columbia, Amazon and New Zealand.

HOBBIES AND OTHER INTERESTS: Writing verse; golf and camping.

BALOW, Tom 1931-

PERSONAL: Born July 2, 1931, in Michigan City, Ind. *Education:* Indiana University, A.B., 1953. *Home:* 333 Southwood Dr., Michigan City, Ind. 46360.

MILITARY SERVICE: U.S. Army, 1954-56.

WRITINGS—All with Allan Carpenter; all juveniles; all published by Childrens Press: *Ecuador,* 1969; *Paraguay,* 1970; *Guyana,* 1970; *British Honduras,* 1971; *Nicaragua,* 1971; *Honduras,* 1971; *Botswana,* 1973; *Lesotho,* 1975.

WORK IN PROGRESS: Algeria.

Children help themselves to food donated by world relief organizations during the long drought in the 1960's. ■ (From *Botswana* by Allen Carpenter and Tom Balow.)

HENRY A. BAMMAN

BAMMAN, Henry A.   1918-

PERSONAL: Born June 13, 1918, in Macon, Mo.; son of Henry A. and Ivy (McAnally) Bamman; married Ruth G. Wiren, June 12, 1948; children: Richard, Elin Kristina. *Education:* Northeast Missouri State Teachers College, B.A., 1945, B.S., 1945; University of Colorado, M.A., 1948; Stanford University, Ed.D., 1952. *Home:* 5718 Monalee Ave., Sacramento, Calif. 95819. *Office:* California State University, Sacramento, Calif. 95819.

CAREER: Public schools, Macon Co., Mo., teacher, 1936-41; University of Colorado, Boulder, instructor in English, 1947-48; Eastern Washington College of Education, Cheney, assistant professor of English, 1948-50; Stanford University, Stanford, Calif., assistant director of counseling center, 1951-55; Sacramento State College, Sacramento, Calif., professor of education, 1955—. *Military service:* U.S. Army Air Forces, European Theater of Operations; received Croix de Guerre. *Member:* National Council of Teachers of English, National Conference on Research in English, International Reading Association (organization chairman, 1962-67), Kappa Delta Pi, Phi Delta Kappa, Blue Key National Honor Fraternity.

WRITINGS: (With Brammer) *How to Study Successfully,* Pacific Books, 1954, 2nd edition, 1969; (with Stroud and Ammons) *Improving Reading Ability,* Appleton, 1955, 2nd edition, 1970; (with Dawson) *Fundamentals of Basic Reading Instruction,* McKay, 1959, 2nd edition, 1962; (with

Hogan and Greene) *Reading Instruction in Secondary Schools,* McKay, 1961; (with Dawson and Whitehead) *Oral Interpretation of Children's Literature,* W. C. Brown, 1964; (with Robert Whitehead) *World of Adventure Series,* Benefic, 1965; (with Dawson) *Basic Science Series,* Century, 1966; (with Whitehead) *Invitation to Adventure Series,* Benefic, 1967; (with Whitehead) *Checkered Flag Series,* Field, 1967-68; (with Whitehead) *Mystery Adventure Series,* Benefic, 1969; (with others), *The Kaleidoscope Readers,* Field, 1969; (with Nordberg and Nordberg) *Free to Choose,* Field, 1969-70; (with Nordberg and Nordberg) *World of Ideas,* Field, 1969-70.

(With Whitehead) *Space Science Fiction* Series, Benefic, 1970; (with Hiyama and Prescott) *Free to Read,* Field, 1970; (with Hiyama and Prescott) *World of Words,* Field, 1970; (with others) *The Cornerstone Readers,* Field, 1970; (with Huus and Whitehead) *Field Literature Program,* Field, 1970-71; (with Dale and O'Rourke) *Techniques of Teaching Vocabulary,* Field, 1971; (with McGovern) *Target Red: Auditory-Visual Discrimination Kit,* Field, 1972; (with Dawson, Hilder and Poe) *Target Yellow: Phonetic Analysis Kit,* Field, 1972; (with Hilder and Poe) *Target Blue: Structural Analysis Kit,* Field, 1972; (with Hiyama and McGovern) *Target Green: Vocabulary Development Kit,* Field, 1973; (with Hiyama and McGovern) *Target Orange: Vocabulary Development Kit, II,* Field, 1973; (with Hancock, Hilder and Poe) *Target Purple: Study Skills Kit,* Field, 1973; (with Edwards, McGovern and Poe) *Target Copper: Comprehension Skills Kit,* Addison-Wesley, 1975; (with Gardiner, Gardner, Hiyama) *Target Mechanics: Guides to Capitalization and Punctuation Kit,* Addison-Wesley, 1975; (with Edwards, McGovern, and Poe) *Target Usage: Guides for Standard English Kit,* Addison-Wesley, 1975; (with Edwards, McGovern and Poe) *Target Spelling: Kits I and II,* Addison-Wesley, 1977; (with Whitehead) *Top Flight Reading Series,* Addison-Wesley, 1977.

SIDELIGHTS: "I was born the seventh child of ten, on a farm in Macon County, Missouri. I learned to read because I was a member of a family whose members all read as soon as they could hold books. As a child, I had the freedom of the fields and the woods, plus an imagination that constantly took me beyond my limited environment. I had excellent teachers, who encouraged me to write, plus a Scottish grandfather who was a marvelous storyteller. I consider writing for children an awesome responsibility—to be honest, faithful to what I believe, and challenging to others' ideas."

Henry Bamman owns a collection of one-hundred-twenty Hogarth originals and holds frequent gallery shows and lectures.

BARISH, Matthew   1907-

PERSONAL: Born October 19, 1907, in Jersey City, N.J.; son of Joseph David (a teacher) and Tillie (Ostrow) Barish; separated; children: David, Emily (Mrs. Clark Josephs). *Education:* City College of New York (now City College of the City University of New York), B.S.S., 1930; New York University, M.A., 1932, further graduate study, 1959-61. *Politics:* Democrat. *Religion:* "Beauty." *Home:* 788 Columbus Ave., New York, N.Y. 10025. *Office:* Parsons School of Design, 2 West 13th St., New York, N.Y. 10011.

CAREER: Public school teacher in New York, N.Y., 1932-33; social worker in New York, N.Y., 1933-36; Hebrew

Lettering comes in two basic types: block letters or print, and script letters. On a card, your letters should not overpower your art work. In a poster, the letters should be outstanding. ■ (From *The Kid's Book of Cards and Posters* by Matthew Barish.)

Publishing Co., New York, N.Y., general manager of Greeting Card Division and member of board of directors, 1936-71; Parsons School of Design, New York, N.Y., teacher of greeting card art, 1974—. Personnel manager for United Transformer, 1944-45; teacher at New York School of Visual Art, 1970—. Volunteer teacher of remedial reading in public schools; executive member of Committee on Returning Veterans (to the electronic industry), 1945-46.

WRITINGS: A Comparative Study of Nine New York City Schools, New York City Board of Education, 1932; *Kids Book of Cards and Posters* (on making greeting cards for people of all ages), Prentice-Hall, 1973.

WORK IN PROGRESS: A slide presentation from his book for high schools and geriatric groups.

SIDELIGHTS: "Most of my adult life has been involved with greeting cards. Its philosophy of communication, love of others has permeated my everyday actions. Starting as a salesman through every step upwards until I became general manager-art director of a greeting card company.

"A few years back in thinking of retiring I decided to think of teaching young people the joy and creativity involved in making greeting cards. I was hired first by the School of Visual Arts and later by the Parsons School of Design to teach a college level course on 'The Greeting Card.' As a result many young people have become free-lance artists and created many saleable greeting cards.

"In 1971 I was asked to write a book on the subject by Prentice-Hall. I fought with them about the title because I thought the book was for people of all ages, but in vain.

"I enjoyed writing the book, though it involved a great deal of research and trying to remember all the details of a varied industry. I had to rewrite it many times which was a struggle. New ideas reminded me of old ideas which I had almost forgotten. Language problems were solved to make complex matters simpler. How to fit hundreds of pages into ninety-six. All forgotten when I saw the first printed copy with my name on the jacket."

HOBBIES AND OTHER INTERESTS: Playing chess and bridge, and travel.

BARTLETT, Robert Merrill 1899-

PERSONAL: Born December 23, 1899, in Kingston, Ind.; son of Robert Alexander (a minister) and Minnie Lou (Dobson) Bartlett; married Theresa Sue Nuckols, August 9, 1923; children: Susan Jane (Mrs. Seward Weber), Mary Warren (Mrs. Fred Stare), Robert Hill. *Education:* Oberlin College, A.B., 1921; Yale University, B.D., 1924. *Politics:* Republican. *Home:* 1660 Bartlett House, Brook Rd., Plymouth, R.F.D. 1, Mass; (winter) 203 Warwick Club, 280 Second Ave. S., Naples, Fla. 33940.

CAREER: Ordained minister of Congregational Church, 1924; Yenching University, Peiping, China, professor of comparative literature, 1924-27; First Congregational Church, Norwood, Mass., minister, 1927-32; First Church of Christ, Longmeadow, Mass., minister, and lecturer at Boston University and Springfield College, 1932-42; Plymouth Congregational Church, Lansing, Mich., minister, and lecturer at Michigan State University, 1942-51; First Congregational Church, Shrewsbury, Mass., minister, 1951-64. New England Theological Library, Boston, Mass., director; Pilgrim Society, lecturer. Lecturer on literature and world affairs at colleges in the United States; member of councils and seminars to Europe, Asia, and South America. Director of Massachusetts chapter, United Nations International Children's Fund; founder of Worcester chapter, National Council of Christians and Jews; chairman, Massachusetts United Church Committee on Church Unity; founder, United Church of Naples, Fla. *Military service:* U.S. Army, World War I, Field Artillery Officers Training.

MEMBER: Society of Mayflower Descendents (elder), Massachusetts Society of Mayflower Descendents (board of assistants), English-Speaking Union, World Congress of Religions, Boston Authors, Pilgrim Society, Society of Descendants of Robert Bartlett (president), Phi Beta Kappa, Boston Fortnightly, Eel River Beach Club. *Awards, honors:* D. D., Yankton College, 1940; Freedoms Foundation Award, 1973.

WRITINGS: The Great Empire of Silence, Pilgrim, 1928; *A Boy's Book of Prayers,* Pilgrim, 1930; *Builders of a New World,* Friendship, 1933; *They Dared to Live,* Association Press, 1934; *Christian Conquests,* Abingdon, 1935; *They Did Something About It,* Association Press, 1937; *Discovery—A Guidebook in Living,* Association Press, 1943; *They Work for Tomorrow,* Association Press, 1944; *The Ascending Trail,* Association Press, 1945; *Sky Pioneer—The Story of Igor I. Sikorsky,* Scribner, 1951; *They*

ROBERT MERRILL BARTLETT, with wife, Sue

Dare to Believe, Association Press, 1952; *They Stand Invincible—Men Who Are Reshaping Our World,* Crowell, 1959; *With One Voice—Prayers From Around the World,* Crowell, 1961; *The Huguenots and Their Cross,* Whittemore, 1965; *Thanksgiving Day,* Crowell, 1965; *Pilgrim Robert Bartlett,* Leyden, 1966; *The Pilgrim Way,* Pilgrim, 1971; *Pilgrim House by the Sea,* Christopher, 1973. Contributor to religious and professional journals.

WORK IN PROGRESS: A biography, *Under Six Flags;* juvenile books; *Ways We Are Alike—The Story of the Great Religions;* a Puerto Rican story, *The House that Juan Built; A Child's First Prayers; The Light Here Kindled—The Faith of the Pilgrims,* a historical work.

BATES, Barbara S(nedeker) 1919-
(Stephen Cuyler, Jim Roberts)

PERSONAL: Born April 28, 1919, in Philadelphia, Pa.; daughter of R. Cuyler (a builder) and Dorothy (Roberts) Snedeker; married Frederick H. Bates, January 20, 1945; children: Susan Penelope, Stephen Cuyler. *Education:* Wellesley College, B.A., 1940. *Religion:* Presbyterian. *Home:* 104 Runnymede Ave., Jenkintown, Pa. 19046.

CAREER: Westminster Press, Philadelphia, Pa., story papers editor, 1941-46, fiction editor, 1944-46, children's book editor, 1967—. Adult education teacher of creative writing in Abington, Pa., Cheltenham, Pa., and Willow Grove, Pa., 1957-66; workshop leader at writers conferences, 1959—, including International Writers Seminar, Green Lake, Wis., 1962. *Member:* American Library Association, Authors Guild of the Authors League of America, Franklin Institute, Abington Library Association, American Association of University Women, National Book Association.

WRITINGS: The Roly Poly Puppy, Grosset, 1950; *The Happy Birthday Present,* Grosset, 1951; *The Real Book of Pets,* Garden City, 1952; (under pseudonym Jim Roberts) *The Real Book of Camping,* Garden City, 1953; *Trudy Phillips, New Girl,* Whitman Publishing Co., 1953; *Trudy Phillips, Headline Year,* Whitman Publishing Co., 1954; *New Boy Next Door,* Broadman, 1965; *Bible Festivals and Holy Days,* Broadman, 1967. Represented in anthologies. Contributor to magazines.

FOR MORE INFORMATION SEE: More Parades, edited by Gray, Monroe, Artley, and Arbuthnot, Scott, 1957.

Something about the Author

BARBARA S. BATES

BEACH, Edward L(atimer) 1918-

PERSONAL: Born April 20, 1918, in New York, N.Y.; son of Edward Latimer (a U.S. naval officer and writer of children's books) and Alice (Fouche) Beach; married Ingrid Schenck, June 4, 1944; children: Inga (deceased), Edward L., Jr., Hubert Schenck, Ingrid Alice. *Education:* U.S. Naval Academy, B.S. (second in class), 1939; National War College, graduate, 1963; George Washington University, M.A., 1963. *Religion:* Presbyterian. *Home:* 29 Gravel St., Mystic, Conn.; currently, 1622 29th St. N.W., Washington, D.C. 20007.

CAREER: U.S. Navy, 1935—, commissioned ensign, 1939, became captain, 1956. Served at sea continuously, 1939-45 (except for three-month period at submarine school), aboard cruiser Chester, destroyer Lea, submarines Trigger, Tirante, Piper. Other major assignments: Commanding officer, USS Amberjack, 1948-49; naval aide and assistant to chairman, Joint Chiefs of Staff, 1949-51; commanding officer, USS Trigger, 1951-53; naval aide to President Eisenhower, 1953-57; commanding officer, USS Salamonie, 1957-58; commanding officer, USS Triton, 1958-61, making 36,000-mile underwater circumnavigation of world, 1960; commander, Submarine Squadron Eight, 1961-62; assigned to Navy Department, Washington, D.C., 1963-66, retired, 1966. Stephen B. Luce chair, U.S. Naval War College, Newport, R.I., 1967-69; staff director, U.S. Senate Republican Policy Committee, 1969-77.

MEMBER: U.S. Naval Institute, National Geographic Society, Naval Historical Association, Metropolitan Club (New York), Cosmos Club (Washington). *Awards, honors*—Military: Navy Cross; Silver Star, twice, Legion of Merit, Bronze Star, twice; Commendation Medal, twice; Presidential Unit citation, three times. Civilian: Sc.D., American International University; Magellanic Premium, American Philosophical Society, 1962; LL.D., University of Bridgeport, 1963.

WRITINGS: Submarine!, Holt, 1952; *Run Silent, Run Deep,* Holt, 1955; *Around the World Submerged,* Holt, 1962; *The Wreck of the Memphis,* Holt, 1966; *Dust on the Sea,* Holt, 1972. Articles for *Argosy, Bluebook, Saturday Evening Post, U.S. Naval Institute, National Geographic, Esquire.* Television script, "Enrico Tazzoli."

SIDELIGHTS: Beach and his crew of 183 officers and men took the Triton on its submerged trip around the world on much the same route followed by Magellan on his 1519-22 voyage. The Triton, world's first sub or ship to be equipped with twin nuclear reactors, left Groton, Conn., on February 16, 1960, and surfaced off Rehoboth Beach, Del., on May 10, 1960. Beach's third book is based on the trip. His second book, *Run Silent, Run Deep,* a war story, was made into the United Artists film with the same title, 1958.

EDWARD L. BEACH

■ (From the movie "Run Silent, Run Deep," copyright 1957 by United Artists Corp., starring Burt Lancaster and Clark Gable.)

BEALS, Carleton 1893-

PERSONAL: Born November 13, 1893, in Medicine Lodge, Kan.; son of Leon Eli and Elvina S. (Blickensderfer) Beals; married Carolyn Kennedy (farmer), June 30, 1956. *Education:* University of California, B.A. (cum laude), 1916; Columbia University, M.A., 1917; additional studies at University of Madrid, 1920, University of Rome, 1922, University of Mexico, 1923. *Politics:* Independent. *Home:* M.R. 2, Box 25, Killingworth, Conn. 06417. *Agent:* Bertha Klausner, 130 East 40th St., New York, N.Y. 10016.

CAREER: American High School, Mexico City, Mexico, principal, 1919-20; correspondent in Spain and Italy, *Nation, Current History,* both of New York, N.Y., 1921-23; New York School Board, New York, lecturer, 1924-25; National University of Mexico, Mexico City, faculty lecturer, 1927; *Nation,* correspondent, Central America, 1926-27; University of California, Berkeley, faculty lecturer, 1932; North American Newspaper Alliance, New York, correspondent, Cuba, 1934; *New York Post,* New York, correspondent, Scottsboro trial, 1935; New School for Social Research, New York, lecturer, 1936; *Nation,* correspondent, Cuba, Haiti, 1957, 1959; *Independent,* New York, correspondent, Cuba, 1960-61, Latin America, 1961. President, *Latin American Digest,* 1932-35; Jacques Romain Committee, chairman, 1935; board of education, New Haven,

Conn., research, 1950-51, 1956-57; public library, Bristol, Conn., research, 1953-54; town of Bristol, Conn., research, 1953-54; Barnes Foundation, Bristol, research, 1953-54; Housing Authority of New Haven, Conn., annual report consultant, 1957-58; Columbia Records, consultant, 1964. Lecturer, fourteen Latin American universities, 1961.

MEMBER: P.E.N. *Awards, honors:* Guggenheim Foundation fellowship to write *Porfirio Diaz,* 1931; award from *Arizona Quarterly,* 1962, for best article of 1961; National Academy of Recording Arts and Sciences, national award, 1966.

WRITINGS: *Mexico,* Huebsch, 1923; *Rome or Death,* Century, 1923; *Brimstone and Chili,* Knopf, 1927; *Con Sandino en Nicaragua,* Comite Pro-Sandino, 1928; *Destroying Victor,* Macaulay, 1929; *Mexican Maze* (Book Club of America selection), Lippincott, 1931; *Banana Gold,* Lippincott, 1932; *Porfirio Diaz,* Lippincott, 1932; *Crime of Cuba,* Lippincott, 1933; *Black River,* Lippincott, 1934; *Fire on the Andes,* Lippincott, 1934; *Story of Huey P. Long,* Lippincott, 1935; *Prologue to Cuban Freedom,* Autenticos, 1935; *The Stones Awake,* Lippincott, 1936; *America South,* Lippincott, 1937; *The New Genius of Roberto de la Selva,* Centro de Estudios Pedagogicos e Hispano Americanos de Mexico, 1937; *The Coming Struggle for Latin America,* Lippincott, 1938, last revision, Halcyon House, 1940; *Glass Houses:*

Something about the Author

Ten Years of Free-Lancing, Lippincott, 1938; *American Earth, The Biography of a Nation,* Lippincott, 1939; *Great Circle,* Lippincott, 1940; *Pan America: A Program for the Western Hemisphere,* Houghton, 1940; *Rio Grande to Cape Horn,* Houghton, 1943; *Dawn Over the Amazon* (Literary Guild selection), Duell, Sloan & Pearce, 1943; *Lands of the Dawning Morrow,* Bobbs, 1948; *Chile: The Long Land,* Coward, 1949.

Our Yankee Heritage: The Making of Greater New Haven, Bradley and Scoville, 1951, revised 1957; *Stephen F. Austin, Father of Texas,* McGraw, 1953; *Our Yankee Heritage: The Making of Bristol,* Bristol Public Library Association, 1954; *Our Yankee Heritage: New England's Contribution to American Civilization,* McKay, 1955; *Adventure of the Western Sea: The Story of Robert Gray,* Holt, 1956; *Taste of Glory,* Crown, 1956; *John Eliot: The Man Who Loved the Indians* (Literary Guild selection) Messner, 1957; *House in Mexico,* Hastings, 1958; *Brass Knuckle Crusade: The Great Know-Nothing Conspiracy,* Hastings, 1959; *Nomads and Empire Builders,* Chilton, 1961; *Cyclone Carry: The Story of Carry Nation,* Chilton, 1962; *Latin America: World in Revolution,* Abelard, 1963; *Eagles of the Andes: South American Struggles for Independence,* Chilton, 1963; *War Within a War,* Chilton, 1965; *Land of the Mayas, Past and Present,* Abelard, 1966; *The Great Revolt and Its Leader,* Abelard, 1966; *Stories Told by the Aztecs,* Abelard, 1970; *Colonial Rhode Island,* Nelson, 1970; *Great Guerrilla Warriors,* Prentice-Hall, 1971; *The Nature of Revolution,* Crowell, 1971; *The Incredible Incas,* Abelard, 1973.

Collaborator, contributor: *Church Problem in Mexico,* 1926; *Genius of Mexico,* Committee on Cultural Relations with Latin America, 1931; *Recovery Through Revolution,* Covici Friede, 1933; *Contemporary Opinion,* Houghton, 1933; *The Writer in a Changing World,* Equinox, 1937; *We Testify,* Smith & Durell, 1941; *What South America Thinks of Us,* McBride, 1945; *The Price of Liberty,* Harper, 1947; *Exploring Life through Literature,* Scott, 1951; *A Treasury of Mississippi River Folk Lore,* Crown, 1955; *Politics U.S.A.,* Macmillan, 1961; *Bits of Silver,* Hastings, 1961.

Writer of introduction: *The Under Dogs,* Cape, 1930; *Memoirs of Jose Luis Blasio,* Yale, 1939; *J'Accuse,* Dial, 1940; *Free Men of America,* Ziff Davis, 1943.

Translations: *Mexiko Och Mexikanska Problem,* Hugo Gebers, 1924; *Enredo de Mexico,* El Universal, 1933; *Porfirio Diaz: Dictader de Mexico,* Universal Illustrado, 1933; *America Ante America,* Zig Zag, 1940; *Panorama Mexicano,* Zig Zag, 1941; *La Proxima Lucha por Latino America,* Zig Zag, 1942; *Fuego Sobre los Andes,* Zig Zag, 1942; *Juan Jose Arévalo, Anti-Kommunism in Latin America,* Lyle Stuart, 1963; *Americo Latina Mundo en Revolucion,* Palestra, 1964; *Nomados y Creadores de Imperios,* University of Buenos Aires Press, 1965.

Contributor to numerous books, pamphlets, encyclopedias, magazines, and newspapers in the United States and other countries. Associate editor, *Mexican Folkways,* 1925-37, *Modern Monthly,* 1943-46, *Controversy,* 1936, *Living Age,* 1936. Columnist, *Independent,* 1961—.

WORK IN PROGRESS: Dream of Marble Halls; The Story of Emperor Maximilian and Carlota; autobiography.

CARLETON BEALS

SIDELIGHTS: "When I was about three, I took my family from Medicine Lodge, Kansas, its big red ants, a local dog-poisoner and Carry Nation, to Pasadena, California. We lived in a white house on a hill beside a cemetery, from which spectres sneaked about at night frightening me. To the north, for miles, stretched fields of golden poppies to the blue mountains beyond. In due time I climbed those mountains with friends, particularly Mount Lowe where stood an astronomical observatory. For a time I wanted to be an astronomer.

"From my earliest years I wanted to be a writer, and about seven, wrote a number of poems. One about a prairie dog who sat at his door in the fog or surveyed the world from a log. Another about a cat who slept on a mat and grew fat. Around twelve I won a prize for a poem sent to a contest held by a Los Angeles daily, and a reporter came out to interview me about what I was going to do with the $5.00 I would receive. I wrote many poems from then on. Had a few of them published; one in the *New Republic,* one in *Pagan,* and later on one in the Irish *Monthly* and another in the London *Times.* One was reprinted in the chief news weekly of that time, the *Review of Reviews,* if I remember correctly.

"My great delight as a boy was my bearded grandfather, a Civil War veteran who rolled about the house in his wheelchair, sick with T.B. He was a one-book man and read and reread *Don Quixote* with such hilarity it often brought on a coughing fit. I read it as a boy and again in Spanish in Mexico and again in Spain, where the great Spanish novelist Valle Incoán recited, to me, the first pages from memory to emphasize the grandeur of its style. In high school I read Washington Irving's *Alhambra,* another glorious book, and swore that the day would come when I would go to Spain. Later I did so twice, and on one occasion lived there for a year. Naturally I read John Dos Passos', *Rosinante to the Road Again* and was happy when I became a good friend of the author.

"In Spain I spent much time in the Alhambra in Granada. Became acquainted with gypsies, who had a settlement out-

Opochtli's body was stained black. About his face hung quail feathers. ■ (From *Stories Told by the Aztecs* by Carleton Beals. Illustrated by Charles Pickard.)

side the town. I wrote my first story, 'The Song of the Whip,' which was published by a Bohemian Paris magazine, *The Broom,* and won three-star mention in O'Neal's annual short story anthology. I also lived for a short time at the Posanda de la Sangre, the Inn of Blood in Toledo, where Cervantes wrote most of his great masterpiece. The inn was later destroyed by the guns of that troglodyte dictator Franco when he took over the country.

"My mother went to the St. Louis World's Fair of 1893 with me in her womb. Her great joy was the extensive exhibits of painting, of which those of New York and Kansas were the most notable. She dreamed that I would be a painter and to promote that she spent most of her time enjoying the art exhibits, an unscientific but laudable hope.

"In Spain, and particularly in Toledo, I became passionately interested in art, and in Toledo, dwelt the spirit and the work of El Greco, who still remains for me the world's greatest painter. Later I spent many happy hours in El Prado, one of the world's great museums, lingering before the canvases of El Greco and Goya and Zubaran and Velasquez. There was a fine-collection of Italian renaissance art, also Titian, Raphael, Tintoretto. When in Italy, where I lived for two years, I made daily visits to the Pitti Palace and Uffizi, the world's finest museum. Later on I spent many hours in the Lateran, the Papal museum, visited the Sistine Chapel, saw

the fine collections in Lucca, Pisa, Bologna, Sienna. Afterwards I visited the remarkable collections in Leningrad and Berlin, and, of course, the Louvre, the most majestic of all.

"I came to appreciate Cimabue, Giotto, Michael Angelo, Pinturrichio, Massacio. (In Florence I had an apartment on the Via Massacio.) And all the time I kept on writing. I received word of the acceptance of my first two books at the American Express Company in Rome, and took the letters up to the Pincio to read them; *Mexico an Interpretation* and *Rome or Death: The Story of Fascism.*

"In the course of my writing, I have visited forty two countries and have met some of the world's great leaders, thinkers, writers and artists.

"Mine has been a full independent life with the customary number of successes and set-backs, ups and downs. I have witnessed numerous revolutions and governmental turnovers in Latin America, Africa and Europe. My life has covered the downfall of European imperialism and serious setbacks to United States imperialism. I have been gladdened by the independence of India, Pakistan, Indo-China, Indonesia, most of Africa, much of Europe, Mexico, Cuba, Jamaica and other peoples of the Caribbean, the various countries of the Near East, of Morocco, Algiers, Tunis, Lybia and Egypt, the end of the Franco dictatorship (but not his system) in Spain, the new democratic regime in Portugal, the overthrow of Mussolini in Italy. I was present at the time of his march on Rome, and at that time prophesied he would last a quarter of a century. I am saddened by the puppet dictatorships of the United States in Chile, Argentina, Uruguay and Brazil, frightful regimes all of them. But more new independent nations have been born during my life time than any time in the history of the world, and a goodly number of them are examples of human freedom. Not since the collapse of the Spanish empire has the phenomenon of human liberation been more in evidence. Meanwhile I can occasionally visit the Metropolitan Museum and the Museum of Modern Art, where, thanks to Ambassador Morrow, a friend of mine, René, became director.

"Being an independent writer, doubly so now, is a thorny path. Sooner or later, one steps on everybody's toes. Being an independent writer means having no fixed address; people pin labels on you, and, when the labels don't fit, they hate you. But there is still a large body of independent thinkers in America; there is a large body of tolerant spirits; there is a large body of people seeking knowledge, truth, moral and spiritual understanding. Such as these are my friends and my readers. Sometimes I fail them but not most of the time.

"I have done most of my writing in Spain, Italy, Mexico and Peru, and in this country, chiefly in New York, later in Guilford, Conn., since 1957 in Killingworth, where I have reconditioned one of the village's first schoolhouses as a study, a big barrel-ceiling room, with seven windows, floor to ceiling book shelves, three metal files, a grand piano, good heat, a radio but no television, water colors of Haiti's painter, Joseph Blanchard, neon lights.

"My wife tends to two horses and five cats. She gets most of the exercise. When I feel the need for exercise, I usually lie down on my studio couch, and it soon goes away. My working hours are about 9:00 to 2:00, occasionally a few hours in the afternoon, 8:30 p.m. to midnight or maybe 3:00 a.m. I read one book a day (included in work time). Most of my reading is in Spanish.''

Carleton Beals has traveled in forty-one countries, frequently as a member of educational and archaeological expeditions. He speaks Spanish, Italian and some German. Has a reading knowledge of French and Portuguese and a smattering of Aztec.

HOBBIES AND OTHER INTERESTS: Chess, horseback-riding.

FOR MORE INFORMATION SEE: Horn Book, April, 1958; *Nation,* August 20, 1960; *New York Herald Tribune Book Review,* August 28, 1960; *Saturday Review,* December 16, 1961, October 12, 1963; *Yale Review,* December, 1963; *Times Literary Supplement,* March 5, 1964.

BEAME, Rona 1934-

PERSONAL: Born December 8, 1934, in New York, N.Y.; daughter of Alvin (a manufacturer) and Frances (Weinberg) Friedman; married Bernard Beame (a film producer; and son of New York City mayor, Abe Beame), June 23, 1963; children: Andrew, Richard, Julia. *Education:* University of Michigan, B.A., 1956; Cooper Union, art certificate, 1962.

Politics: Democrat. *Religion:* Jewish. *Home:* 40 Valley View, Chappaqua, N.Y. 10514. *Agent:* Lucy Goldberg, 255 West 84th St., New York, N.Y. 10024.

CAREER: Nationwide Trade News Service, New York, N.Y., writer, 1956; Earl Wilson (columnist), New York, N.Y., writer, 1957-59; *MD Medical Newsmagazine,* New York, N.Y., picture editor, 1961-67. Free-lance photographer, 1956—.

WRITINGS—All juveniles; all with photographs by author: *Calling Car 24 Frank: A Day with the Police,* Messner, 1972; *Ladder Company 108,* Messner, 1973; *What Happens to Garbage?,* Messner, 1975; *Emergency,* Messner, 1977.

WORK IN PROGRESS: (Writing with Bobbie LoSacco) a contemporary mystery for children that is intertwined with slavery and the underground railroad; a comedy for adults on the life of suburban women.

SIDELIGHTS: ''Ever since I was little, I was a storyteller. I needed to share my experiences with others. The medium didn't matter—it could be talking, writing, photography or painting. What was important was that the retelling clarified my thoughts and satisfied some need to record and pinpoint the interesting and beautiful things that happened to me.

''At various times I studied painting, piano and ballet and writing. I enjoyed them all. Then I went to college (Univer-

RONA BEAME

At 6 A.M., the fire is out. Tired and dirty, Eddie Hand stops for a moment to rest. Then 108 leaves. ■ (From *Ladder Company 108* by Rona Beame. Photographs by the author.)

sity of Michigan) and started to work on the school newspaper (*The Michigan Daily*). And then I learned that journalism was the career for me. I discovered I loved the simplicity, directness and power of good journalistic writing. I discovered I loved meeting people and finding out all about them. How else could I ask people I didn't know, all kinds of questions and not be accused of rudeness?

"My college years were, also, the years of Senator Joseph McCarthy and his Unamerican Activities Committee. It was a terrible time. McCarthy destroyed so many lives and was so powerful that few people in this country dared speak out against him. But the *Michigan Daily* and the people who worked for it did. And I was proud to be a part of it. And I learned that every voice that spoke up was important, no matter how small. Because each voice became part of a tide and when that tide became strong enough, it swept away McCarthy. And so I saw at first hand, what journalism could do at its best.

"During college I decided to take a few photography classes. I thought it would help me get a job later as a journalist. And it did. Eventually photography became as important to me as the writing. When I wrote and took pictures of a subject, it became a complete expression of everything I had to say.

"After college I went through a variety of reporting jobs. When I began having children I decided to find part time work that would fit in with raising a family. I decided to try and write children's books. The first one I wrote was fiction.

The second one was fiction with photographs. Both books collected enough rejection slips from publishers to convince a less hardy soul to find a new career.

"Then one day something clicked in my head. As a beginning author, why was I trying fiction when my own special talents were in journalism? I thought about all the subjects that *I* would really like to know about and decided to do a book on the police.

"I have never been interested in facts and figures, so I decided that my book would be concerned with people—which is what I do care about. I would find out how a policeman felt about his job, what he thought about the people he arrested and when he was scared. I wanted anecdotes and stories and feelings. Because that is what we remember.

"I would like to say that the police book was immediately snapped up by a publisher. Untrue. The police book almost collected as many rejection slips as the first two books. Then just as I was about to give up on the police book *and* my career as a children's author, the miracle happened. Someone wanted to publish my book. Surely, that was one of the best moments of my life.

"After that it all became easy. My publisher, Julian Messner, was interested in doing a series of books on community workers and that was just fine with me. I am now working on my fourth book for them.

"Researching my books is almost the most fun. For the police book I spent two weeks riding in a police car. And it was a fascinating and scarey two weeks.

"For the fireman book I spent weeks living in a firehouse, eating and sleeping there. I was most impressed by the firemen themselves. Each day their lives are filled with danger and adventure. And they thrive on it. They are the most independent and gutsy men I have ever met.

"Now I am working on two books. One is on a hospital's emergency room and the other is a mystery. But even the mystery requires some research. The story takes place in New York City today, but, also, tells about what it was like in the days of slavery. Most of our research was reading—about slavery, the underground railroad and what New York City was like in the 1840's and 50's. But for some of it we had to actually go out and explore very old parts of the city and old buildings. That was fun, too.

"I enjoy what I do. I love finding out about the 'underside' of life. Like suddenly picking up a rock and catching a glimpse of all the creatures that live underneath. I want to find out what is at the end of a siren and where everybody's garbage goes and what it's like to ride inside an ambulance and to know that whether a person lives or dies may depend on how fast you think.

"Writing a book is an adventure. When I start, I never know how it will turn out or which of the strangers that I am meeting will turn out to be the heroes of my book. Doing a book is like walking through a magic mirror into someone else's life—and it has made my life so much richer."

HOBBIES AND OTHER INTERESTS: Travelling, tennis, opera.

BECK, Barbara L. 1927-

PERSONAL: Born March 25, 1927, in Boston, Mass.; daughter of James J. (executive of a restaurant chain) and Frances Louise (Holmberg) Curry; married Andrew De-Young; children (first marriage); Sandra L. Beck. *Education:* Monmouth College, Monmouth, Ill., B.A. *Politics:* "Unreconstructed Republican." *Religion:* Episcopalian. *Home:* Craney Hill, Henniker, N.H. 03242.

CAREER: Free-lance journalist and advertising copywriter in Boston, Mass., 1948-52; John C. Dowd, Advertising, Boston, Mass., research director, 1953-54; self-employed insurance and real estate broker, Scituate, Mass., 1954-57; Ginn and Co. (educational publishers), Boston, Mass., advertising manager, 1957-74. Lecturer on books and traveling. Massachusetts Taxpayers Association, executive director, 1954-55; Town of Scituate, member of personnel board, 1958-59. United Fund of Greater Boston, co-director, 1956.

WRITINGS: First Book of Weeds, 1963, *First Book of Palaces,* 1964, *First Book of the Ancient Mayas,* 1965, *First Book of the Inca,* 1966, *First Book of the Aztecs,* 1966, *First Book of Fruits,* 1967, *First Book of Vegetables,* 1968, *First Book of Columbia,* 1969, *First Book of Venezuela,* 1970, *The Pilgrams of Plymouth,* 1971 (all published by Watts).

WORK IN PROGRESS: Writing on Latin America.

BECKER; John (Leonard) 1901-

PERSONAL: Born December 12, 1901, in Chicago, Ill.; son of Benjamin V. (an attorney) and Elizabeth (Loeb) Becker; married Virginia Campbell (a painter); children: R. Campbell, Haidee Giovanna. *Education:* Phillips Academy, Andover, Mass., graduate, 1919; Harvard University, B.A., 1924. *Home:* 46 Glebe Pl., London SW3 5JE, England.

CAREER: Chicago Daily News, Chicago, Ill., columnist, 1927; John Becker Gallery, New York, N.Y., owner 1929-33; Brattleboro Theatre, Brattleboro, Vt., and Brooklyn, N.Y., co-director, 1935-37. Free-lance writer. American Red Cross, field service in Italy, 1943-44. Director of work for Negro advancement, Council Against Intolerance in America. *Member:* Authors League of America.

WRITINGS: The Negro in American Life, Messner, 1944; (with Georgene Faulkner) *Melindy's Medal* (juvenile), Messner, 1945; *New Feathers for the Old Goose* (poems for children), illustrated by wife, Virginia Campbell, Pantheon, 1956; *Near-Tragedy at the Waterfall* (juvenile), illustrated by V. Campbell, Pantheon, 1964; *Seven Little Rabbits,* Walker, 1973. Contributor of short stories to literary magazines in Italy and *London Magazine.* Writer of plays for private marionette theater.

WORK IN PROGRESS: A children's book entitled *Mirabelle Pirabelle Pickles;* short stories; and commentary for a John Ferno film about Israel, "Tree of Life."

One of the three gateways to Sacsahuaman, the gigantic fortress outside of Cuzco. ■ (From *The Incas* by Barbara L. Beck. Pictures by Page Cary.)

Then
The last little rabbit
Went to sleep--
Shh, don't say "Peep"--
■ (From *Seven Little Rabbits* by John Becker. Illustrated by Barbara Cooney.)

JOHN BECKER

SIDELIGHTS: During the years he owned his art gallery Becker was responsible for introducing to the United States such artists as Arp, Bauchant, Charlot, Noguchi, Helion, Le Corbusier, Leger, and Lurcat.

BELL, Gertrude (Wood) 1911-

PERSONAL: Born January 28, 1911, in Liberty, Mo.; daughter of William Edward and Myrtle (Griffith) Bell. *Education:* William Jewell College, A.B., 1933. *Home:* 30 South Fairview, Liberty, Mo. 64068.

CAREER: Freelance fiction writer, 1954—. *Member:* Authors Guild, National League of American Pen Women, Missouri Historical Society, Missouri Writers Guild, Clay County Museum Association. *Awards, honors:* Missouri Writers Guild award, 1963, for juvenile short story; Midwest section of National League of American Pen Women award, 1963, for teen-age short story; awards from Missouri Writers Guild and National League of American Pen Women, both 1965, for *Posse of Two;* nomination of *First Crop* for 1975 Mark Twain Award; Missouri Library Association literary award, 1975.

WRITINGS: Posse of Two, Criterion, 1964; *Roundabout Road,* Independence Press, 1972; *First Crop,* Independence Press, 1973; *A Ladder for Silvanus,* Independence Press, 1974; *Where Runs the River,* Independence Press, 1976. Contributor of short stories to periodicals.

WORK IN PROGRESS: Sand, Silver, and a Mule Named Mike and *Shannon's Seeking,* both fiction for 10-14-year-old readers.

Something about the Author

SIDELIGHTS: "Since my love affair with books preceded my learning to read, it was an early dream, late realized, that I would be a writer.

"'Write about what you know,' instructors advised.

"What did I know best?

"Well, I had a head full of stories from pre-radio, pre-television days when people 'spun yarns.' Often their tales were of early days, their hardship and drama.

"Thanks to nine enchanted years on a 'family farm' before electricity, before all-weather roads, when the internal combustion engine was still almost a novelty, I was, to a degree, equipped to write about the hard work and sacrifice that went into the creation of our structured society. Most of all, to write about the lives of the people who bequeathed it to us.

"It was a personal commitment. My funny little seventy-year-old house, bulging with books, is less than a block from the 'Kansas Road,' built in early days to connect Liberty with Fort Leavenworth, Kansas. Along that road, in the early 1830's, creaked the covered wagon that carried my Bell great-grandparents from Kentucky to the farm a few miles west where they would rear their family and live out their lives.

The shouts, a scant quarter-mile away, at first seemed scarcely louder than the rustle of the rich green blades of the corn and the thump of a heavy hoe. ■ (From *First Crop* by Gertrude Bell. Illustrated by Susan Hood.)

"From early days two great-great-grandfathers and eight great-grandparents called Clay County, Missouri 'home.' A traditional one-room country school, now closed, carried the Bell name. Great-grandfather Smithey was one of the original trustees of our still-flourishing Methodist church. There are houses in Liberty, still occupied, which he built. Great-great-grandfather Knight was among the first pastors to another early church, now gone.

"They, and thousands of others, created so much for us! It is my privilege and pleasure to write for young people about their struggles and their achievements.

"I have written much of the Civil War period because so little has been written, particularly for young people, about the western war, which was almost a separate conflict. I do not apologize for reminding young readers that wars don't necessarily happen on the other side of the world. One of the wickedest, the Civil War, happened right here. Also, I have a store of true stories that I think worth preserving.

"*First Crop* 'happened' because all my life I have heard about the ancestor who stood on his porch in the little frontier village of Blue Springs and counted the columns of smoke rising as house after house was put to the torch when the infamous General Order No. 11 was carried out. As a farm girl, the burning of houses, the wanton slaughter of livestock, and the destruction of crops impressed me deeply.

GERTRUDE BELL

"Those enchanted years gave me long hours of solitude for observing and dreaming. A creek to fall into . . . trees to fall out of . . . horses to fall off of. . . . Nothing could have better prepared me for welcoming my profession's mandatory solitude. The little girl who was content with only the company of a dog at her heels is now a senior citizen content with her typewriter, weaving tales in which that little girl's experience and observations, often attributed to a boy, may play a part.

"For me a story starts with asking myself, 'What if?' Then, whether it is a few hundred words or many thousands, I plan my ending. Whatever happens in between, and usually I'm not sure, I have two goals for my central character. He will meet and master challenges, and thereby mature and become a better person.

"Autographing books to young readers, I wish them, 'Happy reading,' the best I can wish for them. To me education is learning to communicate. If I can communicate admirable values, I am content."

BENEDICT, Lois Trimble   1902-1967

PERSONAL: Born June 29, 1902, in North Tonawanda, N.Y.; daughter of William D. (a real estate man) and Bertha (Todd) Trimble; married Clinton S. Benedict (a civil engineer); children: Clinton S., Jr. *Education:* Buffalo State Teachers College, Diploma and Life Teaching Certificate, 1923; Simpson College, B.A., 1925. *Religion:* Methodist. *Home:* 23 High St., Katonah, N.Y. 10536.

CAREER: Elementary teacher in Katonah, N.Y., before marriage; operator of private kindergarten in her home, Katonah, N.Y., 1932-40; writer for young people. *Member:* National League of American Penwomen, Woman's Society of Christian Service (secretary of New York conference), Woman's Civic Club (Katonah), Lionets, King's Daughters.

WRITINGS: Canalboat Mystery, Atheneum, 1963. Writer of church school teacher's guides published by Friendship. Contributor of thirty stories and forty articles to *Scholastic Magazine, Boy's Life, Child Guidance, Juniors, Horticulture, Instructor, McCall's Needlework,* and other educational and denominational magazines (Catholic, Jewish, and Baptist, as well as Methodist).

WORK IN PROGRESS: A book on falconry and history of the early settlement of Iceland; a book on scavenger animals, birds, and fish of the world.

(Died April 8, 1967)

BERENSTAIN, Jan(ice)

PERSONAL: Daughter of Alfred J. and Marian (Beck) Grant; married Stanley Berenstain (a cartoonist, illustrator, and author; her collaborator), April 13, 1946; children: Leo, Michael. *Education:* Philadelphia College of Art, 1941-45. *Residence:* Solebury, Pa. *Agent:* Sterling Lord, The Sterling Lord Agency, 660 Madison Ave., New York, N.Y. 10021.

CAREER: Cartoonist, illustrator, and author. Creator, with husband Stanley, of *McCall's* magazine feature, *It's All in the Family* (now appearing in *Good Housekeeping*). Work featured in advertising campaigns and brochures. Calendars and greeting cards for Hallmark, 1962-72. Represented in Metropolitan Museum of Art international exhibition of cartoons; represented in exhibition of British and American humorous art in London. Work is in Albert T. Reid Cartoon Collection at the University of Kansas and the Farrell Library Collection at Kansas State University. Stanley and Janice Berenstain Manuscript Collection established at Syracuse University in 1966.

WRITINGS—All illustrated, all with husband, Stan: *Berenstain's Baby Book,* Macmillan, 1951; *Sister* (cartoons), Schuman, 1952; *Tax-wise,* Schuman, 1952; *Marital Blitz,* Dutton, 1954; *Baby Makes Four,* Macmillan, 1956; *Lover Boy,* Macmillan, 1958; *It's All in the Family* (originally published in *McCall's*), Dutton, 1958; *Bedside Lover Boy,* Dell, 1960; *And Beat Him When He Sneezes,* McGraw, 1960, paperback published as *Have A Baby, My Wife Just Had A Cigar,* Dell, 1960; *Call Me Mrs.,* Macmillan, 1961; *It's Still in the Family* (originally published in *McCall's*), Dutton, 1961; *Office Lover Boy,* Dell, 1962; *The Facts of Life for Grown-ups,* Dell, 1963; *Flipsville-Squaresville,* Dial, 1965; *Mr. Dirty vs. Mr. Clean,* Dell, 1967; *You Could Diet Laughing,* 1969; *Be Good or I'll Belt You,* Dell, 1970; *Education Impossible,* Dell, 1970; *Never Trust Anyone Over 13,* Bantam, 1970; *How to Teach Your Children About Sex,* Dutton, 1970; *How to Teach Your Children About God,* Dutton, 1971; *Are Parents for Real?,* Bantam, 1972.

"Berenstains' Bears Series" (juvenile), all published by Random House: *The Big Honey Hunt,* 1962, *The Bike Lesson,* 1963, *The Bears' Picnic,* 1966, *The Bear Scouts,* 1967, *The Bears' Vacation,* 1968 (published in England as *The Bears' Holiday,* Harvill, 1969), *Inside, Outside, Upside Down,* 1968, *Bears on Wheels,* 1969.

The Bears' Christmas, 1970, *Old Hat New Hat,* 1970, *Bears in the Night,* 1971, *The B Book,* 1971, *C is for Clown,* 1972, *The Bears' Almanac,* 1973, *The Berenstain Bears' Nursery Tales,* 1973, *He Bear She Bear,* 1974, *The Berenstain Bears' New Baby,* 1974, *The Bears' Nature Guide,* 1975, *The Bear Detectives,* 1975.

WORK IN PROGRESS: The Bears' Science Fair; No Such Thing as a Little Bit Pregnant.

SIDELIGHTS: "Stan and I have been doing what it takes two to—for thirty years. Since, individually, each has a serious bent for humor, we hope that when we tango it comes out funny. Our tango consists of a combination of funny pictures and funny words—we both draw, we both write (some times he leads, some times I lead)—and until thirteen years ago, we had an average general readership. (*Everybody* likes cartoons.)

"About that time we got interested in doing children's books. Our own two children had taken to books like ducks to water and we had made some observations about the process of language development and learning to read. I had one of the children on my lap the very first time he put two words together—he had just gotten a toy truck for Christmas and we were in the back seat of the car . . . he was identifying trucks in the traffic and a big truck that was coming toward us was suddenly passing by his window and as it filled the window he said, 'Bi-i-ig truck!' We didn't have to grope long to figure out how to depict a big brown bear in the *B*

Book—we just made sure it *filled the window*. The other one first started using sentences and action phrases while crawling in and out of a big grocery carton. His early experience became Small Bear's in *Inside, Outside, Upside Down*.

"We had books all over the house including lots of excellent childrens books—and—cartoons. They loved cartoons—they loved jokes—they liked to laugh. We could see that children as well as grown-ups would read for the reward of laughter. And with our simple but realistic cartoon style, we felt we could make *anything* clear.

"We were very interested in the Beginner Book program just getting started at Random House. We started doing Beginner Books to give children the extra fun of cartoon humor that had spiced the early reading of our own children. Our bear family—especially Papa Bear—will do anything for a laugh ... from sticking his nose into a skunk's hollow looking for honey to backing into a bolt of lightning looking for the perfect picnic spot. When he gets a laugh he knows someone is having fun reading.

"Stan and I hope the bears give children a little insight into human nature, too—after all, the bears are just exaggerated people—the small ones are alert and smart and learn a lot from the big ones who are very sincere and expert but make a lot of mistakes while trying to impart their vast knowledge to their young.

"In our Bright & Earlies we hope to instill in our small readers carefully programmed number and language concepts that the small bears go all out to demonstrate as they tell their stories:—the concepts of *Inside, Outside, Upside Down* (and how it's possible to be any two or even all three at once)—number concepts in *Bears on Wheels*, where many small bears *add* themselves *to* and *take* themselves *away* from different sets of wheels as they travel the freeways of Bear Country—the use of all kinds of description words (*Old Hat New Hat*) while telling an old hat joke—prepositional phrases that describe movement and direction while telling a spooky bedtime story (*Bears in the Night*)—the *B Book* and *C is for Clown* are a couple of tongue-twisters that encourage the use of phonics in puzzling out new words—and in *He Bear She Bear*, two small bears demonstrate what great fun the residents of Bear Country have not being sexist—some even get to tango."

BERENSTAIN, Stan(ley) 1923-

PERSONAL: Born September 29, 1923, in Philadelphia, Pa.; son of Harry and Rose (Brander) Berenstain; married Janice Grant (cartoonist, illustrator, and author; his collaborator), April 13, 1946; children: Leo, Michael. *Education:* Philadelphia College of Art, 1941-42; Pennsylvania Academy of Fine Arts, 1946-49. *Residence:* Solebury, Pa. *Agent:* Sterling Lord, The Sterling Lord Agency, 660 Madison Ave., New York, N.Y. 10021.

CAREER: Cartoonist, illustrator, and author. Creator, with wife Janice, of *McCall's* magazine feature, *It's All in the Family* (now appearing in *Good Housekeeping*). Cartoons featured in advertising campaigns and brochures. Calendars and greeting cards for Hallmark, 1962-72. Represented in Metropolitan Museum of Art international exhibition of cartoons; represented in exhibition of British and American humorous art in London. Work is in Albert T. Reid Cartoon

Collection at the University of Kansas and the Farrell Library Collection at Kansas State University. Stanley and Janice Berenstain Manuscript Collection established at Syracuse University in 1966. *Awards, honors:* School Bell Award of National Education Association for illustrated article "How to Undermine Junior's Teacher," 1960.

WRITINGS—All illustrated, all with wife, Jan: *Berenstain's Baby Book,* Macmillan, 1951; *Sister* (cartoons), Schuman, 1952; *Tax-wise,* Schuman, 1952; *Marital Blitz,* Dutton, 1954; *Baby Makes Four,* Macmillan, 1956; *Lover Boy,* Macmillan, 1958; *It's All in the Family* (originally published

JAN and STAN BERENSTAIN

Be alert for any
sign or sound--
the wonders of nature

Something about the Author

are all around!

■ (From *The Bears' Nature Guide* by Stan and Jan Berenstain. Illustrated by Stan and Jan Berenstain.)

in *McCall's*), Dutton, 1958; *Bedside Lover Boy*, Dell, 1960; *And Beat Him When He Sneezes*, McGraw, 1960, paperback published as *Have A Baby, My Wife Just Had A Cigar*, Dell, 1960; *Call Me Mrs.*, Macmillan, 1961; *It's Still in the Family* (originally published in *McCall's*), Dutton, 1961; *Office Lover Boy*, Dell, 1962; *The Facts of Life for Grownups*, Dell, 1963; *Flipsville-Squaresville*, Dial, 1965; *Mr. Dirty vs. Mr. Clean*, Dell, 1967; *You Could Diet Laughing*, 1969; *Be Good or I'll Belt You*, Dell, 1970; *Education Impossible*, Dell, 1970; *Never Trust Anyone Over 13*, Bantam, 1970; *How to Teach Your Children About Sex*, Dutton, 1970; *How to Teach Your Children About God*, Dutton, 1971; *Are Parents for Real?*, Bantam, 1972.

"Berenstains' Bears Series" (juvenile), all published by Random House: *The Big Honey Hunt*, 1962, *The Bike Lesson*, 1963, *The Bears' Picnic*, 1966, *The Bear Scouts*, 1967, *The Bears' Vacation*, 1968 (published in England as *The Bears' Holiday*, Harvill, 1969), *Inside, Outside, Upside Down*, 1968, *Bears on Wheels*, 1969.

The Bears' Christmas, 1970, *Old Hat New Hat*, 1970, *Bears in the Night*, 1971, *The B Book*, 1971, *C is for Clown*, 1972, *The Bears' Almanac*, 1973, *The Berenstain Bears' Nursery Tales*, 1973; *He Bear She Bear*, 1974, *The Berenstain Bears' New Baby*, 1974, *The Bears' Nature Guide*, 1975, *The Bear Detectives*, 1975.

WORK IN PROGRESS: The Bears' Science Fair; No Such Thing as a Little Bit Pregnant.

SIDELIGHTS: "The whole business of creating books for children has been a humbling experience. Children do not necessarily approach books as sacred objects which trace their noble lineage back to Gutenberg and the invention of moveable type. Children are like voters at the precinct level. They want to know what you've done for them lately.

"They don't worry much about reviews, best seller lists, or the authors' appearance on last night's Dick Cavett Show. To a child a book is a book is a book . . . and he either likes it—for any of a number of reasons—or he doesn't.

"To a very small child a book isn't even a book. It's just a thing. An object. And not a very promising object at that. It doesn't go up and down on a string like a yo-yo. It doesn't taste terrific like a Tootsie Roll. And it certainly doesn't light up and move and talk and dance and sing like the big color TV in the living room.

"What to do. What can we do to make books and the closely connected, vitally important idea of reading competitive with yo-yos, Tootsie Rolls and television. . . .

"In the course of the fifteen or so beginner and pre-beginner books Jan and I have done since the Bears moved into our studio a dozen years ago, we've come to a few conclusions on the subject of encouraging children to read.

"One thing we can do is make things *perfectly clear.* For most children, learning to read well is a difficult job and they need all the help they can get. One of the most encouraging things that can happen to a child who is learning to read is *success*—as much as possible, as soon as possible.

"Our Bears are sticklers for making things perfectly clear. They insist that we not let the pictures get involved in activities that have little to do with the text. They bring us up short if our sentences get too long. A sentence which may seem quite moderate to an experienced reader can look like the long, long trail awinding to somebody still sounding out 'run' and 'jump.' Sometimes we have to redraw a scene four or five times before the Bears are satisfied—so it's perfectly clear who's talking, for instance. Lose a beginning reader among the he saids and she saids and you may lose him for good. The Bears work endlessly on details like facial expressions, pose and gesture. Because they are hams? Partly . . . but mostly to provide context clues as to words and phrases and ideas.

"Of course, the child needs a variety of print and non-print material of all kinds. There are all kinds of children and a great range of interests and abilities—but at the same time, as soon as possible, as often as possible, give a child a book he can read. A book he can read and enjoy in his own time on his own terms. It's a great, great thing to be able to pick up a book, read it from cover to cover, then brag, 'I read it all by myself!'

"Now, that's a bit of an illusion in our books. He didn't read it *all* by himself. He had help. Lots of help. Because when it comes to helping kids to read, Papa Bear, for instance, is quite dedicated. In the course of his career he has run afoul of owls, porcupines, skunks, bees, crocodiles, thick gooey mud, low-hanging branches, mosquitos, a dump, turtles, whales and irate farmers. He has fallen from cliffs, into chasms and onto rocks. And in his efforts to find his family the perfect picnic spot, he almost makes the supreme sacrifice. He is struck smack in the seat of his overalls by an enormous bolt of lightning. Why does he go through all this? Because he is bound and determined to keep those pages turning!"

BERKOWITZ, Freda Pastor 1910-

PERSONAL: Born October 11, 1910, in Newark, N.J.; daughter of Abe (a builder) and Mary (Lubetkin) Pastor; divorced; children: Ellen (Mrs. Albert S. Carlin), Joan (Mrs.

FREDA PASTOR BERKOWITZ

There is an anecdote about Haydn and his love of the drums. When he was a very small boy, he was asked to beat the drums in a procession. He was so little that the drum had to be lowered to his height and carried in front of him by a hunchback. ■ (From *Unfinished Symphony* by Freda Pastor Berkowitz. Illustrated by Joseph Schindelman.)

Murray R. Schuman). *Education:* Curtis Institute of Music, B.Mus., 1935. *Politics:* Democrat. *Religion:* Jewish. *Home:* 1530 Locust St., Philadelphia, Pa. 19102. *Agent:* Curtis Brown Ltd., 575 Madison Ave., New York, N.Y. 10022. *Office:* Curtis Institute of Music, 18th and Rittenhouse Sq., Philadelphia, Pa.

CAREER: Instructor in piano, Curtis Institute of Music, Philadelphia, Pa., and privately, for forty years; also faculty member at Rutgers University, Camden, N.J.

WRITINGS: Popular Titles and Subtitles of Musical Compositions, Scarecrow, 1962, second edition, 1975; *Unfinished Symphony, and Other Stories of Men and Music,* Atheneum, 1963; *On Lutes, Recorders, and Harpsichords: Men and Music of the Baroque,* Atheneum, 1967.

WORK IN PROGRESS: A book on American music for children.

SIDELIGHTS: "The reason for my writing about nicknamed compositions is that many times a nickname for a piece of music is better known than it's real title. For instance, everyone knows 'The Moonlight Sonata' of Ludwig Van Beethoven rather than its designated title of 'Sonata opus 27 no 2 in C# minor.' This goes for many works of many composers. I thought that young people would like to know how these nicknames came about. Even in real life a child whose name is Gregory, might be nicknamed Butch and he will answer much quicker to his nickname. So with 'Moonlight Sonata.'

"The whole idea came to me when I was practicing the piano for a recital which included 'The Moonlight Sonata,' a piece of Beethoven called 'The Rage Over a Lost Penny,' some Chopin such as 'The Minute Waltz,' also known as 'The Dog Waltz,' 'The Revolutionary Elude' and 'The Raindrop Prelude.'

"Fifty of these are in the book *Unfinished Symphony* specially written for young people. This book, also, has biographical sketches of the composers who wrote the pieces that have nicknames. Somehow the whole idea intrigued my young pupils as well as the older ones.

"Incidentally, a child does not necessarily have to play an instrument to enjoy the book. It is geared to children who like to read."

FOR MORE INFORMATION SEE: Christian Science Monitor, November 2, 1967.

BERNSTEIN, Theodore M(enline)   1904-

PERSONAL: Born November 17, 1904, in New York, N.Y.; son of Saul and Sarah (Menline) Bernstein; married Beatrice Alexander, 1930 (died, 1971); children: Eric M. *Education:* Columbia University, A.B., 1924, B.Litt., 1925.

THEODORE M. BERNSTEIN

Home: 2 Fifth Ave., New York, N.Y. 10011. *Office: New York Times,* Times Square, N.Y., N.Y.

CAREER: Started with *The New York Times,* 1925, served as foreign editor, 1939-48, assistant night managing editor, 1948-51, news editor, 1951-52, assistant managing editor, 1952-69, editorial director, book division, 1969-71, consulting editor, 1971—, columnist, "Bernstein on Words," 1972—. Founding editor, international edition, Paris, 1960. Taught at Columbia School of Journalism, New York, N.Y., as associate, assistant professor, and associate professor, 1925-50. *Member:* Sigma Delta Chi.

WRITINGS: (With Robert E. Garst) *Headlines and Deadlines,* Columbia University Press, 1933, 3rd edition, 1961; *Watch Your Language,* Channel Press, 1958; *More Language That Needs Watching,* Channel Press, 1962; *The Careful Writer,* Atheneum, 1965; *Miss Thistlebottom's Hobgoblins,* Farrar, Straus, 1972; *Bernstein's Reverse Dictionary,* Quadrangle/The New York Times Book Co., 1975. Member of Usage Panel, *American Heritage Dictionary,* member of the Consultant Staff, *Random House Dictionary;* member of editorial advisory board, *Columbia University Forum,* 1961-64.

BERRILL, Jacquelyn (Batsel)   1905-

PERSONAL: Born November 5, 1905, in South Carrollton, Ky.; daughter of Edmond and Mary (Sweetser) Batsel; married Norman John Berrill (a professor of zoology), June 3, 1939; children: Peggy, Elsilyn, Michael. *Education:* University of Toledo, A.B., 1927; attended New York University. *Home:* 410 Swarthmore Ave., Swarthmore, Pa. 19081.

CAREER: Young Women's Christian Association, Jackson and Lansing, Mich., social worker, 1927-39; writer and illustrator, 1950—.

JACQUELYN BERRILL

Today there are no wolves left in forty-five states, and outside of Alaska there are probably less than 500 individual wolves living in Minnesota, Wisconsin, and Michigan together. ■ (From *Wonders of the World of Wolves* by Jacquelyn Berrill. Illustrated by the author.)

WRITINGS—All published by Dodd: *Wonders of the Seashore,* 1951, *Wonders of the Woodland,* 1953, *Wonders of Strange Nurseries,* 1954, *Wonders of the Wild,* 1955, *Albert Schweitzer: Man of Mercy,* 1956, (with N. J. Berrill) *1001 Questions Answered about the Seashore,* 1957, *Wonders of the Antarctic,* 1958, *Wonders of the Arctic,* 1959, *Wonders of the Ponds and Fields at Night,* 1962, *Wonders of the Woods and Desert at Night,* 1963, *Wonders of the Monkey World,* 1967; *Wonders of Animal Nurseries,* 1968; *Wonders of the World of Wolves,* 1970.

WORK IN PROGRESS: Wonders of How Animals Learn.

SIDELIGHTS: "My happy early life centered around the Green River in Kentucky where showboats, paddlewheel steamers, floating sawmills, houseboats, and even floating photography studios made regular stops. Best of all were the stories told by riverboat captains and most frightening were the devasting floods. I tried to capture these fantastic years in my book *River Girl.*

"Long before this, I had written many books. The writing started after I had married a biologist whose research took us to the rocky shores of Maine where we built a cottage when the children were very small. Life was regulated by the tides and I, and three small children, followed along after their father as he collected sea creatures. When a child asked, 'Daddy, how does a star fish walk?' Professor Daddy answered in terms of hydrolics. 'Mummy, what did daddy say?' So it was I who learned and then translated the answers into their language. My first book *Wonders of the Seashore* was the result. I sent the manuscript to the publishers with watercolor illustration and was asked to use a cheaper media and have it ready in six weeks. I turned to scratch-board and learned the art while drawing sea creatures. I perfected the technique when I used it to draw furry animals and have found it very satisfactory.

"When I am asked where I get the ideas for a book I have to admit that the need for a certain book often dictates the subject. Example: the Geophysical Year found no book for children on the Antarctic, so I wrote one and followed it with one on the Arctic. When there was a need for a book on animal migration I wrote one. But sometimes there is a desire on my part to speak up for an endangered creature. The wolf is my favorite animal and so I wrote his story. Raising three children probably suggested the book on monkeys.

"I was very much interested in the philosophy of Albert Schweitzer and when I was asked by high school students, 'What is so wonderful about this man,' I had to try to put his thoughts in their language. Then there is the publishers request: I was asked to write, with my scientific husband, *1001 Questions Answered about the Seashore*. Half of my husbands books are written for the general public, the others are scientific.

"I was an author-illustrator with fifteen books in nineteen years and when my husband retired and we moved to warmer and shorter winters, I have at last had a chance to carry out other dreams. I do pottery, batiking, jewelry, copper enameling (I make coffee tables, *not* ash trays!). Life seems far too short and there are so many things I want to accomplish. We have just returned from Greece where we walked 135 miles in three weeks and I have my pedometer to prove it.

"And when I am asked who I write for, I answer, for anyone who does not know why a horse has a long face or a giraffe a long neck, and it is *not* so they can reach the trees!

"I think the three most thrilling experiences I've had are: I was once 'kissed' by a wild wolf; a hummingbird landed on my knee; and a chipmunk sat on my typewriter while I worked in the garden in Maine."

HOBBIES AND OTHER INTERESTS: Art, jewelry making, ceramics, painting, and sewing.

BIRMINGHAM, Lloyd   1924-

PERSONAL: Born August 23, 1924, in Buffalo, N.Y.; son of William John (in gas industry) and Alma (Luebke) Birmingham; married Gean Taylor, August 29, 1964. *Education:* Studied at Parsons School of Design, 1946-47. *Religion:* Lutheran. *Home and studio:* Peekskill Hollow Rd., Putnam Valley, N.Y. 10579.

CAREER: Free-lance illustrator, 1949—. Has done illustrations for magazines, book publishers and Los Angeles Times-Mirror Syndicate. *Military service:* U.S. Army, 1943-46; became captain. *Member:* Society of Illustrators, American Institute of Graphic Arts, Graphic Artists Guild, Westport Artists.

The moisture in the air is just one part of a great "Water Cycle"--that is, a kind of continuous process in which many things, including you, have an important part. ■ (From *Understanding Weather* by Harry Milgrom. Illustrated by Lloyd Birmingham.)

WRITINGS: Do-It-Yourself with the Handy Family (illustrated by Birmingham in comic strip form), Fleet Publishing, 1960, 2nd edition, New American Library, 1972.

Illustrator: George Daniels, *How to Use Hand and Power Tools,* Popular Science, 1964; R. J. Cristoforo, *How to Build Your Own Furniture,* Popular Science, 1965; Malcolm Weiss, *Clues to the Riddle of Life,* Hawthorn, 1968; Ralph F. Robinett, Paul W. Bell, *English-Target 1,* Harcourt, 1968; Malcolm Weiss, *Man Explores the Sea,* Messner, 1969; Early, Cooper, Santeusanio, Adell, *Reading Skills Two,* Harcourt, 1970; Harry Milgram, *Understanding Weather,* Crowell-Collier, 1970; Dr. Kenneth Bobrowsky, *The Living Scene,* Scholastic, 1971; Dr. Kenneth Bobrowsky, *Power and Man,* Scholastic, 1971; Martin L. Keen, *How it Works,* Grosset, 1972; Vernon G. Abel, Jeffrey C. Callister, *Earth Science,* College Entrance Book Co., 1972; Paul F. Brandwein, *Experience Book: Concepts in Science,* Harcourt, 1972; Paul F. Brandwein, *Classroom Laboratory: Concepts in Science,* Harcourt, 1972; Malcolm Weiss, *Storms From the Inside Out,* Messner, 1973; Clifford R. Nelson, *Investigating the Earth's Living Things,* Harcourt, 1973; Henry Doren, *Unified Chemistry,* College Entrance Book Co., 1973; Donald Cantin, *The Care and Maintenance of Small Boats,* Drake, 1973; Yvonne Young Tarr, *The Complete Outdoor Cookbook,* Quadrangle, 1973; Richard Day, *How to Repair and Maintain Your Car,* Popular Science, 1973.

BISCHOFF, Julia Bristol 1909-1970
(Julie Arnoldy)

PERSONAL: Born March 2, 1909, in Almont, Mich.; daughter of William Howard (a lawyer and farmer) and Charlotte (Kelsey) Bristol; married Francis N. Arnoldy (a major, U.S. Army; died, 1949); married William Henry Bischoff (a newspaper editor, now retired, and a free-lance writer), May 4, 1956; children: (first marriage) Irene Simone (Mrs. Jack North). *Education:* Attended Eastern Michigan University, 1926-27, and University of Grenoble, 1927-28. *Home:* Volcan de Buenos Aires, Costa Rica, Central America.

CAREER: During her early career taught country schools in Almont Township, Mich.; *Detroit News,* Detroit, Mich., travel writer, 1937-39; *Miami News,* Miami, Fla., assistant editor of Sunday Magazine, "Florida Living," 1956-58; free-lance writer. In 1965 retired with her husband to a ranch in Costa Rica, where they both wrote. *Member:* Audubon Society.

WRITINGS: Great-Great Uncle Henry's Cats, W. R. Scott, 1965; *A Dog for David,* W. R. Scott, 1966; *Mystery on El Rancho Grande,* W. R. Scott, 1967; *Paddy's Preposterous Promises,* W. R. Scott, 1968. Author of 150 broadcast

The children had a wonderful time during the next couple of weeks with the stilts. ■ (From *Paddy's Preposterous Promises* by Julia Bristol Bischoff. Illustrated by Ingrid Fetz.)

radio plays, and a three-act play produced by Detroit Community Theatre; contributor of more than three hundred articles and a few short stories to magazines, many of them published under the name of Julie Arnoldy.

WORK IN PROGRESS: A fourth children's book for W. R. Scott.

SIDELIGHTS: Lived in Europe three years; spoke fluent French and Spanish. Her ambition was "to write a series of young people's books with Latin American settings (Latin American history has been my hobby for many years)."

(Died March 10, 1970)

BLACK, Algernon David   1900-

PERSONAL: Born November 19, 1900, in New York, N.Y.; son of Adolph and Sophie (Bellachowski) Black; married Elinor Goldmark, June 18, 1929; children: David Goldmark, Peter Elliott, Jonathan. *Education:* Harvard University, B.A. (magna cum laude), 1923. *Office:* New York Society for Ethical Culture, 2 West 64th St., New York, N.Y. 10023.

CAREER: A leader of the American Ethical-Humanist Movement, teacher of ethics in the Ethical Culture Schools, conducting Sunday meetings of the Ethical Culture Societies, officiating at ceremonies of marriage, funeral and memorial services, and personal counselling. Early experience included living and working in settlement houses in the ethnic ghettos, work with the children of coal miners, studies of the readiness of three Indian tribes for federal termination policy, school segregation, study of the human relations directors and the community relations functions in the public schools of New York City. Co-chairman with Rev. Adam Clayton Powell, Sr. of the City-Wide Citizens' Committee on Harlem (1941-1947); chairman of board of directors, New York State Committee and National Committee Against Discrimination in Housing (1948-1967); chairman of the civilian complaint review board of the Police Department of the City of New York (1966). Member of the Board of Directors of the National Association for the Advancement of Colored People, 1950-1960, and of the American Civil Liberties Union, 1960-1974.

MEMBER: National Association of Intergroup Relations Officials, National Association for the Advancement of Colored People (vice-president), American Scenic and Historic Preservation Society (board of directors), Workers Defense League (national board), Phi Beta Kappa, Overseas Press Club (New York). *Awards, honors:* John Lovejoy Elliott Award, 1961; Abraham Lincoln Award, 1952; Globe News Syndicate Award, 1952.

WRITINGS: The Young Citizens, Ungar, 1962; *The First Book of Ethics* (juvenile), Watts, 1965; *The People and the Police,* McGraw, 1968; *The Woman of the Wood* (Child Study Association book list), Holt, 1973; *Without Burnt Offerings: The Ceremonies of Humanism,* Viking, 1974. Author of pamphlets published by Public Affairs Press, and contributor to Ethical Culture Society publications.

SIDELIGHTS: "I was born in New York City in 1900. The first school I went to was a rough place. If we disobeyed any rule we were punished with a ruler across our hands, or sometimes even worse. The second school I went to was much more quiet and peaceful. We had teachers who opened up a whole new world and tried to find out what each boy and girl was interested in, what he wanted to do, and his talents—painting, music, shopwork, gym. The teachers cared about us and gave us a feeling that they liked us and wanted us to grow and learn and be ready for living in the world.

"In the Boy Scouts I learned about the woods, cooking, camping, and first aid. During World War I, another boy and I worked on a farm. That was the first time I had to clean a horse, take cows out to pasture, harvest potatoes and tomatoes, and cultivate a corn field. I learned about the earth and how things grow. Then I sold newspapers and waited tables in a restaurant at college. I think I learned about people from working with them.

"As a teenager I was an 'extra' in the old Metropolitan Opera in the time of the great singer, Caruso. Loving music,

The tailor made a most beautiful dress and many other clothes for the woman. And the teacher taught her to think. . . ■ (From *The Woman of the Wood* by Algernon Black. Illustrated by Evaline Ness.)

ALGERNON D. BLACK

I played the violin in two teenage orchestras, then sang for four years with the Harvard Glee Club. In my work among the slums of the West Side (Irish and Italian) and the East Side (Jewish) of New York, I thought I might teach the children the music. They taught me more music than I taught them.

"As a teacher I have always loved to tell stories and discuss how people treat each other. (My grandmother came from Russia. She brought her children to this country. She wasn't afraid to do anything or try anything new or go to strange places. One day when I was still a very young boy I asked her, 'Grandma, what do you think is the most important thing in the world?' She said, 'If you have a piece of bread, share it.' That's the way she was all her life until she died.)

"My wife is a teacher and writer. I have three wonderful sons: David produces and directs plays. When he was a boy he always put on plays for the family and friends. Peter loved the woods the way I did. He became a forester interested in the creeks, lakes and rivers. Jonathan writes about people. Each of my eight grandchildren has been growing up with music or theater, fishing or skiing, poetry, dancing, shopwork, selling ice cream, delivering newspapers, and politics.

"My favorite activities are tennis and good neighbors."

BLACKETT, Veronica Heath 1927-
(Veronica Heath)

PERSONAL: Born October 20, 1927, in London, England; daughter of Henry Tegner; married J.H.B. Blackett (a solici-

tor), April 20, 1953; children: Simon, Rupert, Rose, Juliet. *Education:* West Heath School, Kent. *Politics:* Conservative. *Religion:* Anglican. *Home:* West House, Whalton, Morpeth, Northumberland, England.

CAREER: Writer.

WRITINGS—All under name Veronica Heath: *Your Pony,* Cassell, 1954, revised and enlarged edition published as *Ponies,* 1969; *Come Riding With Me,* Muller, 1955, Sportshelf, 1956; *Susan's Riding School,* Chatto & Windus, 1956; *So You Want to Be a Show Jumper,* Colin Venton, 1957; *Ponies in the Heather,* Lutterworth, 1959; *Come Show Jumping with Me,* Muller, 1961; *Come Pony-Trekking with Me,* Muller, 1964; *Ponies and Pony Management,* Arco, 1966; *Beginner's Guide to Riding,* Pelham Books, 1970, Transatlantic Arts, 1971; *The Family Dog,* Transatlantic Arts, 1972; *Let's Own a Pony,* Colin Venton, 1974.

WORK IN PROGRESS: Books on sporting events.

SIDELIGHTS: Veronica Blackett is an active assistant in a local riding group for the disabled. She still goes hunting on horseback, and works in the morning on books and articles.

BLAIR, Ruth Van Ness 1912-

PERSONAL: Born June 9, 1912, in St. Michael, Alaska; daughter of Elmer Eugene (an educator and Presbyterian

RUTH VAN NESS BLAIR

minister) and Eula (McIntosh) Van Ness; married Glenn Myers Blair (now a professor of educational psychology), June 27, 1934; children: Glenn Myers, Jr., Sally Virginia (Mrs. Donald L. Leach). *Education:* Seattle Pacific College, graduate in elementary education, 1932; studied voice privately in Seattle and New York. *Home:* 51 Island Way, Apt. 310, Clearwater, Fla. 33515.

CAREER: Public school teacher in Everett, Wash., 1932-34; kindergarten teacher in Champaign, Ill., 1952-61. Soprano soloist for many years in local churches; played piano for adult education physical-conditioning courses. *Member:* National League of American Pen Women, Chicago Children's Reading Round Table.

WRITINGS: Puddle Duck, Steck, 1966; *A Bear Can Hibernate, Why Can't I?,* Denison, 1972; *Willa-Willa, The Wishful Witch,* Denison, 1972; *Mary's Monster,* Coward, 1975. Contributor to Encyclopedia Britannica Education Corp. reading development program, 1974.

WORK IN PROGRESS: Several other children's books.

SIDELIGHTS: "I was born in St. Michael, Alaska, where my parents were government teachers of the Eskimos in the village of Unalakleet. My father, who loved frontiers, had left his teaching position in a small southern college to come to Alaska. It was he who inspired my lifelong interest in science.

"When I was five, my family moved to Montana and later on to Kissimmee, Florida. After my father's death, my mother, my three brothers and I settled in Everett, Washington. I graduated from Seattle Pacific College in 1932, taught for two years and then married Glenn Myers Blair. We lived in Washington for a time, moved to New York City, where I studied voice and sang in a motet choir of the First Presbyterian Church and my husband completed work on his Ph.D., then moved to Urbana, Illinois, where my husband was professor of educational psychology. From 1952 to 1961, I taught kindergarten in Champaign, and continued for many years as a soprano soloist with church choirs in the Urbana-Champaign area. We love to travel. We have been in Europe many times and I, an enthusiastic 'non-digging archaeologist,' toured Egypt and the Middle East on my own.

"My years of teaching kindergarten was excellent experience for writing children's books. That, plus the fact that I won several prizes in *Writer's Digest* contests, set me to seriously thinking about writing. I set to work. Three books later, a good friend suggested I write a story about Mary Ann Anning. My grandchildren thought a story about monsters would be 'super.' The result: *Mary's Monster.*

"The attitude of my husband, children, and grandchildren has had a great deal to do with whatever success I have attained. My husband, who is an excellent writer, reads my material and constantly encourages me. My son and his wife have done valuable research for me, and my daughter, a high school English teacher, has blue-penciled my work with great care. My grandchildren read my stories and are encouraged to tell me exactly what they think of them.

"I'm still working on children's books, but spend a good deal of time swimming forty lengths a day (⅓ mile) in the beautiful pool of our apartment home on an island a mile and a quarter from Clearwater. I am a few blocks from Clearwater beach where I can spend literally hours feeding the saucy sea gulls. I've become quite enamored of the Florida fauna."

HOBBIES AND OTHER INTERESTS: Archaeology, music, art, and travel.

"One would think that the English were ducks; they are forever waddling to the waters."
■ (From *Mary's Monsters* by Ruth Van Ness Blair. Illustrated by Richard Cuffari.)

Well, when Marco tried to draw his map of the world, he drew in the countries, the sea serpents, the giants and the other things he'd seen with his own good eyes. Mostly, he put them in the right places and got good likenesses--though at times there was a little something wrong about the mouth. ■ (From *Tall Tale America* by Walter Blair. Illustrated by Glen Rounds.)

BLAIR, Walter 1900-

PERSONAL: Born April 21, 1900, in Spokane, Wash.; son of John James and Emma (Merritt) Blair; married Carol Conrad, September 20, 1925; children: Paula (Mrs. Lawrence G. Olinger). *Education:* Yale University, Ph.B., 1923; University of Chicago, M.A., 1926, Ph.D., 1931. *Politics:* Democrat. *Office:* University of Chicago, 1050 East 59th St., Chicago, Ill. 60637.

CAREER: Spokesman-Review, Spokane, Wash., reporter, 1923-25; University of Minnesota, Minneapolis, member of English faculty, 1928-29; University of Chicago, instructor, 1929-30, assistant professor of English, 1930-39, associate professor, 1939-44, professor, 1944-68, chairman of department, 1951-60, professor emeritus, 1968—. Goethe University, Frankfort, Germany, visiting professor, 1949-50; William Beckman lecturer, University of California, Berkeley, 1972. *Member:* Modern Language Association (chairman, American Literature division, 1958), American Studies Association, Phi Delta Theta, National Council of Teachers of English. *Awards, honors:* Thormod Monsen Award of the Society of Midland Authors, 1961, for best mid-western book of the year, for *Mark Twain and "Huck Finn";* Jay B. Hubbell Award for scholarship concerning American Literature, Modern Language Association, 1974; Chaplin Award, American Humor Studies Association, 1975.

WRITINGS: (Editor) *The Sweet Singer of Michigan,* Pascal Covici, 1928; *Two Phases of American Humor,* Duke University Press, 1931; (with F. J. Meine) *Mike Fink,*

King of Mississippi Keelboatmen, Holt, 1933, Greenwood, 1971; (with W. K. Chandler) *Approaches to Poetry,* Appleton, 1935, 2nd edition, 1953; *Native American Humor,* American Book, 1937, revised, Chandler, 1960; *Horse Sense in American Humor,* University of Chicago Press, 1942, Atheneum, 1964; *Tall Tale America,* Coward, 1944, 25th printing, 1973; (editor with Theodore Hornberger and Randall Stewart) *Literature of the United States,* Scott, 1947, 8th edition, 1970; *Davy Crockett: Truth and Legend,* Coward, 1955; (in collaboration with F. J. Meine) *Half Horse, Half Alligator,* University of Chicago Press, 1956.

Mark Twain and "Huck Finn," University of California Press, 1960, revised edition, 1973; (with H. Hill) *The Art of Huckleberry Finn,* Chandler, 1962; (editor) *Selected Shorter Writing of Mark Twain,* Houghton, 1962; (editor with Harrison Hayford) Herman Melville, *Omoo,* Hendricks, 1966; (editor) *Mark Twain's; Hannibal, Huck and Tom,* University of California Press, 1969. Contributor to popular magazines and professional journals. Editorial boards, *American Literature,* 1943-51, *College English,* 1945-48, publications of the Modern Language Association, 1945-51; advisory board, *Encyclopaedia Britannica,* 1951—; co-editor, *Mark Twain Papers,* University of California Press, 1964—; co-editor, *The Works of Mark Twain,* University of California-Iowa University, 1965—; educational collaborator, Coronet Films, "Whitman," 1957, "Mark Twain," 1957, "Poe," 1958.

WORK IN PROGRESS: To Get to the Other Side: Humor in America, A History, for Oxford University Press.

SIDELIGHTS: "Out in the Pacific Northwest where I was born and where I lived until I went away to college, I was lucky enough to get to know a number of fine oral storytellers. These told jokes, yarns and tall stories around campfires or hearths in homes. While I worked my way through college, fellow workmen told stories that I enjoyed—air brake repairers and freight car whackers, for instance. A couple of years after I graduated from college, I worked for a newspaper, and heard more tales told by experts.

"It wasn't until I took graduate work in English that I became interested in oral stories as folklore and important elements in American humor. What I learned about the relationships led me, after that, to do systematically what I'd done haphazardly—collect and study oral and written anecdotes and tales. I became a teacher and began to write and publish articles and books about folklore and American humor. Also I wandered around the country, sometimes as a vacationing traveler, sometimes as a visiting teacher in schools all over the United States—the universities of Arkansas, California, Texas, Wisconsin and New York, in Harvard, Cornell and Stanford. Often I heard new stories and learned something about the art of telling them. I practiced on classes and friends.

"What I learned helped me with my writing. For the most part I published textbooks and scholarly studies. But a couple of books that I wrote largely for the sheer fun of it became, I'm happy to say, popular not only with grown-ups but also with boys and girls: *Tall Tale America,* subtitled *A Legendary History of Our Humorous Heroes* and *Davy Crockett: Truth and Legend*—both collections of oral and written stories put into continuous narratives. The former of these has had a popular reception that pleased me greatly. It was issued in an Armed Service's edition by the United

States Government and circulated among thousands of our soldiers, sailors, marines and airmen. It was translated into German and published in both hardcover and paperback editions as *Das Grosse Lügengarn*. It was chosen by the librarians of the United States as the only representative of folklore in the White House Presidential Library. And over the years, hundreds of kids have written letters to me saying that they enjoyed the book.

"One of these days, I hope to write another book that will please boys and girls. They make a fine audience."

BLISS, Ronald G(ene)   1942-

PERSONAL: Born August 12, 1942, in Atwood, Kan.; son of Wilbur Cyril (a farmer and mechanic) and Mary (Makings) Bliss; married Margaret Jane Keeler (a high school teacher), July 25, 1965; children: Eric Dean, Kirk Ronald. *Education:* Fort Hays Kansas State College, student, 1960-62; Kansas State University, B.A., 1964; University of Missouri, M.A., 1969. *Religion:* Christian Church. *Home:* 620 James, Maize, Kan. 67101. *Agent:* Dorothy Markinko, 18 East 41st St., New York, N.Y. 10017. *Office:* KARD-Television, 833 North Main, Wichita, Kan. 67201.

CAREER: Findlay Republican-Courier, Findlay, Ohio, city hall reporter, 1964; *Colby Free Press-Tribune,* Colby, Kan., news editor, 1964-66; University of Missouri, Columbia, radio and television specialist, 1966-69; Kansas State Network, Wichita, 1969—, began as television investigative reporter, now director of public affairs. Kansas Public Television Commission, 1976-80. *Member:* Kansas Authors

RONALD G. BLISS

Club (vice president, 1973; president, 1974). *Awards, honors:* Citation for best television documentary film, from Kansas Association of Broadcasters, 1972, for "A Look at Child Abuse," and 1974, for "The Battered Child."

WRITINGS: Indian Softball Summer (juvenile novel), Dodd, 1974. Author of scripts for KSN television network. Contributor to *TV Guide, V.F.W., Sign of the Times,* and regional publications.

WORK IN PROGRESS: A juvenile novel; a novel about the life of migrant workers in western Kansas, based on factual information.

SIDELIGHTS: "My writing reflects growing up with many fascinating characters in a small town in northwest Kansas. They have become key personalities in my books of fiction. Jesse Stuart and his tales of the people in the backwoods of Kentucky greatly impressed me as a youth and I think that admiration has made me want to write about common people."

BLOCH, Robert   1917-

PERSONAL: Born April 5, 1917, in Chicago, Illinois; son of Raphael A. and Stella (Loeb) Bloch; married Marion Holcombe, 1940 (divorced); married Eleanor Alexander, 1964; children: Sally Ann. *Education:* Attended public schools in Milwaukee, Wis. *Home:* 2111 Sunset Crest Dr., Los Angeles, Calif. *Agent:* Gordon Molson, 10889 Wilshire Blvd., Los Angeles, Calif.

CAREER: Gustav Marx Advertising, Milwaukee, Wis., copywriter, 1942-53; free-lance writer, 1953—, currently writing for television and films and for book publication. *Member:* Writers Guild of America, Mystery Writers of America (president, 1970-71), Science Fiction Writers of America, National Fantasy Association. *Awards, honors:* World Science Fiction Society Award for best short story, 1959; Screen Guild Award, 1960; E. E. Evans Memorial Award; Mystery Writers of America Special Scroll, 1961; Trieste Science Fiction Film Festival Award, 1965; Ann Radcliffe Memorial Award, 1966; Los Angeles Science Fiction Society Award, 1974; Comicon Inkpor Award, 1975; World Fantasy Convention Life Award, 1975.

WRITINGS: Opener of the Way, Arkham, 1945; *The Scarf,* Dial, 1947; *Spiderweb,* Ace Books, 1954; *The Kidnaper,* Lion, 1954; *The Will to Kill,* Ace Books, 1954; *Shooting Star,* Ace Books, 1958; *Terror in the Night,* Ace Books, 1958; *Psycho,* Simon and Schuster, 1959; *Pleasant Dreams,* Arkham, 1959.

The Dead Beat, Simon and Schuster, 1960; *Firebug,* Regency, 1961; *Nightmares,* Belmont Books, 1961; *More Nightmares,* Belmont Books, 1962; *Yours Truly, Jack the Ripper,* Belmont Books, 1962; *The Couch,* Gold Medal, 1962; *Terror,* Belmont Books, 1962; *Atoms and Evil,* Gold Medal, 1962; *Blood Runs Cold,* Simon and Schuster, 1962; *Eighth Stage of Fandom,* Advent, 1962; *Horrors Seven,* Belmont Books, 1963; *The Bogey-Men,* Pyramid, 1963; *Tales in a Jugular Vein,* Pyramid, 1965; *The Skull of Marquis de Sade,* Pyramid, 1965; *Chamber of Horrors,* Award Books, 1966; *The Living Demons,* Belmont Books, 1968; *Dragons and Nightmares,* Mirage Press, 1968; *Ladies Day & This Crowded Earth,* Belmont Books, 1968; *The Star-*

ROBERT BLOCH

Stalker, Pyramid, 1968; *Bloch and Bradbury,* Tower, 1969; *The Todd Dossier,* Dell, 1969.

It's All in Your Mind, Curtis, 1971; *Sneak Preview,* Paperback Library, 1971; *Night World,* Simon and Schuster, 1972; *American Gothic* (*School Library Journal* book list), Simon and Schuster, 1974; *Contes de Terreur,* Editions Opta, 1974; *The King of Terrors,* Mysterious Press, 1977; (editor) *The Best of Fredric Brown,* Ballantine, 1977; *Cold Chills,* Doubleday, 1977; *The Best of Robert Bloch,* Ballantine, 1977.

Recorded Readings: "Gravely, Robert Bloch," Alternate World Recordings, 1976; "Blood," Alternate World Recordings, 1977.

Screenplays: "The Couch," 1962; "The Cabinet of Caligari," 1962; "Strait Jacket," 1964; "The Night Walker," 1965; "The Psychopath," 1966, "The Deadly Bees," 1967; "Torture Garden," 1968; "The House that Dripped Blood," 1971; "Asylum," 1972. Stories adapted to screen: "Psycho," 1960; "The Skull," 1965.

Writer of radio series, "Stay Tuned for Terror," and numerous television plays. Columnist, *Rogue.* Contributor of five hundred short stories, articles, and novelettes to magazines.

SIDELIGHTS: "I became a professional writer when I was seventeen—just a few months after graduating from high school.

"For several years I'd corresponded with a man named H. P. Lovecraft, and it was he who encouraged me to try my hand at writing short stories. Today Lovecraft has come into his own as one of the great authors of fantasy, but at the time he was known only to a little group of fans. I was one of

them, and his interest and approval meant a great deal to me. Many of my early efforts imitated his style.

"Gradually I broadened my subject matter to include science fiction and mystery-suspense stories, and in 1947 I wrote my first novel, *The Scarf.* By 1959 I had published several hundred stories and a half-dozen books, adapted thirty-nine of my tales for my own radio series, written a monthly magazine column, worked as an advertising copywriter, ghosted speeches for politicians, and could look back on a twenty-five-year career. But I'd little to show for it all in terms of reward or recognition.

"Then I wrote a novel called *Psycho.* It was made into a film, and its success brought me identiy.

"By this time a friend secured me an opportunity to try my hand at television writing. My first efforts met with approval and I moved to Hollywood. Since then television and motion pictures have been a major factor in my professional life, but I've continued to write short stories, articles, essays and novels.

"To me, writing has always been a vehicle for communication and entertainment. And it has opened many doors. It gave me the opportunity to travel—to meet people whom I'd always admired and respected. It brought me lifelong friendships which I treasure.

"When I began, many well-meaning relatives and acquaintances urged me not to waste time working on stories for vulgar pulp magazines with limited readership and payment rates of ½¢ or 1¢ a word.

"But I persisted. Today many of those early stories have been adapted for motion pictures or television for quite respectable sums, and in world-wide showings have probably reached an audience of a hundred million people. My work has been reprinted in thirty-seven countries, to my knowledge—not including what may have been pirated behind the Iron Curtain—and as of this date, I've had stories in three-hundred and fifty anthologies, here and abroad.

"All of which makes a writer's life sound very attractive. The point is, it didn't just happen automatically. I spent my adolescence and early manhood reading, studying, researching and pounding a typewriter while most of my peer-group were enjoying fun and games. I'm still following the same pattern today.

"During the forty-odd years of my professional career I've constantly been confronted with criticism, rejection, frustration, and the daily loneliness which is the working writer's lot—and this too continues.

"Is it worth it? Of course—and I wouldn't trade jobs with anyone in the world. But to anyone contemplating a writing career, I must offer this word of caution. Unless you're a genius, and a lucky one, you'll have to be prepared to face all the occupational hazards I've listed. You must be psychologically adjusted to cope with disappointments and equipped with the self-discipline necessary to keep going. Techniques can be acquired through study, talent can be sharpened through practice, but without the personal characteristics of patience, perseverance, intellectual curiousity and critical objectivity, it would be better just to write for one's own amusement. Besides, plumbers make more money.''

HOBBIES AND OTHER INTERESTS: Silent movies, painting in oil.

BLOCK, Irvin 1917-

PERSONAL: Born April 1, 1917, in Pittsburgh, Pa.; son of Morris and Minnie Block; married Doris Senk, June 6, 1948; children: Jessica, Amy, Rachel, Mark. *Education:* Western Reserve University, A.B. (cum laude), 1938. *Religion:* "Not particularly." *Home:* 2 Carpenter Ave., Sea Cliff, N.Y.

CAREER: U.S. Army, Infantry, 1939-45, leaving service as first lieutenant; free-lance writer, 1946-58; Blue Cross Association, New York, N.Y., public relations manager, 1959-63; New York Governor's Committee on Hospital Costs, editor and researcher, 1964; Schless & Co. (public relations), New York, N.Y., vice-president, 1965; Metropolitan Life Insurance Co., New York, N.Y., editor of "Statistical Bulletin," 1966-68, senior editor of "Hospital Practice," 1968-75. Now consultant in health and medical communications. *Member:* Authors Guild, American Public Health Association, Population Association of America. *Awards, honors*—Military: Purple Heart, Bronze Star with oak leaf cluster, Presidential Unit Citation.

WRITINGS: Real Book About Explorers, Garden City Books, 1952; *Real Book About the Mounties,* Garden City Books, 1952; *Real Book About Christopher Columbus,* Garden City Books, 1953; *People,* Watts, 1956; *Real Book About Ships,* Garden City Books, 1961; *Neighbor to the World* (biography of Lillian Wald), Crowell, 1969; *The Lives of Pearl Buck,* Crowell, 1973. Contributor of fiction to *Saturday Evening Post, Liberty,* and *Maclean's Magazine.*

WORK IN PROGRESS: Books for young people.

SIDELIGHTS: "About myself—I wish I had illuminating things to say about what makes a writer write. Music turns some people on, the smell of ink or the feel of a saw chewing wood does it for others. I'm turned on by the surf and thunder of the written word, and I always was. As a kid I started at 'A' in my neighborhood library and worked my way down the alphabet. I didn't do spectacularly in school, except in English, but I felt I had the approval of Zola, Dostoievsky, Hemingway, and Melville. My discharge pay after leaving the army gave me the opportunity to go to New York and spend time at the typewriter, finally. I scored in some of the popular magazines, wrote true confessions, comic books, and picked up occasional writing assignments for public relations firms.

"I never did write the great novel, but it's been satisfying just being occupied with the act of absorbing material and then spewing it out in organized form on reams of paper. I like the act of it. Children's books were great fun to write, but most of my work now is in science writing, particularly the health sciences, in which I've developed some expertise.

"The things I like are the total private commitments and I have three of these that consume me while I'm at them: my affair with pen and paper; my absorption in sailing; and the classical guitar, which I've taught myself to play badly. Any of these, however, takes second place to my wife and four kids, who collectively are the most exciting things that have happened to me in my life, the most rewarding, the most troublesome, the most exasperating, and the most delicious."

HOBBIES AND OTHER INTERESTS: "Sailing in summer and thinking about sailing in winter."

BOARDMAN, Gwenn R. 1924-

PERSONAL: Born November 16, 1924, in London, England; daughter of Edward and Mabel (Ware) White; married Henry Petersen. *Education:* University of California, Berkeley, B.A. (with highest honors), 1957; Claremont Graduate School, M.A., 1961, Ph.D., 1963. *Home:* 2200 Sacramento St., Apt. 208, San Francisco, Calif. 94115.

CAREER: Worked with South-East European Service of British Broadcasting Corp. while still in teens; University of California Medical School, San Francisco, administrative assistant, Cancer Research Institute, 1952-54; kindergarten and elementary teacher in Riverside, Calif., 1957-59; University of California, Riverside, associate in English, 1959-61; Claremont Men's College, Claremont, Calif., instructor in English, 1961-63; Kobe College, Nishinomiya, Japan, professor of English, 1963-65; University of the Pacific, Raymond College, Stockton, Calif., assistant professor of humanities, 1965; returned to Japan to continue research, 1965; part-time professor of English at Osaka City University and English tutor to physicians and surgeons at the medical schools of Kobe and Osaka universities, 1965-67; University

GWENN R. BOARDMAN

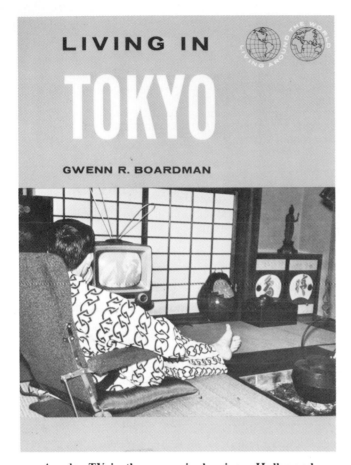

A color TV in the corner is showing a Hollywood movie, with the actors speaking dubbed-in Japanese.
■ (From *Living in Tokyo* by Gwenn R. Boardman. Illustrated by the author.)

of Saigon, Saigon, Vietnam, Fulbright professor of American literature, 1967-68; Immaculate Heart College, Los Angeles, Calif., assistant professor of English literature, 1968-70; International Christian University, Tokyo, Japan, visiting associate professor, 1970-71; United Nations Centre for Regional Development, Nagoya, Japan, editorial and publications officer, 1972-73; University of San Francisco, San Francisco, lecturer in English and Japanese literature, 1973—. Free-lance writer and photographer. Visiting professor at Kwansei Gakuin University, 1965, University of Cape Town, 1968, World Campus Afloat of Chapman College, 1970; visiting lecturer at universities in South Africa, Japan, and for Far East Division, University of Maryland. *Member:* Authors Guild, Modern Language Association of America, International Platform Association.

WRITINGS: Carrying Cargo, Thomas Nelson, 1968; (self-illustrated with photographs) *Living in Tokyo* (young adult book), Thomas Nelson, 1970; *Graham Greene: The Aesthetics of Exploration,* University of Florida Press, 1971; (self-illustrated with photographs) *Living in Singapore* (young adult book), Thomas Nelson, 1971. Contributor to *Critique, Journal of Modern Literature, Renascence* and *Modern Fiction Studies,* and to *Today's Health, RN, Mademoiselle,* and other magazines and newspapers. Presently writes special section for *Student Times* (bilingual junior edition of *Japan Times*).

WORK IN PROGRESS: Study of Japanese women, tentatively titled *Eight Thousand Yen and a Bottle of Scotch;* an introduction to the works of Kawabata, Mishima, and Tanizaki, titled *The Moon in the Water;* a book about China, *Across the Bridge to China.*

SIDELIGHTS: "I've been writing since I was five (my first poem) and earned my first prize for an essay (on kindness to animals) when I was ten, and honorable mention for a photograph when I was eight, so I suppose you could say that it is never too early to start a writing (and photography) career! Actually my writing of children's books is related to my interest in teaching, just as much of my writing and photography is designed to communicate something about unfamiliar worlds and experiences to people who have not shared the actual experiences. In particular, my regular feature for *The Student Times,* published by the *Japan Times* in Tokyo, is a perfect example of this cross-cultural communication, although the column (page) is no longer sub-titled 'Living Here and There.'"

BODIE, Idella F(allaw) 1925-

PERSONAL: Surname is pronounced Body; born December 2, 1925, in Ridge Spring, S.C.; daughter of Robert Grady (a farmer) and Grace Pearl Fallaw; married James E. Bodie (an engineer for DuPont), August 15, 1947; children: Susanne (Mrs. Robert Rhoden), Edwin, John, Beth. *Education:* Mars Hill College, student, 1942-44; Columbia College, B.A., 1946; University of South Carolina, graduate study, 1950-51. *Religion:* Methodist. *Home:* 1113 Evans

IDELLA F. BODIE

Rd., Aiken, S.C. 29801. *Office:* Department of English, Aiken High School-Schofield Campus, 220 Sumter St., Aiken, S.C., 29801.

CAREER: High school English teacher at Kennedy Junior High School, Aiken, S.C., 1960-70, and Aiken High School, Aiken, S.C., 1970—. *Member:* National Education Association, National Council of English Teachers, Association of Teacher Educators, South Carolina Education Association, Poetry Society of South Carolina, Friends of Library (Aiken County), Delta Kappa Gamma.

WRITING: The Secret of Telfair Inn, Sandlapper Press, 1971; *The Mystery of the Pirate's Treasure,* Sandlapper Press, 1973; *Ghost in the Capitol,* Sandlapper Press, 1976. Contributor of poems to *National Poetry Anthology.*

WORK IN PROGRESS: Adventure novel for young readers; entitled *Stranded!;* a suspense novel for teenagers.

SIDELIGHTS: "I was fortunate to live on a farm during my younger years. Although life was sometimes lonely, we always had loads of pets, as well as farm animals. A world of magic and wonder lay in the newly-born calves, piglets, and colts. Once we raised a piglet who suffered a broken leg. My mother let us keep it in a box by the wood stove where we lovingly fed it with a bottle and nipple.

"It was on the farm, too, that I learned to be aware of the beauty of nature. My play-houses were under giant oaks whose surfacing roots made the walls of rooms. Here I entertained make-believe friends who lived on to become characters in my books.

"My mother had a profound influence on my life during these years. She was a great storyteller and lover of nature. She was never too busy to go on hikes and picnics in the woods. We would bring back wild ferns and violets to plant in our yard. Then, too, my mother always had time to listen to the stories I made up, for she said I told 'stories' long before I could write.

"I can't remember when I didn't love books. When my older brother and sister went off to school, I cried every day to go with them. Finally, in exasperation my mother took me to the school house and told the teacher her problem. Miss Grace, the first grade teacher in our small town, kept me at the age of five.

"The most enjoyable part of writing for me is building characters. The people in my books are a blending of real people I know. I never make my characters all good or all bad because real people are not that way. No one is all bad. Perhaps a person has a reason for acting the way he does, and the reader has a chance to find out why and attempt to understand him. Also, no one likes a goody-goody so I never make my protagonist this type.

"After I've gotten to know my characters quite well by thinking about them for a long, long time, then I put them in a setting and the action begins. In fact, I have very little time for the actual writing since I am a school teacher so I do a great deal of thinking and planning while I'm doing household chores and driving to and from school. When I have thoroughly thought through what I'm going to write, I find it goes much faster when I do begin to put it down on paper.

My first drafts are always written by hand because I seem to think better this way. Of course, I always have my manuscripts typed as neatly as possible before sending them to an editor, but this takes many many hours of going over and over my first copies.

"The greatest pleasure I receive from my writing is fan mail from my readers. I'm really pleased to know that I've given someone else the pleasure I have always found in reading. And, I make an attempt to answer all letters I receive."

BOECKMAN, Charles 1920-

PERSONAL: Surname is pronounced Beckman; born November 9, 1920, in San Antonio, Tex.; son of Charles Otto (a salesman) and Elizabeth (Kiesewetter) von Boeckman; married Patricia Ellen Kennelly (a teacher), July 25, 1965; children: Sharla Tricia. *Education:* Attended Texas Lutheran College, 1938-39, and New School for Social Research, 1958. *Religion:* Lutheran. *Home:* 322 Del Mar, Corpus Christi, Tex. 78404. *Agent:* Lenniger Literary Agency, 437 Fifth Ave., New York, N.Y. 10016.

CAREER: Copywriter and advertising account executive in Corpus Christi, Tex., 1947-51; full-time author, 1951—. Teacher of creative writing, Del Mar College, 1955—; instructor in writers' workshops at University of Houston and for Abiline Writers' Guild. *Member:* Authors Guild, Authors League of America, Mystery Writers of America, Corpus Christi Press Club, Corpus Christi Musicians Asso-

CHARLES BOECKMAN

ciation. *Awards, honors:* Short story, "Mr. Banjo" appeared in *Best Detective Stories of 1976.*

WRITINGS: Maverick Brand, Bouregy, 1961; *Unsolved Riddles of the Ages,* Criterion, 1965; *Our Regional Industries,* Criterion, 1966; *Cool, Hot and Blue,* Luce, 1968; *And the Beat Goes On,* Luce, 1972. Author of television plays for "Alfred Hitchcock Presents" and "Celebrity Playhouse." Contributor of short stories to magazines, including *Alfred Hitchcock's Mystery Magazine;* about one thousand stories published since 1940.

WORK IN PROGRESS: Suspense and mystery books.

SIDELIGHTS: "I am fortunate in being part of a generation that has lived through many of the exciting events of the twentieth century. I was a child during the 'Roaring Twenties.' I remember my father taking me to hear the broadcast of a Jack Dempsey fight on one of the first radios in our small Texas town. Thomas Edison, Charles Lindberg and Babe Ruth were my childhood heroes. The movies were silent then. I sat on my mother's lap and she read the captions to me. Then I learned to read and books became my best friends. I read *Tom Swift, The Rover Boys, Tarzan, Robinson Crusoe, Treasure Island.* Then I read them again. I mowed lawns in the neighborhood to earn money to buy more books.

"Then it was the 1930's and the country was in the midst of the Great Depression. Things weren't all that bad for us, though. I put a bicycle together out of spare parts and explored the country lanes, swam in the river, and went hunting with my father and big brother. I built model airplanes, crystal set radios. And when it got dark, I made up ghost stories to tell my playmates in the back yard. (The stories were scary enough to send one youngster running home in tears.)

"My daily chores included chopping kindling wood for the stove that provided our heat, emptying the water pan under the ice box that kept the butter cool, and fetching kerosine oil from the corner store for the stove we cooked on. Our greatest treasure—and I'll never know how my father managed such an extravagant luxury in 1930—was a console Atwater Kent radio. It brought the outside world into our small village. I heard the great radio programs, the news events and the music of the 1930's. Any night we could tune in the famous big bands: Benny Goodman, Artie Shaw, the Dorsey Brothers, Glenn Miller. (Believe it or not, I still have that Atwater Kent radio, and it still plays!)

"Music was an important part of my family life. My big brother was off much of the time, making a living playing the saxophone. He played for the marathon dances of the 1930's. When he came home, he showed me the fingering on his saxophone. That was the extent of my formal music lessons. On Sundays, the whole family gathered around the piano as my sister played and we sang. I taught myself to play clarinet. I played in the high school band. When I was seventeen, I played my first professional dance engagement. Jazz music has been a hobby and an avocation with me ever since. I have my own jazz group now.

"Writing stories was the thing I wanted to do most, though. My first story was published when I was twenty-two. I wrote all kinds of stories: adventure, mystery, westerns for children and adults. Writing became my ticket to the outside world. It gave me the freedom to travel, to see the big cities I'd read about, San Francisco, Los Angeles, Las Vegas, New Orleans. I went to live in New York for a while. But I came back to Texas to live on the sea coast, to write and enjoy my family. My beautiful wife, Patricia, shares my interest in music and writing. And we now have a lovely daughter, Sharla Tricia, born on September 9, 1976.

"My love of music has inspired many of the stories and the books about music I have written for young people. Often I have a glimmer of a story idea from a place I've been, an item in the newspaper or a person I meet. But there is more to it than that. Stories have to have form and purpose, logical motivation for characters and a clearly defined effect upon the reader. A writer must approach his story material with a combination of logic and emotion plus that mysterious, indefinable element of artistic creativity. Factual books require much research so the information in them will be accurate. Putting a story, or a book, together is one of the most demanding and difficult art forms—but one of the most satisfying."

Charles Boeckman's papers and correspondence are now on file in the library at the University of Oregon. He speaks Spanish and some German.

HOBBIES AND OTHER INTERESTS: Travel, jazz music and photography.

BOESCH, Mark J(oseph) 1917-

PERSONAL: Born October 31, 1917, son of Anthony Joseph and Anna (Supancheck) Boesch; married Frances Blackburn, April 2, 1951; children: Mark, David, Anna Marie. *Education:* "High school graduate and that's all any author needs." *Home:* 311 Geneva, Hamilton, Mont. 59840.

CAREER: U.S. Forest Service, fire dispatcher in Hamilton, Mont., 1946-65, press officer in Milwaukee, Wis., beginning 1965; now full-time writer. Member, Environmental Resources group. *Military service:* U.S. Marine Corps, 1942-46; became sergeant; received Purple Heart and Bronze Star. *Member:* Authors Guild.

WRITINGS: The Lawless Land, Winston, 1953; *Beyond the Muskingum,* Winston, 1953; *Fire Fighter,* Morrow, 1954; *The Cross in the West,* Farrar, Straus, 1956; *Kit Carson of the Old West,* Farrar, Straus, 1959; *John Colter,* Putnam, 1959; *The Long Search for the Truth About Cancer,* Putnam, 1960; *The World of Rice,* Dutton, 1967; *Careers in the Outdoors,* Dutton, 1975. Author of brochures; contributor of articles and short stories to *Popular Science, Boy's Life, Better Homes and Gardens,* and *Ford Times.*

WORK IN PROGRESS: Research for several books.

SIDELIGHTS: "I do abide by the old adage that a writer should write about what he knows. For that reason there is a heavy emphasis on the outdoors in all my writing, for all my life I have been an outdoorsman. I still spend a good deal of time roughing it, backpacking in the wilderness, camping, fishing, enjoying nature, combining this with photography.

"I also love history and consider it important, and so write about it, particularly the early history of our country, from

MARK J. BOESCH

the time the settlers moved across the Alleghenies, to the earliest settling of the West. I think this was one of the most exciting periods in world history. I also write much about the Indians, for I consider them outstanding people in many ways even though they were long treated badly by their white contemporaries and the historians who followed. We are just beginning to understand the Indians and give them their fair shake.

"Conservation of natural resources has been my strong professional interest. I spent many years with the U.S. Forest Service, from just before World War II until September, 1971 when I resigned in order to get back to writing full time; being disturbed because I was not able to publish many books during the last ten years or so with the Forest Service, having so much official writing to do for the organization. And so I moved back to Montana where I had spent so many of my good young years, and where I could again follow the kind of outdoor life that appeals to me. The largest wilderness area left in the continental United States is practically in my back yard.

"But, I also travel about the country a good bit, for I consider that important. It helps me to write better about the country and its people.

"I spent slightly more than four years in the Marines during World War II and I think my experiences as a Marine in the South Pacific will reflect more in future writing. It does take time to gain the kind of perspective you need in order to write best about a given period of your life. One must have much patience to succeed at writing.

"I have wanted to be a writer for as long as I can remember. Everything else has been secondary. But a writer must live and experience life in order to write best about it. He must be a good observer, and he must have compassion for people. He must read and read, and write and write and write.

"I have many young friends who help to keep me young, and who help me write what I think young people like to read. I want to entertain them with my writing, but if I can help them too, so much the better.

"But I do not just write for young people. Like Robert Louis Stevenson, one of my favorite writers, though, I do try to write the kind of things young people will particularly enjoy, I do try to appeal to all people, regardless of age.

"I have a strong urge to expose the evils in our society, to champion the underdog, the so-called misnamed 'common man.' Expect this to reflect in my future writing."

BROOKS, Polly Schoyer 1912-

PERSONAL: Born August 11, 1912, in South Orleans, Mass.; daughter of William Edgar and Lucy (Turner) Schoyer; married Ernest Brooks (a foundation president), June 23, 1934; children: Joan B. (Mrs. J. R. McLane III), Peter, Turner, Ernest III. *Education:* Radcliffe College, B.A., 1933. *Home:* 152 Marvin Ridge Rd., New Canaan, Conn. 06840.

WRITINGS: (With Nancy Zinsser Walworth) *The World Awakes: The Renaissance in Western Europe,* Lippincott, 1962; *World of Walls,* Lippincott, 1966; (with Walworth) *When the World was Rome,* Lippincott, 1972. Also contributor to *Junior Encyclopedia Britannica.*

POLLY SCHOYER BROOKS

■ (From *The World Awakes: The Renaissance in Western Europe* by Polly Schoyer Brooks and Nancy Zinsser Walworth.)

WORK IN PROGRESS: Currently working on a book on aspects of living in ancient Rome and the Middle Ages, using characters and episodes to illustrate chapters, some of whose titles are *Better Homes, Spectator Sport, Dining Out,* and *Healing Waters and Dream Cures.*

SIDELIGHTS: "My own interest in history, perhaps first sparked by pouring over a delightfully and dramatically illustrated *History of European Civilization* by Guizot in my early childhood, was increased through my children who were really 'turned on' by the excellent history teaching at the Dalton School in the 1940's. Here they studied areas of history in great depth and with lots of collateral reading. I often read aloud to them or read their books to myself—the Howard Pyle Arthurian cycle, *Men of Iron,* Conan Doyle's *The White Company,* to mention a few historical novels. In the field of genuine history Genevieve Foster's *Augustus' World* and Olivia Coolidge's *Roman People* and *Caesar's Gallic Wars* spring to mind and I firmly believe that history

itself has as much interest and excitement to offer as historical fiction.

"When asked to write a history of the Renaissance for the junior high school, I was eager to prove this. My co-author and I had been asked to write a text book but, finding that too circumscribed by rules of format and by a limited vocabulary, we instead, began writing biographical history. We chose a wide variety of men and women, some of whom had helped shape history (Caesar, Charlemagne and the like) and some less well-known characters whose lives revealed the daily life and culture of their times.

"We did considerable research by traveling abroad to see where and to find out as much as possible how our characters had lived. As history came alive for us, so we felt more able to enliven it for our young readers."

FOR MORE INFORMATION SEE: New York Times, December 3, 1962.

CARAS, Roger A(ndrew)   1928-
(Roger Sarac)

PERSONAL: Born May 24, 1928, in Methuen, Mass.; son of Joseph Jacob (insurance executive) and Bessie (Kasanoff) Caras; married Jill Langdon Barclay, September 5, 1954; children: Pamela Jill, Barclay Gordon. *Education:* Huntington Preparatory School, graduate, 1946; Northeastern University, student, 1948-49; Western Reserve University, student, 1949-50; University of Southern California, A.B. (cum laude), 1954. *Home:* 46 Fenmarsh Rd., East Hampton, N.Y. 11937. *Agent:* Roberta Pryor, International Creative Management, 40 West 57th St., New York, N.Y. 10019.

CAREER: Columbia Pictures Corp., New York, N.Y., assistant to vice-president; Polaris Productions, Inc., and Hawk Films Ltd., England, vice-president, 1965-68. Freelance work in writing, film production; Michael Myerberg Productions, New York, N.Y., director of animation, 1954-55. Radio: "Pets and Wildlife," CBS Radio Network, 1969-72; "Report from the World of Animals," NBC Radio Network, 1973; "Pets and Wildlife" (five times weekly), CBS Radio Network, 1973—; "Roger Caras's Mailbag" (five times weekly), WCBS Radio, N.Y. Plus hundreds of guest appearances in United States and Canadian cities. Television: Has appeared on *Today Show,* NBC-TV (approximately sixty reports as "house naturalist"), 1964-75, *Tonight* (Johnny Carson), *Dick Cavett* (numerous appearances, functioned as guest host), *Mike Douglas.* Currently animal correspondent, two reports weekly for network evening news, ABC-TV Network News and technical advisor and editorial commentator, "Animals, Animals, Animals," ABC-TV Network. Plus most major national, network, syndicated, regional and dozens of local TV shows as guest and/or host. Host for half-hour and hour specials for ABC and CBS. *Military service:* U.S. Army, 1946-48, became staff sergeant; 1950-51, as a sergeant. *Member:* Delta Kappa Alpha (president, 1953-55), Explorers Club, Wildlife Federation, Wilderness Society, East African Wildlife Society, Blue Key.

WRITINGS: Antarctica: Land of Frozen Time (Junior Literary Guild and National Travel Club selection), Chilton, 1962; *Dangerous to Man,* Chilton, 1964; *Wings of Gold,* Lippincott, 1965; (under Roger Sarac) *The Throwbacks,*

ROGER A. CARAS

■ (From *Going to the Zoo with Roger Caras* by Roger Caras. Illustrated by Cyrille R. Gentry.)

Something about the Author

Belmont, 1965; *The Custer Wolf*, Little, Brown, 1966; *Last Chance on Earth*, Chilton, 1966; *North American Mammals*, Meredith, 1967; *Sarang*, Little, Brown, 1968; *Monarch of Deadman Bay*, Little, Brown, 1969; *Source of the Thunder*, Little, Brown, 1970; *Panther!*, Little, Brown, 1970; *Death as a Way of Life*, Little, Brown, 1971; *Venomous Animals of the World*, Prentice-Hall, 1974; *Nature Quiz Book #1*, Bantam, 1974; *Nature Quiz Book #2*, Bantam, 1974; *The Private Lives of Animals*, Grosset, 1974; *Sockeye*, Dial, 1975; *Dangerous to Man: 2*, Holt, 1976; *The Roger Caras Pet Book*, Holt, 1977.

Juvenile: *Vanishing Wildlife*, Westover, 1971; *Animal Children*, Westover, 1971; *Animal Architects*, Westover, 1971; *Birds and Flight*, Westover, 1971; *Protective Coloration*, Westover, 1972; *Animal Courtship*, Westover, 1972; *Boundary: Land and Sea*, Westover, 1972; *Creatures of the Night*, Westover, 1972; *Wonderful World of Mammals: Adventuring with Stamps*, Harcourt, 1973; *Going to the Zoo with Roger Caras*, Harcourt, 1973; *Bizarre Animals*, Barre, 1974; *Venomous Animals*, Barre, 1974; *A Zoo in Your Room*, Harcourt, 1975; *Skunk for a Day*, Windmill, 1975. Contributor to *National Observer*, *Seventeen*, *National Wildlife*, *Instructor*, *Ranger Rick*, *Audubon*, *Family Circle* and other magazines; writer of record album jackets; freelance ghosting on radio and television scripts.

SIDELIGHTS: "I am a communicator. I can't help myself. I have to share enthusiasms with anyone who will read, listen or watch. My life is one big game of 'show and tell.'

"The world around us is alive with wonders, it is never less than exciting and often more than even that. To see it and not share it is a terrible loss for each of us brings ourselves to the task of observation. It, the wonder, plus ourselves combine to create a unique marvel. It is the marvel we share—the world through our eyes and hearts and souls. That is what a writer is and a broadcaster is—one who has learned how to really share. I like to think that is what my life is all about.

"As for how it all started—it was as the sun coming up. It was inexorable. I was born to wonder and born to share that wondering. I would have it no other way.

"As for the animals I write and broadcast about, my love for them is older than my consciousness of self. That was always there. I was surrounded in my dreams and in my childhood, too, with animals and through them I reached out to travel and adventure and the exotic places on this planet. Later they pulled me on, made me reach out and then, in my late teens, I began to travel—to where the wild animals were. The animals have been my teachers and my friends. My wife and kids share that enthusiasm and that feeling and, thank heavens, they share my ferocious determination that one day this earth will be a less cruel place for man and animal alike."

Roger Caras has traveled to Europe, to the Orient nine times, to New Zealand and the South Pole and to Africa eight times.

HOBBIES AND OTHER INTERESTS: Enjoys photography, natural history, archaeology, primitive art, ethnology, rare natural history books. Main research interests are in the fields of natural history and anthropology.

HELEN CASWELL

CASWELL, Helen (Rayburn) 1923-

PERSONAL: Born March 16, 1923, in Long Beach, Calif.; daughter of Odis Claude (a carpenter) and Helen (Kepner) Rayburn; married Dwight Allan Caswell (a research engineer), December 27, 1942; children: Dwight Allan, Jr., Philip Rayburn, Mary Helen, Christopher Edwards, John Albert. *Education:* Attended University of Oregon, 1940-42. *Religion:* Episcopalian. *Home:* 15095 Fruitvale Ave., Saratoga, Calif. 95070. *Agent:* Miss Norma Fryatt, Box 213, Manchester, Mass. 01944.

CAREER: Portrait painter, specializing in studies of children. *Member:* Society of Western Artists, Saratoga Contemporary Artists. *Awards, honors:* James D. Phelen Award for Narrative Poetry; San Francisco Browning Club award for dramatic monologue.

WRITINGS: Jesus, My Son, John Knox, 1962; *A Wind on the Road*, Van Nostrand, 1964; *A New Song for Christmas*, Van Nostrand, 1966; *Shadows from the Singing House*, Tuttle, 1968; *You Are More Wonderful*, C. R. Gibson, 1970; *Never Wed an Old Man*, Doubleday, 1975.

SIDELIGHTS: "I was born in California but grew up in Western Oregon. During the week I went to school in the town of Eugene, where I lived with my mother in a small apartment. Every weekend and all during the summers, I stayed with my grandparents on their farm. My grandfather had about 200 acres, but there were only three fields where he grew vegetables and grain. The rest was made up of hills, thickly wooded with fir trees, vine maples, and hazels.

"My grandfather made his living mostly from the goats he raised. They were angora goats, with long, silky white hair and long, spiralling horns. They were allowed to run wild in the hills all year, except in the spring, when my grandfather and I and the dog would climb the mountain, find them, and herd them down to the barnlot. There, they would be sheared of their long hair, which is used to make mohair. In addition to the goats, there were all the usual farm animals—cows and horses and chickens, and I had a rabbit hutch full of white angora rabbits. There were, also, lots of cats and kittens who lived in the barn.

"My favorite things, when I was growing up, were jumping in the fresh hay when it was first put in the barn in the fall, riding my horse to the mail box, a mile away, and playing in the shallow creek that ran past the house, with wooden boats my grandfather made for me.

"Since I was an only child, I decided at an early age that when I grew up I would have a big family. I also decided that I would be an artist, and a writer. Partly, this was because, even when I was very young, whenever I saw something beautiful—a wild Oregon orchid, an orange salamander beneath the maidenhair fern that edged the creek—I felt very strongly that I had to *do* something about it. I don't think everybody feels this way. I think most people are able simply to enjoy beauty, and that is very sensible of them. Perhaps this rather unreasonable feeling of having to *preserve* beauty is one of the things that makes some people paint pictures and write books. However that may be, when I grew up I did, indeed, become a painter and a writer. I also got married and had five children.

"Now my children are all grown up, with only two living at home, but our big old house is still full of people most of the time. I live in a three-story white house that was built in 1906, and is surrounded by very old live-oak trees. It is not a very tidy house, because we have a lot of cats, and plants, and books, and musical instruments lying around, and someone is always in the middle of some big, untidy project. I spend most of my time painting, because that is the way I make my living, and most of my paintings are of children. Sometimes people commission me to paint portraits of their children, and other times I just paint pictures of children I know, and the pictures are sold at galleries. My studio opens off one end of the family room, where everybody listens to records and practices drums, and so forth. Sometimes, when I have to finish a book, or a lot of paintings for a special show, I go to our beach house, where there isn't even a telephone. Growing up an only child in the country, you learn to value company, but you also learn to value solitude.

"My daughter and four sons are all interested in the arts. My oldest son, Dwight, is a photographer and writer, Philip is an artist and writer, Mary is married to a musician, Matthew Walsh, and is a writer, Christopher is a musician, and John, the youngest, has been interested in print making and makes pottery, but he is really more interested in scuba diving.

"The most exciting and pleasurable parts of my work are the first idea, and getting started on it. I also enjoy it when it is finished and has come out rather well. In between is very hard work indeed. My hobby, if you can call it that, is travelling, and seeing lots of new things I have to *do* something about!"

DAVIS, Daniel S(heldon) 1936-

PERSONAL: Born September 15, 1936, in New York, N.Y.; son of Julius and Ruth (Standig) Davis; married Flora Ball, April 7, 1963 (divorced, 1972); married Yona Nachum, December 21, 1972; children: (first marriage) Rebecca, Jeffrey. *Education:* Hunter College (now Hunter College of the City University of New York), B.A., 1959; also studied at New York University. *Residence:* New York, N.Y. *Office:* National Urban League, 500 East 62nd St., New York, N.Y. 10021.

CAREER: New York Times, New York, N.Y., picture editor for *New York Times Magazine,* 1960-63, editor and writer of "News of the Week in Review," 1964-66; National Urban League, New York, N.Y., associate director of public relations, 1966-70, special assistant to the executive director, 1970—. Associate manager of editorial services for Columbia Broadcasting System, Inc., 1970; speechwriter for Whitney Young, Vernon Jordan, and has written speeches for corporate and political figures. *Awards, honors: Beyond Racism* won the Christophers Award in 1969.

WRITINGS: (Editor) Whitney Young, *Beyond Racism,* McGraw, 1969; *Struggle for Freedom: The History of Black Americans,* Harcourt, 1972; *Marcus Garvey,* Watts, 1972; *Mr. Black Labor: The Story of A. Philip Randolph, Father of the Civil Rights Movement,* Dutton, 1972; *Spain's Civil War: The Last Great Cause,* Dutton, 1975. Author of a film tribute to Whitney Young. Contributor to *Saturday Review, Newsweek, Films in Review,* and other national periodicals.

SIDELIGHTS: "The road to writing lies in reading. I read early and often. Books were for me, as for so many others, a way for the mind to escape a poverty-ridden childhood in a Bronx tenement. Several times a week I would trek the

DANIEL S. DAVIS

Ku Klux Klan members march down Pennsylvania Avenue in Washington, D.C. in 1925.
■ (From *Marcus Garvey* by Daniel S. Davis.)

twenty blocks or so to the nearest public library and bring home an armful of books, to be returned read—indeed, devoured—a few days later.

"I was educated in the New York City school system, and after graduating from Hunter College started a career in journalism which I left to become involved in the civil rights movement as a writer first for Whitney Young, and later, for Vernon Jordan. History was my first love and throughout my life I maintained an interest in the past and in the forces that shape the present.

"Because I wanted to share this enthusiasm with others, especially with younger readers, I started writing books. My aim is to present for younger readers accounts of the past and of the figures that helped make history, that are sound, true, interesting, and stimulating. I am disturbed by the trend of ignoring the past, because we cannot understand where we are or where we are going unless we understand where we've been. History embodies all of man's existence, it takes in economics, sociology, geography, literature and much else.

"While I have no 'ideal' reader in mind when I write, I like to think that, perhaps, my book will find its way into the hands of someone much like myself when I was a boy, someone who will be inspired by what I write to explore the subject more deeply, to think, to probe, and to investigate on his own."

DEAN, Anabel 1915-

PERSONAL: Born May 24, 1915, in Deming, N.M.; daughter of Orlee Eugene and May (Wheeler) Stephenson; married William O. Hummel, March 10, 1933; married second husband, Edward M. Dean (an accountant), September 3, 1949; children: (first marriage) David, (second marriage) Stephen Mason, Denise. *Education:* Humboldt State College, B.A., 1959; further study at Chico State University and University of California. *Home:* 2993 Sacramento Dr., Redding, Calif. 96001.

CAREER: Enterprise Elementary Schools, Redding, Calif., teacher, 1960—. *Member:* National Education Association, California Teachers Association, Enterprise Elementary Teachers Association.

WRITINGS—For children: *About Paper,* Melmont, 1968; *Exploring and Understanding Oceanography,* Benefic, 1970; *Exploring and Understanding Heat,* Benefic, 1970; *Willie Can Not Squirm,* Denison, 1971; *Willie Can Ride,* Denison, 1971; *Willie Can Fly,* Denison, 1971; *Men Under the Sea,* Harvey House, 1972; *Hot Rod,* Benefic, 1972; *Destruction Derby,* Benefic, 1972; *Drag Race,* Benefic, 1972; *Road Race,* Benefic, 1972; *Stock Race,* Benefic, 1972; *Indy 500,* Benefic, 1972; *Pink Paint,* Denison, 1973; *Bats, the Night Fliers,* Lerner, 1974.

Saddle Up, Benefic, 1975; *Junior Rodeo*, Benefic, 1975; *High Jumper*, Benefic, 1975; *Harness Race*, Benefic, 1975; *Steeple Chase*, Benefic, 1975; *Animals that Fly*, Messner, 1975; *Ride the Winner*, Benefic, 1975; *Motorcycle Scramble*, Benefic, 1976; *Motorcycle Racer*, Benefic, 1976; *Baja 500*, Benefic, 1976; *Safari Rally*, Benefic, 1976; *Grand Prix Races*, Benefic, 1976; *Submerge! The Story of Divers and Their Crafts*, Westminster, 1976; *Strange Partners*, Lerner, 1976; *Carnivorous Plants*, Lerner, 1977; *How Animals Communicate*, Messner, 1977; *Fires! How Do They Fight Them?*, Westminster, 1977.

SIDELIGHTS: "When I was young, there was a big depression. Many people, including my father, were out of work. My clothes were shabby and there wasn't enough food. I was always cold. But books helped me escape into a land where I was always well dressed, warm and having wonderful adventures. I paid little attention to my studies unless the subject interested me. I dreamed of being a writer, but was always too busy reading.

"Necessity forced me to go to work in an office. Slowly I climbed in the business world until I had a good job. But something was always missing—I was vaguely dissatisfied. After some years of this, I left a good job and went back to college. The first day there, I felt as if someone had opened a window and let fresh air in on me. There were so many things I wanted to learn. I had always loved to work with children. Now I decided to become a teacher.

"Teaching led to writing for children. As I worked with them, I became aware of their tastes in books. I tried new ideas out on them. I found that there were no books on certain subjects for younger children.

ANABEL DEAN

In the cold, a bird fluffs up its feathers to make its coat as light as the wind but warmer than fur. ■ (From *Animals That Fly* by Anabel Dean. Illustrated by Haris Petie.)

"My books are divided into two categories. Easy to read adventure stories and books on natural science. The fiction seems to come easily as I could always tell stories to children. To get the right background, I read, talk to people, and find out as much as I can about a certain subject before I begin. I also draw from personal experiences. In writing science books I choose a subject which interests me and should interest children. Then I research that subject for months until I feel I know it well enough to write about it.

"I enjoy hearing from children who read my books and always answer letters. These letters make me feel that my books aren't just sitting on a shelf. They are being read."

HOBBIES AND OTHER INTERESTS: "I never have time to do all the things I am interested in doing. I do many different kinds of crafts, take part in efforts to improve our environment, sports and travel. I love to travel—to see how people live. I spend several months each year exploring out of the way places."

de CAMP, Catherine C(rook) 1907-

PERSONAL: Born November 6, 1907, in New York, N.Y.; daughter of Samuel (a lawyer) and Mary E. (Beekman) Crook; married Lyon Sprague de Camp (an author under name of L. Sprague de Camp), August 12, 1939; children: Lyman Sprague, Gerard Beekman. *Education:* Barnard College, B.A. (magna cum laude), 1933; graduate study at Western Reserve University, Columbia University, and Temple University, between 1934-38. *Politics:* "Uncommitted." *Religion:* Episcopalian. *Home:* 278 Hothorpe Lane, Villanova, Pa. 19085.

CAREER: Oxford School, Hartford, Conn., teacher of English, 1934-35; teacher of English and history at Laurel School, Shaker Heights, Ohio, 1935-37, and Calhoun School, New York, N.Y., 1937-39; Temple University, Philadelphia, Pa., instructor in child development, 1949; editor of books and radio scripts for husband, L. Sprague de Camp, 1949-62; writer alone and in collaboration with husband, 1962—. At times, social worker with the handicapped, tutor, and substitute teacher. *Member:* Author's Guild,

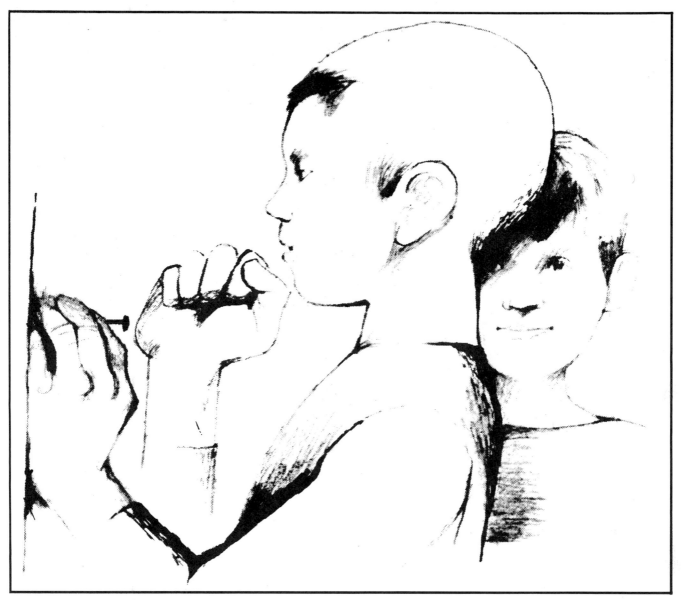

He'd take one in his left hand, hold it to the wood, and bang! bring his fist down on it and drive it home. ▪ (From *Tales Beyond Time* by L. Sprague de Camp and Catherine Crook de Camp. Illustrated by Ati Forberg.)

Academy of Natural Sciences (Philadelphia), University Museum of University of Pennsylvania, Phi Beta Kappa, Barnard Club of Philadelphia (president, 1956-59).

WRITINGS: Scripts on Science for "Voice of America," 1949-50; *The Money Tree,* New American Library, 1972; *Teach Your Child to Manage Money,* Simon & Schuster, 1975; *Creatures of the Cosmos,* Westminster, 1977. Has also done a number of articles on various money-management subjects.

With husband, L. Sprague de Camp: *Ancient Ruins,* retitled *Citadels of Mystery,* Doubleday, 1964, Ballantine, 1973; *Spirits, Stars and Spells,* Canaveral, 1966; *The Story of Science in America,* Scribner, 1967; *The Day of the Dinosaur,* Doubleday, 1968; *Darwin and His Great Discovery,* Macmillan, 1972; *3,000 Years of Fantasy and Science Fiction,* Lothrop, 1972; *Tales Beyond Time,* Lothrop, 1974; *Science Fiction Handbook, Revised,* Owlswick Press, 1975, McGraw, 1977.

WORK IN PROGRESS: Children's stories; more articles on money-management; book in collaboration, *Life on This Planet.*

SIDELIGHTS: "I grew up in a big townhouse in New York City, but it was not a very happy home. Because my mother was ill most of the time, my brothers, sister, and I were brought up by nurses and governesses. Being a frail child with many bad colds, I spent much of each winter in bed, trying to keep up with my school work by doing all the assignments sent home by my teachers. Studying was more fun than simply lying in bed.

"We lived near a park. As soon as the forsythia burst into bloom in April, I knew that the beautiful healthy months were coming. I was very fond of my sister, who was two years younger than I. We used to play and fight with our two brothers and stand together against the grown-ups who were very strict and seldom any fun.

CATHERINE C. DE CAMP

the students to stand up one by one and tell about some interesting thing they had done during the previous summer. When they said they couldn't face an audience, I pointed out that I had faced them all week. I was amused when they replied, 'But you've been doing that for years!'

"After teaching for a few years, I married a free-lance writer. Luckily for me, I had always been good in English, with a bent for writing poetry. However, I majored in economics in college in order to learn how to take care of whatever money I might earn because my widowed mother had handled the family money so badly that we were very poor during my college years. The skills I gained from my work in English and economics have served me well. While my sons were young, I spent my spare time editing my husband's work and keeping the family books. When the boys were grown, I became a full-time writer and my husband's business manager.

"Being a teacher at heart, I have always wanted to share the things I know with young people. That is why most of the books I have written or co-authored have been for children or teen-agers. Although *Teach Your Child to Manage Money* has a title designed to encourage parents to buy the book, the book itself is addressed to readers ten to eighteen. I love science fiction, and with my husband have done two anthologies: *Tales Beyond Time* for readers ten to twelve, and *3,000 Years of Fantasy and Science Fiction* for young adults. *Science Fiction Handbook, Revised* teaches would-be authors almost everything a writer needs to know about creating and selling a story of any type.

"While writing is work that takes self-discipline and a great deal of time, it can be a very satisfying career and a lot of fun."

HOBBIES AND OTHER INTERESTS: Travel, theater, interior decoration, lecturing.

FOR MORE INFORMATION SEE: Philadelphia Sunday Bulletin, December 6, 1964, January 26, 1975; *Main Line Times,* March 3, 1966, June 26, 1975; *The Sunday Bulletin,* January 26, 1975.

"All this changed when I was eleven. The house was sold, and we moved into a hotel. We continued to live in one hotel after another until I finished college. Since my father died two days before I turned sixteen, the hotels we lived in grew more and more shabby. Those were the days of the Great Depression when many families lost all their money and most of their possessions.

"Because I was a shy and awkward young girl, I decided to do everything I could to overcome my handicaps. I begged my mother to let me attend a dancing class. That helped me to stand better. In ballet school, there are long mirrors on the wall so that dancers may see just what they look like as they walk or dance. With the help of those huge mirrors, I learned to straighten my shoulders, hold in my stomach, and move beautifully. I began to feel pretty and be able to smile.

"I found it very hard to answer questions in class. Although I knew the answers, I was embarrassed to speak out when the teachers called on me. One ninth grade teacher told me she thought I would fail my Latin because I hadn't opened my mouth all year. To everyone's surprise, my test paper grade was the highest grade in the class! When at last I was accepted as a day student at Barnard College, I chose all the courses in acting and public speaking that I could find. It was not easy to face an audience, but I persevered. This training paid off when I got my first job, teaching English in a private high school. On Friday of that first week at school, I asked

DEISS, Joseph Jay 1915-

PERSONAL: Surname rhymes with "dice"; born January 25, 1915, in Twin Falls, Idaho; son of Joseph John (a rancher) and Charlotte (Neilson) Deiss; married Catherine Dohoney, August 3, 1937; children: John Casy (deceased), Susanna (Mrs. Eric Chivian). *Education:* University of Texas, B.A., 1934, M.A., 1935. *Home:* Thoreau House, Wellfleet, Mass. 02667.

CAREER: U.S. Government, Washington, D.C., editor and writer, 1936-44; *Executives' War Digest,* New York, N.Y., editor, 1944-46; free-lance writer, 1947-50; Medical & Pharmaceutical Information Bureau (public relations), New York, N.Y., partner, 1950-54; free-lance writer, 1954—. American Academy in Rome, vice-director, 1965-69; writer-in-residence, Currier House, Harvard-Radcliffe, 1975. *Member:* Authors Guild, Thoreau Society, Phi Gamma Delta. *Awards, honors:* Distinguished Alumnus Award, University of Texas, 1970; Cavalier, Order of the Star of Solidarity of Italy, 1971.

JOSEPH JAY DEISS

WRITINGS: A Washington Story (novel), Duell, Sloan & Pearce, 1950; *The Blue Chips* (novel), Simon & Schuster, 1957; *The Great Infidel; Frederick II of Hohenstaufen* (biographical novel), Random House, 1963; *Captains of Fortune—Profiles of Six Italian Condottieri*, Gollancz, 1966; Crowell, 1967; *Herculaneum: Italy's Buried Treasure*, Crowell, 1966; *The Roman Years of Margaret Fuller*, Crowell, 1969; *The Town of Hercules: A Buried Treasure Trove* (young readers), Houghton, 1974. Contributor to national magazines, including *Mademoiselle, Cosmopolitan, Holiday, Harper's, Reader's Digest,* and *American Heritage.*

SIDELIGHTS: "When I was a youngster in Texas, like every boy I played cowboys and Indians. Gradually I became more interested in Indians than in cowboys, because I found arrowheads, camp sites, burial grounds. (I found the bones of a mastodon, too, but that's another story.) These finds were the beginning of my fascination with history and archaeology.

"I knew an old lady who told me about the time, when she was a small girl, that Chief Quanah came unannounced to the family cabin with a band of braves. The settlers were terribly frightened, and my friend hid in a trundle bed. But Chief Quanah and his braves meant no harm—they merely wanted to talk and exchange gifts. When my friend came out from under her parents' bed, she smiled at Chief Quanah and he smiled back. She thought him very handsome. Afterwards, my friend never could understand why people spoke of Indians as blood thirsty. Her story was the beginning of my fascination with historical persons as living people.

"As it turned out, I haven't written any books about cowboys or Indians (though maybe I will someday). I've written mostly about people and places of times past: Roman times or the Middle Ages or the Renaissance in Italy. Unlike America, in Italy the remote past is all around you, and as a writer I found a challenge to bring back the past to seeming

life. I spent so many hours, days, months, years, in ancient Herculaneum that I felt I had grown up there instead of Texas. So when I wrote my books on Herculaneum I knew the people far more intimately than I had known Chief Quanah. It was almost as if I had played in their gardens and eaten at their tables, before the disasterous eruption of Mt. Vesuvius that buried both Pompeii and Herculaneum in 79 A.D.

"Some of the rewards of writing such books are the surprises. One day on my short-wave radio I tuned to the BBC, London, and heard a group of critics discussing *Herculaneum* as one of the twelve outstanding books published in Britain that year. Another day I opened an envelope from England and found an unsolicited letter from the famous scholar Sir Julian Huxley. I had written 'a wonderful book,' he said, '—vivid and historically important. It will be one of my treasured permanent possessions.' The great Irish playwright, Sean O'Casey, also wrote to me about one of my books. Equally unexpected was the opportunity to present personally the Swedish translation of one of my books to Gustavus Adolphus VI, King of Sweden. Such is the encouragement that makes writers—especially young writers—persevere.

"Sometimes I am asked to name the book I found most difficult to write. My answer is: *The Town of Hercules—A Buried Treasure Trove.* It is the version of *Herculaneum* especially for young readers. I invited some kids to serve as editors, and they really took me to task. As a result, I worked harder than I ever worked on any other book, explaining every reference, making every word the right one and every sentence bell clear. I always like to hear from young readers how they feel about the book. And criticism is welcome, because criticism is one of the best ways to learn."

Deiss' books have been translated into nineteen languages.

HOBBIES AND OTHER INTERESTS: Swimming, rowing, tennis.

FOR MORE INFORMATION SEE: John Bainbridge, *Another Way of Living,* Holt, 1968.

DeLAURENTIS, Louise Budde 1920-

PERSONAL: Born October 5, 1920, in Stafford, Kan.; daughter of Louis (a farmer) and Mary (Lichte) Budde; married Mariano A. DeLaurentis (an airline pilot), March 26, 1948; children: Delbert Louis. *Education:* Ottawa University, Ottawa, Kan., B.A., 1942. *Home:* 983 Cayuga Heights Rd., Ithaca, N.Y., 14850.

CAREER: Airport traffic controller with U.S. Civil Aeronautics Administration (now U.S. Federal Aviation Agency) in Buffalo, N.Y., Bangor, Me., and elsewhere in United States, 1943-55; free-lance editor, 1970—. *Member:* Writers Association (Ithaca, N.Y.; president, 1963), National Writers Club. *Awards, honors: Wind, Sun, and Sky* (novel) was awarded third prize in the National Writers Club 1975 Book Contest.

WRITINGS: Etta Chipmunk, Denison, 1962; *A Peculiarity of Direction* (collection of previously published poems), privately printed, 1975. Edited *Gentle Sorcery* (poems by

LOUISE BUDDE DELAURENTIS

Bessie Jeffery), in 1972. "Prairie Blizzard" (a children's story) appeared in *Cricket*, 1975. Other children's stories have been published in *Trailblazer, Five/Six, Grade Teacher, Adventure, Road Runner*. Contributor of poetry to *The New Renaissance, Moondance, Kansas* magazine, *Minnesota Review, Discourse, Quartet, Epoch, Poem, Epos, Womanspirit* and others.

WORK IN PROGRESS: "Honey Locust" (group of adult stories); second poetry collection, *Waiting It Out;* children's stories.

SIDELIGHTS: "An on-going love affair with the chipmunks living around my home in the woods led to the research that culminated in *Etta Chipmunk*. Most of my other children's stories have come as a result of the experiences of my son, when he was younger, and from memories of my life on a farm in western Kansas during Depression and dust bowl days."

HOBBIES AND OTHER INTERESTS: Philosophy, swimming, bicycling, local politics, the women's movement.

DEVANEY, John 1926-

PERSONAL: Born March 15, 1926, in New York, N.Y.; son of John (an engineer) and Delia Devaney; married Barbara Masciocchi (graphic designer), April 16, 1955; children: John, Luke. *Education:* New York University, B.S., 1949. *Politics:* Democrat. *Religion:* Roman Catholic. *Residence:* New York, N.Y. *Office:* 520 LaGuardia Pl., New York, N.Y. 10012.

CAREER: Science Illustrated, New York N.Y., writer, 1948-50; *Quick,* New York, N.Y., medical editor, 1952-54; *Parade,* New York, N.Y., sports editor, 1955-61; free-lance writer, 1961—. *Military service:* U.S. Army, 1944-46.

WRITINGS: Bob Cousy, Putnam, 1965; *The Pro Quarterbacks,* Putnam, 1966; *The Great Olympic Champions,* Putnam, 1967; *Bart Starr,* Scholastic Magazine, 1967; *The Baseball Life of Mickey Mantle,* Scholastic Magazine, 1967; *Greatest Cardinals of Them All,* Putnam, 1968; *Juan Marichal,* Putnam, 1970; *History of the World Series,* Rand, 1971; *Tom Seaver,* Popular Library, 1972; *O. J. Simpson,* Warner, 1973; *Johnny Bench,* Scholastic Magazine, 1973; *Gil Hodges: Baseball Miracle Man,* Putnam, 1973; *History of the Stanley Cup,* Rand, 1975; (with Bob Cousy) *The Killer Instinct,* Random House, 1975; *The Indy 500,* Rand, 1976. Contributor of articles to *Redbook, Saturday Evening Post, Sport, Boys' Life, Scouting, Explorer,* and *Catholic Digest.*

WORK IN PROGRESS: Tiny Archibald for Putnam; *The Harlem Mosque Murder* for Crown.

SIDELIGHTS: "I have always wanted to write almost as far back as I can remember—when I was about nine or ten and living in the Bronx and typing out, one issue at a time, a 'newspaper' for our neighbors on East 139th near Willis Avenue. Unlike many newspapers before and since, that one made money . . . about five cents, as I recall, although it took some strong-arm tactics to sell some of the copies to reluctant playmates.

"About the same time I became interested in sports, enthralled by the New York Giants, and I imagined myself as a

JOHN DEVANEY

The quarterback's skills are the heaviest ingredients when you weigh the total talents of a team. ■ (From *The Pro Quarterback* by John Devaney.)

sportswriter sitting in the press box at the Polo Grounds typing out play-by-play stories of Giant victories. I listened to games on the radio, then wrote stories of the games for my two favorite newspapers—the *Journal American* and the *Daily News*.

"While in the Army, and quite by accident, I became a sportswriter and later, sports editor, of the Army paper, *Stars and Stripes*. Unfortunately I was desk-bound, editing other people's stories, and it wasn't until 1954 that the dream came true and I was sitting in the press box at the Polo Grounds. I was there as the sports editor of a magazine. I never did get to write newspaper stories about what was being played out below me. But since then I have been writing magazine articles and books about sports heroes—not so much about what they do on a playing field, but how they got to where they are and how they feel about their passage to this point and time of their career. Now, I realize, this is where the fun, the craft and perhaps the art really is—not in newspaper reporting of a game but in the less hurried and deeper look at the people who play the game."

DOWDELL, Dorothy (Florence) Karns 1910-

PERSONAL: Surname is accented on first syllable; born May 5, 1910, in Reno, Nev.; daughter of Albert Berdell (a federal employee) and Florence (Lusk) Karns; married Joseph A. Dowdell (a retired college botany instructor), June 21, 1931; children: Joan Eva (Mrs. William R. Moore), John Lawrence. *Education:* Sacramento City College, student, 1927-29; University of California, Berkeley, A.B., 1931;

additional study at Sacramento State College, 1948-50. *Politics:* Republican. *Religion:* Episcopalian. *Home:* 120 Carlton Ave., #4, Los Gatos, Calif. 95030. *Agent:* John Payne, Lenniger Literary Agency, 437 Fifth Ave., New York, N.Y. 10016.

CAREER: Sacramento City Unified School District, Sacramento, Calif., elementary school teacher, 1948-61; full-time writer, 1961—. *Member:* American Association of University Women (member of Sacramento branch board, 1964-65), Authors Guild of Authors League of America, California Writers Club (Sacramento branch president, 1953-54, 1963-64; Peninsula branch vice-president, 1975-76), California Congress P.T.A. (honorary life), P.E.O. Sisterhood (chapter president, 1944-46).

WRITINGS: Karen Anderson, Illustrator (for young adults), Bouregy, 1960; *Strange Rapture* (for young adults), Bouregy, 1961; *Border Nurse* (for young adults), Bouregy, 1963; *Roses for Gail* (for young adults), Bouregy, 1964; *How to Help Your Child in School,* Macfadden, 1964; *Secrets of the ABC's* (juvenile), Oddo, 1965; *Arctic Nurse* (for young adults), Bouregy, 1966; *The Allerton Rose* (for young adults), Dell, 1972; *Hawk Over Hollyhedge Manor,* Avon, 1973; *House in Munich,* Avon, 1975; *Pretty Enough to Kill,* Playboy Press, 1976; *Tahoe,* Playboy Press, 1977.

With husband, Joseph Dowdell: *Tree Farms: Harvest for the Future,* Bobbs-Merrill, 1965; *Your Career in Teaching,* Messner, 1967, revised edition, 1975; *Sierra Nevada: The Golden Barrier,* Bobbs-Merrill, 1968; *Careers in Horticul-*

DOROTHY KARNS DOWDELL

This little girl attends one of the three Chinese schools in New York's Chinatown. The students learn the Chinese language, culture, and writing. In this picture, she is using a brush to write each character. ■ (From *The Chinese Helped Build America* by Joseph & Dorothy Dowdell. Picture by Pak and Wan.)

tural Sciences, Messner, 1969, revised edition, 1975; *The Japanese Helped Build America,* Messner, 1970; *Your Career in the World of Travel,* Messner, 1971; *The Chinese Helped Build America,* Messner, 1972.

WORK IN PROGRESS: The Casino, a suspense for adults.

SIDELIGHTS: "Although I was born in Reno, Nevada, my parents soon moved to the state capital, Carson City, which only had a population of about two thousand at that time. I lived here until I was twelve years old. It always seemed very isolated tucked at the base of the towering Sierra Nevada range, especially in the winter when the Carson Valley and the mountains were covered with snow.

"However, there were many things to do and I don't remember being lonely. We were always fascinated by the Piute Indians who would come into town with their painted faces and meet in a vacant lot. They would form a large circle and sit cross-legged all day gossiping and playing a game with bones. We children stood around and watched them and the Indians seemed as interested in us as we were in them.

"My father owned one of the first automobiles in Nevada, an open Ford touring car with a bright brass band around the radiator. The fifteen-mile trip crawling up the steep grade to Lake Tahoe was an adventure, indeed. There were many stops along the way to change flat tires and to fill the boiling radiator with cold water. Coming down was even more dangerous, especially at night because the slower one drove, the dimmer the headlights became. One night the headlights went out completely and my father walked ahead with a lantern while my mother steered the car down the narrow, twisting road cut out of the cliffs.

"Of course, when the Ringling Brothers circus came to town with the big tents, the wild animals snarling in cages, the calliope leading the parade, we were beside ourselves with excitement. Another highlight was when all the schools were dismissed and we children lined an open field to wait impatiently four hours for the first airplane to land in Nevada.

"There were old mines to explore, endless deserts with the pungent smell of sagebrush to hike in, mountain streams alive with fish to catch, and the United States Mint to visit where coins were made from gold and silver brought from nearby mines.

Something about the Author

"Best of all was the state library, housed in the small capitol building, which had an excellent collection of children's books. I was an insatiable reader and one of the library's most eager patrons from the time I learned to read. Even in those early days, I knew that someday I, too, would write books.

"The nagging desire to write was always with me while I was a child in Nevada and later in California where I went to high school and college. I tried to write articles and stories but had little success.

"As soon as I graduated from the University of California in Berkeley, I married a botany instructor. After our first year of marriage we went to Munich, Germany to study at the university during 1932 and 1933. We were there when Hitler came into power and Jewish persecutions began. It was a frightening time and how glad we were to return to America!

"Even though the United States, like the rest of the world, was going through a terrible depression in the thirties, it was a happy time for us for our two children were born. Later followed World War II and when it was over I started to teach in the elementary schools of Sacramento. During all this time, I was having experiences and absorbing impressions which eventually became grist for my mill as a writer.

"In 1948 I wrote a travel article which was published and that was the beginning of my writing career. At first I wrote articles and stories for magazines, for in the forties and fifties there were hundreds of periodicals on the stands. Later I turned to books and since 1960 have had sixteen books published which has been one of the most fulfilling experiences of my life.

"It is always an exciting adventure to embark on a new book whether it is fiction or non-fiction. Usually there is interesting research to do which expands ones horizons. There is always the challenge of trying to improve ones techniques and writing skills. There is nothing more rewarding to an author than to feel that the latest book is the best one of all."

Dorothy Dowdell lived in Europe for one year and has traveled to Alaska, Hawaii, Canada and throughout the United States studying plant life with her botanist-husband.

HOBBIES AND OTHER INTERESTS: Traveling, reading, meeting with other writers.

FOR MORE INFORMATION SEE: Best Sellers, May 1, 1967, September 1, 1968, April 1, 1969; *Library Journal,* September, 1968, July, 1969, October 15, 1970.

EDELL, Celeste

PERSONAL: Daughter of Julius and Irma (Rothschild) Loeb; married Harold Edell. *Education:* Attended Hunter College, New York University. *Home:* 9472 Bay Dr., Surfside, Fla. 33154.

CAREER: Writer. *Member:* Authors Guild, Women's National Book Association, Professional Writers' Roundtable of New York City.

Jean was at the window crying. ■ (From *A Present From Rosita* by Celeste Edell. Illustrated by Elton C. Fax.)

WRITINGS: A Present from Rosita, Messner, 1953; *Here Come the Clowns,* Putnam, 1958; *Lynn Pamet,* Messner, 1961.

EDWARDS, Herbert Charles   1912-
(Bertram Edwards)

PERSONAL: Born July 22, 1912, in London, England; son of John Quilton and Eliza (Conybeare) Edwards; married Lilian Florence Hinton, December 25, 1937; children: John Charles, Michael Vernon, Nigel Philip. *Education:* Attended Newlands Park Training College, Buckinghamshire, England, and Cambridge Institute of Education. *Religion:* Church of England. *Home:* 20 Whitehurst Ave., Hitchin, Hertfordshire, England. *Office:* Wilshere-Dacre School, Hitchin, Hertfordshire, England.

CAREER: Teacher at Longfield Special School, Stevenage (five years) and Wilshere-Dacre School, both in Hertfordshire, England. *Military service:* British Army, 1940-45; became staff sergeant. *Member:* National Union of Teachers. *Awards, honors:* Runners-up Junior Book award certificate from Boys' Clubs of America for *The Mystery of Barrowmead Hill.*

HERBERT CHARLES EDWARDS

scribed enough money to enable a single-roomed classroom to be built on the edge of the village green. This was opened in 1917 and the two teachers concerned, Mr. and Mrs. Higdon, continued to teach the village children until 1939, when Mr. Higdon died.

"It struck me at once that many of the school children involved would be alive still, with vivid memories of the drama of sixty years ago, memories that they would love to re-live. My search for these wonderful folk, and my documentary research, took me two wonderful years and I don't think I have ever been so fascinated and excited in my life.

"The television producer, Stephen Peet, asked me to co-operate with him on one of his 'Yesterday's Witness' pro-grammes and I took him around Norfolk, Essex, and London, and introduced him to the folk I had traced. They were interviewed on his forty-five minute programme on B.B.C.2. He also borrowed from me the old documents and photo-graphs that I had collected, and the manuscript of my book, which had not yet been published.

"My wife and I still visit many of the old folk several times a year. Two years ago we arranged a 'get-together' for them, over tea, at the Strike School, which is now used for social functions. I have given my documents and photographs to the Norfolk Archives Officer and the school has become a kind of shrine. Senior children at the large Comprehensive School at the New Town of Milton Keynes, Buckingham-shire, made a social study of the strike and their work culmi-nated in a fine play that they produced 'in the round.' This teaching project attracted the interest of the British 'Open University' and a booklet was produced and distributed to students, as an example of how such social conflicts can be made the centre of widening school studies."

WRITINGS—Under pseudonymn Bertram Edwards: *The Restless Valley*, Brockhampton Press, 1956; *Midnight on Barrowmead Hill*, Brockhampton Press, 1957, published in America as *The Mystery of Barrowmead Hill*, McKay, 1959; *Strange Traffic*, Brockhampton Press, 1959, McKay, 1960; *Danger in Densmere*, Thomas Nelson, 1965; *The Rise of the U.S.A.*, Blackie & Son, 1968; "Captain Swing at the Penny Gaff" (play), first produced in London at Unity Theatre, 1971; *The Burston School Strike*, Lawrence & Wishart, 1974.

WORK IN PROGRESS: "I am now working on an adult novel and another documentary study. I have just completed an adventure story for children of ten to fifteen years."

SIDELIGHTS: "The children's story that gave me the most pleasure to write was *The Mystery of Barrowmead Hill*, but the sustained fascination and delight I got from my research into an authentic strike of village school children in 1914, which culminated in my writing *The Burston School Strike*, were immense.

"The children of this Norfolk village, supported by their parents, refused to go to school when the headmistress and her husband, whom they loved, were unjustly dismissed by the school managers. I saw a brief reference to the affair in a book on the history of British education and I was deeply moved by the loyalty of the children and their parents. The strike began in April, 1914, and trade unionists all over Brit-ain, indignant at the treatment of the two teachers, sub-

EDWARDS, Monica le Doux Newton   1912-

PERSONAL: Born November 8, 1912, in Belper, Derby-shire, England; daughter of Harry (a clergyman) and Beryl F. le Doux (Sargeant) Newton; married William Ferdinand Edwards (a retired farmer), 1931; children: Shelley C. Ed-wards Paton, Sean R. *Education:* Attended Beecholm Col-lege, Thornes House School, and St. Brandon's School for the Daughters of Clergy. *Home:* Punch Bowl Farm, Thur-sley, Surrey, England. *Agent:* Curtis Brown Ltd., 13 King St., Covent Garden, London W.C.2, England.

CAREER: Author, mainly of children's books. *Member:* Society of Authors, Royal Horticultural Society, Interna-tional Camellia Society, National Farmers' Union. *Awards, honors:* Co-recipient of Foyles' Children's Book Club Au-thor of the Year designation, 1957.

WRITINGS: *Wish for a Pony*, 1947, *No Mistaking Corker*, 1948, *The Summer of the Great Secret*, 1948, *The Midnight Horse*, 1949, Vanguard, 1950, *The White Riders*, 1949, *Black Hunting Whip*, 1949 (all originally published by Col-lins).

Punchbowl Midnight, 1951, *Cargo of Horses*, 1951, *Spirit of Punchbowl Farm*, 1952, *Hidden in a Dream*, 1953, *The Wanderer*, 1953, *Storm Ahead*, 1954, *No Entry*, 1954, *The Unsought Farm*, M. Joseph, 1954, *Punchbowl Harvest*, 1955, *The Nightbird*, 1955, *Joan Goes Farming*, Bodley Head, 1955, *Rennie Goes Riding*, Bodley Head, 1956,

Frenchman's Secret, 1956, *Strangers to the Marsh*, 1957, *Operation Seabird*, 1957, *The Cownappers*, 1958, *Killer Dog*, 1959 (all published by Collins, except as indicated).

No Going Back, 1960, *The Outsider*, 1961, *The Hoodwinkers*, 1962, *Dolphin Summer*, 1963, *The Cats of Punchbowl Farm*, Doubleday, 1964, *Fire in the Punchbowl*, 1965, *The Badgers of Punchbowl Farm*, Michael Joseph, 1966, *The Wild One*, 1967, *Under the Rose*, 1968, *A Wind is Blowing*, 1969, *The Valley & the Farm*, Michael Joseph, 1971, *Badger Valley*, Michael Joseph, 1976 (all published by Collins, except as indicated).

Author of film script, "The Dawn Killer," for Children's Film Foundation. Contributor of short stories to English magazines.

WORK IN PROGRESS: Research on badgers.

SIDELIGHTS: Twelve books have been translated for publication in other European languages, one transcribed into Braille, some serialized and broadcast.

HOBBIES AND OTHER INTERESTS: Natural history, wildlife conservation, photography, gardening, needlework, riding, music, reading and cats.

EISENBERG, Azriel 1903-

PERSONAL: Born August 29, 1903, in Russia; came to United States in 1914; son of Louis and Mindel (Shpetrik) Eisenberg; married Rose Leibow (a teacher), August 19, 1928; children: Sora (Mrs. Aaron Landes), Judah M. *Education:* Jewish Theological Seminary of America, teachers diploma, 1922; New York University, B.S., 1926; Columbia University, Ph.D., 1935. *Politics:* Liberal. *Religion:* Jewish. *Home:* 68-52 Juno St., Forest Hills, N.Y. 11375.

CAREER: Bureau of Jewish Education, New York, N.Y., director of bureaus in Cincinnati, Ohio, 1935-40, Cleveland, Ohio, 1940-46, and Philadelphia, Pa., 1946-49; Board of Jewish Education, New York, N.Y., executive vice-president, 1949-66; World Council of Jewish Education, New York, N.Y., director, 1966-68. American Jewish Joint Distribution Committee, organized office of Jewish education in Paris, 1956, conducted survey of Jewish education in Iran, 1969. Acting dean of Graetz College, 1946-49; chairman of United Synagogue Commission on Jewish Education, 1968-73; co-chairman of National Zionist Education Commission; organized international conferences.

MEMBER: National Council for Jewish Education (president, 1946-50), Jewish Publication Society, American Jewish Joint Distribution Committee, North Eastern Ohio Religious Education Association (past president), Jewish Teachers Association (New York; past president). *Awards, honors:* D.H.L. from Jewish Theological Seminary of America, 1959; National Jewish Book Council award, 1965, for *Worlds Lost and Found;* D.H.L. (Honoris Causa), Baltimore Hebrew College, 1977.

WRITINGS: Children and Radio Programs, Columbia University Press, 1936; (with Leon J. Feur) *Jewish Literature Since the Bible*, two volumes, Union of American Hebrew Congregations, 1943, new edition, 1946.

AZRIEL EISENBERG

Tze'dakah and Federation, Jewish Education Committee of New York, 1952; *Dear Parents*, Jewish Education Committee of New York, 1952; (with Abraham Segal) *Teaching Jewish History*, Jewish Education Committee of New York, 1954; *The Great Discovery: The Dead Sea Scrolls*, Abelard, 1956; (with Segal) *Presenting Bialik: A Study of His Life and Works*, Jewish Education Committee of New York, 1956; *Teacher's Guide to Modern Jewish Life in Literature*, United Synagogue Commission on Jewish Education, 1956; *Voices from the Past*, Abelard, 1958; (with Jesse B. Robinson) *My Jewish Holidays*, United Synagogue Commission on Jewish Education, 1958; *My Own J.N.F.*, Jewish National Fund, 1958; *The Story of the Jewish Calendar*, Abelard, 1959.

(With Dov Peretz Elkins) *Worlds Lost and Found*, Abelard, 1964; *Feeding the World: A Biography of David Lubin* (youth book), Abelard, 1965; *Fill a Blank Page: A Biography of Solomon Schechter* (youth book), United Synagogue Commission of Jewish Education, 1965; (with Philip Arian) *The Story of the Prayer Book*, Prayer Book Press, 1968; *Jewish Historical Treasures*, Bloch Publishing, 1969.

(With Leah Ain Globe) *Sabra Children*, J. David, 1970; (with Elkins) *Treasures from the Dust*, Abelard, 1972; *The Book of Books: Story of the Bible Text*, Soncino Press, 1974; *The Synagogue through the Ages*, Bloch Publishing, 1974; *Home at Last*, Bloch, 1977; (with Jessie B. Robinson) *Our Living Prayer Book*, Prayer Book Press, 1977.

Editor: *The Bar Mitzvah Treasury*, Behrman, 1952; *The Confirmation Reader*, Behrman, 1953; (with Abraham Segal) *Readings in the Teaching of Jewish History*, Jewish Education Committee of New York, 1956; *Modern Jewish Life in Literature*, Union of American Hebrew Congregations, Volume I, 1956, Volume II, 1968; (with Segal) *Accent on Hebrew*, Jewish Education Committee Press, 1960; (with Joseph Lukinsky) *Readings in the Teaching of Hebrew*, Jewish Education Committee Press, 1961; *Tzedakah: A Way of Life*, Behrman, 1963; *Readings in the Teaching of Prayer and Siddur*, Jewish Education Committee Press, 1964; *The Golden Land: A Literary Portrait of American Jewry, 1654 to the Present*, Yoselof, 1965; (with Leah Ain Globe) *The Bas Mitzvah Treasury*, Twayne, 1965; (and translator with Globe) *The Secret Weapon and Other Stories*, Soncino Press, 1966; (with Jacob Seegar) *World Census on Jewish Education*, World Council on Jewish Education, 1968; *Jerusalem Eternal*, Jewish Education Committee Press, 1971; (with Hannah G. Goodman and Alvin I. Kass) *Eyewitness to Jewish History*, Union of American Hebrew Congregations, 1973; (with Hannah G. Goodman) *Eye Witness to American Jewish History*, Union of American Hebrew Congregations, 1977.

In Hebrew: (Editor) *Yerushalayim*, Jewish Education Committee of New York, 1955; *Kolot mini kedem*, [Tel Aviv], 1962. Also author of *Olamot shenelinu veniglu*.

Author of over a dozen teacher's guides and manuals, and a number of other works, including textbooks. Contributor to journals and magazines.

WORK IN PROGRESS: Heroes of the Holocaust; Children in the Holocaust; Words on Wings: Anthology Post-Biblical Literature (2 vols.) for Union of American Hebrew Congregations; *A Time to Live: On Age and Aging—a Reader.*

SIDELIGHTS: "From my long and varied experiences I should like to submit the following recommendations which I am convinced are relevant to general education:

"1. Approach to teaching history for beginners, especially on secondary school and college levels.

"The best of history text books present generalized and highly condensed materials which can not affect the reader. I have experimented successfully in introducing the student to the study of history through effective eyewitness accounts.

"2. Teaching a second language: comprehensive reading.

"The emphasis on speech in teaching a second language is frustrating and unproductive. We should bring the student as soon as possible to acquire a minimum of vocabulary to *read* in the new language. And we must prepare story books that are attractive for leisurely enjoyable reading. Their vocabulary and syntax must be controlled. Today we have several graded libraries in Hebrew consisting of hundreds of books. The student's acquisition of an evergrowing passive vocabulary activates his speaking ability.

"3. Teaching ritual observances and ceremonies.

"These subjects are still very much alive in the home, church and synagogue as well as the community to be confined within the covers of a book and treated as a subject like civics, history or geography. The approach should be a 'do-it-yourself' basis. Imaginative exercises, group work, projects involving home and school, handcraft activities and the like should be devised in a new kind of text so that school and home compliment each other. This approach has to be examined by studying the series: *My Jewish Holidays, Our Living Prayer Book, My Jewish Heritage,* to be understood and appreciated.

"4. Restore the book as the primary source of learning.

"With the development of visual and aural media we must rally around the book as the timetested generative force in the education of the generations.

"These have been the primary motivations in my writing career in Jewish religious education."

FALKNER, Leonard 1900-

PERSONAL: Born July 7, 1900, in Cleveland, Ohio; son of John (a farmer) and Emma (Piersdorf) Falkner; married Irene Steiner, December 18, 1922; children: Doris Irene (Mrs. James W. Hart). *Education:* Attended public schools in Cleveland, Ohio. *Politics:* Independent. *Religion:* Methodist. *Home:* Candlewood Isle, Conn. *Agent:* Lurton Blassingame, 60 East 42nd St., New York, N.Y. 10017. *Office:* 90 Morningside Dr., New York, N.Y. 10027.

CAREER: American Magazine, New York, N.Y., staff writer, 1930-32; *New York World-Telegram and Sun*, New York, N.Y., news editor, 1937-48, features editor, 1948-65.

WRITINGS: Forge of Liberty, Dutton, 1959; *Painted Lady Eliza Jamel: Her Life and Times*, Dutton, 1962; *The President Who Wouldn't Retire*, Coward, 1967; *John Adams: Reluctant Patriot of the Revolution*, Prentice-Hall, 1969; *For Jefferson and Liberty*, Knopf, 1972. Contributor of articles and short stories to *American Heritage, Reader's Digest, Redbook,* and *Liberty*.

Ostrich

The ostrich can outrun any animal that threatens it.
■ (From *The Land, Wildlife, and Peoples of the Bible* by Peter Farb. Illustrations by Harry McNaught.)

FARB, Peter 1929-

PERSONAL: Born July 25, 1929, in New York, N.Y.; son of Solomon and Cecelia (Peters) Farb; married Oriole Horch (a museum director and painter), February 27, 1953; children: Mark Daniel, Thomas Forest. *Education:* Vanderbilt University, B.A. (magna cum laude), 1950; Columbia University, graduate study, 1950-51. *Politics:* Independent. *Home:* 39 Pokeberry Ridge, Amherst, Mass. 01002.

CAREER: Argosy, New York, N.Y., feature editor, 1950-52. Free-lance writer on a variety of subjects, 1953—. Columbia Broadcasting System, New York, N.Y., editor-in-chief of Panorama (publishing project), 1960-61; Riverside Museum, New York, N.Y., curator of American Indian cultures, 1964-71; Yale University, New Haven, Conn., visiting lecturer, 1971-72, fellow, Calhoun College, 1971—. Consultant, Smithsonian Institution, 1966-71; judge, National Book Awards Committee, 1971. Member of board of directors, Allergy and Asthma Foundation of America, 1970-73; trustee, University of Massachusetts Library. *Member:* American Association for the Advancement of Science (fellow), American Anthropological Association, Society of American Historians (fellow), New York Entomological Society (former secretary), P.E.N., Phi Beta Kappa, Omicron Delta Kappa.

WRITINGS: Living Earth, Harper, 1959; *The Story of Butterflies and Other Insects,* Harvey, 1959; *The Insect World,* Constable, 1960; *The Story of Dams,* Harvey, 1961; *The Forest,* Time, Inc., 1961; (co-editor) *Prose by Professionals,* Doubleday, 1961; *The Insects,* Time, Inc., 1962; *The Story of Life,* Harvey, 1962; *Ecology,* Time, Inc., 1963, revised edition, 1970; *Face of North America: The Natural History of a Continent* (Book-of-the-Month Club selection), Harper, 1963, young reader's edition, 1964; *The Land and Wildlife of North America,* Time, Inc., 1964; (with John Hay) *The Atlantic Shore,* Harper, 1966; *The Land, Wildlife, and Peoples of the Bible,* Harper, 1967; *Man's Rise to Civilization as Shown by the Indians of North America from Primeval Times to the Coming of the Industrial State,* Dutton, 1968, 2nd revised edition, 1977; *Yankee Doodle,* Simon & Schuster, 1970; *Word Play,* Knopf, 1974; *The Human Equation,* Houghton, 1977.

Columnist, *Better Homes and Gardens,* 1959-63, and contributor of science and nature articles to *Reader's Digest* and other national magazines.

WORK IN PROGRESS: A textbook of general anthropology.

SIDELIGHTS: President Kennedy presented *Face of North America* to the heads of one hundred foreign governments, and its author was hailed by Secretary of the Interior Stewart Udall in 1964 as "one of the finest conservation spokesmen of our period." Farb's books have been translated into more than fifteen languages and have set something of a sales record for works on natural history subjects by living writers.

FOR MORE INFORMATION SEE: Book of the Month, February, 1963, October, 1968.

Something tilted up to meet them, and they were both falling. She felt that they were tumbling through endless, black space. They landed with a bump.
■ (From *The Ghost Garden* by Hila Feil. Illustrated by Thomas Quirk.)

FEIL, Hila 1942-

PERSONAL: Born June 29, 1942, in New York, N.Y.; daughter of Robert (a writer) and Dorothy (a writer; maiden name, Crayder) Newman; married Gerald Feil (a film director), February 2, 1967; children: Anna. *Education:* Attended Barnard College, 1960-62. *Office:* c/o Feil Productions, 36 West 62nd St., New York, N.Y. 10023.

CAREER: Columbia Broadcasting System (CBS) News, New York, N.Y., editorial staff of "The 20th Century" and "The 21st Century" series, 1964-68. *Member:* Writers Guild of America-East.

WRITINGS: The Windmill Summer (juvenile), Harper, 1972; *The Ghost Garden* (juvenile), Atheneum, 1976.

Translator: Shel Silverstein, *The Giving Tree (l'Arbre au Grand Coeur),* Harper, 1973. Also author and co-narrator for "New Guinea: Patrol into the Unknown," a special program for National Broadcasting Co. (NBC).

HILA FEIL

SIDELIGHTS: In 1969, Hila Feil accompanied her husband to New Guinea to film traditional ceremonies and cultures of the inhabitants, and on an expedition to establish contact with a group of people who had never seen anyone from the outside.

FIJAN, Carol 1918-

PERSONAL: Born February 18, 1918, in Milwaukee, Wis.; daughter of Philip Paul (a furrier) and Julia (Hauler) Fijan; married Herman Starobin (an economist and professor), September 12, 1956; children: Christina Fijan. *Education:* Hunter College (now of the City University of New York), B.A., 1939. *Politics:* None. *Religion:* None. *Home:* 58 Rose Ave., Great Neck, N.Y. 11021.

CAREER: Puppet Associates, New York, N.Y., director, 1949-70; National Theatre of Puppet Arts, New York, N.Y., director, 1971—. Teacher of puppetry for Columbia Broadcasting System and Public Broadcasting Service, 1969, and National Educational Television, 1973; has performed as a television puppeteer, 1972-74. *Member:* Union Internationale de la Marionnette, Puppeteers of America (member of board, 1968-70), Actors Equity Association, Ontario Puppetry Association (honorary member), Puppet Guild of Long Island, Great Neck Arts Council. *Awards, honors:* National citation from Puppeteers of America, 1974 and 1976, for contributions to the art of puppetry.

WRITINGS: Making Puppets Come Alive, Taplinger, 1974. Contributor to *Journal of Puppeteers of America* and other puppetry journals throughout the world.

WORK IN PROGRESS: Research on acting with puppets, the change in technique throughout the ages; a book of playlets, skits, and sketches on puppet plays relating to the Bicentennial for grade school level; a book on puppetry as an educator's tool.

FOSTER, Elizabeth Vincent 1902-

PERSONAL: Born June 18, 1902, in Wilkes-Barre, Pa.; daughter of George E. (an educator) and Louise (Palmer) Vincent; married Maxwell E. Foster (a retired lawyer) June 9, 1926; children: Maxwell E., Jr., Vincent. *Education:* Bryn Mawr College, A.B., 1923. *Politics:* Independent.

CAREER: Director of the Massachusetts Audubon Society, 1936-66.

WRITINGS: Lyrico, Gambit, 1970.

SIDELIGHTS: "The first story I remember beginning to write was just after I learned my letters, sitting on the floor beside my grandmother's bed and asking her how each word was spelled. Story telling and reading aloud were an important part of life in those far-off pre-television days. In subsequent decades I started many other stories, but it wasn't until I was over sixty that I finally was able to stay in the house long enough to finish one. I doubt if I will ever do another.

"*Lyrico* embodies most of the interests and enthusiasms of a happy childhood—horses, of course (I was born loving horses), camping in the West (I was taken on the first of many pack trips at six years old), mountain climbing (my mother was a mountaineer), birds, wildflowers, wild animals, every aspect of nature in every season.

"Later, becoming aware of growing threats to America's natural beauty and wild places, I joined the Massachusetts Audubon Society's pioneering work in conservation educa-

ELIZABETH VINCENT FOSTER

... an old prospector, who used to go off for months and years to live with the Indians, or maybe alone, with only animals for friends, got lost in a snow storm. ■ (From *Lyrico* by Elizabeth Vincent Foster. Illustrations by Joy Buba.)

tion in the public schools. As a result *Lyrico* includes a certain amount of propaganda for leaving natural areas undeveloped and unspoiled—but not so insistent and didactic as to interfere with the story. For the story was my main concern—I wanted it to be an entertaining one which children would read and enjoy, and which parents who read it aloud to their younger children could enjoy too.''

FOX, Charles Philip 1913-

PERSONAL: Born May 27, 1913, in Milwaukee, Wis.; son of George William and Mary (Romadka) Fox; married Sophie Zore, 1942; children: Barbara, Peter. *Home:* 132 Grant Rd., Winter Haven, Fla. 33880.

CAREER: Circus World Museum, Baraboo, Wis., museum director, 1960-72; Ringling Brothers and Barnum & Bailey Circus, director of circus research and circus historian, 1972—. Writer of circus histories and children's photo books.

WRITINGS: Circus Trains, Kalmbach, 1948; *Circus Parades,* Century House, 1953; *A Ticket to the Circus,* Superior Publishing Co., 1959; *Frisky, Try Again,* Reilly & Lee, 1959; *Pictorial History of Performing Horses,* Superior Publishing Co., 1960; *A Fox in the House,* Reilly & Lee, 1960; *Come to the Circus,* Reilly & Lee, 1961; *Mr. Stripes, the Gopher,* Reilly & Lee, 1962; *When Winter Comes,* Reilly & Lee, 1962; *Mr. Duck's Big Day,* Reilly & Lee, 1963; *Birds Will Come to You,* Reilly & Lee, 1963; *Snowball, the Trick Pony,* Reilly & Lee, 1964; *When Spring Comes,* Reilly & Lee, 1964; *When Summer Comes,* Reilly & Lee, 1966; *When Autumn Comes,* Reilly & Lee, 1966; *Opie Possum's Trick,* Reilly & Lee, 1968; (with Tom Parkinson) *The Circus in America,* Country Beautiful, 1972. Contributor of photostories to national magazines.

WORK IN PROGRESS: Circus—World's Greatest Show and *The Circus Moves.*

SIDELIGHTS: "Having been born with an inherent interest in animals, I naturally found myself at the show-

Barbara and Peter met the clowns. ■ (From *Come to the Circus* by Charles Phillip Fox. Photographs by the author.)

grounds when the circus arrived in town. This interest became more intense after I acquired a camera and began to photograph the animals—especially the beautiful draft horses which I enjoyed more than any other animal.

"All of this activity exposed me to the fascinating aspects of the circus—circus trains, circus tents, putting up the circus, the menagerie etc.

"As I accumulated more and more photos I realized I could share them with others if I compiled them into book form.

"It was all this studying the circus, photographing the circus, reading books about the circus and writing books about the circus that resulted in my present position of circus historian for the 'Greatest Show On Earth—Ringling Brothers and Barnum & Bailey Circus.'"

Something about the Author

CHARLES PHILIP FOX

GARDEN, Nancy   1938-

PERSONAL: Born May 15, 1938, in Boston, Mass. *Education:* Columbia University, B.F.A., 1961, M.A., 1962. *Residence:* Carlisle, Massachusetts. *Agent:* Dorothy Markinko, McIntosh & Otis, Inc., 475 Fifth Ave., New York, N.Y. 10017.

CAREER: "Knocked around theater a good deal in the past, as an actress, lighting designer, and jack-of-all trades; have taught, in one way or another, all levels, including adult; have worked as a writer and editor for a national magazine, as an editor for major publishers, and have done free-lance editorial work for various publishers."

WRITINGS—For young people: *What Happened in Marston,* Four Winds, 1971; *Berlin: City Split in Two,* Putnam, 1971; *The Loners,* Viking, 1972, Avon, 1974; *Vampires,* Lippincott, 1973; *Werewolves,* Lippincott, 1973; *Witches,* Lippincott, 1975; *Devils and Demons,* Lippincott, 1976. Former book reviewer for magazines, including *American Observer.*

WORK IN PROGRESS: A young adult novel; an adult novel; several shorter books for children.

SIDELIGHTS: "I started writing when I was eight—poems, mostly, although I remember one story vividly. It was called 'The Hill That Turned Into a Valley.' I got the idea while playing with a salt cellar at dinner one night. First I piled the salt up at one end of the container, making a 'hill' there and leaving a 'valley' at the other end. Then I took salt from the hill and put it in the valley—presto! Another hill! That made me think up a story about some people who lived on a hill and thought they were better than their neighbors in the valley because they were higher. One night it snowed—and snowed—and snowed—until the valley was higher than the hill, and the hill dwellers could no longer be snobs. (I guess the storm was *only* in the valley, and that the original valley dwellers must somehow have managed to scramble up above the snow as it piled up.)

"When I was twelve or so I wrote a long adventure story for school, which prompted my English teacher to suggest that I might become a writer someday. I felt very flattered, but by then there were lots of other things I thought I might be—a veterinarian, for one. Nevertheless, I went on writing. One of the pieces I worked on hardest was a 'book' called 'Dogs I Have Known,' a collection of biographies of every dog I'd ever met. That was no small number, because I was always seeking dogs out. A lot of the characters in 'Dogs I Have Known' I met during World War Two's housing shortage when my parents and I had to live in a couple of rooms in

A factory for elf arrows. ■ (From *Witches* by Nancy Garden.)

someone else's house and my dog, Muggins, had to be boarded. I missed him so much I made friends with all the dogs in the neighborhood.

"When I got to high school, I became very interested in theater, first in acting, then in lighting design and directing. I went on writing and had a couple of things published in the school literary magazine, but I was pretty sure I wanted to go into theater. Part of the reason for this decision was that I felt I could always go on writing anyway no matter what else I did—and that's just the way things turned out.

"One reason, I think, why books and writing were always so important to me is that they were important to my family. My parents always read aloud to me and, when I was older, we sometimes all read aloud to each other. My father wrote a wonderful story for me when I was very little, called 'Josephine the Ostrich,' so writing seemed like a natural thing to do. Then, too, I was an only child, and my family moved a lot so I was always having to leave old friends and make new ones. That wasn't always easy, because I was shy, and I think I often took refuge in books, in writing, and in telling long stories to myself and sometimes acting them out.

"People often ask writers where they get their ideas. I get mine from many different places, and I'm sure other writers do also. I wrote my first published book, *Berlin: City Split in Two*, at least partly because my mother's side of the family was German (although not from Berlin). *What Happened in*

Marston, my second book, was prompted partly by the racial tension of the 1960's; the idea for *The Loners,* my second novel, came out of interviews I did for *Junior Scholastic* magazine with teenagers who had trouble with drugs. My four occult books for Lippincott's 'Weird and Horrible Library' began more or less by accident. The originator of the series, Barbara Seuling, is a friend of mine, and when she told me about it, I jokingly suggested she do a book on vampires (in which I'd become interested at a summer theater some years earlier) and werewolves. One thing led to another and I ended up doing four books for the series.

"I do sometimes get ideas from newspaper stories, and I keep a file of clippings and notes about subjects that I think I might want to write about someday. But sometimes, too—perhaps more often—my ideas, especially for fiction, come from people, from places, and from feelings. Often something or someone in my own experience will make me think of an idea for a book, but usually by the time the book is written, there's very little left in it of the original experience or character.

"If anybody who reads this is young and wants to write, I'd like to say to him or her that one of the best ways to learn about writing is to write. Reading, of course, is important too—vital. But if you want to be a writer, don't just think about it as some future thing that will happen when you have time for it. A lot of adults have said to me, 'Oh, I'd love to write, but I just don't have the time.' If you want to be a

NANCY GARDEN

writer, you have to *make* the time, no matter what else you want to do or have to do. You have to sit down at that desk (or table or packing case) regularly and write, even if when your writing time comes you'd rather play ball or walk the dog or go to the movies. That's hard sometimes, but so is writing itself. The wonderful part is that there's nothing more rewarding, at least to me, when the day's work goes well!''

Nancy Garden is a refugee from New York City, living ''happily in the country surrounded, after fifteen years of concrete, with dogs and cats and trees and fresh air.''

HOBBIES AND OTHER INTERESTS: Gardening, weaving, walking, cross-country skiing, the Carlisle *Mosquito* ("a local newspaper whose board I'm on, for which I was once consulting editor, and to which I occasionally contribute").

GILBREATH, Alice 1921-

PERSONAL: Born April 8, 1921, in Montpelier, Idaho; daughter of Alfred and Nanna (Nielsen) Thompson; married Rex E. Gilbreath (an employee of Phillips Petroleum Co.), March 17, 1945; children: Rex E., Jr., Sue. *Education:* Studied at College of Idaho, 1938-40, University of Tulsa, 1949, and Trinity University, 1951. *Religion:* Protestant. *Home:* 1100 Grandview, Bartlesville, Okla. 74003.

WRITINGS: Beginning-to-Read Riddles and Jokes, Follett, 1967; *Beginning Crafts for Beginning Readers,* Follett, 1972; *God Is with Me,* Gibson, 1972; *Spouts, Lids, and Cans,* Morrow, 1973; *Fun and Easy Things to Make,* Scholastic, 1974; *Making Costumes for Parties, Plays, and Holidays,* Morrow, 1974; *Candles for Beginners to Make,* Morrow, 1975; *Fun with Weaving,* Morrow, 1976; *More Beginning Crafts for Beginning Readers,* Follett, 1976; *I Like to Talk with God,* Standard, 1976. Contributor of stories, plays, and craft articles to children's magazines.

SIDELIGHTS: "I grew up in a small town in Idaho where my dad, like almost everyone else, worked for the Union Pacific Railroad. Our lives centered around our church, school, the railroad, and home.

"'Home' included parents, a brother and sister, horses, cows, chickens, pigs, dogs, cats, and sometimes more unusual pets such as geese, badgers, and an ornery goat—my favorite pet. Our home had lots of laughter, and I still consider happy laughter as one of the most beautiful sounds in the world. Perhaps this is why my first book was *Beginning-to-Read Riddles and Jokes*.

"As a child during the depression, if I wanted something, I made it out of whatever was available around home. It never occurred to me to buy it. So the craft books I write come quite naturally. I'm a 'packrat,' can't bear to throw anything away that can be used, so there is always something available for making any craft.

"My husband and children have 'gone the second mile' in their encouragement, inspiration, and research. Once, when I was writing about volcanoes, our daughter searched out and recorded for me the sounds of an actual volcano, so I could get it 'right.'"

HOBBIES AND OTHER INTERESTS: Traveling, sewing, gardening.

ALICE THOMPSON GILBREATH

What number is not hungry?
  8(ATE)
■ (From *Beginning to Read Riddles and Jokes* by Alice Thompson Gilbreath. Illustrations by Susan Perl.)

GLADSTONE, Gary 1935-

PERSONAL: Born July 8, 1935, in Philadelphia, Pa.; son of Milton Stanley (an advertising man) and Bernice (Bayuk) Gladstone; married Meredith Townsend (a fashion designer), July 7, 1967; children: Gregory Townsend. *Education:* Attended Art Students' League of New York, 1953-55. *Agent:* McIntosh & Otis, 475 Fifth Ave., New York, N.Y. 10017. *Office:* The Gladstone Studio Ltd., 237 East 20th St., New York, N.Y. 10003.

CAREER: Westchester News, White Plains, N.Y., photographer and columnist, 1955-56; *New York Daily News,* New York, N.Y., photographer, 1957-58; Norton O'Neil Co., Inc. (industrial theater), New York, N.Y., producer, 1963-68. *Member:* American Society of Magazine Photographers. *Awards, honors: New York Daily News* annual free-lance award, 1956; *Popular Photography* yearbook design and photography award, 1960, 1961; Printing Industries of America yearbook design and photography award, 1964, 1965, 1966; Art Directors Club of New York, merit award, 1975; *Art Direction* magazine, certificate of distinction, 1976.

Probably the last place you will find dune buggies is on the dunes. ■ (From *Dune Buggies* by Gary Gladstone. Illustrated by the author.)

GARY GLADSTONE

WRITINGS—Self-illustrated juveniles: *Hey, Hey, Can't Catch Me,* Van Nostrand, 1970; *Needle Point Alphabet Book,* Morrow, 1972; *Dune-Buggies,* Lippincott, 1973. Member of editorial board, *Infinity* (American Society of Magazine Photographers publication), 1961-62.

WORK IN PROGRESS: Children's Cities, a photographic essay, completion expected in 1978.

GOETTEL, Elinor 1930-

PERSONAL: Surname is pronounced Go-*tell;* born August 14, 1930, in Bangkok, Siam; daughter of Otto (assistant post-master general under President Woodrow Wilson and known as the "father of airmail") and Carrie Will (Coffman) Praeger; married Gerard Goettel (U.S. district judge), June 4, 1951; children: Sheryl, Glenn, James. *Education:* Duke University, A.B., 1951. *Home:* 6 Chamberlain St., Rye, N.Y. 10580.

MEMBER: Phi Beta Kappa.

WRITINGS: Eagle of the Philippines: President Manuel Quezon (juvenile), Messner, 1970; *America's Wars—Why?,* Messner, 1972. Wrote filmstrips for Educational Audio Visual Co., "The U.S. as World Leader" (8 parts, 1968), "From Johnson to Ford" (3 parts, 1975), "The Civil War: Two Views" (4 parts, 1977). Contributor to *Merit Student Encyclopedia, Columbia Encyclopedia, Columbia Viking Desk Encyclopedia,* and *Reader's Digest Almanac.*

ELINOR GOETTEL

LOUIS HABER

SIDELIGHTS: "I love to work with primary sources and visit historical places. The Civil War and World War II are my primary areas of interest. Have toured and re-toured most of the Civil War Battlefields. My chief interest is in making history as exciting for my readers as it is for me."

HABER, Louis   1910-

PERSONAL: Born January 12, 1910, in New York, N.Y.; son of Jacob (in real estate) and Lena (Turim) Haber; married Blanche Steinberg, December 27, 1937; children: Richard Jay. *Education:* City College, New York, N.Y., B.S., 1932, M.S., 1939; New York University, Ed.D., 1960. *Home:* 3000 Bronx Park E., New York, N.Y. 10467.

CAREER: Woodlands High School, Hartsdale, N.Y., chairman of science department, 1960-73. Pace College-Westchester, adjunct professor of sciences, 1965-74; College of White Plains, N.Y., director of teacher education, 1973-75. *Military service:* U.S. Army, 1943-46; became captain. *Member:* National Science Teachers Association, National Education Association, New York State Sciences Supervisors Association. *Awards, honors:* U.S. Office of Education research grant, 1966.

WRITINGS: (Editor) *Discovery Problems in Biology,* College Entrance Publications, 1958; (with Lawrence Samuels) *How to Study Science,* College Entrance Publications, 1959; *Black Pioneers of Science and Invention* (juvenile), Harcourt, 1970. Contributor to science education journals.

WORK IN PROGRESS: Writing in the field of the history of science.

HAIG-BROWN, Roderick (Langmere) 1908-1976

PERSONAL: Born February 21, 1908, in Lancing, Sussex, England; son of Alan Roderick, (an Army officer), and Violet M. (Pope) Haig-Brown; married Ann Elmore (a high school librarian), January 20, 1934; children: Valerie Joan, Mary Charlotte (Mrs. F. O. Bowker), Alan Roderick, Evelyn Celia (Mrs. Ted Vayro). *Education:* Attended Charterhouse School, Godalming, England. *Home:* R.R. 2, Campbell River, British Columbia, Canada. *Agent:* Harold Ober Associates, 40 East 49th St., New York, N.Y. 10017.

CAREER: Logging, fishing, and trapping, Washington State and British Columbia, Canada, 1926-30, 1931-34; writer in London, England, 1930-31; full-time writer, 1934-76. Provincial magistrate and judge of Children's and Family Court, 1940-76. Commissioner, Federal Electoral Boundary Commission, 1965-66 and 1975; member of International Pacific Salmon Fisheries Commission, 1970-76; member of Fisheries Development Council. Director of conservation societies. Consultant for National Film Board, Canadian Broadcasting Corp., Vancouver Public Aquarium. *Military service:* Canadian Army, 1939-45; served overseas; became major; assigned to Royal Canadian Mounted Police, 1944.

MEMBER: Authors Guild, Canadian Authors Association, Society of Authors, Playwrights and Composers (British). *Awards, honors:* LL.D., University of British Columbia, 1952; Canadian Library Association Medal, 1947, for *Starbuck Valley Winter;* Governor General's Award, 1948, for *Saltwater Summer;* Crandall Conservation Trophy, 1955; University of Alberta National Award in Letters, 1956; Canadian Library Association Medal, 1963, for *The Whale People;* Barien Library Award, 1964, for *Fisherman's Fall;* Vicky Metcalf Award for juvenile writing, 1965; Conservation Award, Trout Unlimited, 1965.

WRITINGS: Silver, A. & C. Black, 1931; *Pool and Rapid,* J. Cape, 1932; *Ki-Yu,* Houghton, 1934; *The Western Angler,* Derrydale, 1939; *Return to the River,* Morrow, 1941; *Timber,* Morrow, 1942; *Starbuck Valley Winter,* Morrow, 1943; *A River Never Sleeps* (autobiographical), Morrow, 1946; *Saltwater Summer,* Morrow, 1948; *On the Highest Hill,* Morrow, 1949.

Measure of the Year, Morrow, 1950; *Fisherman's Spring,* Morrow, 1951; *Mounted Police Patrol,* Morrow, 1954; *Fisherman's Winter,* Morrow, 1954; *Captain of the Discovery,* Macmillan (Canada), 1956; *Fisherman's Summer,* Morrow, 1959; *The Farthest Shores,* Longmans, Green (Canada), 1960; *The Living Land,* Macmillan (Canada), 1961; *Fur and Gold,* Longmans, Green (Canada), 1962; *The Whale People,* Morrow, 1963; *A Primer of Flyfishing,* Morrow, 1964; *Fisherman's Fall,* Morrow, 1964; *Panther,* Collins, 1967.

Contributor: *The Face of Canada,* Clarke, Irwin, 1959; *The Pacific Northwest,* Doubleday, 1963. Contributor to *Atlantic Monthly, New Yorker, Sports Illustrated, Life,* other publications.

WORK IN PROGRESS: View from a Low Bench.

RODERICK HAIG-BROWN

FOR MORE INFORMATION SEE: British Columbia Library Quarterly, July, 1958; *Canadian Children's Literature,* Summer, 1975.

(Died October 9, 1976)

HALLWARD, Michael 1889-

PERSONAL: Born October 2, 1889, in London, England; son of Reginald Francis (an artist) and Adelaide (an artist; maiden name, Bloxam) Hallward; married Jean McDougal, 1910; married second wife, Penelope Alice Bradley, October 18, 1934; children: (first marriage) Joy Hallward Mitchum, Gloria Hallward Ray (stage name Gloria Graham); (second marriage) Penelope (Mrs. Richard Gase), Peter Michael. *Education:* Attended Royal Institute of British Architects. *Home:* 14446 Valverde Ct., San Diego, Calif. 92129.

CAREER: Haslemere Craft Group, Surrey, England, owner, 1907-1910; Michael Hallward, Inc., Boston, Mass., president, 1940-54. Executive director of New Bedford Industrial Development Commission, 1954-59; founding trustee and director of American Design Institute. *Military service:* Canadian Army, 1912-16.

WRITINGS: The Enormous Leap of Alphonse Frog (juvenile), Nash Publishing, 1972. Also author of short stories. Contributor to magazines.

WORK IN PROGRESS: A Nation of Usurers; The Economics of Corruption; The Small Elf Persons, a sequel to *The Enormous Leap of Alphonse Frog;* an autobiography; revising "The Directors Meet," a play; "Before the Fall," a play.

The deer was suddenly uneasy. All five heads were raised. ■ (From *Panther* by Roderick L. Haig-Brown. Illustrated by Ben F. Stahl.)

SIDELIGHTS: "My parents' home at Brush Green was dedicated to the aesthetic and nothing catered it, guests, furniture and decor that did not meet my parents exacting stan-

The Boss Frog leaned forward. "You'll take," he told his bodyguard, "your regular allowance--no more, no less. Ten flies, ten gnats and twenty midges. That's what you got coming and that's what you gets."
■ (From *The Enormous Leap of Alphonse Frog* by Michael Hallward. Illustrated by Sharleen Pederson.)

dards of perfection. Only artists, authors and others of the same ilk were admitted. As a result, my earliest recollections were of men like Shaw, Oscar Wilde, Archer, etc., who belonged to the group which made famous the Sunday afternoon gatherings at the home of William Morris. While still very young, my father took me to the homes and studios of artists and other intellectuals such as G. F. Watts, Chesterton, Dressler (sculptor and author of *The Curse of Machinery*). The turn of the century was a time when art was spelt with a capital 'A' and of great men whose names were mentioned with awe. I was well into my teens before I met my first so called business man. I have been married twice.

"My education was unique, included little formal schooling and consisted of a series of governesses, tutors, etc. As a result, at twelve years old I had read, at my parents insistence, such books as *The Rise and Fall of the Roman Empire,* much of Emerson and vast amounts of poetry, but was incapable of solving the simplest problems in arithmetic. I should, perhaps, add that at the age of four I spent a few days at the first of the Montessori schools.

"I have written since I was very small, short stories, plays and much poetry, all of the latter destroyed in the interest of posterity. Made no effort to publish until after my retirement

in 1976. I write mostly for children for two reasons. The first I like children and don't much care for adults. The second, it permits me to attack the soft, underbellies of their parents' thought by indirection. I also write on subjects of social significance that arouse my indignation."

HAMILTON, Dorothy   1906-

PERSONAL: Born September 25, 1906, in Monroe Twp., Delaware County, Ind.; daughter of Garry C. (a farmer) and Mary (Bartle) Drumm; married Harry D. Hamilton (a farmer), September 29, 1927; children: Dale, Kathryn (Mrs. Malcolm Julian), Carolyn (Mrs. Bill Necessary), Lois (Mrs. Leonard Benson), Stephen, Frances (Mrs. John Parkison), David. *Education:* Attended Ball State University, 1924-26, and correspondence courses at Indiana University, 1961, 1965, writing courses at Writer's Digest Schools. *Home address:* R.R. 1, Box 351, Selma, Ind. 47383.

CAREER: Liberty-Perry School Corp., Selma, Ind., private tutor, 1964—. Teacher of writing classes for YWCA in Muncie and community education program of Muncie Community Schools; member of planning committee, teacher, and co-director of Midwest Writers' Workshop, Ball State University. *Member:* Women in Communications (Eastern Indiana Chapter), Delta Kappa Gamma.

DOROTHY HAMILTON

Something about the Author

The wind carried kite gave little tugs on the string which was wrapped around Jody's hand. ■ (From *The Blue Caboose* by Dorothy Hamilton. Illustrated by Jerry Needler.)

WRITINGS—Young people's books; published by Herald Press: *Anita's Choice*, 1971, *Charco*, 1971, *Christmas for Holly*, 1971, *Jim Musco*, 1972, *Tony Savala*, 1972, *The Blue Caboose*, 1973, *Kerry*, 1973, *Mindy*, 1973, *Jason*, 1974, *Gift of a Home*, 1974, *Busboys at Big Bend*, 1974, *Cricket*, 1975, *Neva's Patchwork Pillow*, 1975, *Linda's Raintree*, 1975, *Winter Girl*, 1976, *Straight Mark*, 1976, *Rosalie*, 1977.

Adult; published by Herald Press: *The Killdeer*, 1972, *Settled Furrows*, 1972, *The Quail*, 1973, *The Eagle*, 1974.

WORK IN PROGRESS: Mary Jane: A Bound Girl; Daniel Forbes: Frontier Boy; Maris Mountain; Rosalie at Eleven; Bittersweet Days.

SIDELIGHTS: "The words of the poem, *The Chambered Nautilus,* have often been in my thoughts. And now it seems that my life experience resembles the design of the spiral-shelled mollusk. Each stage opens to a wider sphere.

"I've used the positive experiences of my childhood as a guide in being mother to my children. These seven individuals gave me insights needed in tutoring 350 people, and the knowledge gained from these experiences contributes to the store of material used in the books written after my children were grown.

"The compassion I feel for young people has led to appearances in more than 200 schools in Indiana, Pennsylvania, Tennessee, and in London and Kitchener in Canada.

"Every group hears my reasons for the visits; that I want to help them see that what they're learning will help them do something as what I learned helps me write books. This idea is also presented, 'books are doors that open to new ideas,

new places, new people.' I'm a little emphatic when I make this statement, 'I tell my writing classes that people who write books about young people should like them, care what happens to them, go where they are, and above all, they should *listen* to them.'

"The fourth reason for the visits (for which I do not take money) is that I've learned so much from my children, my grandchildren, the people I've tutored, and the Chicano children with which I work every summer, that my visits are a way of saying 'thank you.'

"The young people are told to think of questions they wish to ask while I show them a kit containing handwritten manuscripts, typed pages, royalty agreements, galley proofs, original drawing of a front cover, completed cover, signature (sixteen pages on a large sheet) dummy copy and completed book.

"The response is lively, the questions are searching and the communication is clear. I could fill a book with testimonies that a caring, honest, person bridges any generation gap. One answer may summarize the total rapport. A sixth grade girl asked, 'Why do you write more books for us than for grown-ups?'

"'Could you guess?'

"She smiled before saying, 'Because you like us?'

"'Because I like you.'

"These visits reinforce me in my resolve to offer positive thinking to young people. The trend toward realism is erasing two important qualities, inspiration and imagination, qualities which make the realities more bearable. I hear such sentences as, 'Your books make me feel good inside,' and 'I'm glad you don't use dirty words'; and 'I feel like I'm learning good things I might never know any other way.'"

Dorothy Hamilton published her first book at the age of 65. "In a television interview I was asked, 'How do you account for the late blooming of your writing career?' My answer was 'Prayer, persistence and the resolve to work to attain a professional attitude.' My urge to write was inborn. My material is people and a kind of total immersion in my setting. My goal is to make each book better than the one before."

HANO, Arnold 1922-

PERSONAL: Surname is pronounced *Hay*-no; born March 2, 1922, in New York, N.Y.; son of Alfred Barnard (a salesman) and Clara (Millhauser) Hano; married second wife, Bonnie Abraham, June 30, 1951; children: (first marriage) Stephen, Susan; (second marriage) Laurel. *Education:* Long Island University, A.B., 1941. *Politics:* Democrat. *Religion:* Jewish. *Home:* 1565 Bluebird Canyon Dr., Laguna Beach, Calif. 92651.

CAREER: New York Daily News, New York, N.Y., copy boy and junior reporter, 1941-42; New York State Department of Labor, New York, N.Y., editor of news bulletin, 1946-47; Robert Louis Stevenson School, New York, N.Y., teacher, 1947-48; Bantam Books, New York, N.Y., editor, 1948-50; Magazine Management Co., New York, N.Y., editor, 1950-54; free-lance writer, 1954—; University of California, Irvine, instructor in writing, 1966—. Founder, Laguna Beach Interracial Citizens Committee, 1963-64; member of local executive board, National Association for the Advancement of Colored People, 1962; member, Laguna Beach Greenbelt Committee, 1969, Laguna Beach Chamber of Commerce, 1970-72, Laguna Beach Board of Adjustment and Design Review, 1971-73. *Military service:* U.S. Army, 1942-46; became second lieutenant; awarded combat ribbons for Pacific Theater, Bronze Arrowhead for Kwajalein. *Member:* Society of Magazine Writers. *Awards, honors:* Sidney Hillman Foundation Prize Award, 1963, for an article on California farm labor; selected magazine sportswriter of the year, National Sportscasters and Sportswriters Association, 1963; Boys' Clubs of America junior book award, 1967.

WRITINGS: (Editor) *Western Roundup,* Bantam, 1948; *The Big Out* (novel), A. S. Barnes, 1951; *A Day in the Bleachers,* Crowell, 1955; *Willie Mays: The Say-Hey Kid,* Bartholomew House, 1961, reissued as *Willie Mays,* Grosset, 1966; *The Executive* (novel), New American Library, 1964; *Sandy Koufax, Strikeout King,* Putnam, 1964, revised edition, 1967; *Marriage, Italian Style,* Popular Library, 1965; *Bandolero,* Popular Library, 1968; *Greatest Giants of Them All,* Putnam, 1968; *Roberto Clemente, Batting King,* Putnam, 1968; (with William Gargan) *Why Me?,* Doubleday, 1969; *Running Wild,* Popular Library, 1973; *Kareem,* Putnam, 1975; *Muhammed Ali: The Champion,* Putnam, 1977. Represented in *Best Sports Stories of the Year, 1963, 1965, 1967,* edited by Irving T. Marsh and Edward Ehre, Dutton, 1963, 1965, 1967, and in other anthologies. Book reviewer, *New York Times;* contributor of short stories and articles to magazines.

SIDELIGHTS: "When I write a book about an athlete, what I am trying to do is *explain* that person to the reader. Who is he? How did he get to be a great pitcher or a famous boxer or whatever? What makes him tick, as a human being? I am not so interested in his exploits. You can read about them in your daily newspaper. But who is he, really? That is what I am after. Sometimes I seem to be successful; sometimes not so. And in the process of discovering another human being, I find I am also discovering myself. The more you dig into another person's drives, manner, needs, and appetites, the more you find yourself making comparisons with your own drives and appetites and needs. So this sort of writing has been, for me, an exploration into myself. I suppose all writing is such an exploration; this time, however, it seems more conscious, more obvious."

HARDWICK, Richard (Holmes, Jr.) 1923-
(Rick Holmes)

PERSONAL: Born June 28, 1923, in Atlanta, Ga.; son of Richard Holmes (an insurance executive) and Caroline (Shivers) Hardwick; married Margaret Wilkins (now a secretary), March 14, 1951; children: Amy, Caroline, Lynn. *Education:* Emory University, student, 1940-42; University of Georgia, student, 1942-43, B.S., 1947. *Politics:* Independent. *Religion:* Episcopalian. *Home:* 374 East Paces Ferry Rd. N.E., Apt. 707, Atlanta, Ga. 30305. *Agent:* Scott Meredith Literary Agency, Inc., 580 Fifth Ave., New York, N.Y. 10036.

CAREER: Owner of forty-foot ketch, sailing and chartering in the Caribbean, 1946-48; Peachtree Trust Co., Atlanta, Ga., assistant cashier, 1948-50; Lockheed Aircraft, Marietta, Ga., industrial engineer, 1950-51; Cutter's Inc. (boats), Atlanta, Ga., vice-president, 1951-55; Surfside Motel, Saint Simon Island, Ga., co-owner, 1955-60; free-lance writer, 1960—. *Military service:* U.S. Army, 1942-46; Japanese-English interpreter; also trained as pilot in Air Corps Reserve. *Member:* Mystery Writers of America, Authors Guild.

WRITINGS: Skin and Scuba Diving, Monarch Books, 1963; *The Plotters,* Doubleday, 1965; *The Season to be Deadly,* Doubleday, 1966; *Flipper and the Mystery of the Black Schooner* (juvenile), Whitman Publishing Co., 1967; *Charles Richard Drew: Pioneer in Blood,* Scribner, 1967. Contributor to *Alfred Hitchcock Mystery Magazine, Yachting, Man's Magazine, Toronto Star Weekly, Manhunt, Saint Mystery Magazine, Mister, Sir, Man to Man, True Men,* other magazines.

Paperback novels under name Rick Holmes: *Tropic of Cleo,* 1962, *New Widow, Love Under Capricorn,* 1963, *Man Crazy, Child Woman, Riverfront Girl,* 1965 (all published by Monarch Books).

WORK IN PROGRESS: A mystery novel; several nonfiction books; short stories and magazine articles.

HOBBIES AND OTHER INTERESTS: Sailing, golf, fishing, bridge.

HARNAN, Terry 1920-
(Eric Traviss Hull)

PERSONAL: Born February 1, 1920, in New York, N.Y.; daughter of Thomas (a jeweler) and Edna Irene (Ahrens) Harnan. *Education:* Montclair State College, B.A. (cum laude), 1941; further study at New York University, 1942-43, and at Urbino, Italy, in study program of State University of New York, 1976. *Politics:* Independent. *Home:* Horton's Point, Southold, N.Y. 11971. *Agent:* McIntosh & Otis, Inc., 475 Fifth Ave., New York, N.Y.

CAREER: Look magazine, New York, N.Y., assistant editor, 1943-46; *Life* magazine, New York, N.Y., editorial staff, 1949-65. Instructor in creative writing, Dowling College, Oakdale, N.Y., 1976. *Member:* League of Women Voters, Environmental Defense Fund, Sierra Club, Nature Conservancy, North Fork Audubon Society.

WRITINGS—Adult: (Under pseudonym Eric Traviss Hull) *Murder Lays a Golden Egg,* Doubleday, 1944; *Signal for Danger,* Doubleday, 1946; (contributor) *The Coming Victory over Polio,* Simon and Schuster, 1954; (contributor) *The World We Live In,* revised edition, Time, Inc., 1955.

Juvenile: *Gordon Parks: Black Photographer and Film Maker,* Garrard, 1972; *African Rhythm, American Dance* (biography), Knopf, 1974. Contributor of articles to *Travel and Camera,* and *Suffolk Times.*

SIDELIGHTS: "I came late to writing books for children since my early writing experience was in journalism on *Look* and then *Life* magazines. Yet, I was unconsciously heading that way since I specialized in those 'back of the book' series of articles so appealing to young people that thousands of reprints were requested for use in American high school and college classrooms.

"Parental influence aroused very early the love of books and the desire to be a writer. My father brought from Ireland tales of Irish myths and legends which he told as bedtime stories. I still remember how thick and slow the snowflakes fell the day my mother trudged with me through city streets to the children's reading room of the local library. It was in the tower of an old building, an enchanting place that seemed part of the castles in the fairy tales the librarian read to us. From then on I was hooked.

"But only in recent years have I had the time and opportunity to try writing for children. I was moved by two immediate stimuli. One was the injustice of the way blacks had been treated, and the other was the desire to show blacks how their handicaps could be, and had been, overcome by members of their own race. The black photographer, Gordon Parks, had been an associate of mine with whom I'd worked on many assignments at *Life* and I felt that the story of his life would be an inspiration. It was written for nine-to-twelve-year-old children.

The accomplishments and struggles of the gifted black dancer, Katherine Dunham, became the next book, written

TERRY HARNAN

Sweating and trembling with a sense of the evil he was about to do, Gordon slowly rose from his seat.
■ (From *Gordon Parks, Black Photographer and Film Maker* by Terry Harnan. Illustrated by Russell Hoover.)

for the young adult group who might be interested in dancing as a career. Letters received from boys and girls who read these books show that the aim in writing them is apparently being achieved. Both books were selected for the recommended lists published by the New York Public Library in 1974 and 1975. I spoke over 'Teen Age Book Talk' on Station WNYC in 1975.

"Now, a new generation of black writers is developing who, understandably, want to write about their own people and themselves. So I doubt that I shall go along that line again.

"At present, I am working on a biography of a Renaissance woman and again I have a double purpose: to show how women lived in other ages, and to prove that history is not the dull chronicle of events many present-day students seem to think. I feel freer to tell stories from my own childhood experiences. And I keep being impelled to weave a tale, in form like the legends of my father's Ireland, about the seven ages of man.''

HOBBIES AND OTHER INTERESTS: Sailing, travelling, gardening, painting.

There was a sudden lovely thought in the boy's mind: perhaps these were the tongues of flame that the teachers had so often spoken of. The sign of the spirit of the one holy God. Yet even as he watched, the flickering flames grew ugly, spreading and belching smoke. And then he saw fire in the schoolhouse, too, and he knew that Salem was burning. ■ (From *The Valley of the Shadow* by Janet Hickman. Jacket design by Richard Cuffari.)

Something about the Author

HICKMAN, Janet 1940-

PERSONAL: Born July 8, 1940, in Kilbourne, Ohio; daughter of Bernard Franklin (a plumber) and Pauline (Williams) Gephart; married John D. Hickman (a teacher), January 14, 1961; children: John H., Holly. Education: Ohio State University, B.Sc., 1960, M.A.Ed., 1964. Religion: Presbyterian. Home: 356 Gudrun Rd., Columbus, Ohio 43202.

CAREER: Junior high school teacher in the public schools of Whitehall, Ohio, 1961-64; Ohio State University, Columbus, part time instructor in children's literature, 1968-73; researcher for textbook authors. Member: National Council of Teachers of English, Ohio Historical Society.

WRITINGS: The Valley of the Shadow (juvenile), Macmillan, 1974; The Stones, Macmillan, 1976. Contributor to Ohio Reading Teacher.

WORK IN PROGRESS: Manuscript tentatively titled Zoar Blue, concerns a communal settlement of German Separatists at Zoar, Ohio during Civil War; current research on several aspects of Ohio history.

SIDELIGHTS: "When I was little I liked to read and tell myself stories, but I never thought seriously about writing for children. Then when I became a teacher one of the first assignments in my eighth graders' history book was to write a short story based on the information in the chapter they had just read. They complained so much that I promised I would do the assignment too, just to prove it wasn't so bad. The resulting story was a big hit with my students, and I was later able to sell it to a magazine.

"Luckily my family has been able to put up with my interest in history, which has grown over the years. Our children do find it easier to share my passion for museums than for old cemeteries ('Oh no, not another one!' they call from the back seat. 'Please Dad, don't stop!'). But all in all, it's been a bonus; we've managed to turn most research trips into short-term family vacations."

HILL, Lorna 1902-

PERSONAL: Born February 21, 1902, in Durham, England; daughter of G. H. and Edith (Rutter) Leatham; married V. R. Hill (a clergyman); children: Shirley Victorine (Mrs. E. F. Emley). Education: University of Durham, B.A., 1926. Religion: Anglican. Home: Brockleside, Keswick, Cumberland, England.

CAREER: Author of children's books.

WRITINGS: The Vicarage Children, Evans Brothers, 1961; More About Mandy, Evans Brothers, 1963; The Secret, Evans Brothers, 1964; The Vicarage Children in Skye, Evans Brothers, 1966; La Sylphide: The Life of Maria Taglioni, Evans Brothers, 1967.

"Marjorie" series: Marjorie & Co., Art & Education, 1948, Thomas Nelson, 1956; Stolen Holiday, Art & Education, 1948, Thomas Nelson, 1956; Border Peel, Art & Education, 1950, Thomas Nelson, 1956; No Medals for Guy, Thomas Nelson, 1962.

"Sadler's Wells" series: A Dream of Sadler's Wells, Evans Brothers, 1950, Holt, 1955; Veronica at the Wells, Evans Brothers, 1951, published as Veronica at Sadler's Wells, Holt, 1954; Masquerade at the Wells, Evans Brothers, 1952, published as Masquerade at the Ballet, Holt, 1957; No Castanets at the Wells, Evans Brothers, 1953, published as Castanets for Caroline: A Story of Sadler's Wells, Holt, 1956; Jane Leaves the Wells, Evans Brothers, 1953; Ella at the Wells, Evans Brothers, 1954; Return to the Wells, Evans Brothers, 1955; Rosanna Joins the Wells, Evans Brothers, 1956; Principal Role, Evans Brothers, 1957; Swan Feather, Evans Brothers, 1958; Dress Rehearsal, Evans Brothers, 1959; Back Stage, Evans Brothers, 1960; Vicki in Venice, Evans Brothers, 1962.

"Patience" series, published by Burke Publishing: They Called Her Patience, 1951; It Was All Through Patience, 1952; Castle in Northumbria, 1953; So Guy Came Too, 1954; The Five Shilling Holiday, 1955.

"Dancing Peel" series, published by Thomas Nelson: Dancing Peel, 1954; Dancer's Luck, 1955; The Little Dancer, 1956; Dancer in the Wings, 1958; Dancer in Danger, 1960; Dancer on Holiday, 1962.

SIDELIGHTS: "I began to write stories when I was about twelve years old. I wrote them at school when I ought to have been doing math and Latin; I illustrated them myself too. It came easy to me because I was born into a literary

LORNA HILL

and artistic family. My mother, Edith Rutter Leatham, was a poet and wrote the world famous 'Child's Grace', which begins: 'Thank you for the world so sweet—.'

"I read English and philosophy at Durham University and obtained my degree. A short time afterwards I married a clergyman and had one daughter. When she was ten years old, she discovered one of the stories I had written at school and demanded more. So I sat down on the old-fashioned steel fender in front of the kitchen fire and wrote her *Marjorie & Co.,* an adventure story about children and their ponies in that wild and undiscovered part of England. This book (which, incidentally was written in a hard-backed exercise book, illustrated by myself) was so popular with Vicki and her school friends that I just went on writing, never thinking of publication, but just for love and the joy of writing.

"One week-end we had a playwright staying with us. He happened to have been a publisher's reader, so was interested in our book-cases and their contents. He was fascinated by the hand-written *Marjorie* books (there were eight of them by now) and asked me if I had done anything with them. When I said 'no', he scribbled the name of a literary agent on the back of an envelope and said: 'Send them here.' I sent up the first of the series, just as it was, and got a reply from the agent saying that they didn't usually deal with hand-written manuscripts, but since my story was at least in book form, they were making an exception in my case, and had sent it to a publisher. A few days later, I got a letter from the publisher saying that he was interested in the book and he understood that I had another one. I wrote back and said: 'Yes—seven more!'. His reply was a telegram saying: "Come up to London and bring the lot.' Mine was 'Sorry—can't. Poor clergyman's wife.' His reply to *that* was a cheque for fifty pounds—a lot of money in those days.

"I went up to London, weighed down with books, and returned to my remote Northumbrian vicarage with a contract for all the eight in my shabby handbag. That was how I began my literary career.

"My ballet books are another story altogether, and just as romantic I might say. My daughter, Vicki, became a dancer with the Royal Ballet, and an artist. She illustrated most of my ballet books."

HOBBIES AND OTHER INTERESTS: Scottish dancing, fell walking, swimming, gardening, photography, music.

HILL, Robert W(hite) 1919-

PERSONAL: Born September 12, 1919, in Richmond, Va.; son of Dudley J. and Mary (Banks) Hill; married Barbara Whitall, October 20, 1956; children: Matthew Banfield, Elizabeth Brinton, Anthony Whitall. *Education:* Haverford College, B.A., 1944, M.A., 1947. *Home:* 156 De Forest Rd., Wilton, Conn. *Office:* Association Press, 291 Broadway, New York, N.Y. 10007.

CAREER: Harcourt, Brace and Co. (publishers), New York, N.Y., sales representative and editorial reader, 1948-53; free-lance editor and Book-of-the-Month Club reader, 1953-54; John Day Co., Inc. (publishers), New York, N.Y., associate editor, 1955-58, secretary of corporation and

ROBERT W. HILL

member of board of directors, 1958, managing editor, 1959, vice-president, 1960-66; J. B. Lippincott, Co., New York, N.Y., editor-in-chief, 1967-68; Association Press, New York, N.Y., director, editor-in-chief, 1969—. Wilton Public Library, member of book selection committee; founding member, Wilton (Conn.) Land Trust, 1960—; American Field Service, home selection committee, 1961-65. *Military service:* U.S. Navy, 1943-46; became lieutenant junior grade. *Member:* Beta Rho Sigma, Publishers' Lunch Club, Wilton (Conn.) Riding Club, Saunderstown (R.I.) Yacht Club.

WRITINGS: What Colonel Glenn Did All Day, John Day, 1962; *What the Moon Astronauts Do,* John Day, 1963, revised, 1971; *The Chesapeake Bay Bridge Tunnel,* John Day, 1972.

SIDELIGHTS: "I lived in a small town in Virginia until I was nine years old, when my father moved his family to Washington, D.C. The change from a rural environment to a busy city brought an introduction to many new areas of experience. From the first I had a strong interest in mechanical things and how they operated, as well as in nature and writing.

"One of my keenist boyhood fascinations was aviation, beginning with the collecting of pictures of and the building of models of early airplanes. With the coming of World War II, I enlisted in the Naval Air Corps where I learned to fly. Since that time I have maintained a private pilot's license.

"Although my publishing career has been involved with a wide range of literary subjects, including fiction, history, biography, anthologies, some poetry, and many how-to books, I have retained my liking for aviation.

     Something about the Author

"A natural extension of that interest was the United States space program. In February, 1962, I watched on television the first manned orbital space flight of this nation, which inspired my book *What Colonel Glenn Did All Day.* About fifteen months later I attended the launching of astronaut Gordon Cooper into space at the National Aeronautics and Space Administration flight center at Cape Canaveral, Florida. I later wrote *What the Moon Astronauts Do,* and after touring the Chesapeake Bay Bridge-Tunnel, a book on that great engineering achievement.

"The challenge of all three books was to make a very complex technical program understandable to both young readers and adults whose knowledge of the workings of such matters is, as expected, limited. Acknowledging the ancient Chinese recognition that a picture is worth a thousand words, I combined carefully chosen photographs and line drawings with word text that allows the reader to follow step-by-step a process that otherwise would be nearly impossible to grasp. These books have had considerable success. This has made the experience all the more enjoyable, for, as a fellow publisher once aptly observed, 'writers and publishers are all teachers at heart.''

HODGE, P(aul) W(illiam)   1934-

PERSONAL: Born November 8, 1934, in Seattle, Wash.; son of Paul H. and Frances (Bakeman) Hodge; married Ann Uran, June 14, 1961; children: Gordon, Erik, Sandra. *Education:* Yale University, B.S., 1956; Harvard University, Ph.D., 1960. *Residence:* Seattle, Wash. *Office:* Astronomy Dept., FM 20, University of Washington, Seattle, Wash. 98105.

CAREER: Harvard University, Cambridge, Mass., lecturer in astronomy, 1960; University of California, Berkeley, assistant professor of astronomy, 1961-65; University of Washington, Seattle, associate professor, 1965-69, professor of astronomy, 1969—. Physicist at Smithsonian Astrophysical Observatory. *Member:* American Astronomical Society, American Geophysical Union, International Astronomical Union, Committee on Space Research of International Council of Scientific Unions. *Awards, honors:* National Science Foundation fellow, 1960-61.

WRITINGS: (With J. C. Brandt) *Solar System Astrophysics,* McGraw, 1963; *Galaxies and Cosmology,* McGraw, 1965; *The Magellanic Cloud,* Smithsonian Press, 1967; *Concepts of the Universe,* McGraw, 1969; *The Revolution in Astronomy,* Holiday House, 1970; *Galaxies* (revised edition of H. Shapley's classic), Harvard University Press, 1972; *Astronomy Study Guide,* McGraw, 1973; *Slides for Astronomy,* McGraw, 1973; *Concepts of Contemporary Astronomy,* McGraw, 1974; (with F. W. Wright) *The Small Magellaine Cloud,* University of Washington Press, 1977.

WORK IN PROGRESS: The Andromeda Galaxy; Interplanetary Dust; Islands in Space.

SIDELIGHTS: "My non-technical books are motivated by a desire to share the excitement of astronomy with others and to help others to enjoy the magnificence of the universe. For professional reasons, I have traveled extensively to Europe, South America, Africa, Australia, and Asia.''

P. W. HODGE

HOGAN, Bernice Harris   1929-

PERSONAL: Born January 24, 1929, in Philadelphia, Pa.; daughter of Robert H. (a salesman) and Lily (Garrison) Harris; married Donald Thomas Hogan (a minister), June 30, 1951; children: Carol Louise, Robert Lawrence, Susan Lynn. *Education:* Ursinus College, student, 1947-49; Bethany College, Bethany, W.Va., A.B., 1951; graduate study, Western Illinois University, 1968-72; Kearney State College, M.S. in Ed., 1977. *Religion:* Disciples of Christ. *Home:* 1014 East 33rd St., Kearney, Neb. 68847.

CAREER: Teacher at Abingdon Grade School, Abingdon, Ill., seven years; teacher of English and journalism of Axtell Community School, Axtell, Neb.; Central Nebraska Emergency Medical Services, Kearney, Neb., consumer information coordinator, 1976—; writer. Japan International Christian University, member of women's planning committee, 1963—; Illinois Disciples of Christ, district chairman of children's work, 1964-65, district chairman, 1965-66. *Member:* Pi Chapter of Alpha Delta Kappa, Community Concert Association (board member), Axtell Education Association (secretary), Nebraska State Education Association, National Education Association, National Council of Teachers of English.

BERNICE HARRIS HOGAN

WRITINGS—All published by Abingdon, except as indicated: *Abingdon Party Parade*, 1954; *Abingdon Shower Parade*, 1957; *Pre-School Party Parade*, 1958; *More from Your Class Meetings*, 1959; *Now I Lay Me Down to Wonder* (children's book), 1961; *Grains of Sand* (devotional), 1961; *Deborah* (children's book), 1964; *Listen for a Rainbow!* (devotional), Revell, 1965; *Party Planner*, Revell, 1967; *A Small Green Tree and a Square Brick Church* (chil-

dren's book), 1967; *Fun Party Games*, Revell, 1969; *Party Planner*, Baker Book, 1975.

SIDELIGHTS: "I grew up on 60th Street in Philadelphia and rode two trolley cars downtown to the Philadelphia High School for Girls at 17th and Spring Garden Streets, just across from the Philadelphia Mint, although both buildings have now moved.

"Downtown in the city, I was delighted with sauerkraut on a hot dog on a bun, especially if I could put ketchup on top of the sauerkraut! People in Illinois and Nebraska think it most strange to have mustard on pretzels, but Philadelphia venders had the most delicious, soft, unsanitary pretzels with mustard anyone can imagine!

"One of the biggest thrills was selling my first poem when I was just sixteen for the magnificent sum of 65c!

"I liked being a Junior-Senior high teacher of English, but I was aghast at all the books I had NOT read and all the poetry and short stories I had not analyzed.

"It was good to look backwards in literature to those who had already described their skylarks and urns and heroes, but English has present value for all persons who use this language to compile research, combat propaganda, buy hamburgers, make love and conjecture about the right place for a comma!

"May all of you who read this enjoy commas in your sentences and mustard on your pretzels!"

HOOVER, Helen (Drusilla Blackburn) 1910- (Jennifer Price)

PERSONAL: Born January 20, 1910, in Greenfield, Ohio; daughter of Thomas Franklin (a factory manager) and

**My brother and I went skipping, hopping, leapfrogging, but slowly. . .
but slowly. . .
because it was a hot summer day, and we had licked almost all of our ice-cream cones.**
■ (From *A Small Tree and a Square Brick Church* by Bernice Hogan. Illustrated by Meg Wohlberg.)

While the other animals stood in an anxious group, he walked slowly and silently into the clearing. "I can help you," he said as softly as he could. ■ (From *Great Wolf and the Good Woodsman* by Helen Hoover. Illustrated by Charles Mikolaycak.)

Hannah (Gomersall) Blackburn; married Adrian Everett Hoover (an illustrator), February 13, 1937. *Education:* Ohio University, student, 1927-29; took special and night courses in sciences at De Paul University and University of Chicago, 1943-49. *Address:* P.O. Box 89, Ranchos de Taos, N.M. 87557. *Agent:* Brandt & Brandt, 101 Park Ave., New York, N.Y. 10017.

CAREER: Henry Paulsen and Co., addressograph operator, 1929-31; Audit Bureau of Circulations, Chicago, Ill., proofreader, 1931-43; Pittsburgh Testing Laboratory, Chicago, Ill., analytical chemist, 1943-45; Ahlberg Bearing Co., Chicago., Ill., metallurgist, 1945-48; International Harvester Co., Chicago, Ill., research metallurgist, 1948-54; free-lance writer for general, nature, and juvenile magazines, Minnesota and New Mexico, 1954—. Patentee of agricultural implement discs.

MEMBER: Mystery Writers of America, Authors Guild, International Council for Bird Preservation, International Union for Preservation of Nature, National Audubon Society, Society for Animal Rights, Humane Society of the United States, Wilderness Society, Defenders of Wildlife, Committee for Preservation of the Tule Elk, Fauna Preservation Society, Save-the-Redwoods League, Jersey Wildlife Preservation Trust, Minnesota Ornithologists Union, Minneapolis Audubon Society, Sierra Club. *Awards, honors:* Annual Achievement Award of Metal Treating Institute, 1959; Blue Flame Ecology Salute, 1973; Zia Award, New Mexico Press Women, 1973; Brooklyn Art Books for Children citation, 1977.

WRITINGS: The Long-Shadowed Forest, Crowell, 1963; *The Gift of the Deer,* Knopf, 1966; *Animals at My Doorstep* (juvenile), Parents Magazine Press, 1966; *Great Wolf and the Good Woodsman* (juvenile fiction), Parents Magazine Press, 1967; *A Place in the Woods,* Knopf, 1969; *Animals Near and Far* (juvenile), Parents Magazine Press, 1970; *The Years of the Forest,* Knopf, 1973. Regular contributor of feature, 'Nature Story,' to *Humpty Dumpty,* 1959-69, and column, 'Wilderness Chat,' to *Defenders of Wildlife News,* 1963-73. Also contributor of articles and features to magazines, including *Audubon, American Mercury, Gourmet, Organic Gardening and Farming, Saturday Review, Living Wilderness,* and *Woman's Journal* (London). Also, other nature publications and some religious magazines. Some fiction, juvenile magazine and book-length adult romance, under pseudonym, Jennifer Price.

WORK IN PROGRESS: Possible book on the whys and wherefores of life-style changes, based on the author's own varied and numerous dwelling places. Might cover long period, from 1929 to present.

SIDELIGHTS: "The little town where I grew up was full of Victorian houses, great trees from the original forest, and people with circumscribed minds. The urge to write came to me when I was nine and discovered *The Circular Staircase* and *Tarzan of the Apes.* I was constantly scribbling and my mother was as constantly chasing me out to play with other children. Since I was older mentally and very near-sighted, I was hardly a success at games. This was no disappointment because I liked to read and write and think. I kept on doing these happy mental things until the activities and challenges of study took up my energies. I entered college as a classic language major—school teaching was the only respectable occupation for a woman according to the *mores* of the town—but changed to physical sciences in my second year. When the Depression interrupted my education I had a heavy background in physics, chemistry, and mathematics.

"I worked at anything I could during the lean years, in Chicago, because my father died of a heart attack when he lost his money and my mother was unable to support herself in any way; and little towns offered little in the way of employment, even in good times. I went into chemistry, then metal-

HELEN HOOVER

lurgy on the wings of World War II and continued that until after my mother's death. Then my husband, an artist whom I had met and married in Chicago, and I decided to strike out on our own, for a number of reasons, one of the most important to me being his health, which was not good in the flu-and-cold atmosphere of the city.

"We moved to our log cabin on the Canadian border of Minnesota and there, under the grim necessity of earning money or starving, I began to write seriously, not the mysteries I had yearned to do long before, but articles on the natural world around us. These led, after some time, to my wonderful literary agent who took *The Gift of The Deer,* which my husband illustrated (my husband illustrated all my adult books), and its sale to the Reader's Digest Condensed Books. We had been totally isolated for some years and our phone was a very new thing when it rang and I got the overwhelming thrill of learning about the book club sale, which meant that the long hard years were over.

"Gradually the isolation that had made the atmosphere from which my North Woods books came gave way to more and more people and the accompanying disturbances of city and town living. So, although the area was still, to those who had never known it in its almost pristine state, very wild and remote, it was no longer safe for animals to share our clearing. We felt it was time to see a bit more of the United States while we were still young enough to enjoy it. Young is relative because we had moved to the woods when we were forty-four and had not left it for thirteen years.

"So we headed for the southwestern areas. *The Years of the Forest* was written in Taos, New Mexico, where another author and illustrator cause no stir whatsoever. And this gave us the needed privacy for concentration. One thing and another has led us from place to place and delayed our return to the North, where the little log house waits patiently for our return.

"As to how I write, I am not sure. I have had no training in any phase of it. The 'Animal' books were built up from my nature story in *Humpty Dumpty*—selected, arranged, tied together with a suitable theme, with beginning, connections, and ending added. This was easy. *Great Wolf* popped into my head on a Christmas Eve when I heard a wolf howling and realized that his song sounded much like a long, drawn-out, 'Noel.' The other books just seemed to suddenly be in my mind, and when that happened I knew I was ready to sit down and get them on paper.

"*The Gift of the Deer,* written for adults I thought, has turned out to be a favorite with youngsters, some quite young. A teacher in Kentucky developed a whole course of study for her third-year class, using the book as a guide not only to nature study but to such things as bread baking, old time records, etc. I have a treasured folder sent by her and her class, with pictures of the children, letters from each one; which gives me a fine overall view of how *Gift* was used.

"All of the adult books have been published abroad, with *Gift* leading the list. I have copies of editions in all the languages of Western Europe, as well as Japanese, Kannadu (southern India), and Thai (U.S. Information Service). It has, also, appeared in Mexico, South America, South Africa, Australia, and New Zealand. *Place* and *Forest* also have European and other foreign publications, some still to come."

FOR MORE INFORMATION SEE: *Farm Implement News,* March 20, 1958; *Implement and Tractor,* May 20, 1964.

HOPE SIMPSON, Jacynth 1930-

PERSONAL: Born November 10, 1930, in Birmingham, England; daughter of Frank and Mabelle (Brooks) Cureton;

JACYNTH HOPE SIMPSON

And Baba Yaga, gnashing her teeth and screaming with rage and disappointment, turned round and drove away home to her little hut on hen's legs.
■ (From *A Cavalcade of Witches* edited by Jacynth Hope-Simpson. Illustrated by Krystyna Turska.)

married Dermot Hope Simpson (a headmaster), August 3, 1955; children: Elinor. *Education:* University of Lausanne, student, 1949; Oxford University, M.A. and Diploma of Education, 1953. *Religion:* Church of England. *Home:* The Red House, Hartley Rd., Plymouth, England.

CAREER: Teacher of senior English at Bournemouth School for Girls, Bournemouth, Hampshire, England, 1953-54, at Croham Hurst School, Croydon, Surrey, England, 1954-57; examiner for Cambridge and Oxford General Certificates of Education, 1957-58; author, 1958—.

WRITINGS—Novels: *The Bishop of Kenelminster,* Putnam, 1961; *The Bishop's Picture,* Putnam, 1962; *The Unravished Bride,* Putnam, 1963.

Children's books—All published by Hamish Hamilton, except as indicated: *Anne, Young Swimmer,* Constable, 1959, *The Stranger in the Train,* 1960, *Young Netball Player,* Constable, 1961, *The Great Fire,* 1961, *Danger on the Line,* 1962, *The Man Who Came Back,* 1962, *The Ice Fair,* 1963, *The Ninepenney,* 1964, *The Witch's Cave,* 1964, (editor) *Hamish Hamilton Book of Myths and Legends,* 1963, *The Edge of the World,* 1965, Coward, 1966; (editor) *A Cavalcade of Witches,* 1966, Walck, 1967; (editor) *The Hamish Hamilton Book of Witches,* 1966; *The Unknown Island,* 1968, Coward, 1969; *The Curse of the Dragon's Gold: European Myths and Legends,* Doubleday, 1969; *Elizabeth I,* 1971; (compiler) *Tales in School: An Anthology of Boarding-School Life,* 1971; *The Gunner's Boy,* Heinemann, 1973; *Save Tarranmoor!,* Heinemann, 1974; *Who Knows?,* Heinemann, 1974; *The Hijacked Hovercraft,* Heinemann, 1975; *Always on the Move,* Heinemann, 1975; *Black Madonna,* Heinemann, 1976; *Vote for Victoria,* Heinemann, 1976.

WORK IN PROGRESS: An illustrated history of industrial changes, *Men and Machines.*

SIDELIGHTS: "As a person, I have a very strong sense of place. My own roots are in the English Midlands, a very mixed scene. Part of it is entirely pastoral. I spent many happy hours in my childhood on the river Avon, seven miles from Stratford where Shakespeare was born, and later lived on the Malvern Hills, which greatly influenced the composer Elgar and are the very essence of 'Englishness.' The rest of my youth was spent in Birmingham, a busy industrial city, still full of relics of the early nineteenth-century industrial revolution. For this reason, I have welcomed a recent suggestion that I should write a large scale work (for school libraries and similar public) on the Industrial Revolution.

"Nowadays I live in Plymouth between the sea and Dartmoor which is one of the last areas of 'wilderness' in our tiny, highly populated British Isles. Two of my recent books (*They Sailed from Plymouth* and *The Gunner's Boy*) have been based on local seafarers and one (*Save Tarranmoor*) on the need to preserve Dartmoor.

"Another area to which I am very responsive is the Balkans—Greece, Yugoslavia, Turkey. One of my recent books is based on a recent visit to Macedonia, one of the least developed, but at the same time most vivid and picturesque parts of Europe. I collect antiquarian travel books on this area, and often find them a better guide than more recent writings.

"As you will see from this, I am, also, a person to whom a sense of the past is important. I like living in places with many associations. As a result of this, I very much think of my books, from the earliest stage, not only as stories about people but about people in a particular setting.

"I believe tremendously strongly in the importance of children's writing, both as an influence on children and as a craft in its own right, and have several times spoken about this on radio and television. I think that children are a very alert, very critical audience (more so than many adults) and one must *never* approach children's books on the principle that anything is good enough for a juvenile readership. To me, the chief difference in writing for children and writing for adults is in matters like length, vocabulary, sentence structure and so on, but certainly not in accuracy, quality of imagination or anything like that."

HOBBIES AND OTHER INTERESTS: Foreign travel, especially with reference to art and architecture.

HORNER, Dave 1934-

PERSONAL: Born December 13, 1934, in Lynchburg, Va.; son of L. David, Jr. (a banker) and Katherine (Byers) Horner; married Jayne Bond, September 10, 1955; children: Valerie Jayne, Victoria Lynn, Julie Bond. *Education:* University of Virginia, student, 1952-56; Rutgers, The State University, graduate study in banking, 1965—. *Politics:* Conservative Republican. *Religion:* Methodist. *Home:* 121 Variety Tree Circle, Altamonte Springs, Fla. 32701.

CAREER: Banker; current president of Southeast National Bank, Orlando, Fla.; Maritime Explorations Ltd. (professional diving equipment), Virginia Beach, consultant. Has been diving for twenty years in the North Atlantic, Mediterranean, and Caribbean; certified SCUBA instructor; underwater photographer, doing commercial work as well as photographs used in own lectures on diving and treasure hunting. *Military service:* U.S. Navy, 1956-58.

The word "scuba" is an abbreviation made up of the first letters in the words Self-Contained Underwater Breathing Apparatus, which includes an air tank, regulator, and harness. ■ (From *Better Scuba Diving for Boys* by Dave Horner. Photo by Paul Tzimoulis.)

WRITINGS: Key to Good Diving, Maritime Explorations, 1963; *Shipwrecks, Skin Divers and Sunken Gold,* Dodd, 1965; *Better SCUBA Diving for Boys,* Dodd, 1966; *The Blockade Runners,* Dodd, 1968; *The Treasure Galleons,* Dodd, 1971. Contributor to *Commonwealth* and to skin-diving journals.

WORK IN PROGRESS: Three books, *Diving for Phantom Gold, Northeast Shipwreck,* and *Treasure Below.*

SIDELIGHTS: "Am actively engaged in underwater exploration and salvage of historical shipwrecks, such as vessels of Cornwallis' fleet sunk by General Washington and the French at Yorktown in 1781, Civil War vessels including the 'Monitor' off Cape Hatteras, some forty blockade runners off Cape Fear, and a Spanish galleon. My goal is to accumulate enough underwater historical items, treasure, relics to build a museum of sunken treasure." Speaks Spanish.

HUNTER, Kristin (Eggleston) 1931-

PERSONAL: Born September 12, 1931, in Philadelphia, Pa.; daughter of George Lorenzo and Mabel (Manigault) Eggleston; married John I. Lattany, June 22, 1968; stepchild: John, Jr. *Education:* University of Pennsylvania, B.S. in Ed., 1951. *Address:* P.O. Box 8371, Philadelphia, Pa. 19101. *Agent:* Harold Matson Co., Inc., 22 East 40th St., New York, N.Y. 10016.

CAREER: Pittsburgh Courier, Philadelphia (Pa.) edition, columnist and feature writer, 1946-52; copywriter for Lav-

KRISTIN HUNTER

enson Bureau of Advertising, Philadelphia, Pa., 1952-59, Wermen & Schorr, Inc., Philadelphia, 1962-63; City of Philadelphia, Philadelphia, Pa., information officer, 1963-64, 1965-66, free-lance writer, 1964—; Temple University, Philadelphia, Pa., director of comprehensive health services, 1971—. Instructor in creative writing, University of Pennsylvania, 1972-73. *Member:* Philadelphia Art Alliance, University of Pennsylvania Alumnae Association (director, 1970-73). *Awards, honors:* Fund for the Republic prize for television documentary, "Minority of One," 1955; John Hay Whitney "opportunity" fellowship, 1959-60; Philadelphia Athenaeum award, 1964; National Council on Interracial Books for Children award, 1968, for *The Soul Brothers and Sister Lou;* Sigma Delta Chi reporting award, 1968; Mass Media Brotherhood Award from National Conference of Christians and Jews, 1969, for *The Soul Brothers and Sister Lou;* Lewis Carroll Shelf Award, 1971, for *The Soul Brothers and Sister Lou;* Book World Children's Spring Festival, first prize, 1973; National Book Award finalist, 1974, and Christopher Award, 1975, for *Guests in the Promised Land.*

WRITINGS—All published by Scribner: *God Bless the Child* (adult), 1964; *The Landlord* (adult), 1966; *The Soul Brothers and Sister Lou* (juvenile), 1968; *Boss Cat* (juvenile), 1971; *Guests in the Promised Land* (juvenile), 1973; *The Survivors* (adult), 1975. Poems, short stories, book reviews and articles have appeared in the *Philadelphia Bulletin* and in *The Nation, Essence, Rogue, Black World, Good Housekeeping, Seventeen* and other publications. Articles include "Pray for Barbara's Baby," *Philadelphia Magazine,* June, 1968 (reprinted in *Reader's Digest,* January, 1969) and "Soul City North," *Philadelphia Magazine,* May, 1972.

SIDELIGHTS: "As an only child of school teacher parents whose friends were mostly childless, I was thrown back early on my own imaginative resources of fantasy and reading. I believe these circumstances—onliness, loneliness and resultant fantasizing and omnivorous reading—are the most favorable for producing writers (when they do not produce hopeless schizophrenics). Since ours was a middle-class family, and since the only playmates available to me were the children of relatively poor blacks, their sharply different values, speech patterns and habits and, above all, their seemingly greater freedom, made them irresistibly fascinating to me as people, and, later, as subjects for stories.

"For most of my life, until a few years ago, I believed, perhaps a bit romantically, that the inner city, the so-called 'ghetto' or 'slum,' was the only place to find black people and themes worth writing about. But now, after living for five years in the Philadelphia 'ghetto' and writing six books mainly located there, I find myself turning to other, neglected areas I find equally worthy and interesting—i.e. the black middle class from which I came, and suburban and even rural locations. I am hopeful that 'humor, warmth and humanity,' the words most often used to describe my writings to date, will be abundantly present in these future works too.

"Oddly enough, I never intended to write for children. *The Soul Brothers and Sister Lou* came about only because my publisher's juvenile editor asked me to consider writing a children's book. I considered this an outlandish suggestion at first, but something in the back of my mind filed it away, then went to work on it without my conscious knowledge. Then came a summer of listening to some talented young

GUESTS IN THE
PROMISED LAND
Stories by Kristin Hunter

HUNTER Guests in the Promised Land SCRIBNERS

CHILDRENS SPRING FESTIVAL
1973
PRIZE
BOOK
Chicago Tribune

It ain't no promised land at all if some people are guests and others are always members.
■ (From *Guests in the Promised Land* by Kristin Hunter. Jacket photograph by Terry Smith.)

street singers in the alley below my inner-city apartment, and the story of *The Soul Brothers and Sister Lou,* a young singing group, followed.

"Two more children's books, *Boss Cat* and *Guests in the Promised Land* have appeared since, and I am planning a fourth after I complete the adult novel I am currently writing, which takes place in a small black town that is technically a Northern suburb but has a strong Southern and rural flavor. My husband of over seven years, John Lattany, is the most enthusiastic and supportive partner a woman writer could hope for, as well as a very sympathetic and capable human being. He tells everyone, proudly, about my books; goes with me to the all-too-many public functions to allay my nervousness; and even at times takes over the kitchen, where he is a far more skilled performer than I. (I am a fairly good basic cook, but my husband, among his many other skills, is a trained *grand chef.*) Instant motherhood was one of the many blessings my marriage brought me, and until last year, when John, Jr. enlisted in the Coast Guard, my life and my understanding of children were immeasurably enriched by the presence of both his sons in our household. I also gain much understanding and excitement from contact with the young people to whom I teach creative writing at the University of Pennsylvania."

The book *The Landlord* was filmed by United Artists, released in 1970.

FOR MORE INFORMATION SEE: Top of the News, January, 1970.

HURWOOD, Bernhardt J. 1926-
(Mallory T. Knight, D. Gunther Wilde, Father Xavier)

PERSONAL: Born July 22, 1926, in New York, N.Y.; married. *Education:* Northwestern University, B.S., 1949. *Residence:* New York, N.Y. *Agent:* John Cushman Associates, Inc., 25 West 43rd St., New York, N.Y. 10036.

CAREER: U.S. Merchant Marine, seaman, 1945-47; film editor with Television Arts Productions, Berkeley, Calif., 1949, Chicago Film Laboratory, Chicago, Ill., 1950, and National Broadcasting Co. (news and special events), New York, N.Y., 1951-52; miscellaneous "insignificant" jobs, and free-lance film editing, writing, and public relations work, 1952-62; full-time professional writer, 1962—. *Member:* Writers Guild of America, East, Authors Guild, American Society of Journalists and Authors.

WRITINGS: Terror by Night, Lancer, 1963; (with F. S. Klaf) *A Psychiatrist Looks at Erotica,* Ace Books, 1964; (translator with Klaf) *The Hundred Merry Tales,* Citadel, 1964; *Monsters Galore,* Fawcett, 1965; *Golden Age of Erotica,* Sherbourne, 1965; *Strange Lives,* Popular Library, 1966; *Monsters and Nightmares,* Belmont Books, 1967; *Strange Talents,* Ace Books, 1967; (translator) *The Facetiae of Poggio Bracciolini,* Award Books, 1968; (editor) *The First Occult Review Reader,* Award Books, 1968; *Vampires, Werewolves and Ghouls,* Ace Books, 1968; *Torture Through the Ages,* Paperback Library, 1969; (editor) *The Second Occult Review Reader,* Award Books, 1969; (with Frank Grosfield) *Korea: Land of the 38th Parallel,* Parents Magazine Press, 1969; *Dracutwig,* Award Books, 1969;

Society and the Assassin, Parents Magazine Press, 1970; *The Two-Sided Triangle,* Ace Books, 1970; *The Hag of the Dribble and Other True Ghosts,* Taplinger, 1971; *The Invisibles,* Fawcett, 1971; *Ghosts, Ghouls, and Other Horrors,* Scholastic, 1971; *Life, the Unknown,* Ace, 1971; *Rip-Off,* Fawcett, 1972; *Passport to the Supernatural,* Taplinger, 1972; *Vampires, Werewolves, and Other Demons,* Scholastic, 1972; *Haunted Houses,* Scholastic, 1972; *Chilling Ghost Stories,* Scholastic, 1973; *Eerie Tales of Terror and Dread,* Scholastic, 1973; *The Mindmaster,* Fawcett, 1973; *The Bisexuals,* Fawcett, 1974; (under pseudonym "Father Xavier") *Casebook: Exorcism and Possession,* NAL, 1974; *Born Innocent,* Ace, 1975; *Strange Curses,* Scholastic, 1975; *The Whole Set Catalogue,* Pinnacle, 1975 (for complete bibliography see *Contemporary Authors,* 25/28).

Films: "The Creatures from the Negative," produced by Ram Films; about two-hundred short motion picture scripts for animated cartoons. Numerous magazine pieces, including film reviews, book reviews, personality pieces, have been published in *Forum, Genesis, Travelscene, Vogue, Saturday Review, New York, Penthouse* and others. A column of personal opinion in the short-lived, defunct *Writer's World,* called "Writer at Large."

SIDELIGHTS: "My thinking is eclectic and my interests cover a wide spectrum. If I had sufficient time, I would take up painting and sculpture as adjuncts to writing. I would probably, also, read more fiction and much more history, but somehow, my leisure reading (what little there is) follows the

BERNHARDT J. HURWOOD

non-fiction patterns of my required reading. It is difficult to find anything more stimulating than reality.

"I am a competent photographer—technically professional—but far from a fanatic. My background in the motion picture industry is so extensive that I will always retain an involvement of some sort with it.

"Having gone to sea during a period that was neither war nor peace was extremely valuable to me. I learned at an early age that the differences between nations and cultures are insurmountable, despite the fact that the similarities between individuals are far greater than the differences. For this reason (among others) I tend to be slightly cynical and iconoclastic.

"I earn my living as a writer because the thought of wearing another man's collar is abhorrent to me. For the most part I write about subjects that interest me, and in which I can interest publishers. I have frequently turned down large sums of money to do things that I did not believe in, or did not find interesting. I write about many subjects, I am not a specialist, although my credits would tend to indicate that I am. I find it annoying that writers, like performers tend to be typecast, yet, I know that as my career progresses, my work improves. Therefore, I can be certain that in time I can break any molds that others tend to cast about me.

"For the record I have been in all of the states except Alaska and Hawaii. I have been to England, France, Italy, Germany, Holland, Spain, Ireland, Iceland, Canada, Nova Scotia, Newfoundland, Cuba, Chile, Curacao, Panama, Trinidad and Tobago (where I was once shipwrecked) and West Africa.

"I was once fairly competent in Spanish, although, now it would be positively fractured if I attempted to use it. I feel that I could translate anything with a Latin base if given sufficient time and dictionaries.

"I do not believe that poverty enriches, ennobles, or strengthens character. It destroys the body and the spirit. At the other end of the spectrum I regard excessive materialism as unwise and stultifying in its own way, even dangerous if carried to excess. I agree with the late Winston Churchill that Democracy is the worst form of government, but better than all the others. Ours has fallen far short of complete success, yet, it survives because all the others have fallen even farther from the mark. The same thing goes for our economy. It is utterly ridiculous, yet, somehow, it has managed to make us the richest nation in the world. Whether this justifies it or not, remains to be seen.

"I firmly believe that there will never be universal love or peace in the world because we humans are too human. Henry James put it succinctly when he said that man is 'the most formidable of all beasts of prey and indeed the only one that preys systematically on its own species.'

"The things that bother me most of all are hypocrisy and the growing depersonalization and dehumanization of our society. The thing I value most is freedom to be an individual and to express myself as I see fit. If all writers would continue to attack hypocrisy and defend individuality and freedom, not only would they be able to sleep nights, they might in the long run succeed in extending that gift to millions of others."

ROBIN P. HYMAN

HYMAN, Robin P(hilip)   1931-

PERSONAL: Born September 9, 1931, in London, England; son of Leonard and Helen Hyman; married Inge Neufeld; children: James, Peter, Philippa. *Education:* University of Birmingham, B.A. (honors), 1955. *Home:* 101 Hampstead Way, London N.W.11, England. *Office:* Evans Brothers Ltd., Montague House, Russell Square, London W.C.1, England.

CAREER: Evans Brothers Ltd. (publishers), London, England, 1955—, presently managing director. Council, Publishers Association, 1975—. *Member:* Garrick Club.

WRITINGS: (Compiler) *A Dictionary of Famous Quotations,* Evans Brothers, 1962, published in the United States as *The Quotation Dictionary,* Macmillan, 1967; (with John Trevaskis) *The Boys' and Girls' First Dictionary,* Evans Brothers, 1967, published in the United States as *The Young Readers Press First Dictionary,* Young Readers Press, 1972; (with wife, Inge Hyman) *Barnabas Ball at the Circus* (juvenile), Evans Brothers, 1967; (with Hyman) *Runaway James and the Night Owl* (juvenile), Evans Brothers, 1968; (with Hyman) *Run, Run, Chase the Sun* (juvenile), Evans Brothers, 1969.

(Compiler) *Three Bags Full* (juvenile), Evans Brothers, 1972; (with Hyman) *Happy with Hubert* (juvenile), Evans

Brothers, 1972; (with Hyman) *The Hippo Who Wanted to Fly* (juvenile), Evans Brothers, 1973; *The Fairy Tale Book* (juvenile), Evans Brothers, 1974; (with Hyman) *Casper and the Lion Cub* (juvenile), Evans Brothers, 1974; (with Hyman) *The Magical Fish* (juvenile), Evans Brothers, 1974; (with Hyman) *Casper and the Rainbow Bird* (juvenile), Evans Brothers, 1975; *Universal Primary Dictionary*, Evans Brothers, 1976. Member of editorial board, *World Year Book of Education*, 1969-73.

HOBBIES AND OTHER INTERESTS: Theater, travel, reading.

ILSLEY, Velma (Elizabeth) 1918-

PERSONAL: Born August 6, 1918, in Edmonton, Alberta, Canada; daughter of Rowland Sutherland and Lily E. (Thomas) Ilsley; married James W. Ledwith (a physician), May 1, 1962. *Education:* Studied at Douglass College, 1936-38, Moore School of Art, 1938-40, Art Students League, Sculpture Center, New School of Social Research, and Hunter College. *Politics:* Independent. *Home:* 59 East Shore Rd., Huntington, N.Y.

CAREER: Writer and illustrator of children's books, painter, sculptor. *Member:* Society of Illustrators, Authors League.

WRITINGS—All self-illustrated: *The Pink Hat*, Lippincott, 1956; *A Busy Day for Chris*, Lippincott, 1957; *The Long Stocking*, Lippincott, 1959; *Once Upon a Time* (baby record book in verse), C. R. Gibson, 1960; *M Is for Moving*, Walck, 1966.

Illustrator: Elizabeth Honness, *Mystery of the Doll Hospital*, Lippincott, 1955; Gladys Adshead, *Brownies, It's Christmas*, Oxford University Press, 1955; Mabel Leigh Hunt, *Miss Jellytop's Visit*, Lippincott, 1955; Mabel Leigh Hunt, *Stars for Cristy*, Lippincott, 1956; Joan Lowery Nixon, *Mystery of Hurricane Castle*, Abelard, 1956; Elizabeth Honness, *Mystery in the Square Tower*, Lippincott, 1957; Sybil Conrad, *Enchanted Sixteen*, Holt, 1957; Emma Atkins Jacob, *For Each a Dream*, Holt, 1958; Mabel Leigh Hunt, *Cristy at Skippinghills*, Lippincott, 1958; Norma Simon, *My Beach House*, Lippincott, 1958; Gladys Adshead, *Brownies, Hurry*, Walck, 1959; Rebecca Caudhill, *Time for Lisa*, Thomas Nelson, 1960; Alice P. Miller, *The Heart of Camp Whipporwhill*, Lippincott, 1960; Molly Cone, *Only Jane*, Thomas Nelson, 1960; Gladys Adshead, *Smallest Brownie's Fearful Adventure*, Walck, 1961; Helen D. Olds,

What's a Cousin, Knopf, 1962; Alma Powers, *Waters, the Giving Gift*, Farrar, Straus, 1962; Duane Bradley, *Mystery at the Shoals*, Lippincott, 1962; Beman Lord, *Our New Baby's ABC*, Walck, 1964; Nan Hayden Agle, *Kate and the Apple Tree*, Seabury, 1965; Nan Hayden Agle, *Joe Bean*, Seabury, 1966; Margaret Hodges, *Sing Out Charley*, Farrar, Straus, 1968; Anne Houston, *The Cat Across the Way*, Seabury, 1968; Rosalie K. Fry, *Mungo*, Farrar, Straus, 1972; Dorothy Crayder, *She, the Adventuress*, Atheneum, 1973; Tanith Lee, *Princess Hynchatti and Some Other Surprises*, Farrar, Straus, 1973; Dorothy Crayder, *She and the Dubious Three*, Atheneum, 1974; Anne Alexander, *To Live a Lie*, Atheneum, 1975. Has illustrated more than twenty jacket covers.

SIDELIGHTS: "*M is for Moving,* the title of my alphabet book, could have been the title for the first five years of my childhood. In 1920, my father died and we moved from British Columbia to Nova Scotia, then to California and finally to Lakewood, New Jersey where I had most of my schooling. I have very few memories of my early years. The highlights were gathering hailstones in San Bernardino and 'sailing over our sea lawn' in a rocking washtub.

"My interest in the arts started in Lakewood. My father, formerly a teacher and owner of a men's clothing store, had come from a family of artists. Our small apartment was full of my mother's paintings; though now being the sole supporter of three daughters, she spent most of her time sewing.

There was a white blanket of snow tucked around it and a snow pillow, soft and thick, on it's roof. ■ (From *Brownies--It's Christmas!* by Gladys L. Adshead. Pictures by Velma Ilsley.)

VELMA ILSLEY

My older sister and I made up stories and illustrated them for our own amusement. All of us drew. With a small jigsaw we cut out wooden dolls that we later painted, shellacked and sold. We, also, spent hours dancing to Ned Wayburn records and were usually on the school entertainment programs either as acrobatic, toe or tap dancers: my mother, the choreographer. Though not a professional dancer it was through her dancing graces and some wonderful influential friends: namely, Caroline Fuller, an author and Katherine Hinsdale, the librarian, that made it possible for us to spend enjoyable hours on some of the loveliest estates in Lakewood. I remember playing games and having lunch with the Arthur Brisbane children, to whom my mother taught dancing, having tea with Mrs. Charles Lathrop Pack in her garden and dining with John D. Rockefeller, Sr. It was because of these friends that we were able to vacation in Nova Scotia on the Bay of Fundy where my father had spent his boyhood.

"After college and art school I became a fashion artist in Philadelphia, then Miami and eventually New York, where I continued in that career as free-lancer until I lost the Saks Fifth Avenue children's account. This was a turning point in my life—I decided to be an illustrator of children's books. Eunice Blake, then children's editor of Lippincott, gave me my first chance and a short time later Ursula Nordstrom of Harper & Row suggested I write my own picture books. It was thanks to some severe criticism from the poet, Horace Gregory, who was teaching a course I took at The New School that prompted me to analyze the drawing style of my, as yet unsold picture book, *The Pink Hat,* rewrite it completely except for the opening two lines and sell it to Lippincott. The children who had been models for my fashion drawings became models for my stories, illustrations and paintings for many years. Now, I mostly create my own.

"The subjects of my books are usually based on personal feelings, experiences, habits or chance happenings. *The Pink Hat* resulted from paintings I had done of my models in a hat; *A Busy Day for Chris* from a drawing I had made of a little girl contentedly lying in a meadow and my own love for the outdoors—whether it was 'opening windows wide' to look out on the green parks in Tudor City where I lived, or riding through the Connecticut countryside in an old M.G. with the windshield down. *M is for Moving* was written after my marriage and more moving, culminating in our present nineteenth-century house in Huntington Harbor. Here, I paint, sculpture and fill a 'LONG STOCKING' with stories, just begun, half finished or being revised."

HOBBIES AND OTHER INTERESTS: Ship travel, beach combing, chess and dancing with my husband.

ISRAEL, Elaine 1945-

PERSONAL: Born January 24, 1945, in New York, N.Y.; daughter of Otto (in electrical devices business) and Kate (Mendle) Israel. *Education:* Bronx Community College, A.A., 1964; University of Rhode Island, B.A., 1966. *Home:* 20 Continental Ave., Forest Hills, N.Y. 11375. *Office:* Scholastic Magazines, 50 West 44th St., New York, N.Y. 10036.

ELAINE ISRAEL

One February day, Ginny Cook sat in an icy-cold Kansas classroom. She was wearing a winter jacket and muffler. The school thermostat had been turned down, and she couldn't keep warm.
■ (From *The Great Energy Search* by Elaine Israel.)

CAREER: *Long Island Star Journal,* Long Island, N.Y., reporter, 1966-68; Scholastic Magazines, New York, N.Y., writer and associate editor of *Newstime,* 1968—.

WRITINGS: *The Great Energy Search* (juvenile), Messner, 1974; (with Essie E. Lee) *Alcohol and You,* Messner, 1975; *The Hungry World,* Messner, 1977.

SIDELIGHTS: "Loving to write has been the one constant in my life. There was never a time when I didn't do some kind of writing. As a child, I wrote rather melodramatic short stories. At home I used reams of paper for a newspaper only a few understanding friends were allowed to read. My first ambition was to be a great reporter, like the late war correspondent Marguerite Higgins. I kept diaries and wrote endless letters to friends in anticipation of such writings being useful when I became famous!

"I still haven't written fiction for publication, which is something I'd really like to do. But I have worked as a reporter on a city newspaper. I now write for a national children's magazine, *Newstime.* It is work that is fulfilling and fun.

"The three non-fiction books I've had published were written after work and on weekends. I'm lucky to live in New York City, which is one big library. I'm, also, lucky to live in surroundings that are conducive to creativity. My apartment is in a rambling old building that looks very much like a castle. My windows face a walled garden full of big old trees.

"It would be wonderful if something I've written—or will write—becomes as important and permanent as those trees."

HOBBIES AND OTHER INTERESTS: Travel, photography.

HELEN HULL JACOBS

JACOBS, Helen Hull   1908-
(H. Braxton Hull)

PERSONAL: Born August 6, 1908, in Globe, Ariz.; daughter of Roland Herbert and Eula (Hull) Jacobs. *Education:* Attended Anna Head School for Girls and University of California, Berkeley, 1926-29, College of William and Mary, 1942. *Religion:* Episcopalian. *Home:* Egypt Close, East Hampton, N.Y. 11937.

CAREER: Former national and international tennis star, and senior editor, Grolier Council for Educational Research, New York, N.Y. U.S. tennis titles include junior champion, 1924-25, women's singles champion, 1932-35, women's doubles champion (with Sarah Palfrey), 1932, 1934, 1935, mixed doubles champion (with George Lott), 1934; in international tennis was finalist at Wimbledon, England, six times, Wimbledon singles champion, 1936, member of Wightman Cup team for thirteen consecutive years, 1927-39, and winner of titles in Egypt, Austria, Switzerland, and Greece. Formerly designer of women's sports clothes. *Military service:* U.S. Naval reserve, on active duty, as commandant of seamen and public relations officer at WAVES Training School, New York; public information officer and administrative assistant, Naval Gun Factory, Washington, D.C., 1943-45, Naval Proving Ground, Dahlgren, Va., 1949-54; retired as commander, 1968.

MEMBER: National Geographic Society (honorary), Mark Twain Society (honorary), English Speaking Union (honorary), Eugene Field Society (honorary), California Writers' Club, Kappa Alpha Theta, Oakland Junior League (charter), All England Lawn Tennis and Croquet Club (honorary), Nice Tennis Club (France; honorary), Women's Athletic Club (Oakland), San Francisco Press Club (honorary),

Berkeley Tennis Club (California; honorary). *Awards, honors:* Inducted into Lawn Tennis Hall of Fame, Newport, R.I., 1962; Tennis Immortal award, Tennis Writers Association of America, 1968.

WRITINGS: Modern Tennis, Bobbs-Merrill, 1933; *Improve Your Tennis,* Methuen, 1936; *Beyond the Game: An Autobiography,* Lippincott, 1936; (under pseudonym H. Braxton Hull) *Barry Cort,* Faber, 1938; *Tennis,* A. S. Barnes, 1941; *"By Your Leave, Sir": The Story of a WAVE,* Dodd, 1943; *Storm Against the Wind,* Dodd, 1944; *Laurel for Judy,* Dodd, 1945; *Adventure in Blue-jeans,* Dodd, 1947; *Gallery of Champions,* A. S. Barnes, 1949.

Center Court, A. S. Barnes, 1950; *Judy, Tennis Ace,* Dodd, 1951; *Proudly She Serves: The Realistic Story of a Tennis Champion Who Becomes a WAVE,* Dodd, 1953; *Golf, Swimming and Tennis,* Creative Educational Society, 1961;

Besides teaching you balance and counter-balance, the squat exercise will develop strength in your feet, legs, ankles, and thighs. ■ (From *Better Physical Fitness for Girls* by Helen Hull Jacobs. Photographs by Peter Schroeder.)

The Young Sportsman's Guide to Tennis, Thomas Nelson, 1961; *Famous American Women Athletes,* Dodd, 1964; *Better Physical Fitness for Girls,* Dodd, 1964; *Courage to Conquer,* Dodd, 1967; *The Tennis Machine,* Scribner, 1972; *Famous Modern American Women Athletes,* Dodd, 1975; *Beginner's Guide to Winning Tennis,* Wilshire, 1975. Contributor of articles to major American magazines, to *Sketch, Country Life,* and *Britannia* in England, and to newspapers in United States, England, and Egypt.

SIDELIGHTS: "I was born in Arizona and grew up in San Francisco, and Berkeley, California. I attended the University of California at Berkeley and the College of William and Mary in Williamsburg, Virginia. I am a descendant, through my mother, of Carter Braxton, a signer of the Declaration of Independence from Virginia.

"When I was sixteen and seventeen, I won the National Junior Tennis Championships and in 1927 joined the American Wightman Cup team, retaining my membership for twelve years. When I was twenty-four years old, I won the United States women's singles championship and, as no other person has done since, held my title for four consecutive years. As a fitting climax to my sports career, I was presented at the Court of St. James in 1935 and won the World Championship at Wimbledon in 1936.

"I have, also, won championships in United States doubles and mixed doubles competitions, and in Egyptian, Greek, Austrian, and Swiss games. I was the first player to be named an honorary member of the All-England Lawn Tennis and Croquet Club before actually winning the Wimbledon cup. A member of numerous tennis clubs, I was inducted into the National Lawn Tennis Association's Hall of Fame in 1962.

"Tennis is just one of my careers, for I am, also, a retired Commander in the United States Naval Reserve. I served during World War II as Commandant of Seamen, United States Naval Training School, and as a public relations officer and administrative assistant during that and the Korean War. I have, also, designed active sportswear for Izod and for Harrods in London, and for Lord & Taylor and other specialty department stores in the United States, and was a senior editor at Grolier, Inc., for four years.

"My father's mother, Helen Single, was an English writer. I may have inherited the interest from her. I began writing stories at twelve and first wrote seriously for the McClure Syndicate in 1927. I have been writing ever since. It was my first 'love,' long before I started tournament tennis. My tennis fiction and non-fiction are derived from my own experience; historical fiction from research. *Storm Against the Wind* began as a biography of my ancestor, Carter Braxton. Too little on his youth was extant, so I fictionalized the story. When I am working on a book, as I am now, I write from 8:30 a.m. to noon, and about two hours in the afternoon."

FOR MORE INFORMATION SEE: John Durant and Otto Bettman, *Pictorial History of American Sports: From Colonial Times to the Present,* A. S. Barnes, 1952; John Durant, editor, *Yesterday in Sports: Memorable Glimpses of the Past as Selected from the Pages of Sports Illustrated,* A. S. Barnes, 1956; Parke Cummings, *American Tennis: The Story of a Game and Its People,* Little, Brown, 1957; *Best Sellers,* January 1, 1968; *National Observer,* January 15, 1968; *Women Sports,* April, 1977.

DANIEL JACOBSON

JACOBSON, Daniel 1923-

PERSONAL: Born November 6, 1923, in Newark, N.J.; son of Samuel and Mary (Siegel) Jacobson; married Iris Blachman (a counselor), August 18, 1957; children: Lisa, Darryl, Jerrold. *Education:* New Jersey State Teachers College, Montclair, B.A., 1947; Clark University, graduate study, 1947-48; Columbia University, M.A., 1950; Louisiana State University, Ph.D., 1954. *Politics:* Democrat. *Religion:* Jewish. *Home:* 1827 Mirabeau Dr., Okemos, Mich. 48864. *Office:* 518 Erickson Hall, Michigan State University, East Lansing, Mich. 48824.

CAREER: University of Kentucky, Lexington, instructor in geography, 1952-55; Brooklyn College (now of the City University of New York), Brooklyn, N.Y., instructor in geology, 1955-57; New Jersey State College, Upper Montclair, associate professor of geography, 1957-66; Michigan State University, East Lansing, visiting professor, 1966-67, professor of geography and education, 1967—, adjunct professor of anthropology, 1974—. *Military service:* U.S. Army Air Forces, 1943-46. *Member:* Association of American Geographers, American Geographical Society, National Council for Geographic Education (president, 1968), American Anthropological Association, American Society for Ethnohistory, Society for American Archaeology, Histor-

When he heard the flapping of a bird's wings nearby he looked up, watched a blackbird circle the hillside, and then fly right toward him. The young man, now in tears, covered his eyes! He fell stunned atop his bison robe. ■ (From *The Hunters* by Daniel Jacobson. Illustrated by Richard Cuffari.)

ical Society of Michigan, New Jersey Historical Society. *Awards, honors:* Awards from National Council for Geographic Education, 1965, for "The Role of Historical Geography in the American School."

WRITINGS: The Story of Man, Home Library Press, 1963; (with Stanley N. Worton and others) *New Jersey: Past and Present,* Hayden, 1964; (contributor) John Morris, editor, *Methods of Geographic Instruction,* Ginn, 1968; *Teaching the American Indian in the American School: An Adventure in Cultural Geography,* National Council for Geographic Education, 1969; *The First Americans,* Ginn, 1969.

Great Indian Tribes, Hammond, Inc., 1970; (with Ralph H. Marsh and Howard N. Martin) *Alabama-Coushatta (Creek) Indians,* Garland Publishing, 1974; *The Hunters,* F. Watts, 1974; *The Fishermen,* F. Watts, 1975; *The Gatherers,* F. Watts, 1977. Contributor to *New Book of Knowledge,* and to *Journal of Geography.* Editor of *Peninsular* (of Michigan Council for Geographic Education).

WORK IN PROGRESS: The Farmers, publication by Watts expected in 1978; research on the Jewish community of Lansing, Michigan—the significance of the city in historical geography.

SIDELIGHTS: "I was fortunate enough, years ago, to have audited a course on the American Indians with Fred Kniffen at the Louisiana State University. That course led to my life-long interest in the Indian. It led to my research on the Coushatta, my Ph.D., my writings in education, geography and ethnohistory and particularly to the juveniles of which I am most proud.

"For two wonderful years I travelled back and forth between the campus at Baton Rouge and the Coushatta community on Bayou Blue. I talked with the old timers, Ency Abbott and Kinney Williams (both are no longer with us), with the younger folk, Bel and Nora Abbey. Marie and Sam Thompson, Loris Langley, and with the then very young—Joyce, Wilma and Myrna Abbey. I had long conversations with Paul Leeds, the Congregationalist minister, who preached at the Coushatta church. I learned much about the Coushatta lifeway and many words and phrases in the Coushatta tongue.

"And I read widely—everything I could get my hands on about the Indians north of Mexico.

"At Montclair State College (New Jersey) I introduced a course on the 'Geography of the American Indian.' And while serving as geography editor for the *New Book of Knowledge* was asked to contribute (by Martha Schapp and Dorothy Furman) an article on the Indians of North America. The article was edited by Claudia Cohl who was to become a good friend.

"The article in the *New Book of Knowledge* was woven around the theme of the hunters, the gatherers, the fishermen and the farmers—a theme that has become the cornerstone of my writing about the Indians for young people. The theme, it seems to me, is simple, meaningful, easy to grasp. It provides an evolutionary approach. It is ahistorical yet lends itself well to the historical approach as we move with the evolving economies—and other cultural items—through time.

"*New Book of Knowledge* editors working later for Ginn brought me the contract to do *The First Americans.* One of the chapters in it—on the Creeks with an inside look at the Coushatta. And one of the characters *Skalapista*—mosquito in Coushatta—is none other than Myrna Abbey herself!

"Meanwhile, Martin Bachellor of Hammond, Inc. (I am on their publications advisory board) asked me to do a book on the Indians for their 'Profile Series.' Because it was for a somewhat older age group I used the *culture area* approach, developed by the anthropologists, rather than the hunters, gatherers, fishermen, farmers theme. The book was a joy to write.

"For some years I had been at Michigan State University. From my seminars, serious students of American Indian culture change were sent out to the far flung portions of North America. To Alaska to study the Tlingit, to British Columbia to look into the Haida, to Montana for the Crow, to Arizona for the Papago, to Pelly Bay for an Eskimo group. Fine Ph.D. dissertations were the result.

"And I continued to write. Claudia Cohl, then at Franklin Watts, interested me in the possibilities of a five-volume set on the Indians. The springboard would be my old theme for the young folks. Thus was born *The Hunters,* and *The Fishermen* (it carries in part the work of my graduate students) and *The Gatherers.* In summer, 1976, I started work on *The Farmers*—a work that centers on the pueblo at Cochiti on the Rio Grande.

"My greatest reward? In 1972 the Coushatta intervened in the Caddo case before the Indian Claims Commission. Their lawyers needed an 'expert' to testify in Washington. I was summoned. And with elation I returned to the Coushatta haunts in Texas and Louisiana. I shed tears with Joyce and spent the happiest of hours with Bel, Nora, Sam, Marie, Loris and others in the community. An embrace with Bel at the old church will remain one of the happiest moments in my life.

"I will continue to research and write. Ethnicity, the urban world, the historical geography of the United States are, perhaps, my new frontiers. But I will always have a soft spot inside for the Indians of North America and how to interpret their lifeway—past and present—for children."

JOHNSTON, Johanna

PERSONAL: Born in Chicago, Ill.; daughter of John F. (a lawyer) and Florence (Bell) Voigt; divorced; children: Abigail. *Education:* Attended University of Chicago, 1934-36, and Art Institute of Chicago, 1936-38. *Residence.* New York, N.Y.

CAREER: CBS Television and Radio, New York, N.Y., staff writer, 1951-60. *Awards, honors:* Thomas Alva Edison Award, 1962, for *Thomas Jefferson: His Many Talents.*

WRITINGS—Adult biographies: *Runaway to Heaven: The Story of Harriet Beecher Stowe and Her Era,* Doubleday, 1964; *Mrs. Satan: The Incredible Saga of Victoria Woodhull,* Putnam, 1967; *The Heart That Would Not Hold: The Life of Washington Irving,* M. Evans, 1971.

Juvenile books: *Sugarplum* (novel), Knopf, 1956; *Stories of the Norsemen,* Doubleday, 1961; *Hannibal,* Doubleday, 1962; *Sugarplum and Snowball* (fiction), Knopf, 1963; *Thomas Jefferson: His Many Talents,* Dodd, 1962; *Joan of Arc,* Doubleday, 1963; *Edie Changes Her Mind* (novel), Putnam, 1964; *The Challenge and the Answer* (history), Dodd, 1964; *Together in America* (history), Dodd, 1967; *A Special Bravery* (biographies), Dodd, 1967; *That's Right, Edie* (novel), Putnam, 1967; *The Eagle in Fact and Fiction,* Crown, 1967; *The Connecticut Colony* (history), Macmillan, 1969.

(With Murry Karmiller) *All Kinds of Kings in Fact and Legend: From Hammurabi to Louis XIV,* Norton, 1970; *Paul Cuffee: America's First Black Captain,* Dodd, 1970; *Speak Up, Edie* (novel), Putnam, 1970; *The Indians and the Strangers* (history), Dodd, 1972; *Women Themselves* (biographies), Dodd, 1973; *Who Found America?* (history), Golden Gate, 1974; *Frederick Law Olmstead: Partner with Nature* (biography), Dodd, 1975.

He stopped on a rise of land to look out over the acres that had been acquired for a park. He looked east and west and north and south. He thought about the land, and what it may become. ■ (From *Frederick Law Olmstead* by Johanna Johnston. Jacket design by Deanne Hollinger.)

KATZ, Bobbi 1933-

PERSONAL: Born May 2, 1933, in Newburgh, N.Y.; daughter of George and Margaret (Kahn) Shapiro; married Harold D. Katz (an optometrist), July 15, 1956; children: Joshua, Lori. *Education:* Goucher College, B.A. (with honors), 1954; also studied at Hebrew University, Jerusalem, Israel, 1955-56. *Politics:* Peace Activist, registered Democrat. *Religion:* Unitarian. *Home and office:* 205 Main St., Cornwall, N.Y. 12518. *Agent:* Curtis Brown, Ltd., 575 Madison Ave., New York, N.Y.

CAREER: Began career as a free-lance writer and fashion editor in New York, N.Y., 1954-55; Department of Welfare, Newburgh, N.Y., social worker, 1956-59; Headstart, Newburgh, N.Y., social worker, 1966-67. Greater Cornwall School District, creative writing consultant; Arts in Action, chairman, 1969-71; Newburgh NAACP, education chairman, 1964-67; Orange County Sanc and Citizens for Peace, chairman, 1960-61. *Member:* Authors Guild, Phi Beta Kappa.

WRITINGS: I'll Build My Friend A Mountain, Scholastic Book Services, 1972; *Nothing But a Dog,* Feminist Press, 1972; *Upside-Down and Inside-Out,* Watts, 1973; *The Manifesto and Me-Meg,* Watts, 1974; *1,001 Words,* Watts, 1974; *Rod and Reel Trouble,* Albert Whitman, 1974; *Snow Bunny,*

JOHANNA JOHNSTON

How was Debbie ever going to be one of them? Not by being the biggest bunny on the baby slope. That much she knew for sure. ■ (From *Snow Bunny* by Bobbi Katz. Illustrated by Michael Norman.)

Albert Whitman, 1976. Contributor of poetry to anthologies and magazines.

WORK IN PROGRESS: "I'm currently working on a series of supplementary reading books about the adventures of a fictional family traveling around the United States. In the process I'm discovering America myself."

SIDELIGHTS: "My training was as an art historian and I specialized in rare books. I've been a fashion editor, social worker and full time mom. For a number of years I had a weekly radio program called 'Arts in Action.'

"I feel a deep commitment to people and to places, and I've worked hard to create happenings to sensitize people to each other and the community and natural beauty they share. (Such events include The Hudson River Sloop Festival, 'Weed-Ins' in parks, street fairs, etc.)

"My poetry always comes from inside—from my deep need to express a feeling. The child in me writes picture books. My fiction is almost not mine. The characters emerge and seem to tell their own stories. Even when writing within rigid boundaries that editors sometimes set, I find the characters become very real to me. I care what happens to them.

"I write only for children because I desperately want to return childhood to them. I hope to join those writers and artists who delight, sensitize, and give hope to children."

Bobbie Katz has reading and speaking competence in French, Spanish, and Hebrew.

KERIGAN, Florence 1896-
(Frances Kerry)

PERSONAL: Born December 4, 1896, in Haverford, Pa.; daughter of John Joseph and Elizabeth (Harvey) Kerigan. *Education:* Attended high school in Lower Merion, Pa. *Politics:* Democrat ("usually voting independently"). *Religion:* Presbyterian. *Home and office:* 128 Arnold Rd., Ardmore, Pa. 19003.

CAREER: American Sunday School Union, Philadelphia, Pa., editorial work, 1924-45; David C. Cook Publishing Co., Elgin, Ill., editor of juveniles, 1945-46; free-lance writer, Haverford, Pa., 1946-59; Family Service of Chester County, West Chester, Pa., secretary, 1959-66; secretary for a social service group, Philadelphia, Pa., 1966-67; retired, 1967, but still does free-lance writing. *Member:* Professional Writers' Club of Philadelphia (current president), Penn Laurel Poets (past president), Philadelphia Writers' Conference (founder and past president), Main Line Writers' Club (current vice-president).

WRITINGS: June's Quest (juvenile), Lothrop, 1931; *The Secret of the Maya Well* (teen book), Dodd, 1936; (under pseudonym Frances Kerry) *Three on a Honeymoon*, Gramercy House, 1942; *Inspirational Talks for Women's Groups,* Standard Publishing, 1951; *Time and the Rivers,*

FLORENCE KERIGAN

Concordia, 1960; *Runaway from Romance,* Bouregy, 1971; *The Romance of the Moss Agate,* Bouregy, 1972; *Passion Under the Flamboyante,* Bouregy, 1974; *Hearts in Jeopardy,* Bouregy, 1975. Contributor of poetry, plays, articles, fiction, and travel pieces (more than one-thousand items in all) to magazines.

SIDELIGHTS: "I don't remember learning to read, nor when I first knew I had to write. I was about three when I asked my mother how I was going to write books when I couldn't even write, so she taught me how, and I published my first story, titled 'Elsie' at the age of five, in a children's page of a Philadelphia newspaper *(The North American).* From then on I wrote part-time, becoming actively selling when I was twenty-three. And I am still at it.

"I have given up my beloved live pets, mostly cats, and give my time aside from writing to raising house plants as my garden is a little too strenuous a job for me. My specialty is begonias, with African violets running a close second.

"Also, in my years after middle age, I have become interested in psychic phenomena because of personal experiences."

HOBBIES AND OTHER INTERESTS: Music, travel, photography, gardening.

KINES, Pat Decker 1937-
(Pat Decker Tapio)

PERSONAL: Born December 22, 1937, in Grangeville, Idaho; daughter of Floyd E. (a farmer) and Minette (Foster) Decker; married William Robertson, August 20, 1960 (divorced, August, 1965); married Einar Tapio, February 16, 1968 (divorced, February, 1975); married Clifford Kines (a personnel officer for a fire department), July 12, 1975; children: (first marriage) Diana Rose Robertson, Katherine A. Robertson, (second marriage) E. Markus Tapio. *Education:* University of Idaho, B.S.Ed., 1959; graduate study at University of Washington, Seattle, University of Alaska, and De Anza College. *Religion:* Protestant. *Residence:* San Jose, Calif.

CAREER: Teacher, 1959-61, 1965-68; composition reader in public schools in Santa Clara County, Calif., 1973—.

WRITINGS: The Lady Who Saw the Good Side of Everything, Seabury, 1975. Contributor to children's magazines.

WORK IN PROGRESS: One book similar to one already published; a juvenile book on California riverboats, illustrated by husband, Clifford Kines.

"Oh well," she said. "I always wanted to take a trip down the river." ■ (From *The Lady Who Saw the Good Side of Everything* by Pat Decker Tapio (Kines). Illustrated by Paul Galdone.)

PAT DECKER KINES

SIDELIGHTS: "The major motivation behind most of my writing is to instill a happy sort of optimism in children. I enjoy reading my material to classes everywhere and trying to encourage young writers in the joy of setting thoughts to paper."

HOBBIES AND OTHER INTERESTS: Square dancing, sewing, traveling.

KING, Billie Jean   1943-

PERSONAL: Born November 22, 1943, in Long Beach, Calif.; daughter of Willis B. (a fireman) and Betty (Jerman) Moffitt; married Larry W. King (a lawyer, promoter, and publisher), September 17, 1965. *Education:* Attended California State College (now University), Los Angeles, 1961-64. *Religion:* Protestant. *Office:* King Enterprises, 1660 South Amphlett Blvd., Suite 266, San Mateo, Calif. 94402.

CAREER: Professional tennis player, 1968—. Publisher, *Women Sports* magazine, San Mateo, Calif., 1974—. Player-coach, Philadelphia Freedoms of the World Team Tennis League, 1973-74, player, New York Sets, 1975—. *Member:* Women's Tennis Association (president, 1973-75). *Awards, honors:* Named "Sportsperson of the Year" by *Sports Illustrated,* 1972.

WRITINGS: (With Kim Chapin) *Tennis to Win,* Harper, 1970; (with Chapin) *Billie Jean,* Harper, 1974.

SIDELIGHTS: Billie Jean King began playing tennis at the age of eleven, and by the time she was eighteen had upset top-ranking Margaret Smith Court at Wimbledon. By 1974 she had won five Wimbledon singles championships and two at Forest Hills. She holds the distinction of being the first woman in tennis history to win $100,000 prize money in one year (1971), a figure exceeding the amount won by any American tennis player, male or female, at that time.

"Money is everything in sports. Big money is the common denominator. The guy in the factory can relate to me. He says, 'If she makes all that much, she *must* be good.'" Long active in improving the lot of women in tennis, she was one of nine women founding the Virginia Slims pro tour in 1971.

FOR MORE INFORMATION SEE: Owen Davidson and C. M. Jones, *Great Women Tennis Players,* Pelham Books, 1971; Phyllis Hollander, *American Women in Sports,* Grosset, 1972; Barbaralee Diamonstein, *Open Secrets,* Viking, 1972; *Ladies' Home Journal,* April, 1974.

BILLIE JEAN KING

JEAN STOUT KINNEY

KINNEY, Jean Stout   1912-

PERSONAL: Born March 17, 1912, in Waukon, Iowa; daughter of C. A. (a dentist) and Bernadette (Mooney) Stout; married William H. Brown, 1937; married second husband, C. Cleland Kinney (an artist and author), June 10, 1960; children: (previous marriage) Susan (Mrs. Thomas Fisher), Dina (Mrs. Ernest Anastasio; (stepchildren) Gwen Kinney Ryan, Peter, Thomas, Charles. *Education:* University of Iowa, B.A. in Journalism, 1934. *Politics:* Independent. *Religion:* Episcopalian. *Home and office:* P.O. Box 222, Gaylordsville, Ct. 06755.

CAREER: Biow Agency (advertising firm), copy writer, 1948-53; Grey Agency (advertising firm), copy supervisor, 1953-55; Benton & Bowles Advertising Agency, New York, N.Y., vice-president, 1956-61; Knox Reeves Advertising Corp., Minneapolis, Minn., vice-president, 1964-67; now advertising consultant and writer. Consultant, Dorland Agency, Paris, France, 1964. *Member:* Fashion Group of New York, Theta Sigma Phi. *Awards, honors:* Cited by *Printers' Ink* as one of eighteen top advertising women of all time; Jane Arden Award, State of Iowa, 1968.

WRITINGS: What Does the Tide Do?, illustrated by husband, Cle Kinney, Young Scott Books, 1966; *What Does the Sun Do?*, illustrated by Cle Kinney, Young Scott Books, 1967; *What Does the Cloud Do?*, illustrated by Cle Kinney, Young Scott Books, 1967; *Start with an Empty Nest*, Harcourt, 1968; *Living with Zest in an Empty Nest*, Hawthorn, 1970.

With Cle Kinney: *How to Tell a Living Story with Home Slides*, Rosen Press, 1963; *Who Does the Baby Look Like?*, Rosen Press, 1963; *97 Special Effects for Your Home Slide Shows*, Rosen Press, 1964; *The Neurotic Inanimates*, Rosen Press, 1964; *How to Get 20 to 90½ Off on Everything You Buy*, Parker Publishing, 1966; *21 Sure-Fire Ways to Double Your Income in One Year*, Parker Publishing, 1970; *How to Beat the High Cost of Medical Care by Treating Yourself at Home as Doctors Recommend*, Parker Publishing, 1972; *21 Kinds of American Folk Art and How to Make Each One*, Atheneum, 1972; *Fifty-Seven Tests That Reveal Your Hidden Talents*, Hawthorn, 1972; *How to Make 19 Kinds of American Folk Art from Masks to TV Commercials*, Atheneum, 1973; *23 Varieties of Ethnic Art and How to Make Each One*, Atheneum, 1976; *47 Creative Homes that Started as Bargain Buildings*, Funk & Wagnalls, 1975; *Death to Willy Wolfe*, Simon & Schuster, in press. Contributor to popular magazines.

SIDELIGHTS: "In fourth grade in Cedar Rapids, Iowa, I wrote a theme which I was allowed to read aloud. This heady experience made me know that I was going to be a writer, and from that moment on, I walked with sure-footed steps to what I am now. At the State University of Iowa, where I took journalism, I became 'campus newscaster' on WSUI, the educational radio station, and after graduation, got a job at WOC in Davenport where I wrote everything that went on the air for eighteen hours a day—all commercials, fashion shows, newscasts and special sports vignettes for a young sports announcer named Dutch Reagan who later became Ronald Reagan, Governor of California.

"Except for a trip to Chicago and another to Minneapolis, I had never been out of the state of Iowa until long after I had married, had two daughters and was divorced, but I learned early to use life as I knew it in Iowa in the stories and radio shows that I wrote. And this paid off. In my first year, when I was in my early thirties, I sold twelve short stories about a young woman who worked in a radio station and six network shows about this same woman in one year's time. I, also, wrote a better breakfast book for Kellogg Cereals which brought an invitation for me to go to New York where I became publicity director for an ad agency, but soon crossed over to do ads, television commercials and radio commercials for national accounts. Eventually, I became a vice-president of a major agency where I handled the creative work for $18 million worth of billing and had seven copywriters working for me. Twenty years went by, and, then, with my daughters through school, I remarried and left New York to live in Connecticut where for some time I have done special assignments for advertising agencies and written books, too. By now, I have produced more than twenty.

"I am fortunate that I like to write and like the research, too, without which no writing has meat. I have not looked ahead and said 'two years from now, I will be writing the great American novel' or anything like that. I have just put my foot down for one step and the back foot has come forward to take me where I wanted to go next."

KIRKUP, James   1927-
(James Falconer, Andrew James)

PERSONAL: Born April 23, 1927, in South Shields, County Durham, England; son of James Harold and Mary (Johnson) Kirkup. *Education:* King's College, University of Durham,

"Well, it's time to be going," he sighed, standing up and tucking the bamboo handle of the fan into the back of his kimono sash. His summer kimono was of fine black gauze. ■ (From *Insect Summer* by James Kirkup. Illustrated by Naoko Matsubara.)

JAMES KIRKUP

B.A. (double honors), 1941. *Agent:* Dr. Jan van Loewen, 81/83 Shaftesbury Ave., London W.C.1. *Office:* BM-Box 2780, London WCIV 6XX, England.

CAREER: University of Leeds, Leeds, England, Gregory Fellow in Poetry, 1950-52; Bath Academy of Art, Bath, England, visiting poet, 1953-56; Swedish Ministry of Education, traveling lecturer, 1956-57; University of Salamanca, Salamanca, Spain, professor of English, 1957-58; Tohoku University, Sendai, Japan, professor of English, 1959-61; University of Malaya, Kuala Lumpur, lecturer in English literature, 1961-62; visiting professor, Japan Women's University, 1964-69; Amherst College, Amherst, Mass., visiting poet, 1968-69; University of Nagoya, Nagoya, Japan, professor of English literature, 1969-72; Sheffield University, Sheffield, England; Yorkshire Arts Association, Fellow in creative writing, 1974-75; Ohio University, Athens, Ohio, Morton visiting professor in international literature, 1975—. *Member:* Royal Society of Literature (fellow). *Awards, honors:* Atlantic Award in literature, Rockefeller Foundation, 1950; Mildred Batchelder Award for Kästner translation of *The Little Man and the Big Thief,* 1970; Keats Prize for poetry, 1975.

WRITINGS—Poetry: (With Ross Nichols) *The Cosmic Shape,* Forge Press, 1946; *The Drowned Sailor and Other Poems,* Grey Walls Press, 1947; *The Creation* (epic poem), Lotus Press, 1948; *The Submerged Village and Other Poems,* Oxford University Press, 1951; *A Correct Compas-* sion and Other Poems, Oxford University Press, 1952; *A Spring Journey and Other Poems,* Oxford University Press, 1954; *The Descent Into the Cave and Other Poems,* Oxford University Press, 1957; *The Prodigal Son: Poems, 1956-1959,* Oxford University Press, 1959; *Refusal to Conform: Last and First Poems,* Oxford University Press, 1963; *Japan Marine,* Japan P.E.N. Club, 1965; *Paper Windows: Poems from Japan,* Dent, 1968; *White Shadows, Black Shadows: Poems of Peace and War,* Dent, 1969; *The Body Servant: Poems of Exile,* Dent, 1971; *A Bewick Bestiary,* MidNag Publications, 1971, 2nd edition, 1977; *Zen Gardens,* Circle Press, 1977; *Scenes from Sessku,* Circle Press, 1977; *Scenes from Sutcliffe,* MidNag Publications, 1977.

Other writings: *Upon This Rock* (play), Oxford University Press, 1965; *The Only Child: An Autobiography of Infancy,* Collins, 1957; *Sorrows, Passions, and Alarms* (autobiography), Collins, 1959; *The Love of Others* (novel), Collins, 1962; *These Horned Islands: A Journal of Japan,* Macmillan, 1962; *Tropic Temper: A Memory of Malaya,* Collins, 1963; *England, Now,* Seibido (Tokyo), 1964; *Japan Industrial,* Volumes I and II, PEP Publications (Osaka), 1964-65; *Tokyo,* Phoenix House, 1966; *Frankly Speaking,* Eichosha (Tokyo), 1966; *One Man's Russia,* 1967; *Shepherding Winds* (children's poetry anthology), 1967; *Songs and Dreams* (children's poetry anthology), 1970; *Filipinescas: Travels in the Philippines,* 1970; *Bangkok,* 1971; *Hong Kong and Macao,* 1971; *Streets of Asia,* 1971; *Insect Summer* (children's novel), Knopf, 1971; *Japan Behind the Fan,* 1972; *The Magic Drum* (children's novel), Knopf, 1973. *Heaven, Hell and Hara-Kiri: The Rise and Fall of the Japanese Superstate,* Angus and Robertson, 1975; *Anthology of Modern Japanese Poetry,* University of Queensland Press, 1978.

Translator: (With Julian Shaw) Paul Christian (real name, Christian Pitois), *The History and Practice of Magic,* Forge Press, 1952, revised by Ross Nichols, Citadel, 1963; Camara Laye, *Dark Child,* Noonday, 1954 (published in England as *The African Child,* Collins, 1965); Doan-Vinh-Thal, *Ancestral Voices,* Collins, 1956; Camara Laye, *Radiance of the King,* Collins, 1956; Arnoul and Simon Greban, *The True Mistery of the Nativity,* Oxford University Press, 1956; Bertolt Brecht, "Mother Courage and Her Children," [unpublished], 1957; P. Boileau and T. Narcejac, *Evil Eye,* Hutchinson, 1959; H. T. von Gebhardt, *Girl From Nowhere,* Criterion, 1959; Simone de Beauvoir, *Memoirs of a Dutiful Daughter,* World, 1959; Heinrich von Kleist, "The Prince of Homburg" [and] Friedrich von Schiller, "Don Carlos," in *Classic Theatre of Germany,* edited by Eric Bentley, Anchor, 1959; Heinrich E. Klier, *Summer Gone,* Bles, 1959; Jeanne Loisy, *Don Tiburcio's Secret,* Pantheon, 1960; Ernst von Salomon, *The Captive,* Weidenfeld & Nicolson, 1961; Margot Benary-Isbert, *Dangerous Spring,* Harbrace, 1961; Herbert Wendt, *It Began in Babel,* Houghton, 1962; Fritz Brunner, *Trouble in Brusada,* Verry, 1962; *The True Mistery of the Passion* (adaptation of French medieval mystery cycle by Arnoul and Simon Greban), Oxford University Press, 1962; (with Oliver Rice and Abdullah Majid) *Modern Malay Verse,* Oxford University Press, 1963; Fritz Habeck, *Days of Danger,* Harbrace, 1963; Ralph Adams Cram, *Sins of the Fathers,* Weidenfeld & Nicolson, 1963; Jacques Heurgon, *Daily Life of the Etruscans,* Macmillan, 1964; J. Andrzejewski, *The Gates of Paradise,* Weidenfeld & Nicolson, 1964; Erwin Wickert, *The Heavenly Mandate,* Collins, 1964; James Kruess, *My Great-Grandfather and I,* University of London Press, 1964; Friedrich Durrenmatt, *The*

Physicists, Grove, 1964; Camara Laye, Jean Robiquet, *Daily Life in the French Revolution*, Macmillan, 1965; *Tales of Hoffmann*, Blackie, 1965; Theodor Storm, *Immensee*, Blackie, 1965; Erich Kaestner, *The Little Man*, J. Cape, 1966.

Unpublished plays: "Masque, the Triumph of Harmony," performed at Albert Hall (London), 1955. Stage productions of new versions of: Durrenmatt, *Play Strindberg*, 1971, 1973, 1974; *Peer Gynt*, 1972; *The Magic Drum* (from a Japanese noh play), 1972-3; *Cyrano de Bergerac*, 1974; *Don Carlos*, 1975; *Prince of Homburg*, 1975; Durrenmatt, *The Conformer*, 1975; *Frank the Fifth*, 1977; *Portrait of a Planet*, 1973-77; Kleist, *Prince of Homburg*, 1977 (Chelsea Theatre Center and CBS-TV film).

Television plays: "Peach Garden," BBC TV, 1954; "Two Pigeons Flying High," BBC TV, 1955; "The True Mistery of the Passion," BBC TV, 1960, 1961. Contributor to *New Poems, New Yorker, Botteghe Oscure, The Listener, New Statesman, Spectator, Times Literary Supplement, Realites, Japan Quarterly*, and other periodicals. Former editor of *Orient/West*.

SIDELIGHTS: Kirkup is a pacifist.

FOR MORE INFORMATION SEE: Horn Book, October, 1971, February, 1974.

KISHIDA, Eriko 1929-

PERSONAL: Born January 5, 1929; daughter of Kunio (a dramatist and novelist) and Tokiko Kishida; married; children: Michi, Koto. *Education:* Graduated from Tokyo Art Academy. *Home:* Yanaka, 5, 9, 4, Daito-Ku, Tokyo, Japan.

CAREER: Poet and author of children's books.

WRITINGS: The Forgotten Autumn (poetry), Shoshi Eureka, 1955; *A Tale of a Lion* (poetry), Shoshi Eureka, 1957; *Jiojio's Crown*, Fukuinkan, 1960; *Tram-car in the Forest*, Fukuinkan, 1961; *Wake Up, Hippo*, Fukuinkan, 1962; *Hippopotamus*, translated from the Japanese by Masako Matsuno, Prentice-Hall, 1963; *The Hippo's Boat*, Fukuinkan, 1964, World, 1968; *The Goat of Mons. Seguin*, Kaiseisha, 1964; *Red Balloon*, Kaiseisha, 1966; *The Birth of Japan*, Iwasaki-Shoten, 1967; *Noah's Boat*, Iwasaki-Shoten, 1969; *Colour Books*, Sekai Shuppan Sha, 1969; *Tea Time of Winnie and Squirrel*, Sekai Shuppan Sha, 1969; *Miss Crabby*, Sekai Shuppan Sha, 1970; *The Birthday of Jiojio*, Akane Shobo, 1970; *P. I. Tchaikovsky's Swan Lake*, translated from the Japanese by Ann King Herring, Gakken, 1970.

A Camel with a Hump Was Waiting, Komine Shoten, 1971; *Helicopter of Onimaru*, Sekai Shuppan Sha, 1971; *Baby's Picture Books*, Hikari no Kuni sha, 1971; *I Love Walking*, Hikari no Kuni sha, 1971; *The Sea*, Hikari no Kuni sha, 1971; *Elephant, the Baker*, Hikari no Kuni sha, 1971; *Everyone Ran Away*, Hikari no Kuni sha, 1971; *Hallo, Hallo*, Hikari no Kuni shu, 1971; *All Are Friends*, Hikari no Kuni sha, 1972; *Ripen Red Apples*, Hikari no Kuni sha, 1972; *Ball's Rolling*, Hikari no Kuni sha, 1972; *How Heavy!*, Hikari no Kuni sha, 1972; *Who's It?*, Hikari no Kuni sha, 1972; *Sock is Out*, Hikari no Kuni sha, 1972; *Picture Books of Baby's Life*, Shufu to Seikatsu sha, 1972;

ERIKO KISHIDA

Thank You, Shufu to Seikatsu sha, 1972; *Hallo, Friend*, Shufu to Seikatsu sha, 1972; *Sleepy Cat*, Shufu to Seikatsu sha, 1972; *The Fox That Has Got Home*, Kodansha, 1973; *Jiojio the Baker*, Akane Shobo, 1975.

SIDELIGHTS: "I was born in a suburb of Tokyo, where you could see farms and fields spreading wide so far. My father was a dramatist, who had studied dramaturgy, under J. Copeau and G. Pitoëff in France, wrote many plays, some novels and, later, essays. As my mother, studying English literature, had once helped to translate *Mother Goose's Melody*, she led us children—my only sister Kyoko and me—into the world of old songs of England and Scotland. Father would tell us stories of France, particularly 'La chevre de M. Seguin' out of *Lettres de mon Moulin* by A. Daudet. We just put ourselves in M. Seguin's place, when he called for his goat with his horn, and in the kid's when the wolf emerged.

"And so, thanks to our parents, we were able to read some of the foreign juvenile stories and nursery rhymes, though there were so few of them rendered into Japanese.

"Every year we spent our summer vacation at our villa in Kita-Karuizawa at the foot of Mt. Asama. The life there was such a great influence upon us children that it has haunted us ever since; little wild animals, birds and insects; trees with their boughs stretching out in the fragrant air, mountains that rise one above another, and deep valleys and streams with cool water.

"What a wonderful idea!" The little bird hopped up and down with excitement. "My eggs would be quite safe in your crown." ■ (From *The Lion and the Bird's Nest* by Eriko Kishida. Illustrated by Chiyoko Nakatani.)

"First, when I was a student at Tokyo Art Academy, the tree was the 'Leitmotiv' for me. And then as I was forced to leave oil-painting with illness, tuberculosis, I began to write verses that I had been so strongly attracted by since childhood, and chanced to write the verses of 'Animals Twelve Months,' an LP record, where I depicted different animals; of which 'Hippo' called a picture book *Wake Up, Hippo* came into being, with lovely pictures illustrated by Mrs. Chiyoko Nakatani, a classmate at the Art Academy.

"There had been two picture books by us before 'Hippo' and many followed it thereafter: *Hippo's Boat, The Fox That has Got Home, The Goat of Mons. Seguin,* etc. It was not only because there was none for little children adapted from 'La chevre de M. Seguin' that I did it, but, also, on account of its irresistible charms enticing us into making a picture book. *The Fox That has Got Home* is a work after my heart in these days; where a tree, a fox and a flying squirrel of my beloved Kita-Karuizawa make their appearances; Mrs. Nakatani drew beautiful pictures with coloured pencils for the first time."

KONKLE, Janet Everest   1917-

PERSONAL: Born November 5, 1917, in Grand Rapids, Mich.; daughter of Charles A. (a high school principal) and Minnie (Koegler) Everest; married Arthur J. Konkle (a lumber dealer), February 14, 1941; children: Kraig Everest,

Jill Marie, Dan Jackson. *Education:* University of Michigan, student, 1937-38; Western Michigan University, B.S. in Ed., 1939. *Politics:* Republican. *Religion:* Methodist. *Home:* 1360 Oakleigh Rd., N.W., Grand Rapids, Mich.

CAREER: Grand Rapids (Mich.) schools, elementary teacher, 1939-41, 1952-60, kindergarten teacher, 1960—. *Member:* Council of Performing Arts for Children (director, 1969-71), National Education Association, Michigan Education Association, Michigan Association for Childhood Education (president, 1969-71; state board), Grand Rapids Education Association, Grand Rapids Association for Childhood Education (kindergarten vice-president, 1962-64; newsletter editor, 1964-65; president, 1965-67), Amateur Photo Club (president, 1950-52), Grand Rapids Camera Club (secretary, 1950-53), Western Michigan Cat Society (secretary, 1959, president, 1963), Delta Kappa Gamma (Eta chapter president, 1968-70), Delta Delta Delta (president, 1964-65). *Awards, honors:* Named "Photographer of the Year" by Grand Rapids Camera Club, 1951, 1953; *J. Hamilton Hamster* chosen by the English-Speaking Union, 1957, as ambassador book to be sent overseas.

WRITINGS: Once There Was A Kitten, 1951, *The Kitten and the Parakeet,* 1952, *Christmas Kitten,* 1953, *Easter Kitten,* 1955, *Tabby's Kittens,* 1956, *J. Hamilton Hamster,* 1957, *The Sea Cart,* Abingdon, 1961, *Susie Stock Car,* 1961, *Schoolroom Bunny,* 1965, *The Raccoon Twins,* 1972 (all published by Childrens, except as indicated). Contributor to *Childcraft.*

So it was the happiest Christmas of all! ■ (From *Christmas Kitten* by Janet Konkle.)

JANET EVEREST KONKLE

SIDELIGHTS: "I was born in Grand Rapids and grew up loving books. The neighborhood school I attended, fortunately, had a library which was open evenings. A highlight in those days was going back to school after dinner and choosing a book to read from the library. Many times I would re-choose an old favorite and read it over and over. I loved fairy tales and stories of long ago and far-off places at that time. In school I liked to write original stories, yet I disliked reading them aloud in class. I always felt they were too private to share with others.

"It happened that I was chosen to be senior class historian, so I was first 'published' writing the history for the yearbook, 'The Legend' a la Hiawatha style. At the same time my interest in photography was awakened. Selected to be the yearbook snapshot editor, I had to learn to take pictures in school using time exposures, because flash bulbs were not available for amateurs at that time. I also learned how to develop pictures in a makeshift darkroom (on the back porch after dark) at our cottage on Lake Michigan. My first pictures were, as I remember, dune grass shadows on the sand, waves against the pier, and children playing in the sand and water.

"Later when I married and had my own children, these two hobbies merged. Seeing photo illustrated books for children on the library shelves, the spark of creativity was ignited and I tried my hand at writing and illustrating. Luckily my first attempt, *Once There Was a Kitten,* was accepted for publication. In it I used my daughter, Jill, and a family of kittens we had. In later books my other children and other family pets were used."

All but one of Janet Konkle's books have been illustrated with her own photographs; her photography has won many national awards and has been included in photographic magazines and books. Family pets have included cats, kittens, parakeets, hamsters, chickens, rabbits, a duck and a horse, and several of these have been subjects for her book illustrations. She has been a judge at the annual Western Michigan Cat Show since 1962. Other interests are antiques, square dancing, swimming, and traveling.

KRANTZ, Hazel (Newman) 1920-

PERSONAL: Born January 29, 1920, in Brooklyn, N.Y.; daughter of Louis John and Eva Newman; married Michael Krantz, 1942; children: Laurence Ira, Margaret Ann, Vincent. *Education:* New York University, B.S., 1942; Hofstra College, M.S., 1959. *Home:* 875 Leeds Dr., North Bellmore, Long Island, N.Y. 11710. *Agent:* McIntosh & Otis, Inc., 18 East 41st St., New York, N.Y. 10017.

CAREER: Fashion co-ordinator, copywriter, New York, N.Y., 1942-45; elementary school teacher, Nassau County, N.Y., 1957-68; *True Frontier* magazine, editor, 1969-72; *db, The Sound Engineering Magazine,* Plainview, N.Y., copy editor, 1973—. *Member:* New York Ontological Society.

WRITINGS: Hundred Pounds of Popcorn, Vanguard, 1961; *Freestyle for Michael,* Vanguard, 1964; *The Secret Raft,* Vanguard, 1965; *Tippy,* Vanguard, 1968; *A Pad of Your Own,* Pyramid Communications, 1973.

WORK IN PROGRESS: Windows: The Art of Creative Living for Girls; Herkimer and the Computer Plant.

SIDELIGHTS: "I grew up in the suburbs of New York City, in Westchester County, and since I grew up I have lived in another New York suburb, Nassau County. So one might say that I'm an expert on crab grass and Little League, etc. My father was an engineer and my mother interested in

HAZEL KRANTZ

Something about the Author

The popcorn factory was located in the Taylor kitchen. But very soon it became clear that Mrs. Taylor's chicken frying pan would never be able to make fifteen hundred bags of popcorn fast enough. ■ (From *100 Pounds of Popcorn* by Hazel Krantz. Illustrated by Charles Geer.)

local politics. They believed that a girl should educate herself to her full capacity and do work in the world as well as keep a home.

"My teachers, from earliest elementary school, encouraged my writing. When it was time for me to teach school, I tried to do that with my students too. From the time I was six years old until the present, it was important for me to have a 'reading book.' If I can't get to the library, I feel frustrated. Although my parents weren't much interested in religion, they permitted me to go to religious school for nine years and this very excellent school run by Temple Israel, in New Rochelle, N.Y., had a profound influence on my life.

"I always had the feeling that if people lived the way they were intended, most of the world's troubles just wouldn't exist. Much to my joy, my son, Larry, discovered the Ontologists, a group of people from many backgrounds who have one common aim, to allow the truth of themselves to express itself in every moment. I'm grateful that I have the opportunity, through writing for young people, to show them that they are beautiful and that there is a way to make their light shine through. My husband believes this too, and encourages my work. I am very proud of my children, who have chosen to serve others. My son, Larry, is a medical doctor and Margie is a psychologist. Vincent is studying nutrition.

"I think the most important thing anyone ever said to me about writing is 'what if.' That is all writing comes to after all. You start with an idea and then go on to 'what if this happened, then what would follow?' For example, *Hundred Pounds of Popcorn* came from the fact that my husband really did find a hundred-pound bag of popping corn in the street. I started thinking 'what if people found that and decided to sell it' and the rest of the story wrote itself. Often, the characters in a story come alive and they just seem to speak by themselves. It's exciting to write; even though you're the author, you don't really know what's going to happen next."

HOBBIES AND OTHER INTERESTS: Gardening, sewing, tennis, the Women's Movement, free-lancing articles and stories, writing for *Emissary,* the magazine of the Ontological Society.

KUMIN, Maxine (Winokur) 1925-

PERSONAL: Born 1925, in Philadelphia, Pa.; daughter of Peter and Doll (Simon) Winokur; married Victor M. Kumin, 1946; children: Jane, Judith, Daniel. *Education:* Radcliffe College, A.B., 1946, A.M., 1948. *Home and office:* 40 Bradford Rd., Newton Highlands, Warner, N.H. 03278. *Agent:* Curtis Brown Ltd., 575 Madison Ave., New York, N.Y. 10025.

CAREER: Scholar of the Radcliffe Institute for Independent Study, 1961-63; visiting professor, University of Massachusetts, Columbia, Princeton, 1970—. *Member:* Poetry Society of America, Radcliffe Alumnae Association. *Awards, honors:* Pulitzer Prize for poetry, 1973.

WRITINGS:—Poetry: *Halfway,* Holt, 1961; *The Privilege,* Harper, 1965; *The Nightmare Factory,* Harper, 1970; *Up*

Even in fine weather, the water rises and falls with a great sucking surge. ■ (From *When Great-Grandmother was Young* by Maxine Kumin. Illustrated by Don Almquist.)

Country, Harper, 1972; *House, Bridge, Fountain, Gate*, Viking, 1975.

Novels: *Through Dooms of Love*, Harper, 1965; *The Passions of Uxport*, Harper, 1968; *The Abduction*, Harper, 1971; *The Designated Heir*, Viking, 1974.

MAXINE KUMIN

Juvenile: *Sebastian and the Dragon*, Putnam, 1960; *Spring Things*, Putnam, 1961; *A Summer Story*, Putnam, 1961; *Follow the Fall*, Putnam, 1961; *A Winter Friend*, Putnam, 1961; *Mittens in May*, Putnam, 1962; *No One Writes a Letter to the Snail*, Putnam, 1962; (with Anne Sexton) *Eggs of Things*, Putnam, 1963; *Archibald the Traveling Poodle*, Putnam, 1963; (with Anne Sexton) *More Eggs of Things*, Putnam, 1964; *Speedy Digs Downside Up*, Putnam, 1964; *The Beach Before Breakfast*, Putnam, 1964; *Paul Bunyan*, Putnam, 1966; *Faraway Farm*, Norton, 1967; *The Wonderful Babies of 1809*, Putnam, 1968; *When Grandmother was Young*, Putnam, 1969; *When Mother was Young*, Putnam, 1970; *When Great Grandmother was Young*, Putnam, 1971; (with Anne Sexton) *Joey and the Birthday Present*, McGraw, 1971; (with Anne Sexton) *The Wizard's Tears*, McGraw, 1975.

WORK IN PROGRESS: A novel; children's books.

FOR MORE INFORMATION SEE: Kirkus, January 15, 1961; *Library Journal*, April 1, 1961, November 1, 1971; *Saturday Review*, May 6, 1961, December 25, 1965, March 25, 1972; *Christian Science Monitor*, August 9, 1961; *Choice*, January, 1966; *Boston Globe*, October 12, 1972, September 28, 1971, June 8, 1975; *New York Times Book Review*, November 19, 1972.

KURATOMI, Chizuko 1939-

PERSONAL: Born March 30, 1939, in Tokyo, Japan; daughter of Kazuma and Matsuko (Kawamura) Kuratomi. *Education:* Attended Aoyama Gakiun Women's College, 1957-59, 1963-64. *Home:* 17-9 2-chome, Shinmachi, Setagaya-ku, Tokyo, Japan.

CAREER: Shiko-sha Co., Ltd. (publisher), Tokyo, Japan, editor of children's books, 1964—. *Awards, honors:* Sankei Press prize for *Mr. Bear Goes to Sea*, 1968.

WRITINGS—All originally published by Shiko-sha: *Okasan wa doko* (title means "Where is Mother?"), 1966;

CHIZUKO KURATOMI

Donkumasan, 1966, English translation published as *Remember Mr. Bear*, MacDonald, 1968; *Chisana ohanashi* (title means "The Little Stories," parables from the Bible), 1966; *Boku Hanataro* (title means "I Learned That"), 1967; *Donkumasan umi e iku*, 1967, English translation published as *Mr. Bear Goes to Sea*, MacDonald, 1968; *Ohayo* (title means "Good Morning"), 1968; *Donkumasan sora o tobu* (title means "Mr. Bear Goes to Fly"), 1968.

Donkumasan no rappa, 1970, English translation published as *Mr. Bear's Trumpet*, Macdonald; *Donkumasan no otetsudai*, 1971, English translation published as *Mr. Bear and the Robbers*, Dial, 1975; *Donkumasan wa ekicho*, 1972, English translation published as *Mr. Bear, Station-Master*, Macdonald; *Norainu*, 1973, English translation published as *Pim and the Fisherboy* by Nancy Chambers, Macdonald, 1975; *Jam-jam Donkumasan*, 1973, English translation published as *Mr. Bear and Apple Jam*, Macdonald; *Donkumasan no Christmas*, 1974, English translation published as *Mr. Bear's Christmas*, Macdonald, 1974; *E-o-kaku Donkumasan*, 1975, English translation published as *Mr. Bear's Drawing*, Macdonald; *Donkumasan no komoriuta*, 1976, English translation published as *Mr. Bear, Babyminder*, Macdonald, 1976. Editor and contributor of poems for children to *Kodomo-no-Sekai* (a children's pictorial magazine).

LASHER, Faith B.   1921-

PERSONAL: Born January 26, 1921, in Lincoln County, Mont.; daughter of Benjamen and Clara (Weaver) Nelson; married Richard L. Hoppie, 1944 (died, 1958); married Don R. Lasher, 1962; children: Michael Jay. *Education:* St. Patrick's School of Nursing, Missoula, Mont., R.N., 1944. *Religion:* Protestant. *Home:* 119 Water St., Gaithersburg, Md. 20760.

CAREER: Registered nurse and licensed real estate saleswoman. *Member:* Women in Communications.

WRITINGS: Hubert Hippo's World (juvenile), Childrens Press, 1971. Contributor of fiction, poems, and articles to *Primary Treasure, Happy Times, Wee Wisdom, Rotarian, Bottle News,* and other magazines.

FAITH B. LASHER

Hippo means horse, and potamus means river. ■ (From *Hubert Hippo's World* by Faith B. Lasher.)

Something about the Author

WORK IN PROGRESS: Articles for collectors and antique magazines.

HOBBIES AND OTHER INTERESTS: Photography, vegetable gardening.

FOR MORE INFORMATION SEE: National Antiques Review, September, 1975.

LAUGHBAUM, Steve 1945-

PERSONAL: Surname pronounced Loff-baum; born August 24, 1945, in Nashville, Tenn.; son of Harry Kenneth (an artist) and Junita Laughbaum; married August, 1971 (divorced, 1974). *Education:* Auburn University, BFA; attended University of Tennessee, two years. *Religion:* Lutheran. *Office:* United Methodist Publishing House, 201 8th Avenue, S., Nashville, Tenn. 37202.

CAREER: Illustrator. *Military service:* U.S. Navy. *Member:* Art Directors Club.

ILLUSTRATOR: Presentness, Abingdon, 1974; *God Made Me, I've Got to be Me,* 1975; *Super Food Cookbook for Kids,* Review & Herald, 1976; *Weather or Not,* Abingdon, 1976; *Television: A Guide for Christians,* Abingdon, 1976; *Love is a Magic Penny,* Abingdon, 1977.

SIDELIGHTS: "I enjoy most anything creative; stained glass, clothing design, leather work, sculpture, welding, painting, sailing, camping, photography and print making."

STEVE LAUGHBAUM

LEFLER, Irene (Whitney) 1917-

PERSONAL: Born May 29, 1917, in Hominy Falls, W.Va.; daughter of Hughie Mac and Mary Magdalene (Whitney) Jamison; married James Cameron Lefler, December 2, 1939 (divorced, 1964); children: Mary Ellen (Mrs. Norman Wilson), James M., John G. *Education:* Mid-Ohio Practical Nurse program, graduate, 1965; Oakland Community College, graduate, 1975. *Politics:* Democrat. *Religion:* Seventh-Day Adventist. *Home and office address:* Box 292, Pontiac, Mich. 48056. *Agent:* Dorothy Markinko, McIntosh & Otis, Inc., 18 East 41st St., New York, N.Y. 10017.

CAREER: Licensed practical nurse, 1965; Pontiac State Hospital, Pontiac, Mich., practical nurse, 1968-71; Starr Commonwealth for Boys, Albion, Mich., housemother, 1965; Pontiac General Hospital, Pontiac, Mich., practical nurse, 1965-67; free-lance writer, 1967—. *Member:* International Philosda Club, American Museum of Natural History, National Historical Society, National Geographic Society, Audio-Visual Association, Smithsonian Associates, Michigan Library Association, International Platform Association, Puppeteers of America, Public Health Services of Seventh-Day Adventists, Fellowship of Christian Puppeteers, Christian Writers, Oakland Writers' Workshop.

WRITINGS: Bessie Bee, Southern Publishing, 1972. Contributor of radio scripts, short stories, poetry, and articles to *Guide, Primary Treasure, Our Little Friend, Teen Power, Stories for Children, Your Story Hour, The Secret Place,* and *Pontiac Times.*

WORK IN PROGRESS: Annie Ant for Southern Publishing; a complete nature series for Southern Publishing; *Princess of Aracoma; Balto.*

SIDELIGHTS: "All my adult life I've enjoyed working with and writing for children, whether it be in my church, a youth camp, or in schools.

"While doing research for a short story, I read an informative statement about honeybees, which led me to study them, and become 'hooked' on the subject. Since I write for children, I checked and learned an in-depth study was needed on bees and other wild creatures, so I began writing my nature series. All my creatures will live in Clover Meadow, an area in West Virginia, where I was born and reared. *Bessie Bee* came off the press in 1972, and other books in this series will be *Annie Ant, Humphrey Humming Bird, Beverly Beaver, Melody Meadowlark,* etc.

"Other books in progress are: *Race to Rome,* to show how sled dogs saved the day during an epidemic in Alaska, and to teach children about Eskimoes through the eyes of an Eskimo boy. *Pony Trail to Wyandotte* is ready to go to my agent. This book will cover the life of Shawnee Indians, as seen through the eyes of an Indian boy. I lived in areas this nomadic tribe survived in, and, also, lived in a town my hero, finally settled in.

"I slant my writings toward junior aged young people, and endeavor to teach them more about life of the past, and how to cope with problems of growing up in today's world. My materials are derived from my own personal experiences and experiences of people I know, and from pages of history. I may use as characters some of the patients I've taken care of

IRENE LEFLER

as a nurse, or use incidents that happened to me or others in the field of medicine, or while a housemother in a private school for boys.

"I am a puppeteer, and write my own religious and education scripts, which will be used in churches and schools where I'll be taking my puppet theater. I recently completed a workshop that enables me to now conduct my own workshops in puppetry and record my own programs, and will, hopefully, conduct such workshops in schools, clubs, and hospitals, etc."

FOR MORE INFORMATION SEE: Pontiac Press, April 3, 1971; Oakland Press, April 3, 1971, September 6, 1972; West Virginia Hillbilly, Spring, 1971.

LESTER, Julius B. 1939-

PERSONAL: Born January 27, 1939, in St. Louis, Mo.; son of W. D. (a minister) and Julia (Smith) Lester; married Joan Steinau (a researcher), December 22, 1962; children: Jody Simone, Malcolm Coltrane. Education: Fisk University, B.A., 1960. Home: Amherst, Mass.

CAREER: Singer-songwriter, recorded two albums for Vanguard Records; host-producer of live radio show, WBAI-FM, New York, N.Y., 1968-75; co-host of weekly television show, WNET, New York, N.Y., 1970-72; instructor, Black History, New School for Social Research, New York, N.Y., 1968-70; associate professor, Department of Afro-American Studies, University of Massachusetts,

Amherst, Mass., 1971—. Awards, honors: To Be a Slave was a Newbery Honor Book, 1969, and received the Nancy Bloch Award, 1969; Long Journey Home received the Lewis Carroll Shelf award, 1972 and was a National Book Award finalist, 1973.

WRITINGS: (With Pete Seeger) The 12-String Guitar as Played by Leadbelly, Oak, 1965; Look Out, Whitney! Black Power's Gon' Get Your Mama, Dial, 1968; To Be a Slave (ALA Notable Book), Dial, 1968; Revolutionary Notes, Richard Baron Publishing Co., 1969; Black Folktales, Richard Baron Publishing Co., 1969; Search for the New Land, Dial, 1969; The Seventh Son: The Thought and Writings of W.E.B. Du Bois, two volumes, Random House, 1971; (compiler with Rae Pace Alexander) Young Black in America, Random House, 1971; Long Journey Home, Dial, 1972; Two Love Stories, Dial, 1972; The Knee High Man and Other Tales (ALA Notable Book), Dial, 1972; (with David Gahr) Who I Am, Dial, 1974. Associate editor, Sing Out, 1964—; contributing editor, Broadside of New York, 1964—; contributor to Sounds & Fury.

WORK IN PROGRESS: Compiling a Peter La Farge songbook; a book of interviews with twelve Negro traditional singers; a book on black power, for International Publishers.

FOR MORE INFORMATION SEE: New York Times Book Review, November 3, 1968, November 9, 1969, February 4, 1973; The Nation, June 22, 1970; Horn Book, October, 1972, April, 1973, June, 1975.

JULIUS B. LESTER

It is estimated that some fifty million people were taken from the continent during the years of the slave trade. These fifty million were, of course, the youngest, the strongest, those most capable of bringing great profit, first to the slave trader, and later to the slave owner.■ (From *To Be a Slave* by Julius Lester. Illustrated by Tom Feelings.)

I. E. LEVINE

LEVINE, I(srael) E. 1923-

PERSONAL: Born August 30, 1923, in New York, N.Y.; son of Albert E. and Sonia (Silver) Levine; married Joy Elaine Michael, 1946; children: David Myer, Carol Lynn. *Education:* City College of New York, Bachelor of Social Science, 1946. *Home:* 140-41 69th Rd., Flushing, N.Y. 11367. *Office:* City College Public Relations, Convent Ave. at 138th St., New York, N.Y. 10031.

CAREER: City College of New York, New York, N.Y., publicity assistant, 1946-50, assistant director of public relations, 1950-54, director of public relations, 1954—. *Military service:* U.S. Army Air Forces, 1943-45; became second lieutenant; received Air Medal with four oak leaf clusters, European Theater ribbon with three battle stars, Presidential Unit citation. *Member:* Authors Guild, Metropolitan College Public Relations Council (treasurer, 1959), American College Public Relations Association, American Alumni Council, City College Alumni Association, Queens Valley Home Owners Association.

WRITINGS: (Co-author) *Techniques of Supervision,* National Foremen's Institute, 1954.

Youth books: *The Discoverer of Insulin: Dr. Frederick Banting,* Messner, 1959; *Conqueror of Smallpox: Dr. Edward Jenner,* Messner, 1960; *Behind the Silken Curtain: Townsend Harris,* Messner, 1961; *Inventive Wizard: George Westinghouse,* Messner, 1962; *Champion of World Peace: Dag Hammarskjold,* Messner, 1962; *Miracle Man of*

Printing: Ottmar Mergenthaler, Messner, 1964; *Electronics Pioneer: Lee DeForest,* Messner, 1964; *Young Man in the White House: John Fitzgerald Kennedy,* Messner, 1964; *Oliver Cromwell,* Messner, 1966; *Spokesman for the Free World,* Messner, 1967; *Lenin: The Man Who Made a Revolution,* Messner, 1969; *The Many Faces of Slavery,* Messner, 1975. Contributor to *This Week, Better Homes and Gardens, Writer's Digest, Nation's Business, The Rotarian.* Executive editor, *City College Alumnus,* 1954-74.

SIDELIGHTS: "I was born and brought up in New York City where I attended DeWitt Clinton High School and The City College of New York. Both schools have had a long tradition of educating future journalists and other professional writers. In college I majored in physics, but in my junior year, the writing bug infected me, and I changed my course of study to English and the social sciences. However, I never regretted my science studies, for as it turned out a number of articles and books I have written have dealt with scientific subjects, within a biographical or historical framework.

"It seems to me that books of biography and history have a special importance for young people today. The world is complicated and uncertain. Youngsters are desperately searching for guideposts that will help them shape their aspirations and ideals and aid them in finding a way not only of making a living, but of making a life. Biography, which sets forth in an honest and realistic way the example of men and women who have tried to meet this challenge, and history, which places our life and times in a broader perspective, are sorely needed by modern youth. They offer truths that are timeless and universal.

"If the subject is interesting to me and to my own children, I feel he will be interesting to others as well. . . . My children have taught me that the greatest sin is to be patronizing, to write down. Youngsters today are astute enough to recognize . . . a life story which the author has carefully filtered through rose-tinted lenses."

HOBBIES AND OTHER INTERESTS: Golf, music, gardening.

FOR MORE INFORMATION SEE: Long Island Press, June 10, 1962.

LIEBERS, Arthur 1913-

PERSONAL: Born January 7, 1913, in New York, N.Y.; son of Meyer (a merchant) and Marie (Kaplan) Liebers; married Ruth Lampert (now a teacher and writer), December 22, 1951. *Education:* Attended New York University, 1929-31, Columbia University, 1931-33. *Home:* Halsey La., Remsenburg, N.Y. 11960.

CAREER: Free-lance writer, part-time, 1940-52, full-time, 1952—. *Civil Service Leader,* member of editorial staff, 1942-46; *Boxoffice* (motion picture trade paper), member of editorial staff, 1946; Spadea Schools of New Jersey and New York, head of civil service department, 1948-52. Special writing projects for Laird, Bissell & Meeds, New York, N.Y., and for *Scholastic Magazines* and Scholastic Books Services. *Member:* American Newspaper Guild, Dog Fanciers Luncheon Club, Suffolk Dog Obedience Training Club (Long Island). *Awards, honors:* Book, *Companion Dogs,*

This young woman is a working lineman, demonstrating the safety equipment used in climbing utility poles. ■ (From *You Can be an Electrician* by Arthur Liebers. Photo by American Telephone and Telegraph Company.)

named book of the year by Dog Writers Association of America, 1960.

WRITINGS: (With C. Vollmer) *Investigator's Handbook,* 1954, *Pharmacist License Tests,* 1955, *Oil Burner Installer,* 1956, *Insurance Broker, Fire, Casualty, and Allied Lines,* 1957, *Insurance Agent and Broker,* 1957, *Life Insurance Agent,* 1957, *Notary Public,* 1957, *How to Take Tests and Pass Them,* 1958, *Insurance Agent, Accident and Health,* 1958 (all published by Arco); *Police Civil Service Manual,* Allcat; *Inventor's Complete Guide Book,* Ottenheimer, 1959; *Real Estate Salesman and Broker,* Arco, 1959; *How to Get a Civil Service Job,* Ottenheimer, 1959; *Free!,* Arco, 1959.

Relax with Yoga, Sterling, 1960; *How to Pass Employment Tests,* Arco, 1960, 3rd edition, 1967; *Companion Dogs,* A. S. Barnes, 1960; *Guide to North American Coins,* Arco, 1961; *Refrigeration License,* Arco, 1961; *Encyclopedia of Pleasure Boating,* A. S. Barnes, 1961; *Motorboat Owner's Handbook,* Ottenheimer, 1961; *Complete Book of Winter Sports,* Coward, 1964; *United States Coins,* Putnam, 1965;

Engineers' Handbook Illustrated (ALA book list), Key Publishing Co., 1968; *Fifty Favorite Hobbies,* Hawthorn, 1968; *Complete Book of Sky Diving,* Coward, 1968; *How to Start a Profitable Retirement Business,* Pilot, 1968; *How to Get the Job You Want Overseas,* Pilot, 1968.

Starting Your Own Business, Pilot, 1972; *Complete Book of Cross Country Skiing and Touring,* Coward, 1973; *Jobs in Construction,* Lothrop, 1973; *You Can Be a Carpenter,* Lothrop, 1973; *You Can Be a Plumber,* Lothrop, 1973; *You Can Be an Electrician,* Lothrop, 1974; *You Can Be a Mechanic,* Lothrop, 1975; *You Can Be a Machinist,* Lothrop, 1976; *You Can Be a Printer,* Lothrop, 1976; *You Can Be a Professional Driver,* Lothrop, 1976; *Liebers' Guide to Organizing and Running a Club,* Morrow, 1977.

Series on training dogs: (With Dorothy Hardy) *How to Raise and Train a Basset Hound,* 1959, *How to Raise and Train a Dalmatian, How to Raise and Train a German Short-haired Pointer, How to Raise and Train a Maltese, How to Raise and Train a Pedigreed or Mixed Breed Puppy,* 1958, *How to Housebreak and Train Your Dog,* (author with Georgie Sheppard) *How to Raise and Train a Pomeranian,* (with Paul Jeffries) *How to Raise and Train a Weimaraner,* 1959, (with Dana Miller) *How to Raise and Train a Yorkshire Terrier,* 1959 (all published by Sterling). Contributor to *Book of Knowledge, New York Sunday Times, Nation,* and other periodicals.

Editor: *Laughs for Teens,* Grosset; *Wit's End,* Grosset, 1963. Former managing editor, *Police and Fireman National Press;* editor, *Legislative Conference News,* 1963—; editor, hobby and humor section, Scholastic Publishing Co., *Newstime,* 1965-66.

SIDELIGHTS: "After a while, book writing becomes routine. You learn what makes a good book and then you repeat it. After I finish a book, I forget all about it. If people call me up or write to me for facts, I refer them to my books. Some of the subjects I write about interest me personally as hobbies. The others are just assignments."

LOBSENZ, Amelia

PERSONAL: Born in Greensboro, N.C.; daughter of Leo (a furniture manufacturer) and Florence Freitag; married Norman Lobsenz (divorced); married Harry H. Abrahams (chief of surgery, Syosset Hospital); children: Michael, Kay. *Education:* Attended Agnes Scott College. *Home:* The Columns, Red Ground Rd., Old Westbury, N.Y. *Office:* Lobsenz-Stevens, Inc., 645 Madison Ave., New York, N.Y. 10022.

CAREER: Edward Gottlieb and Associates, New York, N.Y., director of magazine and book department, 1949-56; Lobsenz Public Relations Co., Inc., New York, N.Y., president, 1956-75; Lobsenz-Stevens, Inc., New York, N.Y., chairman of the board and chief executive officer, 1975—. Free-lance writer for magazines. National Cultural Center, Long Island chairman; Hofstra University, council member. *Member:* Public Relations Society of America (New York chapter board of directors), National Association of Science Writers, American Society of Journalists and Authors, American Women in Radio and Television, Mystery Writers of America, Overseas Press Club, Long Island Public Relations Association, Publicity Club of Chicago.

AMELIA LOBSENZ

"The second book, *Kay Everett Works DX,* carries my characters into new adventures. This one is set in North Carolina where I was born. Thus, I have the tendency to use what I have experienced, coupled with my imaginings.

"Today, I have a teen-age daughter whom I named Kay, after the character in the books. She's not a ham, but a ranking tennis player.

"I divide my time between writing and running a large public relations firm, Lobsenz-Stevens, Inc., so I am busy indeed. Of course, the writing ability and the imagination of an author are valuable in doing public relations, too, so my life seems to continue to build upon my experiences."

LORD, (Doreen Mildred) Douglas   1904-

PERSONAL: Born September 25, 1904, in Portsmouth, Hampshire, England; daughter of John and Gertrude (DeTopp) Lord. *Education:* Educated privately. *Religion:* Roman Catholic. *Home:* Nazareth House, Lawrence Rd., Southsea PO5 1NW, Hants., England.

CAREER: Isle of Wight Times, Ryde, Isle of Wight, reporter, 1921-26; full-time writer, except for periodic secretarial jobs, 1926—. *War service:* Women's Royal Naval Service, writer, 1939-41; invalided out. *Member:* Romantic Novelists' Association, Poetry Society, Catholic Poetry Society, Women's Press Club of London, Portsmouth Soroptimists, Portsmouth Dickens Fellowship. *Awards, honors:* Second prize, Romantic Novelists' Association, 1960, for *Yellow Flower;* Catholic Women of the Year as children's author, 1970.

WRITINGS: Kay Everett Calls CQ (Junior Literary Guild selection), Vanguard, 1951; *Kay Everett Works DX* (Junior Literary Guild selection), Vanguard, 1952. Some of her "How to Write . . ." articles have been anthologized including "How to Write the 'How to' Article," originally published in *Scribner's,* and "How to Write the Medical Article" and "How to Write the Personality Profile," first published in *Writer's Digest.* Contributor of some three hundred articles to *Coronet, Reader's Digest, This Week, Pageant, Nation's Business, Parade, American Weekly, McCall's, Better Living, Collier's, Woman's Home Companion, Family Circle, Woman's Day, Ladies Home Journal, Redbook,* and other magazines.

SIDELIGHTS: "In many ways Kay Everett, the heroine of my two teen-age books, is a facsimile of myself as a teen-age girl. I was adventuresome and yearning for travel. I became a radio ham just like Kay and entered ham contests. The very trip that Kay and her friends took across the country follows a trip I took by car as a free-lance magazine writer. The interesting thing is that I have the character Kay using a trailer, and I must have been unconsciously yearning for a recreational vehicle because years later I bought a Travco motor home to go out West.

"In fact, my family and I traveled the *Kay Everett Calls CQ* route in our Travco motor home! Of course, the actual adventures in the book are fiction, but the terrain, background, scenery are authentic and accurate as I viewed them:

(DOREEN MILDRED) DOUGLAS LORD

136   Something about the Author

WRITINGS—All children's books except as indicated: *Spirit of Wearde Hall,* Carey Press, 1927; *Doreen Douglas, Schoolgirl,* Pilgrim Press, 1933; *Joan at Seascale,* Warne, 1936; *Lynnette at Carisgate,* Epworth, 1937; *Margery the Mystery,* Epworth, 1939; *Yellow Flower* (adult novel), Ward, Locke, 1961; *Kiwi Jane,* Odhams, 1962; *The Cypress Box,* Geoffrey Chapman, 1963; *To Win Their Crown,* Geoffrey Chapman, 1963; *Children at the Court of St. Peter,* Geoffrey Chapman, 1963; (translator from the French) Henry Daniel-Rops, *The Wonderful Life of St. Paul,* Geoffrey Chapman, 1965.

Poem anthologized in *Spring Anthology,* Volume I, Mitre Press, 1963. Contributor of poems, plays, and articles to periodicals, 1927—, stories to *Guide* and *Catholic Fireside,* 1934-61, quizzes on Catholic history to *Universe,* 1960-61. Writer of radio scripts, "Five to Ten Stories" and "Silver Lining," for British Broadcasting Corp. Co-editor, *Senior Citizen,* 1963-65.

WORK IN PROGRESS: John Pounds, pioneer of Ragged Schools, Portsmouth.

SIDELIGHTS: "Orphaned very early, I was brought up among much older busy people, so must find my own amusements. I cannot remember when the beauty of my home (the Isle of Wight) first struck me, but by the time I was seven years old I was trying to get it down on paper. I asked questions of those who knew about natural history, and backed this up by reading. Someone gave me Gilbert White's *Natural History of Selborne* and that clinched the matter. The American writer, Gene Stratton Porter, was, also, a major influence. My poems are almost all on nature, and in my stories I have studied to be correct about birds, animals, flowers, etc. Toys meant less to me than my little garden plot. The island was rich in legends, another source for stories. When I went to New Zealand in 1950, I collected Maori myths for the same purpose. Nature there was so lush that ideas came crowding.

"In my teens I became a newspaper reporter which proved a rich experience in studying people young and old. Because I was such a lonely child I think I tend to write for lonely children, as in *Kiwi Jane.* A catholic, I have written of saints and martyrs as a child sees them—not impossibly holy, but brave and resourceful, introducing fictional children into their factual events.

"How do I begin? Some fact—lovely, curious, provoking—strikes me. I frame that fact as an influence on characters, and the characters take over. I am the channel sharing enjoyment. Long illness gave me boundless time for research, and regular working hours, above all, time for thought. Thought is the real cradle of stories and poems for me, and young readers' letters are inspiration."

The Douglas Lord exhibition is in the du Grummond Collection at the University of Southern Mississippi.

HOBBIES AND OTHER INTERESTS: Books, music, nature study—"not as an expert, but as one perennially interested."

FOR MORE INFORMATION SEE: Presswoman, April, 1963.

DORIS LUND

LUND, Doris (Herold) 1919-

PERSONAL: Born January 14, 1919, in Indianapolis, Ind.; daughter of Don (a writer, humorist, and cartoonist) and Katherine (Brown) Herold; married Sidney C. Lund (now an industrial writer), January 6, 1945; children: Meredith (Mrs. James Cohen), Eric, Mark, Lisa. *Education:* Wellesley College, student, 1935-37; Swarthmore College, B.A. (high honors), 1939. *Home:* 9 Sunwich Rd., Rowayton, Conn.

CAREER: Young & Rubicam, Inc. (advertising agency), New York, N.Y., copywriter, 1940-46; William Esty, Inc. (advertising agency), New York, N.Y., copywriter, 1946-47; free-lance copywriter and layout artist; cartoonist and illustrator. *Member:* Authors Guild.

WRITINGS: Did You Ever?, Parents' Magazine Press, 1965; *The Attic of the Wind* (verse), Parents' Magazine Press, 1966; *Did You Ever Dream?,* Parents' Magazine Press, 1967; *Hello, Baby!,* C. R. Gibson, 1968; *I Wonder What's Under,* Parents' Magazine Press, 1970; *The Paint-Box Sea,* McGraw, 1973; *You Ought to See Herbert's House,* Watts, 1973; *Eric,* Lippincott, 1974. Contributor of poems, series verse, and cartoons to *Ladies' Home Journal, Look,* and *Advertising Age.*

WORK IN PROGRESS: Two adult books.

SIDELIGHTS: "*Eric* is the story of my son, Eric, who lived four and a half very intense years with leuke-

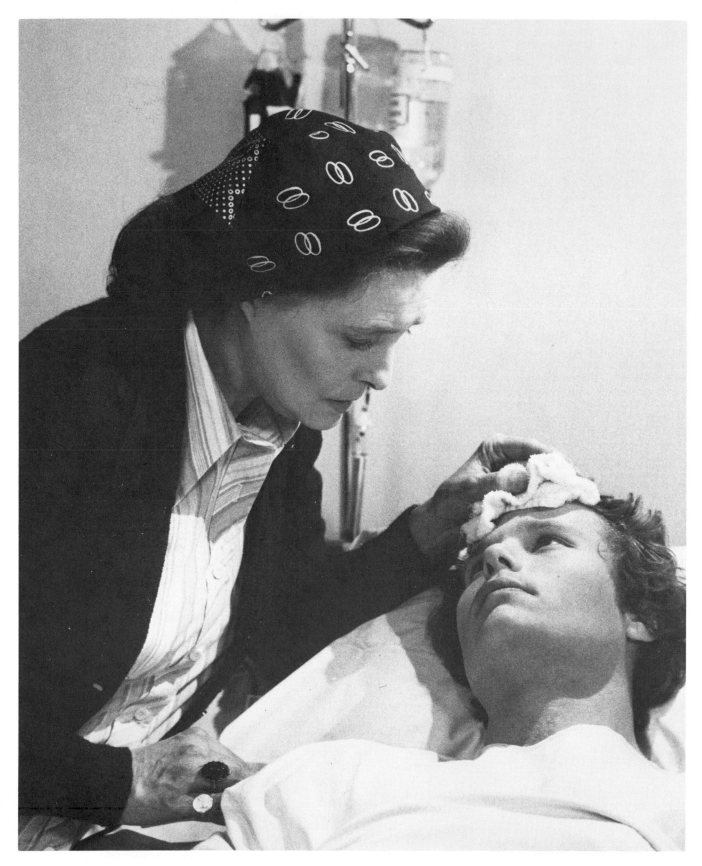

In the hour of his death, I searched Eric's face with wonder and awe, much as I searched it the day he was born. ■ (From the "Hallmark Hall of Fame" presentation of "Eric," NBC-TV, starring Patricia Neal.)

Something about the Author

**Birthday paints
On a little tray:
Jane was painting
Penobscot Bay.**
■ (From *Paint-Box Sea* by Doris Herold Lund. Pictures by Symeon Shimin.)

mia—enjoying a great deal of life and fighting furiously to survive every time he had a setback. It is, also, the story of the mother-son struggle which occurs in every household when the waves of adolescence begin to pound against the walls. And so while Eric demanded his independence, even though he was ill, I had to overcome my need to mother him too much—let him go even though he might be dying. In other words we *both* grew up—in different ways.

"It seems my whole life has been one long struggle to develop the kind of courage that I needed every minute during Eric's losing battle. But the rewards of having independent children are great. Eric's life was a beautiful whole, with many achievements, although cut short. His younger brother Mark is graduating from Yale this year, a goal he set out for himself although neither of us knew where the money would come from when he started out. My older daughter, Meredith, is happily married and becoming an artist. The younger one, Lisa, has been teaching three piano students for three years and is trying to figure out a way to combine college without abandoning her pupils.

"My husband, Sidney, free-lances now doing technical writing. Our lives have been very changed because of *Eric*. There will be a Dell paperback edition soon, the book has been condensed for Reader's Digest Book Club, it was, also, a choice of three other book clubs, including an alternate featured by Book-of-the-Month. And it will eventually be in fifteen foreign editions. We are both *busier*—and more free.

"Of particular interest to young people might be the film strip developed for high school use by Guidance Associates. There are now many courses on 'Living and Dying' for young people in schools and *Eric*'s story will form a section (biographical) of the Guidance package on this subject.

"Lorimar Productions filmed a television special for NBC. (Subsequently expanded into a full-length movie for Southeast Asia, Europe and French Canada.) However, it differed quite a bit from the book. One of the author's woes."

Attic of the Wind has been made into an audio-visual film strip (record and slides) and a fully animated movie by Weston Woods Studios. *Eric,* starring Patricia Neal, was broadcast on NBC's "Hallmark Hall of Fame," November 10, 1975.

HOBBIES AND OTHER INTERESTS: "My husband and I both love the ocean—he's a fantastic swimmer, but I'm not. My other favorite pastimes are listening to opera and nearly all sorts of music, dancing in the kitchen when I cook, beach-walking and studying art and printmaking."

MARKS, Mickey Klar

PERSONAL: Born January 9, in Brooklyn, N.Y.; daughter of Barnet J. and Pauline (Finklestein) Klar; married Nathan Harold Marks, 1935; children: Andrew Roger. *Education:* New York University, student, three and a half years; Co-

Trini and Mr. Kane began to read the play. Trini wasn't aware of showing off. She wasn't aware of coveting a role or wanting to be an actress. ■ (From *Straw Hat Theater* by Mickey Klar Marks. Illustrated by Jacqueline Tomes.)

MICKEY KLAR MARKS

lumbia University, student, two years. *Home:* North Greenwich Rd., Armonk, N.Y. 10504.

CAREER: Writer. *Awards, honors:* Petry Prize, American Sonnets and Lyrics; Parents Book Club award.

WRITINGS: Hucklebones, Whitman, 1950; *Let's Go to the Fair,* Whitman, 1951; *Little Peter What's My Name,* Book Creators, 1953; *Over the Shoulder Book,* Whitman, 1953; *Oh Susanna!,* Mattel; *Fish on the Tide,* Children's Press, 1956; *Fine Eggs and Fancy Chickens,* Holt, 1956; *The Holiday Shop,* Holt, 1958; *Strawhat Theater,* Knopf, 1960; *What Can I Buy?,* Dial, 1962; *Sand Sculpturing,* Dial, 1962; *Slate Sculpturing,* Dial, 1963; *Wax Sculpturing,* Dial, 1964; *Painting Free,* Dial, 1965; *Collage,* Dial, 1968; (with Edith Alberts) *Op-Tricks,* Lippincott, 1972; (with Werner) *The Adventures of Edam Stilton* (musical), Pioneer Drama, 1973; *The Spell of Malatesta* (comedy), Pioneer Drama, 1975; *Is It Soup Yet?,* Contemporary Drama, 1976.

SIDELIGHTS: "Personally I don't think it matters very much to the reader what an author is like or how and why he or she started writing. What is important is the result. If an author can achieve the kind of story that a reader is reluctant to put down; that's what writing is all about and that's what this particular writer aims for; that extension from one mind to another.

"After many books and hundreds of short stories, I have returned to my first interest, the theatre; not as a performer but as a playwright. For the past few years I have been working with high school student-actors not only writing some of the plays for the troupe, but, also, going on tour with them."

Mickey Klar Marks is represented in the de Grummond Collection, University of Southern Mississippi.

HOBBIES AND OTHER INTERESTS: Gardening, swimming, tennis.

MARZANI, Carl (Aldo) 1912-

PERSONAL: Born March 4, 1912, in Rome, Italy; son of Gabriel (a miner) and Enrica (Gorga) Marzani; married first wife, Edith Eisner (an actress), 1937, (deceased); married Charlotte Pomerantz (a writer of children's books), November 12, 1966; children: (first marriage) Judith Enrica (Mrs. Alan Spector), Anthony H.; (second marriage), Ga-

CARL MARZANI

brielle Rose, Daniel Avram. *Education:* Williams College, B.A., 1935; Oxford University, B.A., 1938. *Politics:* Independent socialist. *Religion:* None. *Home:* 260 West 21st St., New York, N.Y. 10011.

CAREER: Volunteer in Spanish Civil War, 1936-37; New York University, New York, N.Y., instructor in economics, 1939-41; U.S. Office of Strategic Services, Washington, D.C., member of staff, 1942-45; U.S. Department of State, Washington, D.C., deputy division chief, 1945-46; independent film producer, New York, N.Y., 1946-49; convicted in federal court of hiding Communist affiliation during a loyalty test while with Department of State, he spent 1949-51 as prisoner in Lewisburg Penitentiary, Lewisburg, Pa.; United Electrical, Radio and Machine Workers of America, New York, N.Y., co-director of education, 1951-54; Marzani & Munsell (publishers), New York, N.Y., president, 1954-67; engaged in real estate operations as owner and builder, New York, N.Y., 1967-70; InterAmerican University, Puerto Rico, professor of world politics, 1974-77. *Military service:* U.S. Army, Office of Strategic Services, 1943-45; became master sergeant. *Member:* Veterans of the Abraham Lincoln Brigade.

WRITINGS: We Can Be Friends (on relations with Russia; foreword by W.E.B. DuBois), Topical Books, 1952, reprinted with new introduction by Barton J. Bernstein, Garland Press (New York), 1972; *The Open Marxism of Antonio Gramsci,* Cameron Associates, 1957; *The Survivor* (novel), Cameron Associates, 1958; (with Victor Perlo) *Dollars and Sense of Disarmament,* Marzani & Munsell, 1960; (translator) Giuseppe Boffa, *Inside the Khrushchev Era,* Marzani & Munsell, 1960; (with Robert E. Light) *Cuba versus CIA,* Marzani & Munsell, 1961; (editor and contributor) *The Shelter Hoax,* Marzani & Munsell, 1962; *The Wounded Earth: An Ecological Survey,* Addison-Wesley, 1972. Writer of film scripts for "War Department Report," 1944, "Deadline for Action," 1946, and "The Threat of American Neo-Fascism," American Film Documentary, 1974.

WORK IN PROGRESS: Beyond 1984: Spain, Orwell, and the Neo-Orwellians.

SIDELIGHTS: Dollars and Sense of Disarmament was published in Moscow, 1961; *The Survivor* was published in England, 1960, and Czechoslovakia, 1962. Marzani has visited "most socialist countries, including Cuba," traveled all over Europe, and in the Near and Far East.

HOBBIES AND OTHER INTERESTS: Reading, fishing, and carpentry.

MATSON, Emerson N(els)   1926-

PERSONAL: Born May 23, 1926, in Seattle, Wash.; son of Nils Isaac (a draftsman) and Anna E. (David) Matson; married JoAnne Riley (a secretary), July 19, 1947; children: William Brock, Robert Emerson, Mariellen Kay. *Education:* Studied at University of Washington, Seattle, 1947, and Metropolitan Business College, Seattle, Wash., 1948. *Religion:* Lutheran. *Home:* 11015 Bingham Ave. E., Tacoma, Wash. 98446. *Office:* David W. Evans, Inc., 190 Queen Anne Bldg., Seattle, Wash. 98109.

CAREER: Bon Marche (department store), Tacoma, Wash., buyer and merchandiser, 1953-59; KMO-Radio, Tacoma, Wash., advertising broadcaster, 1959-60; free-lance writer, 1960-61; KTVW-Television, Tacoma, Wash., program director, 1961-65; Pierce County Publishers, Tacoma, Wash., managing editor, 1965-70; David W. Evans, Inc. (advertising and public relations firm), Seattle, Wash.,

EMERSON N. MATSON

vice-president, 1970—. *Military service:* U.S. Army, 1944-47; received Combat Infantry Badge. U.S. Army National Guard, 1947-57; became first lieutenant. *Awards, honors:* Washington Education Association's better understanding award, 1968, for editorial writing; Pacific Lutheran University's certificate of merit, 1969, for sports writing.

WRITINGS: Longhouse Legends, Nelson, 1968; *Legends of the Great Chiefs,* Nelson, 1972. Writer of industrial motion picture scripts.

WORK IN PROGRESS: They Came on Burros; a novel about the gold rush into the Black Hills.

SIDELIGHTS: "I believe the future of this nation is dependent upon agriculture . . . in fact, more so than industry. If we wiped out our giant industrial complex, another would be built to fill the void almost overnight. However, if we lost our farmland we would lose the nation. Yet, thousands of acres of farm land are being converted into sprawling suburbs, industrial parks, and factory sites . . . all under the heading of progress. As our population explodes, our ability to feed future generations shrinks. . . . As the above indicates, I'm a farmer at heart. We have a few acres and have horses and ducks."

MATUS, Greta   1938-

PERSONAL: Born November 13, 1938, in New York, N.Y.; daughter of Irving L. (an architect) and Helen (Silverman) Levett; married Stanley Matus (an account executive); children: Adam, Jason. *Education:* Attended Cooper Union, New York, New York, 1956-1959; California School of Fine Arts, 1959-1962. *Home:* 3608 Noble Avenue, Richmond, Va. 23222. *Office:* Richmond Newspapers, 333 E. Grace St., Richmond, Va. 23219.

CAREER: New York Public Schools, New York, N.Y., art teacher, 1963-65, painting & sculpture teacher, 1967-1973. Free-lance illustrator, 1973—; Richmond Newspapers, Richmond, Va., research copywriter, 1975—.

WRITINGS—Self-illustrated: *Where are You, Jason?,* 1974.

Illustrator: Genevieve Gray, *Ghost Story,* Lothrop, 1975.

SIDELIGHTS: "I work in different mediums depending on the visual I want to communicate. When I paint landscapes I work in oils. Natural forms, rocks in streams, mountains, trees and the effect of light on these forms are my basic subjects. On canvas these shapes take on a sculptural, impressionistic look, often bordering on the abstract, with movement, light and brushwork giving power and direction to the paintings.

"My illustrations are the opposite of my paintings, they are detailed and contain humour. I like to mix words and graphics similar to Steinberg's statements. When I was a student I fell in love with the Flemish and Dutch painters who often painted a miniature city through a window as a secondary subject to the main theme. This creating of worlds from the primary focus to the secondary details is, I think what gives an illustration credibility, for it evokes mood, atmosphere and a time and place. For children it's important because they have not yet learned to 'abstract' or to see in whole dimensions and their visual experience is made up of minute details.

"As a child I loved to build life-like settings. I was brought up on pop-up picture books and many of my most memorable color dreams are set in similar disney-like two dimensional landscapes. During the years when I was at home

He was caught in a storm.

■ (From *Where Are You, Jason?* by Greta Matus. Pictures by the author.)

GRETA MATUS

raising two young children I became involved with creating family portraits for friends. They were three-dimensional recreations of rooms with stuffed sculpture facsimilies of the subject and their families. The 'dolls' were clothed and drawn on somewhat like a marisol figure. The statement was often satiric.

"At the present time I'm working for money and learning a highly marketable trade—advertising copy writing. As far as consistent jobs go its fairly creative. On the side I'm having fun doing a consumer column for A. H. Robbins Pharmaceuticals. I'm having fun with these full-color illustrations, a sort of visual history of the lovely times I've spent with my own children as they were growing up."

If you know the game well, you will be amazed at how well you can do it without a ball, bat, mitt, or bases. ■ (From *Act Now!* by Nellie McCaslin. Illustrated by Daty Healy.)

NELLIE McCASLIN

McCASLIN, Nellie 1914-

PERSONAL: Born August 20, 1914, in Cleveland, Ohio; daughter of Paul G. and Nellie McCaslin. *Education:* Western Reserve University (now Case-Western Reserve University), B.A., 1936, M.A., 1937; New York University, Ph.D., 1957. *Politics:* Democrat. *Religion:* Presbyterian. *Home:* 40 East Tenth St., New York, N.Y. 10003. *Office:* Mills College of Education, New York, N.Y. 10011.

CAREER: Tudor Hall, Indianapolis, Ind., teacher of dramatic arts, 1937-44; National College of Education, Evanston, Ill., instructor in drama and English, 1944-56; Mills College of Education, New York, N.Y., drama instructor and dean of students, 1957-72; New York University, professor, 1972—. Instructor, Columbia University, part-time, 1961-67. *Member:* American Theatre Association (fellow), American Association of University Professors, Children's Theatre Association (former regional governor; president, 1973-75). *Awards, honors:* Jennie Heiden Award, 1968, for excellence in theatre for children.

WRITINGS: Legends in Action, Row-Peterson, 1945; *More Legends in Action,* Row-Peterson, 1950; *Tall Tales and Tall Men,* Macrae, 1956; *Pioneers in Petticoats,* Row-Peterson, 1961; *Little Snow Girl,* Coach House Press, 1963; *The Rabbit Who Wanted Red Wings,* Coach House Press, 1963; *Creative Dramatics in the Classroom,* McKay, 1968, 2nd edition, 1974; *Theatre for Children: A History,* University of Oklahoma Press, 1971; *Act Now!,* S. G. Phillips, 1975.

HOBBIES AND OTHER INTERESTS: Going to galleries, doing crafts, and baking.

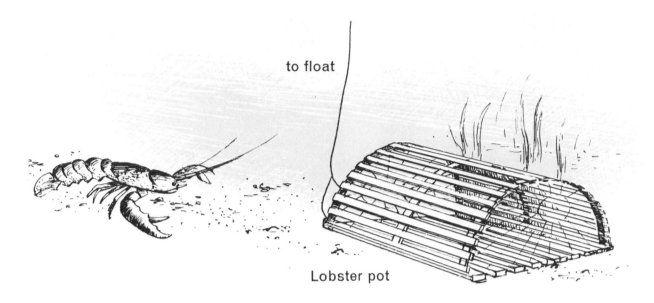

to float

Lobster pot

The standard commercial harvesting of lobsters has centered around the use of pots or traps. ■
(From *Underwater Continent* by Christie McFall. Illustrated by the author.)

CHRISTIE McFALL

McFALL, Christie   1918-

PERSONAL: Born July 5, 1918, in Cincinnati, Ohio; son of Ralph Roscoe (a furniture dealer) and Grace (McChristie) McFall; married Olga Di Domizio, April 3, 1948; children: Ralph, Glenn. *Education:* Miami University, Oxford, Ohio, B.F.A., 1940; Central Academy of Commercial Art, student, 1940-41; New York University, M.A., 1950. *Religion:* Presbyterian. *Address:* 4345 Majestic Lane, Fairfax, Va. 22030.

CAREER: Free-lance commercial artist, New York, N.Y., 1946-50, Levittown, N.Y., 1950-54, Hackettstown, N.J., 1954-67; Naval Photographic Center, Washington D.C., writer and storyboard artist for training films, 1968—. *Military service:* U.S. Army, 1942-46.

WRITINGS—All self-illustrated: *Our Country America*, Macmillan, 1953; *A Book About Hawaii*, Maxton, 1959; *Maps Mean Adventure*, Dodd, 1961, revised and enlarged, 1972; *Wonders of Snow and Ice*, Dodd, 1964; *Wonders of Sand*, Dodd, 1966; *Wonders of Stones*, Dodd, 1969; *Underwater Continent*, Dodd, 1975.

SIDELIGHTS: Has a cartographer's interest in relief and vegetation maps and in landforms; also doing a continuing study of the coastal zone through research and photographs.

McNULTY, Faith   1918-

PERSONAL: Born November 28, 1918, in New York, N.Y.; daughter of Joseph Eugene (a judge) and Faith (Robinson) Corrigan; married John McNulty, 1945 (died, 1956); married Richard H. Martin, 1957; children: (first marriage) John Joseph. *Education:* Attended Barnard College, 1937-38. *Address:* Box 370, Wakefield, R.I. 02880. *Office: The New Yorker,* 25 West 43rd St., New York, N.Y. 10036.

**But their mother does not forget
to watch for danger.**
■ (From *Woodchuck* by Faith McNulty. Pictures by Joan Sandin.)

FAITH McNULTY

CAREER: The New Yorker, New York, N.Y., staff writer, 1953—. *Awards, honors:* Dutton Animal Book Award, 1966, for *The Whooping Crane;* D.H.L., University of Rhode Island.

WRITINGS: (With Elisabeth Keiffer) *Wholly Cats,* Bobbs-Merrill, 1962; *The Whooping Crane: The Bird That Defies Extinction,* introduction by Stewart L. Udall, Dutton, 1966; *Must They Die? The Strange Case of the Prairie Dog and the Black-Footed Ferret,* Doubleday, 1971; *The Great Whales,* Doubleday, 1974. Articles and fiction for *The New Yorker.*

For children: *The Funny Mixed-up Story,* Wonder Books, 1959; *Arty the Smarty,* Wonder Books, 1962; *When a Boy Gets Up in the Morning,* Knopf, 1962; *When a Boy Goes to Bed at Night,* Knopf, 1963; *Prairie Dog Summer,* Coward, 1972; *Woodchuck,* Harper, 1974; *Whales: Their Life in the Sea,* Harper, 1975.

McQUEEN, Mildred Hark   1908-
(Mildred Hark)

PERSONAL: Born October 19, 1908, in LaMoure, N.D.; daughter of William F. and Mabel (Bailey) Hark; married Noel McQueen (died, 1960). *Education:* College of Music, Cincinnati, Ohio, student, 1927-30; studied drama and literature under private tutors. *Politics:* Democrat. *Religion:* Church of the New Jerusalem (Swedenborgian). *Home and office:* 111 East Chicago Ave., Chicago, Ill. 60611.

CAREER: Author of children's books and plays; part-time research editor and writer of reports on educational subjects for Science Research Associates, Inc., Chicago, Ill., 1952-1973; writer of guidance booklets and other materials for school use. *Member:* Children's Reading Round Table.

WRITINGS—With husband, Noel McQueen; under name Mildred Hark, except as indicated: *A Toast to Christmas* (one-act play), Play Club, 1946; *Special Plays for Special*

MILDRED HARK McQUEEN

Days, Plays, 1947; *The Good Luck Cat,* Medill McBride, 1950; *Modern Comedies for Young Players,* Plays, 1951; *Twenty-Five Plays for Holidays,* Plays, 1952; *Make Your Pennies Count,* Science Research Associates, 1953; *Junior Plays for All Occasions,* Plays, 1955, revised edition, 1969; *Miss Senior High* (one-act comedy), Baker's Plays, c.1957; *Teen-Age Plays for All Occasions,* Plays, 1957; *Tomorrow Is Christmas* (one-act comedy), Baker's Plays, c.1958; *A Home for Penny,* F. Watts, 1959; *Romance for Dad* (one-act comedy), Baker's Plays, c.1959; *Doll House Tea Party,* Avon, 1960; (sole author under name Mildred McQueen) *Improved Guidance for Elementary Schools* (pamphlet), Science Research Associates, 1960; (sole author under name Mildred McQueen) *Identifying and Helping Dropouts* (pamphlet), Science Research Associates, c.1961; *Mary Lou and Johnny: An Adventure in Seeing,* F. Watts, 1963.

Under Mildred Hark McQueen: *Who's the President?* (one-act play about John F. Kennedy inaugural), Plays, 1961; *Mother's Choice,* Plays, 1961; *The Musicians of Bremen* (dramatization of Grimm's story), Plays, 1962; *A Visit to the White House* (copy. in Library White House Historical Association), Plays, 1965; *Spring Tonic,* Plays, 1965; *The Christmas Bear,* Plays, 1969; *Neighbors to the North,* Plays, 1970; *Bibliography: Careers,* Science Research Associates, 1974.

Joint author with Noel McQueen of more than two hundred plays for children, about forty of them reprinted in twenty-one anthologies, including reading-improvement books. Contributor of plays (formerly joint authorship, now as sole author) to *Plays Magazine,* and of poems and stories to children's magazines. Author of about two hundred research reports on honors programs, creativity, dropout problem, and related subjects. Former editor with Noel McQueen, *Guidance Index.*

WORK IN PROGRESS: "Children's plays; special children series, fictional stories to help so-called normal children understand those with handicaps; and a book that combines a fictional story with a specific era in the life of our country and its effect on one little girl."

SIDELIGHTS: "I live near the historic Chicago Water Tower. The old tower, set in its own little park, looks like a castle. You can see it from my windows. Some of the friends who visit call my apartment *Castleview,* and the little children love the tower. It is like a castle in fairyland, especially at Christmas time when it often snows and there are tiny white Italian lights on all the trees along Michigan Avenue and around the tower. One little boy calls me 'Millie, the Queen,' because I live near a castle and my name is Mc-Queen. 'Oh, look,' he says in delight as he runs to the windows to see the castle. Later he is sure to say, 'Read me a story.'

"Sometimes you find that the children know your stories better than you do. I was actually 'telling' *Doll House Tea Party* to my godchild, Margaret Scott. I planned to leaf through and tell the story so Margaret's mother could take a picture, so I began, 'Up in the attic in Mary's house was a wooden chest with a hinged top.' Margaret looked up quickly, and said '*Box,* Aunt Millie, not chest.' I looked down at the page. She was right. It *was* box. *Doll House Tea Party* has been translated into Finnish, Dutch, Spanish and sold in Great Britain. Now Margaret can read, although she is not yet six, as I write. It wouldn't surprise me if she read me the Finnish version one day in the future.

"When my husband and I wrote together, people were always asking me how we did it. Collaboration seems to be a mysterious art. 'Do you write a line or a paragraph, and then does he write a line and a paragraph?' 'Do you plan together and then one of you writes the plan?' People would ask. Answers would be: 'Well, yes and no to both. And yes, sometimes it's one way and sometimes another.'

"Once a little girl wrote me a letter after my husband died (she did not know of his death) and said: 'I was wondering how you happened to meet your partner. I think you two make a great team.' I guess that's the secret of writing together. I liked the letter.

"One day some children who came to visit my apartment said, 'This is like Mrs. Santa Claus' house.' (One year on Valentine's Day, I played the part of Mrs. Santa Claus on an educational cassette.) It was at Christmas time when all the music boxes, angels, and chimes were set out. Some of the music boxes and angels are put away after the holidays. I never *planned* to collect music boxes, but somebody gave me one, and then others began to do it. Now my home is full of music boxes, books, and bluebirds. Fortunately the music boxes are small and the bluebirds decorate cups and other bits of china, notepaper, and a small needlepoint pillow made by Margaret's mother. Gifts *need* to be small now. I like to keep an uncluttered look. As a sixteen-year-old friend said, 'If you give Aunt Mil anything, it had better be small or expendable, because she doesn't have room for many more things.'

"One ingenious friend now gives me presents I can give away to my children: reproductions of English paper dolls and Kate Greenaway books, and candy pops in tins decorated with Beatrix Potter characters.

"The pictures on my walls could tell a story. If you sit on the sofa and look to the right, you see a wonderful white rabbit picture in the hall. It was done by a little girl named Ann when she was seven (now eleven). No matter how downhearted you feel, a glimpse of that rabbit makes you feel better. He has pink ears and wears a yellow bow. There are Easter eggs, and a big jolly sun, and a carrot wearing a pink ribbon. Farther down the hall there is a watercolor of three children making a snowman that I did when I was ten years old. Over one bookcase there is a picture of a beautiful woodland done by the minister who married Noel and me. He and his wife brought it as a gift when they came in to visit two days after our wedding. Then there is a pastel drawing of John F. Kennedy, Jr., on his third birthday, saluting the flag-draped coffin of his father.

"There is a special music box in my apartment that is never put away. It looks like a Swiss chalet. When the music plays a little man and a little lady dance around and around in front of it. Once a little girl who was visiting said, 'Do they ever go inside the house?' I answered, 'Not when I've been watching, but maybe they go inside when I'm asleep.'

"Another music box, finished in black lacquer with bright painted flowers, came from Japan, and no one knows what it plays. A young man who had lived in Japan listened to it and said he could not remember the name of the song but it was often played at weddings and, also, used as a lullaby to sing to babies. Inside that box I put some rose-colored glasses, the kind that come out of crackerjacks. Some children once took them out, looked through them at the old Water Tower, and were delighted. The rosy color gave it an added enchantment. So I kept them—for the children. But now they are almost worn out. I'm looking for a new pair and I'm sure they will turn up.

"Sometimes you find that the 'long arm of coincidence' operates in real life, although you are told to avoid it in fiction.

"One day some friends brought a charming young woman from India, who was most interested in a small book I had from her own country. It was an anthology of works by writers from all over the world—Tolstoy, Hans Andersen, Tagore, Tennyson, Shakespeare, and a McQueen play called *Merry Christmas Customs*. Whenever I look at that little book, I feel proud to be in such distinguished company. It turned out that the young woman knew one of the editors of the anthology. They were close friends! So a young woman comes from a far off land to observe our educational methods and is taken to visit. . . . Well, you see what I mean by coincidence in real life!"

FOR MORE INFORMATION SEE: *Philadelphia Evening Bulletin*, January 2, 1948, June 6, 1953; *Chicago Schools Journal*, May-June, 1951; *Children's Reading Round Table Bulletin*, November, 1955, March, 1975; *Researchin' Around*, Science Research Associates, December, 1957, August, 1959.

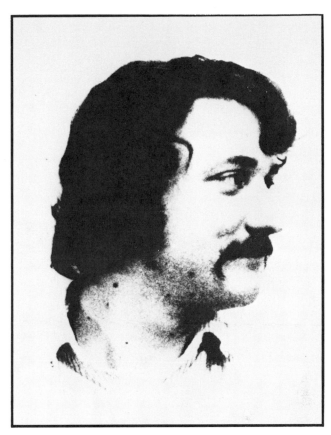

LOUIS A. MEYER

MEYER, Louis A(lbert)   1942-

PERSONAL: Born August 22, 1942, in Johnstown, Pa.; son of Louis Albert (a retired career soldier) and Martha (Keytack) Meyer; married Annetje Lawrence (a teacher), May 28, 1966; children: Matthew, Nathaniel. *Education:* University of Florida, A.B., 1964; Boston University, M.F.A., 1973. *Home:* 191 Captain Pierce Rd., Scituate, Mass. 02066.

CAREER: Painter. Currently teaching at Rockland High School, Rockland, Mass. *Military service:* U.S. Navy, 1964-68; became lieutenant. *Member:* Boston Visual Artists Union.

WRITINGS—Self-illustrated, for children: *The Gypsy Bears*, Little, Brown, 1970; *The Clean Air and Peaceful Contentment Dirigible Airline*, Little, Brown, 1971.

WORK IN PROGRESS: A juvenile novel dealing with the Impressionist period in France.

SIDELIGHTS: "Sorry, but for one who deals so extensively with words, I find myself curiously non-verbal on the subject of myself. I can only say that I have a reasonably active fantasy life which sometimes results in books and paintings."

MICKLISH, Rita   1931-

PERSONAL: Surname is accented on first syllable; born February 7, 1931, in Maywood, Calif.; daughter of Herbert W. (an artist) and Dorothy (Robbeloth) Ryan; married

"It's an egg, a fancy one," Stephanie said. **"I know. Momma told me she was getting it. What's inside?"** ■ (From *Sugar Bee* by Rita Micklish. Illustrated by Ted Lcvin.)

Something about the Author

RITA MICKLISH

Donald Charles Micklish (a state tax supervisor), January 28, 1950; children: David, Janice, Peter, Sharon. *Education:* High school diploma. *Religion:* Roman Catholic. *Home:* 6530 Zena Dr., San Diego, Calif. 92115.

CAREER: Certified instructor in methodology for San Diego Catholic Diocese, San Diego, Calif., 1964—, member of Board of Education, 1963-69. Member of American Red Cross Youth Advisory Board, San Diego County, Calif., 1961-67; para-professional lecturer in San Diego city and county schools. *Member:* American Red Cross, Pro-Life League (San Diego, Calif.). *Awards, honors:* Pius X Award from Confraternity of Christian Doctrine, 1964.

WRITINGS: Sugar Bee, Delacorte, 1972. Contributor of articles and short stories to *Religion Teachers Journal, U.S. Catholic, Nursing Outlook, St. Anthony Messenger,* and *The Southern Cross.*

WORK IN PROGRESS: Cloud Queen, Tio, Winds of Witch Creek, Dream Rider, Storm Summer, and *Ride the Wind West,* all novels for young people.

SIDELIGHTS: "'When did you start writing?' That's almost always the first question when I visit a classroom. I answer simply, 'When I was very young, just like you.' And it's true. My lefthand scrawl filled pages and pages with poetry, plays and stories even in second grade.

"I grew up half city, half country kid, at home in a green, hill-ringed place called Spring Valley and attended school eleven miles away in town. My family lived for a short but exciting time in a giant, flapping tent while my father built our lovely gabled home with his own hands. My mother let me explore and learn from the valley. She passed on her own love of books which we share to this day.

"When I write I try to show the strength and goodness of ordinary people who in small ways change themselves and their small worlds for the better. The experience of *Sugar Bee* is drawn from the too common cruelties and loneliness that face children of all colors and circumstances.

"I am 'town bound' now, three children grown and gone and one daughter in grade school. I see from my window the peak of Cowles mountain, our sleek trunked eucalyptus and the spring roses.

"Any stories underway are drawn from unique places we visited as a family on vacation, where some bit of history struck the flint of my imagination and set new ideas flying like sparks."

FOR MORE INFORMATION SEE: Horn Book, June, 1972.

MILLAR, Barbara F.   1924-

PERSONAL: Born August 26, 1924, in Bay City, Mich.; daughter of William John and Cathryn (Gaffney) Finn; married Stewart Wilson Millar (an audiologist), January 24,

BARBARA F. MILLAR

1953; children: Bruce (died, 1971), Barbara, David, Cass. *Education:* University of Miami, Coral Gables, Fla., A.B., 1963. *Politics:* Democrat. *Religion:* Roman Catholic. *Home:* 16357 Redington Dr., Redington Beach, Fla. 33708.

CAREER: Berkeley Preparatory School, Tampa, Fla., teacher of English, Latin, and creative writing, 1968-75. *Military service:* Women's Army Auxiliary Corps, 1945-47. *Awards, honors: Wheels for Ginny's Chariot* was the winner of the first Edith Busby Award given by Dodd, Mead & Co.

WRITINGS: (With Earlene W. Luis) *Wheels for Ginny's Chariot,* Dodd, 1966; (with E. W. Luis) *Listen, Lissa,* Dodd, 1968.

WORK IN PROGRESS: "Currently up-dating a book about a Cuban refugee while working on several ideas for new books."

SIDELIGHTS: "Although I had been an avid reader and struggling writer, it wasn't until I began teaching the physically handicapped at Bayside School, Tampa, Florida, that I became interested in writing for young people. One of my students, a wonderful boy, became ill and died. Both Mrs. Luis (who was, also, a teacher at that school) and I thought Russell and the other children should have some sort of memorial. So we wrote *Wheels for Ginny's Chariot.* We have received many responses from young people which make the writing effort worthwhile.

"My husband and children think it's rather weird, but nice, to have a mom who writes rather than plays bridge or whatever. I finished my M.A. at the University of South Florida and have moved permanently to the beach."

FOR MORE INFORMATION SEE: Young Readers' Review, May, 1966.

MILLER, Albert G(riffith)   1905-

PERSONAL: Born December 28, 1905, in Philadelphia, Pa.; son of Albert Griffith and Mabel (Morris) Miller; married Mary Susan Horney, 1928. *Education:* University of Pennsylvania, A.B., 1927. *Home:* 440 East 79th St., New York, N.Y. 10021.

CAREER: N. W. Ayer & Son, New York, N.Y., writer, 1928-33; free-lance writer, 1933—. *Military service:* U.S. Navy, became lieutenant. *Member:* Writers' Guild of America, Dramatists Guild, Authors League.

WRITINGS: (Editor) Emidio Angelo, *The Infernal Revenue* (cartoons), Nelson, 1959; *Fury, Stallion of Broken Wheel Ranch,* Holt, 1959, Grosset, 1972; *Fury and the Mustangs,* Holt, 1960, Grosset, 1963; *Silver Chief's Big Game Trail,* Holt, 1961, Grosset, 1961; *Fury and the White Mare,* Holt, 1962, Grosset, 1963; *Pop-Up Hide & Seek: A Child's First Counting Book,* Random House, 1966; *Pop-up Mother Goose,* Random House, 1966; *Pop-Up Sound-Alikes,* Random House, 1967; *The Wonderful Magic Motion Machine,* Random House, 1967; *The Tournament of Magic,* Random House, 1967; *The Magic Motion Martian Book,* Random House, 1967; *The Pop-Up Color Book,* Random House, 1967; *Doctor Dolittle,* Random House, 1967; *My Friend the Dragon,* Random House, 1967; *How Many Tadpoles?,* Random House, 1967; *A Magic-Scope Visit to Other*

ALBERT G. MILLER

Lands, Random House, 1967; *Who Popped Out?,* Random House, 1967; *The Dog That Said Wow-Bow,* Random House, 1967; *The Clock Book,* Random House, 1968; *The Wishing Ring,* Random House, 1968; *Chitty Chitty Bang Bang* (pop-up and flat), Random House, 1968; *The Wizard of Oz,* Random House, 1968; *Pinocchio,* Random House, 1968; *Cinderella,* Random House, 1968; *Alice in Wonderland,* Random House, 1968; *Robin Hood,* Random House, 1968; *20,000 Leagues Under the Sea,* Random House, 1968; *The Circus Book,* Random House, 1968; *The Book of Left & Right,* Random House, 1968; *Captain Whopper,* Astor-Honor, 1968; *More Captain Whopper Tales,* Astor-Honor, 1968; *Ring of Bright Water,* Golden Press, 1969; *A Friend for Shadow,* Singer, 1969; *The Biggest Book,* Random House, 1969; *The Pop-Up Book of Flying Machines,* Random House, 1969; *Book of Knock-Knocks,* Random House, 1969; *Snow-White and the Seven Dwarfs,* Random House, 1969; *Noah and the Ark,* Random House, 1969; *David and Goliath,* Random House, 1969; *The Birth of Jesus,* Random House, 1969; *The Three Little Pigs,* Random House, 1969; *Hansel & Gretel,* Random House, 1969; *Little Red Riding Hood,* Random House, 1969; *The Emperor's New Clothes,* Random House, 1969.

Pop-Up Story of the Nativity, Random House, 1970; (editor) *Pop-Up Aladdin & the Wonderful Lamp,* Random House, 1970; *King of the Grizzlies,* Golden Press, 1970; *The Sesame Street Story Book,* Random House, 1971; *Pop Corn* (jokes), Random House, 1972; (editor) *Pop-Up Book of Boats,* Random House, 1972; *Walt Disney's Bambi Gets Lost,* Random House, 1973; *Mark Twain in Love,* Harcourt, 1973; *Backward Beasts,* Bowmar, 1973; *Our Friends the ABC's,* Bowmar, 1973; *26 Riddles, (From A to Z),* Bowmar, 1973; *Talking Letters,* Bowmar, 1973; *Where Did That Word Come From?,* Bowmar, 1973; *The ABC Dog Show,* Bowmar, 1973. Has also researched twelve gift books for Norcross.

**And since he's almost 12 feet high,
You cannot look him in the eye.**
■ (From *The Pop-Up Biggest Book* by Albert G. Miller. Illustrations by Gwen Gordon and Dave Chambers.)

MOORE, John Travers   1908-

PERSONAL: Born August 24, 1908, in Wellston, Ohio; son of Thomas Emmet (a lawyer and editor) and Mary (Tripp) Moore; married Margaret Rumberger (an author), June 16, 1928. *Education:* University of Dayton, LL.B., 1933. *Home:* Poethaven, 525 Ehringhaus, Hendersonville, N.C. 28739.

CAREER: Practice of law, 1933-38; successively associate editor of youth publications for G. A. Pflaum (publisher), managing editor of Army Air Forces technical journal,

Plane Facts, during World War II; editorial associate, *Writer's Digest;* now poet.

WRITINGS: A Child's Book of Psalms, Hobbyhorse, 1946; *Near Centerville,* privately printed poetry chapbook, 1950; *Poems,* Halcyon (London), 1955; *Modern Crusaders,* Farrar, Straus, 1957; *God's Wonderful World* (poetry), Augsburg, 1964; *The Story of Silent Night,* Concordia, 1965; *My Prayer* (poetry), Guild-Golden, 1965; *When You Walk Out in Spring* (poetry), Helicon, 1965; *Cinnamon Seed* (poetry), Houghton, 1967; *Town and Countryside Poems,* A. Whitman, 1968; *There's Motion Everywhere* (poetry), Houghton,

JOHN TRAVERS MOORE, bronze head by Robert J. Smith

1970; *Poems: On Writing Poetry*, Libra, 1971; *We Are Like Wine* (poetry), Droke House/Hallux, 1972; *All Along the Way* (poetry), Carolrhoda, 1973.

With wife, Margaret R. Moore: *Sing-Along Sary*, Harcourt, 1951; *Little Saints*, Grail, 1953; *Big Saints*, Grail, 1954; *The Three Tripps* (Parents' Magazine Book Club selection, Calling All Girls Book Club selection), Bobbs, 1959; *On Cherry Tree Hill*, Bobbs, 1960; *The Little Band and the Inaugural Parade* (Junior Literary Guild selection), A. Whitman, 1968; *Certainly Carrie, Cut the Cake* (poetry), Bobbs, 1971; *Pepito's Speech at the United Nations*, Carolrhoda (published with the cooperation of the United Nations), 1971.

Poetry in *New York Times, Saturday Evening Post, Good Housekeeping, Horn Book, Child Life,* other magazines, newspapers, and anthologies, readers, and texts (all including poetry by John Travers Moore): *Modern American Poetry,* Galleon, 1933; *Ohio Poets: Eminent American Poets,* Empire, 1933; *We Are Neighbors,* Ginn, 1957; *Poems for Seasons Celebrations,* World, 1961; *Your Poetry Book,* Gage, 1964; *Arrow Book of Poetry,* Scholastic, 1965; *Focus: Themes in Literature,* McGraw, 1969; *Language and How to Use It Book,* Scott, Foresman, 1969; *Teacher's Guide,* United Presbyterian Board, 1970, (revised) 1972; *Language and How to Use It, Book 2,* Scott, Foresman, 1970, 1973; *Teacher's Edition for a World of Surprises and Reading Skills Five,* Harcourt, 1970; *Keep a Poem in Your Pocket,* Scott, Foresman, 1971; *Just My Size,* Scott, Foresman, 1971; *Sing a Song of People,* Scott, Foresman, 1971; *Air Pudding and Wind Sauce,* Economy, 1972; *Teacher's Read-Aloud Anthology* (Level 8), Scott, Foresman, 1972; *Teach-er's Read-Aloud Anthology* (Level 11), Scott, Foresman, 1972; *Time to Shout, Poems for You,* Scholastic, 1973; *The Way of the World,* Holt, 1973; *Explore, Express,* Alberta Education, 1974; *Self Expression and Conduct, The Humanities,* Harcourt, 1974; *Patterns of Language, Teacher's Edition,* American Book Co., 1974; *Composing Language, Changes,* Macmillan, 1974; *Views,* Macmillan, 1974; *Patterns of Language,* American Book Co., 1974; *Sports and Games in Verse and Rhyme,* Laidlaw, 1975; *Sniff Poems,* Scholastic, 1975; *Prisms,* Heath, 1975; *Teacher's Edition, Green Geese,* Laidlaw, 1976; *Tapestry,* Houghton, 1976; *Wide-Eyed Detectives,* 1976; *Poetry 1,* Education Department, Tasmania, 1976.

SIDELIGHTS: "A compulsive writer, I gave up the practice of law for the pursuit of literature. I have spent a dedicated lifetime at it, full time. My interest is progressing in an art field—the writing of poetry, though I know I am doomed to failure. The artist—I use the word to embrace the poet, sculptor and painter, musician (and others in some cases)—can seldom reach the ultimate in art for art is the ultimate: There is always something ahead. Perhaps that is what makes it so fascinating.

"I know of no life better spent than serving, through a search for something on a higher plane. Not that this is a smug observation but rather touched with some humility, for any truly outstanding worker in the field is not vain. He may be confident, through experience, and yet I am inclined to think even then he knows he is subject to his lucky moments. When the 'art-piece' 'comes off' it is his joy and, perhaps, his best satisfaction. It does not matter to him too much—though he feels it—if a young lady just out of school reviews his book as 'pedestrian' or not so good 'of the genre.' If it is good, he knows it. And the world, being selfish in a way, is going to utilize his work, too, if it holds merit. There are enough about who know better than those offering an idle critique through lack of experience or otherwise.

"I really feel today something should be done about not telling a reviewer how to review, but rather setting up suggested guidelines to avoid cliches and unfair and subjective reviews which are costing authors and publishers millions of dollars. In fact, I am making the suggestion to the various interested parties, whether or not I receive bad reviews or good, and I have received both of course, depending on to whom the book was sent, for in such judgment the quality of the work depends on the taste of the judge.

"Most of my material is inspired, I like to feel, or rather factually I have so found. When one has learned to trust the subconscious ninety-odd per cent and leave the balance to the 'front of the brain' as Galsworthy expressed it and bring up the superior from the 'deep wellsprings of the subconscious' he may improve. I touched on this in my book, *Poems: On Writing Poetry.* As to for whom the books of an author are intended, I remember hearing a young person ask Ralph Hodgson, the late British lyrist, for whom he wrote, and he replied, 'For myself.' The young lady did not understand and said, 'That's selfish.' I suppose there must be a measure of selfishness in an artist. He cannot brush aside the Madonna of Art for 'more important things' or he is not an artist. But there is a measure of selflessness inherent too, for I know of few who give more to the world than those so dedicated. In that is the warmth of accomplishment, though the path can be very lonely.

**A kitten is for playing with
And keeping on the floor.**
▪ (From *Certainly, Carrie, Cut the Cake* by Margaret and John Travers Moore. Illustrated by Laurie Anderson.)

"Many of the 'distinguished' posts are held by those who work at it—the writer is busy writing. And writers for children are much neglected in that general literature, manned in some areas by the pedantic, is actually unaware that in some instances, particularly poetry, the work to obtain the desired result in the area of children's literature is much more difficult to do than the catch-as-catch-can, contrived sort which crops up as a school in each respective period. Yesterday it was the gilt cupid of the Victorians; today it is the emaciated madonna. I doubt very much if you will find a children's author in the National Institute of Arts and Letters, the Academy of American Poets and the like, but you will find novelists of many a novel long dead or parliamentary professors who write poetry as a hobby, while the children's work, years later, is still utilized. Immodestly, but factually I mention that the *Poetry Society of America* Bulletin once noted I was one of the leading children's poets of America (I must confess I quit the society long ago because I could not accept the fact that the officers ran for office unopposed), and the observation seems to be borne out by the inclusion of my poetry in numerous reprint items. . . .

"What do I think of life? It is a search, with enjoyment along the way—there is no sin in a smile or the joy of freedom and expression. Life is a building, a doing of what you want to do (for me it is), and as long as you have done your best with the best you have to do it with, how can anyone fail to stand upright, unafraid, and walk through and out of life into whatever. If youth reads this, I would recommend travel, before age, a sipping of the splendor of the earth, a drinking of it, if need be, and the joy of love and companionship (which it was my pleasure to enjoy for, now, almost a half century). Yet I am not old. It is only the body that holds me. I look to the same old sun with the same old dream. I drink the wine of grape and life, eat the good food, and sit by the fireplace. That, coupled with creativity—the right of it, the pleasure of it, causes me to forget (somewhat) the beating I took by being an artist. I see boxers make five million dollars a fight, while poets starve in a society which makes choices. And I understand it. That is why it is wise to get into the eye of the hurricane, if you follow the road I took, and concentrate on your work. As to serving youth, I know of no greater pledge than to guide young eyes to the miracle of the stars."

HOBBIES AND OTHER INTERESTS: Formerly mountain climbing; now enjoys gourmet cooking.

FOR MORE INFORMATION SEE: Cincinnati Post and Times-Star, September 24, 1958; *Cincinnati Enquirer,* May 17, May 24, May 31, 1959, September 15, 1963; *Hendersonville Times-News* (N.C.), October 17, 1972.

MOORE, Margaret R(umberger)   1903-

PERSONAL: Born June 28, 1903, in DuBois, Pa.; daughter of George Francis and Euphrasia (Means) Rumberger; married John Travers Moore (an author; poet), 1928. *Education:* Syracuse University, Syracuse, N.Y., B.S. in L.S., 1926. *Home:* 525 Ehringhaus St., Hendersonville, N.C. 28739.

CAREER: Dayton Public Library, Dayton, Ohio, children's librarian, 1928-1940; free-lance writer, 1941-46; Xavier University, Cincinnati, Ohio, assistant library director, 1947-69, consultant, 1970-71, author and poet, 1971—.

WRITINGS: Here, Kitty, Whitman, 1966; *They Saw Him Fly,* Whitman, 1966.

With husband, John Travers Moore: *Sing-Along Sary,* Harcourt, 1951; *Little Saints,* Grail, 1953; *Big Saints,* Grail, 1954; *The Three Tripps* (Parents' Magazine Book Club selection, Calling All Girls Book Club selection), Bobbs, 1959; *On Cherry Tree Hill,* Bobbs, 1960; *The Little Band and the Inaugural Parade* (Junior Literary Guild selection), Whitman, 1968; *Certainly, Carrie, Cut the Cake* (poetry), Bobbs, 1971; *Pepito's Speech at the United Nations,* Carolrhoda (published in cooperation with the United Nations), 1971. Contributor of many poems, stories and articles to juvenile and professional publications.

WORK IN PROGRESS: New naturalist series for North Carolina Wildlife Resources Commission; working on other volumes of prose and poetry.

SIDELIGHTS: "Since high school days I had been 'dabbling' in poetry. And then, one day an editor of a children's magazine came into the library and asked help in finding a March poem to fit a photograph he had with him. It was a picture of a little lamb following a lion. We found several poems about March coming in like a lion and going out like a lamb, but none quite fit the photo. A librarian hates to give up on a reference question, so that evening I wrote a poem which was appropriate for the picture and mailed it to the magazine. Not having known my name, the editor did not associate the poem with the librarian and his staff thought some kind of a miracle had happened. That was my first sale. Subsequently, they sent me many photos needing poems. I had embarked in children's literature.

"I have seen many changes and trends in the field. Perhaps the most prevalent is the disparaging attitude toward books which promote any sentiment or moral or constructive theses. Properly and competently done, I can see no objection to teaching kindness, understanding, compassion and other characteristics which we like to feel are inherent human qualities. I believe that children respond to beauty and goodness in what they read as well as to violence and scheming. And I believe that what they read is instrumental in forming their adult character."

FOR MORE INFORMATION SEE: Cincinnati Post and Times Star, September 24, 1958; *Cincinnati Enquirer,* April 19, 1959; *Hendersonville Times-News,* N.C., October 17, 1972.

MARGARET R. MOORE

"Do they sing?"
    "Well, they try—"
Midnight magic makes mice merry
    when the moon is high.
■ (From *Certainly Carrie, Cut the Cake: Poems A to Z* by Margaret and John Travers Moore. Illustrated by Laurie Anderson.)

LUCILLE BURNETT MULCAHY

MULCAHY, Lucille Burnett (Helen Hale)

PERSONAL: Born November 10, in Albuquerque, N.M.; daughter of Harry Leland and Grace (Lomax) Burnett; married C. D. Mulcahy, Jr. (an engineer), September 1, 1939, divorced May 1, 1957; children: Burnette (Mrs. John Grega), Dee Ann Eileen (Mrs. James Maestri). *Education:* Attended New Mexico State University, 1947, and University of Albuquerque, 1972-75. *Home:* 425 Western Skies Dr., S.E., Albuquerque, N.M. 87123.

CAREER: Free-lance writer, 1952—. New Mexico Book Co., Albuquerque, N.M., clerk, 1959-62; Albuquerque Public Library, Albuquerque, N.M., procurement aide, 1963-76.

WRITINGS: Dark Arrow, Coward, 1953; *Pita,* Coward, 1954; *Magic Fingers,* Nelson, 1958; (under pseudonym Helen Hale) *Dale Evans and Danger in Crooked Canyon,* Whitman, 1958; *Blue Marshmallow Mountains,* Nelson, 1959; *Natoto,* Nelson, 1960; *Fire on Big Lonesome* (on Zuni Indian fire fighters), Children's Press, 1967. Contributor to juvenile magazines.

WORK IN PROGRESS: Flying Eagle Puppet Plays; a play, "The Broken Reed,"; an adult historical novel, *Taken at the Flood.*

SIDELIGHTS: "The last several years my grandchildren and I have developed an amateur group called 'Flying Eagle Puppets and Puppeteers.' We have performed plays at schools, churches, and libraries consisting of stories woven around ancient Indian legends. Our set of string puppets are characters taken from my first book, *Dark Arrow.* There is a grandfather, Big Little Man, who is the village story teller, and Flying Eagle, his grandson. An uninvited house guest by the name of Hosteen Mouse makes his home with them."

RUTH HILL MUNCE

MUNCE, Ruth Hill   1898-
(Ruth Livingston Hill)

PERSONAL: Born January 24, 1898, in Philadelphia, Pa.; daughter of Franklin G. (a clergyman) and Grace (Livingston) Hill; married Gordon Munce, October 19, 1923 (deceased); children: Gordon, Robert Livingston. *Education:* Swarthmore College, student, 1914-17; Wheaton College, Wheaton, Ill., B.A., 1953; Florida State University, graduate study, 1958. *Politics:* Republican. *Home:* 1255 Pasadena Ave. S., St. Petersburg, Fla. 33707.

CAREER: Swarthmore School of Music, Swarthmore, Pa., co-owner and teacher, 1918-40; Grace Livingston Hill Memorial School (now Keswick Christian School), St. Petersburg, Fla., founder and teacher, 1953-62; Hope Bible Institute, Kenya, East Africa, 1968-75.

WRITINGS: (With Grace Livingston Hill) *Mary Arden,* Lippincott, 1948; (with Hill) *Miss Lavinia's Call,* Lippincott, 1949; *Morning Is for Joy,* Lippincott, 1949; *John Neilson Had a Daughter,* Lippincott, 1950; *Bright Conquest,* Lippincott, 1951; *Jeweled Sword,* Lippincott, 1955; *The South Wind Blew Softly,* Lippincott, 1959; *This Side of Tomorrow,* Zondervan, 1962. Contributor of stories and articles to *His, Sunday School Times,* and *Eternity.*

SIDELIGHTS: "Writing and teaching were the last things I ever wanted to do when I was young, yet they are the two things I have done most. Possibly because I was brought up to the sound of typewriter keys, and literally watched over my mother's shoulder as her stories developed on the page, I absorbed something of her interest in storytelling. After her death, the publisher encouraged me to complete a manuscript she had started, and then to launch out on my own.

"I consider writing hard work, as is anything worthwhile. There comes a point in every manuscript where the writer must practically strap himself into his chair until it is finished.

"As for my mother's books, and my own, she and I both considered that they were a means of sharing with others our living faith in the real and living Saviour, Jesus Christ, and our often confirmed conviction that His Word is true and He does undertake in the lives of those who trust Him."

NAYLOR, Phyllis Reynolds   1933-

PERSONAL: Born January 4, 1933, in Anderson, Ind.; daughter of Eugene S. and Lura (Schield) Reynolds; married Rex V. Naylor (a speech pathologist), May 26, 1960; children: Alan Jeffrey, Michael Scott. *Education:* Joliet Junior College, diploma, 1953; American University, B.A., 1963. *Politics:* Independent. *Religion:* Unitarian Universalist. *Home:* 9910 Holmhurst Road, Bethesda, Md. 20034.

CAREER: Elementary teacher in Hazelcrest, Ill., 1956; Montgomery County Education Association, Rockville, Md., assistant executive secretary, 1958-59; National Education Association, Washington, D.C., editorial assistant with *NEA Journal,* 1959-60; full-time writer, 1960—. Active in civil rights and peace organizations. *Member:* Authors Guild of America, Children's Book Guild (Washington, D.C.).

WRITINGS: The Galloping Goat, Abingdon, 1965; *Grasshoppers in the Soup,* Fortress, 1965; *The New Schoolmaster,* Silver Burdett, 1967; *A New Year's Surprise,* Silver Burdett, 1967; *Jennifer Jean, the Cross-Eyed Queen,* Lerner, 1967; *Knee Deep in Ice Cream,* Fortress, 1967; *To*

PHYLLIS REYNOLDS NAYLOR

Shake a Shadow, Abingdon, 1967; *What the Gulls Were Singing,* Follett, 1967; *When Rivers Meet,* Friendship, 1968; *The Dark Side of the Moon,* Fortress, 1969; *The Private I,* Fortress, 1969; *To Make a Wee Moon,* Follett, 1969; *Meet Murdock,* Follett, 1969; *Making It Happen,* Follett, 1970; *Ships in the Night,* Fortress, 1970; *Wrestle the Mountain,* Follett, 1971; *No Easy Circle,* Follett, 1972; *How to Find Your Wonderful Someone,* Fortress, 1972; *To Walk the Sky Path,* Follett, 1973; *An Amish Family,* O'Hara, 1974; *Witch's Sister,* Atheneum, 1975; *Walking Through the Dark,* Atheneum, 1976; *Getting Along in Your Family,* Abingdon, 1976; *Crazy Love,* Morrow, 1972; *Witch Water,* Atheneum, 1977; *How I Came to be a Writer,* Atheneum, in press; *The Witch Herself,* Atheneum, in press. Contributor of short stories and articles to magazines.

SIDELIGHTS: "When I was small, the thought of being a writer—a paid, professional author—never entered my mind. Writing books on scratch paper was something I did because it was fun and immensely satisfying. We were raised on Mark Twain, the *Bible Story Book,* and Grimm's fairy tales, with occasional desserts such as *The Wind in the Willows* and *Alice in Wonderland* thrown in. My mother, and sometimes my father, read to us each night till we were well into our teens, though I would never have admitted it to anyone.

"At sixteen, I received a letter from a former teacher who had become the editor of a children's Sunday school paper. She said she remembered that I had always liked to write stories, and wondered if I would write one for her. I did, and she bought it for $4.67. I was thrilled, and couldn't imagine being paid for something that was so much fun to do. From then on, very slowly, with many rejections along the way, I began branching out to other magazines, other age levels. By the time I got to college, studying to be a clinical psychologist, I was able to pay a large share of the tuition by writing stories on the side, and when I graduated, I realized that writing was really my first love, so I gave up plans to go to graduate school and began writing seriously for the first time. Two years later my first book was published.

"I like to write about many different things for all ages. After writing an adventure book for younger children, I may write a poem or article for retired people. Then I might write a humorous novel for teenagers, followed by a nonfiction book for their parents. Some of my books are sad, some scary, many of them are funny, and some are all three.

"All of my books begin with a mood—a feeling—which captures me and won't let go till the story is down on paper. It is far more difficult to keep new ideas from crowding in on old ones than it is to get an idea in the first place.

"There is a part of me in every book I write. It may be a big part or a small part. It may be simply a place I have been or someone I have known or something that has happened to me all mixed up with things I just imagine. Some books take a great deal of research—my stories of a Seminole Indian boy, a coal miner's family in West Virginia, or a girl growing up during the Depression. Others are mostly fun and are written 'off the top of my head.' And some books, like *Witch's Sister,* give me goose bumps when I write them, even though I know how the story will turn out.

"Our whole family enjoys books. My boys help not only by counting words in manuscripts for me and proof-reading, but

The hair on the back of Lynn's neck seemed to rise two inches. ■ (From *Witch's Sister* by Phyllis Reynolds Naylor. Illustrated by Gail Owens.)

in giving me ideas for other stories by sharing their own experiences with me. My husband is a chess player in his spare time, and can happily spend an evening over the chess board while I am at the typewriter. But he is my most severe critic, and though I am not always happy with his comments about my characters or plot, his suggestions are always helpful. We enjoy traveling, too, and can spend long hours exploring old villages or beachcombing along the ocean.

"Through my books I can be many different people, living many different places and doing all kinds of interesting things. I can recapture feelings from childhood or project myself into the future. Or I can take a real problem I may be experiencing and work it out on paper. Writing, for me, is the best occupation I can think of, and there is nothing in the world I would rather do."

NEGRI, Rocco 1932-

PERSONAL: Born June 26, 1932, in Italy; son of Salvatore (a barber) and Adele (Plattaroti) Negri; married Joan (Becky) Stewart, March 25, 1958; children: Ronald, Gene. *Education:* Aurel Kessler Academy, Buenos Aires, Argentina, 1953-54; attended Art Students League, New York, N.Y., 1959-60, School of Visual Arts, New York, N.Y.,

1960-64, Pratt Graphic Center, New York, N.Y., 1974-75. *Home and office:* 1668 Norman Street, Ridgewood, N.Y. 11227. *Agent:* Shirley Reece, 39 West 32nd St., New York, N.Y.

CAREER: Artist-illustrator. Vanderbilt Automotive Center, art director, 1970-73. *Exhibitions:* Main Stream, Westhampton Beach, N.Y., 1973; Ratafia Gallery, Ft. Lauderdale, Fla., 1973; The Painter's Mill, Rochester, N.Y., 1974-76; Studio Gallery, Greenport, N.Y., 1975-76.

ILLUSTRATOR: Robert Burch, *Renfroe's Christmas,* Viking, 1968; Mary S. Steele, *Journey Outside,* Viking, 1969; Adrien Stoutenburg, *Fee, Fi, Fo, Fum,* Viking, 1969; Betsy C. Byars, *Trouble River,* Viking, 1969; Rama Mehta, *Life of Keshav: A Family Story from India,* McGraw, 1969; Nardi Reeder Campion, *Casa Means Home,* Holt, 1970; Nancy Garfield, *The Dancing Monkey,* Putnam, 1970; F. N. Monjo, *The One Bad Thing About Father,* Harper, 1970; John Gordon, *The Giant Under the Snow,* Harper, 1970; Don J. Manuel, *Tales from Count Lucanor,* Dial, 1970; Ian Serrailler, *Heracles the Strong,* Walck, 1970; Virginia Holladay, *Bantu Tales,* Viking, 1970; Sarah Abbott, *Where I Begin,* Coward, 1970; Quail Hawkins, *Androcles and the Lion,* Coward, 1970; Francine Jacobs, *The Legs of the Moon,* Coward, 1971; Humphrey Harman, *Men of Masaba,* Viking, 1971; Beman Lord, *On the Banks of the Hudson,* Walck, 1971; Gloria Skurzynski, *The Magic Pumpkin,* Four Winds, 1971; Marietta Moskin, *Toto,* Coward, 1971; James Reeves, *Maildun the Voyager,* Walck, 1971; Laura Fisher, *Charlie Dick,* Holt, 1972; Toby Talbot (editor), *Coplas,* Four Winds, 1972; Johanna Johnston, *The Indians and the Strangers,* Dodd, 1972; Monica Dickens, *The Great Fire,* Doubleday, 1973; Harold Courlander, *The Son of the Leopard,* Crown, 1974; Mirra Ginsburg, editor, *Pampalche of the Silver Teeth,* Crown, 1976.

SIDELIGHTS: "The first three years of my life I lived in Reggio Calabria (Italy), my birthplace. Then my family immigrated to Buenos Aires (Argentina) which I considered to be more my country than my own, for there I grew and developed my personality with the Argentinian idiosyncrasy with a certain touch of the Italian village morality.

"As far as I can remember I was always very quiet just on the surface though, for I was always boiling with the Italian temper inside. I never verbalized with people in general, I don't know whether because of my inability or desire to do so. I communicated more in writing.

I used to express my feelings poetically, especially in the subject of romance. In those days I aspired to become a writer. Fortunately or unfortunately, I never pursued it further, mostly because I hated the academic training.

"My artistic career began during my early twenties, after trying a couple of professional schools unsuccessfully. I was motivated by the desire to find a profession that could grow along with me. I used to dread the idea of becoming part of a 'live-picture' which I think inspired me to become an artist. It impressed me quite deeply to observe how many 'old-people' just sat on park benches day after day, idle, absent-minded, living from past memories, seemingly waiting for death. . . .once people, now just existing, a future certainly not for me. And so it was that after much thinking and perhaps subconsciously, driven by an innate talent (99% perspiration and 1% inspiration talent), I decided art was, besides writing, the one profession I would enjoy enormously. It would provide the opportunity to survive simultaneously with the material and ethereal world.

"Aurel Kessler Academy first introduced me into the world of Art, a whole new universe for me.

ROCCO NEGRI

Peter was alone in the world. ■ (From *The Great Fire* by Monica Dickens. Illustrated by Rocco Negri.)

"After I got married, my wife Becky and I decided to come to the United States to complete our education. We now make our home here with our two boys. After a few years of art training I tried my luck in book illustration. A tough field to get in as well as to get out. You just don't want to.

"Illustration in my case was the product of the School of Visual Art and the influence the instructors who were and still are top-artist illustrators, had on me. I particularly enjoy book illustration because of the ample area of freedom of expression, exposure and recognition as well, to feed the ego.

"My goal for the future is to contribute in my own personal way artistically for the benefit of future artists and art lovers. My philosophy is that illustration in general artistically performed, is just as fine art as fine art itself.

"In addition to my art, carpentry is another vocation that I enjoy and possibly an occupation I would have chosen.

"I haven't done much travelling yet, except visiting now and then Argentina, Brazil, Paraguay, some small islands on my way to them and Canada two or three times a year; but do hope to reach every existing place in this 'mad, mad world of ours.'

"The languages that I speak besides art, are Italian, Spanish and English. The artist that influenced me in feeling and technique was Vincent Van Gogh.

"One of my greatest satisfactions in life is illustrating childrens' books, because children are so pure in appreciation and perception. They have no inhibition or discrimination to cloud their minds or hearts."

NICHOLS, Cecilia Fawn   1906-

PERSONAL: Born March 6, 1906, in Bellevue, Neb.; daughter of Robert Cleveland (a railroad engineer) and Ellen (McGinley) Nichols. *Education:* University of Omaha, B.S., 1938; also studied at University of Nebraska and University of Southern California. *Religion:* First Church of Mystic Christianity. *Home:* Star Rte 1, Box 435, Apt. 2-G, Yucca Valley, Calif. 92284. *Agent:* Georgia Nicholas, Nicholas Literary Agency, 161 Madison Ave., New York, N.Y. 10016.

CAREER: Elementary teacher, 1927-36, high school teacher, 1936-42 (both in Omaha, Neb.); elementary teacher, 1942-43, high school teacher, 1945-51 (both in California); civil service employee at air bases in California, 1943-45, 1951-60, with posts including director of security education at Maywood Air Force Base, 1953-59; teacher of adult education classes in creative writing at Mount San Antonio College, Pomona, and other schools in San Gabriel Valley, Calif., 1960-63; free-lance writer, 1963—. Twentynine Palms Community Council, member. *Member:* Armed Forces Writers League (regional director for Southern California, 1960-64; chairman of editors jury, 1972—), California Retired Teachers Association (regional first vice-president), Twentynine Palms Women's Club (publicity chairman). *Awards, honors:* First prize, Pomona Writers Club, for short story, "The Man Who Went to Hell," 1962; 87th prize, *Writer's Digest* contest, 1964; *Boy's Life* certificate of merit for story, "A Penny's Worth of Boy."

WRITINGS: The Goat Who Ate a Cow, Bruce, 1964. Author of short stories and plays.

SIDELIGHTS: "My parents discovered I loved drama when I was but eighteen months old. They hadn't been near a theater from the day I was born and they both loved stage plays. So they went to see 'Gyp, the Cowgirl' and were told there was a big shooting scene and 'if the baby cries you'll have to leave and your money won't be refunded.' I loved the show and when the shooting took place I applauded it. My delighted parents looked at each other and said, 'We can go to shows from now on.'

"Nickelodeons became my next love. When I was two we lived in a district of moving-picture shows. Whenever my mother took me for a walk and we got near one I darted quickly through the door. I could get in free but Mama had to plunk down a nickel for a ticket to get me, and she couldn't get me out until I had seen the show over at least three times.

"An avid reader, having taken to reading like a bird to the sky, at age nine I decided to become a writer—a playwright. My mother had joined a community players' group and took me with her to all the rehearsals. Thrilled by watching a play

CECILIA FAWN NICHOLS

in production, I wrote my first play—a skit, entitled 'The Tea Party' and the characters were to be three little girls dressed in their mother's clothes playing 'grown-up.' The director liked my play and said when the big production was over she'd direct my little play for a school show. Before my big moment could happen, the players got into some kind of hassle and the group broke up.

"I did no more play-writing until 1939, when I was teaching at South High School in Omaha, Nebraska and, having observed the immense amount of talent among the students, I decided to write a musical play in which all this talent could be used. I spent two years writing the play and I wrote ten songs, both music and lyrics. A Western, the setting was a Southern Arizona ranch. In Act I there was a big fiesta scene to encompass all that beautiful talent I knew existed in South. I finished the play by the fall of 1941. The two Glee Club teachers liked it and were willing to help me produce it. I was still trying to get our principal's approval when boom! the whole thing blew up with Pearl Harbor. No gatherings for the duration of the war.

"In 1948 I was teaching in the high school at Delano, California where I also sponsored the Harlem Club. The Harlem Club had to put on a show for the school before the year ended and one member, seventeen-year-old DeArmond Tarkington, suddenly developed 'playwright-fever' and brought his symptoms to me which consisted of six acts with the curtain going up and down on the few lines of dialogue in each act. However, the few lines of dialogue were like discovering a rich vein of gold and his characters were 'seeable' individuals. His title 'The Diary of Belle La Rue' aroused my imagination. His plot was shorter than his acts, so I took over and built a plot and changed six-acts to three. Every word of dialogue was his and it was marvelous, but he

couldn't produce a single skit for the night club acts in Act I. I had to think up the entire performance and my skit that made the big hit was 'Red Riding Hood and the Wolf.' Delano business men said our show was the best put on in the high school in several years and various organizations asked us to repeat the night club performances, especially 'Red Riding Hood and the Wolf.' We performed for the Kiwanis Club, the Lion's Club and the Royal Neighbors of America. The students even went to Bakersfield for a performance there.

"Later when I was teaching fourth and fifth grades in Moorpark, California, I was scheduled to put on a show in March. For this I wrote a three-act musical about banshees, will-o-the-wisp, talking trees, fairies, elves and a lively potato that refused to be cooked and eaten—setting Ireland, title 'The Irish Potato.' The play was presented on St. Patrick's Day. Between Acts I and II my skit 'Red Riding Hood,' etc., was re-enacted under the title 'Green Riding-Hood and the Irish Wolf' and dialogue was changed to Irish brogue and Irish wit. The Ventura newspaper photographed the skit. As for the play I sold it to *Grade Teacher* and it was published March, 1960. It's my only published play.

"My writings are all dramatically written. 'A Penny's Worth of Boy' is so dramatic the taped radio production is exactly word for word as originally written.

"My life has been, and continues to be, as dramatic as my writings."

HOBBIES AND OTHER INTERESTS: Creative art—painting, wood carving, mask-making, acting in amateur theatricals. Cecilia Nichols had her first art shows in 1975.

FOR MORE INFORMATION SEE: University of Omaha Alumni Newsletter, January, 1965.

NOWELL, Elizabeth Cameron (Elizabeth Cameron, Elizabeth Clemons)

PERSONAL: Daughter of Alfred George and Edith (Catton) Cameron; married Arthur Granville Robinson (vice admiral), 1961 (died, January, 1967); married Nelson T. Nowell, February 15, 1969 (died, September, 1973). *Education:* San Jose State College, A.B., 1928; Stanford University, M.A., 1937; graduate work at Columbia University, University of Minnesota, Oxford University, University of Pennsylvania. *Address:* P.O. Box 686, Carmel, Calif. 93921. *Agent:* Dorothy Markinko, McIntosh & Otis, 18 East 41st St., New York, N.Y. 10017.

CAREER: San Jose State College, San Jose, Calif., education department, 1928-39; University of California Extension Department, in-service education, 1939-42; John C. Winston Co., elementary editor, 1942-43; Silver Burdett Co., elementary editor, 1943-44; D. C. Heath and Co., elementary editor, 1944-46; University of Minnesota, Minneapolis, English department, 1947; General Mills Corp., writer and editor, 1947-50; free-lance writer, 1950—. Community Hospital Auxiliary, member, board of directors, 1962; Visiting Nurse Association, member of board of directors, 1965; Harrison Memorial Library board, 1971—; St. Dunstan's Episcopal Church, vestry, 1974-76; executive board, Monterey chapter of Embroiderers' Guild of America, 1975-77.

Member: National League of American Penwomen, League of Women Voters, International Platform Association, Soroptomist International, Pi Lambda Theta, Delta Phi Upsilon, Kappa Delta Pi, Delta Kappa Gamma, Kappa Alpha Theta, Republican Club, Woman's City Club, Monterey Peninsula Country Club, Commonwealth Club, Casa Abrego Club.

WRITINGS—Under professional name Elizabeth Clemons: *The Pixie Dictionary*, John C. Winston, 1953, revised edition, 1965; *The Catholic Child's First Dictionary*, John C. Winston, 1954; *The Winston Dictionary for Canadian School Children*, John C. Winston, 1955; *Wings, Wheels and Motors*, Grosset, 1957; *Rodeo Days*, Lane, 1960; *Shells Are Where You Find Them*, Knopf, 1960; *Rocks and the World Around You*, Coward, 1960; *Big and Little*, Holt, 1961; *Tide Pools and Beaches*, Knopf, 1964; *Waves, Tides, and Currents*, Knopf, 1967; *Near & Far Stories, Now & Then Stories, Here & There Stories*, (all published by Franklin, 1967); *A Source Book for the Teaching of Literature for Children*, Franklin, 1967; *The Seven Seas*, Knopf, 1971; *What I Like*, Harcourt, 1971; *The Friendly Frog*, Harcourt, 1971.

Under maiden name Elizabeth Cameron: *Away I Go, All About Baby, I Live on a Farm, A Wish for Billy*, (all published by Grosset, 1956); *The Big Book of Real Fire En-*

ELIZABETH CAMERON NOWELL, (on left)

gines, The Big Book of Real Trains, The Big Book of Real Trucks, (all published by Grosset, 1958). Contributor of articles to *Better Homes and Gardens, American Home,* and other national magazines. Associate editor, *California Home* (California edition of *American Home*), 1965—.

SIDELIGHTS: "There have been few times in my life when I have lived far from the sea. I am a third generation Californian, but I have lived in several middlewestern and eastern states. Probably two of my hobbies, shell collecting and travel, have intensified my love of the sea.

"My interest in shell collecting began when I was a young girl. Through this interest on my travels, I have collected shells from all over the world. I wrote *Shells Are Where You Find Them* because there was no authentic book on shells that elementary school boys and girls could read to help them accurately identify the shells they collected. The book is simply written, but it is used by many adults because the information is arranged with scientific names as well as the more common names for easy reference. This is true of *Tide Pools and Beaches* as well.

"*Waves, Tides, and Currents* was begun after a trip to the beach with several young friends. When one of the boys asked me what caused the waves to roll in, I found that I could not explain in simple terms . . . and he told me he could not understand the information he had found in books. The book took four years to write, and I hope it is a good introduction for anyone who wants to understand the mysteries and wonders of the sea.

"The books I have written have all been about things in which I am interested—animals, rodeos, seas and beaches, rocks, transportation, travel, stories of people in other lands, and canvas work embroidery (more commonly called needlepoint in the United States). Most of my books are factual but I have written a few simple fiction books for young people.

"My house is on the beach in Carmel-by-the-Sea. From the large windows I can watch the waves roll in with each tide, find shells along the waters edge, and walk on the beach with my two Welsh Corgi dogs, Happy Talk and Little Sister, who love the beach as much as I do."

Experiences as a writer and editor of children's books led to a concern with helping children who have reading problems.

HOBBIES AND OTHER INTERESTS: Shell collecting, travel, and canvas work embroidery.

O'DELL, Scott   1903-

PERSONAL: Born May 23, 1903, in Los Angeles, Calif.; son of Bennett Mason and May Elizabeth (Gabriel) O'Dell. *Education:* Attended Occidental College, 1919, University of Wisconsin, 1920, Stanford University, 1920-21, and University of Rome, 1925.

CAREER: Formerly a cameraman and a book editor for Los Angeles newspaper; full-time writer, 1934—. *Military service:* U.S. Air Force. *Awards, honors:* Rupert Hughes award, 1960, John Newbery medal, 1961, Southern California Council on Literature for Children and Young People notable book award, 1961, Hans Christian Andersen award of merit, 1962, William Allen White award, 1963, German Juvenile International Award, 1963, and Nene award, 1964, all for *Island of the Blue Dolphins;* Newbery honor award, 1967, and German Juvenile International Award, 1969, both for *The King's Fifth;* Newbery honor awards, 1968, for *The Black Pearl,* and 1971, for *Sing Down the Moon;* Hans Christian Andersen medal, 1972; University of Southern Mississippi medallion, 1976.

WRITINGS: Representative Photoplays Analyzed: Modern Authorship, Palmer Institute of Authorship, 1924; *Woman of Spain: A Story of Old California* (novel), Houghton, 1934; *Hill of the Hawk* (novel), Bobbs-Merrill, 1947; (with William Doyle) *Man Alone,* Bobbs-Merrill, 1953; *Country of the Sun: Southern California, an Informal History and Guide,* Crowell, 1957; *The Sea Is Red: A Novel,* Holt, 1958; (with Rhoda Kellogg) *The Psychology of Children's Art,* Communications Research Machines, 1967.

Juvenile literature—All published by Houghton: *Island of the Blue Dolphins,* 1960; *The King's Fifth,* 1966; *The Black Pearl,* 1967; *The Dark Canoe,* 1968; *Journey to Jericho,* 1969; *Sing Down the Moon,* 1970; *The Treasure of Topo-el-Bampo,* 1972; *The Cruise of the Arctic Star,* 1973; *Child of Fire,* 1974; *The Hawk That Dare Not Hunt by Day,* 1975; *Zia,* 1976; *The 290,* 1976; *Carlota,* 1977.

SIDELIGHTS: "Los Angeles was a frontier town when I was born there around the turn of the century. It had more horses than automobiles, more jack rabbits than people. The very first sound I remember was a wildcat scratching on the roof as I lay in bed.

"My father was a railroad man so we moved a lot, but never far. Wherever we went, it was into frontier country like Los Angeles. There was San Pedro, which is a part of Los Angeles. And Rattlesnake Island, across the bay from San Pedro, where we lived in a house on stilts and the waves came up and washed us under every day. And sailing ships went by.

"That is why, I suppose, the feel of the frontier and the sound of the sea are in my books.

"*Island of the Blue Dolphins,* my first story for children, came directly from the memory of the years I lived at Rattlesnake Island and San Pedro. From the days when with other boys of my age I voyaged out on summer mornings in search of the world.

"We left the landlocked world and went to sea, each of us on separate logs. The logs had been towed into the harbor in great rafts bound together from the forests of Oregon. They

■ (From the movie "Island of the Blue Dolphins," copyright © 1964 by Universal International.)

Something about the Author

SCOTT O'DELL

were twelve feet long or longer, rough with splinters, and covered with tar. But to each of us young Magellans they were proud canoes, dugouts fashioned by ax and fire, graceful, fierce-prowed, the equal of any storm.

"We freed them from the deep-water slips where they waited for the sawmill. Paddling with our hands, we set to sea, to the breakwater and even to Portuguese Bend. We returned hours later, the watery world encompassed.

"Other mornings, in sun or rain, we went to Dead Man's Island, a rocky islet near the entrance to San Pedro Harbor. There we pried abalones from the crevices and searched for devilfish in the sea-washed caves.

"The memory of these times also went into the writing of *Island of the Blue Dolphins*.

"One of those summers my mother and I traveled across the country to visit an aunt and uncle who lived in a small coal-mining town in West Virginia. The miners with lamps on their caps, the blind mules that shoved the carts back and forth in the mine, the electric dolly that hauled the coal out of the mine and the small steam engine that pulled it away to the railroad tipple—all these things fascinated me. Remembering them and that long-ago summer, I wrote *Journey to Jericho*.

"Grammar and high school fascinated me, too. But not college, not Occidental nor Stanford nor the University of Wisconsin. By this time I had my heart set upon writing. However, most of the courses I was forced to take to graduate had little to do with learning to write. So I forgot graduation and took only the courses I wanted—psychology, philosophy, history and English.

"I therefore have a sense of comradeship with the students of today. I agree with those who say that they feel like pris-

oners marching in lockstep toward some unknown goal. I agree that classes are often too large, for I remember a Stanford class in Shakespeare which numbered seventy-six, seventy-five of whom were girls. What can you learn about Shakespeare in such surroundings, even if you're a girl?

"After college I was a cameraman on the second company of the original motion picture of *Ben Hur,* carrying the first Technicolor camera, made by hand at M.I.T., around the Roman countryside. I spent a year with the Air Force in Texas during World War II, several years as a book editor on a Los Angeles newspaper. The past twenty years I have devoted to writing, ten of these years writing for adults and the last ten for children.

"To say that my books were written *for* children is not exactly true. In one sense they were written for myself, out of happy and unhappy memories and a personal need. But all of them lie in the emotional area that children share with adults.

"Writing for children is more fun than writing for adults and more rewarding. Children have the ability, which most adults have lost, the knack to be someone else, of living through stories the lives of other people. Six months after the publication of an adult book, there's a big silence. Or so it is with me. But with a book for children it's just the opposite. If children like your book they respond for a long time, by thousands of letters. It is this response, this concern and act of friendship, that for me makes the task of writing worth the doing.

"There are, of course, a few letters that you would never miss. The letter, for example, from the girl in Minnesota who wrote, asking a dozen or more questions. To have answered them all would have taken two hours, which I didn't have. After a week or so, when she failed to hear from me, she wrote again. She said among other things: '. . . if I don't get a reply from you in five days I will send a letter to another author I know. Anyway, I like her books better than yours.'

"In their letters children ask dozens of questions. Some are personal, like 'How much money do you make?' but mostly they want to know how you work, how stories are put together, how long it takes to write a story, and what is the most important thing a writer should have.

"Anthony Trollope, the great English storyteller, said that the most important thing was a piece of sealing wax with which to fasten your pants to a chair. And I agree with him.

"Writing is hard work. The only part of it I really enjoy is the research, which takes three or four months. The story itself as a rule takes about six months.

"I write, when I do write, which is about half my time, from seven in the morning until noon, every day of the week. I use an electric typewriter, because when you turn it on it has a little purr that invites you to start writing instead of looking out the window. I sometimes use a pen and work very slowly. But I can write with anything and anywhere and have—in Spain and Italy, Germany and France and England and Mexico, in Rancho Santa Fe, a beautiful place in southern California, within sight of the sea, where I now live.

"When I am not writing I like to read and work in the sun. I like to garden, to plant trees of all kinds, to be on the sea, fishing some, watching the weather, the sea birds, the whales moving north and south with the seasons, the dolphins, and all the life of the changing waters."

The Island of the Blue Dolphins was filmed by Universal in 1963 and *The Black Pearl* in 1976. "Meet the Newbery Author" is a Scott O'Dell filmstrip available from Miller-Brody Productions.

FOR MORE INFORMATION SEE: John Rowe Townsend, *A Sense of Story,* Lippincott, 1971; *Horn Book,* October, 1972; *New York Times Book Review,* March 25, 1973; *American Libraries,* June, 1973; *Authors' Choice 2,* Crowell, 1974; *The Pied Pipers,* Paddington Press, 1974.

PAUL, Aileen   1917-

PERSONAL: Born June 2, 1917, in Waycross, Ga.; daughter of John Preston (a railroad dispatcher) and Edna (Samuelson) Phillips; married Sol Paul (a television magazine owner and publisher), June, 1943; married second husband, Fred Bartholomew (a television producer and former child star), December 12, 1953; children: (first marriage) Celia; (second marriage) K. T., Frederick. *Education:* Attended schools in the southwestern United States. *Religion:* Unitarian-Universalist. *Residence:* Leonia, N.J.

AILEEN PAUL

If your youngster is interested in camping, your principal role should be advisory. ■ (From *Kids Camping* by Aileen Paul. Illustrated by Bert Devito.)

CAREER: Aileen Paul has worked for various radio stations as a promotion writer, researcher and writer of news material, production assistant, and saleswoman of commercial time; she produced and hosted "New York Cooks," a thirty-minute daily cooking program, for WPIX-Television, 1952-53; WNYC-Radio, New York, N.Y., hostess for "Children's Center," a weekly calendar, 1972-73. She has worked as a public relations representative and publicist for firms including Proctor & Gamble, Bristol-Myers, and the Dow Chemical Co. She prepares food for photographs, and for television commercials and conducts workshops in cooking and gardening for children. She was education director of Northern Valley Consumers Cooperative (supermarkets in Leonia and Ridgefield) for eight years, now serves as vice-president, and continues as consultant to cooperatives.

MEMBER: Authors Guild, Academy of Television Arts and Sciences, American Women in Radio and Television, International Radio and Television Society, Cooperative Institute Association, National Organization for Women (NOW). *Awards, honors:* American Women in Radio and Television and SESAC (Society of European State Authors and Composers) "AM Broadcaster of the Year" awards.

WRITINGS: (With Arthur Hawkins) *Kids Cooking: A First Cookbook for Children,* Doubleday, 1970; *Kids Gardening: A First Indoor Gardening Book for Children,* Doubleday, 1972; *Kids Camping,* Doubleday, 1973; (with Arthur Hawkins) *Candies, Cookies, Cakes,* Doubleday, 1974; *Kids Cooking Complete Meals,* Doubleday, 1975; *Kids Cooking Without a Stove,* Doubleday, 1975; *Kids 50-State Cook-*

book, Doubleday, 1976; *Kids Outdoor Gardening,* Double-day, 1973. Writer on assignment for several newspapers, including the *Christian Science Monitor.*

SIDELIGHTS: Aileen Paul was born in Waycross, Georgia, but spent much of her childhood growing up in Texas, New Mexico, and Colorado, spending her summers with her Swedish grandparents on a farm in Nebraska. "My family encouraged me to participate in many phases of family life—cooking, gardening, and being part of important decisions . . . I think we had a mutual respect for each other. Perhaps that's one reason I never hesitate to share decision-making with children; I have a great respect for kids, their common sense, and their natural abilities."

She feels children are often excluded from suitable adult activities which would give them support in decision-making and finds her work with young people helps to strengthen the bridge between their lives and the adult world. She is unusually active, but has said, "I'm a Gemini, and Geminis are known to be happiest when we're kept busy doing many things."

HOBBIES AND OTHER INTERESTS: Travel, crewel embroidery, and bridge.

FOR MORE INFORMATION SEE: New York Times, February 10, 1968; *American Home,* June, 1972.

PELAEZ, Jill   1924-

PERSONAL: Surname is pronounced Pel-*eye*-eth; born April 24, 1924, in Santurce, P.R.; daughter of Walter Keaton (a citrus grower) and Sybil Nice (Wende) Fletcher; married Emmanuel Antonio Pelaez (executive director, Mental Health Assoc., Orange County), December 22, 1945; children: Jill (Mrs. Martin Baumgaertner), Gay Wende (Livingston), David. *Education:* Attended Rollins College, 1944-45, B.A., 1973, M.A.T., 1976, and University of Oklahoma,

JILL PELAEZ

A group of singers serenaded her. A troup of gypsies danced for her. But she could not see or hear. She was crying too hard. ■ (From *Donkey Tales* by Jill Pelaez. Drawings by Jim Padgett.)

1956-57; also studied art at Prado Museum, Madrid, Spain, 1962-64, and dance in Santurce, P.R., 1941, and at Chalif School of Ballet, New York, N.Y. 1943. *Home:* 3018 Westchester Ave., Orlando, Fla. 32803.

CAREER: Free-lance writer. Teacher at Lake Highland Preparatory School, (Lower School), Orlando, Fla.; creative writing teacher, Rollins Summer Academy. *Member:* Armed Forces Writers' League, National League of American Penwomen, Authors Guild, Kappa Delta Pi.

WRITINGS: (Contributor) Johnson, Kress, et al, *Ideas and Images 32,* American Book Co., 1968, 1976; *Donkey Tales,* Abingdon, 1971. Contributor of short stories to *Humpty Dumpty* and *Highlights for Children,* of articles to *U.S. Lady,* and of poetry to *Stars and Stripes.* Fiction editor, *Flamingo* (Rollins College publication), 1944.

WORK IN PROGRESS: A historical novel about Florida and a three-act play from that novel; a novel about the storks of Spain for young people.

SIDELIGHTS: "Recently, I have followed in my daughters' footsteps, having returned to school, so I too, could become a teacher. My oldest daughter, Jill, is working on her doctorate and teaching at Emory University, while Gay Wende is a special education teacher.

"I love being with young people and have found the greatest joy in my new career, teaching all reading, English and composition in departmentalized sixth grades. We do a lot of exciting things, publishing our own newspaper and literary magazine."

Jill Pelaez, whose husband is a retired Air Force colonel, has lived in Puerto Rico, Spain, Germany, and ten of the fifty United States, and traveled in Mexico, England, France, Italy, Czechoslovakia, Poland, and Russia.

QUARLES, Benjamin 1904-

PERSONAL: Born January 23, 1904, in Boston, Mass.; son of Arthur Benedict and Margaret (O'Brien) Quarles; married Ruth Brett, 1952; children: (first marriage) Roberta; (second marriage) Pamela. *Education:* Shaw University, B.A., 1931; University of Wisconsin, M.A., 1933, Ph.D., 1940. *Home:* 2205 Southern Ave., Baltimore, Md. 21214. *Office:* Morgan State University, Baltimore, Md. 21239.

CAREER: Shaw University, Raleigh, N.C., instructor of history, 1934-38; Dillard University, New Orleans, La., professor, 1938-46, dean, 1946-53; Morgan State College (now University), Baltimore, Md., professor of history, and head of department, 1953—. *Awards, honors:* Guggenheim Fellow, 1958-59.

WRITINGS: Frederick Douglass, Associated Publishers, 1948; *The Negro in the Civil War,* Little, Brown, 1953; *The Negro in the American Revolution,* University of North Carolina Press, 1961; *Lincoln and the Negro,* Oxford University Press, 1962; (editor) *Narrative of the Life of Frederick Douglass,* 1962; *The Negro in the Making of America,*

Macmillan, 1964; (collaborator) *Lift Every Voice,* Doubleday, 1965; (editor) *Frederick Douglass, "Great Lives Observed" Series,* Prentice-Hall, 1968; *Black Abolitionists,* Oxford University Press, 1969; (editor) *Blacks on John Brown,* University of Illinois Press, 1972; *Allies for Freedom: Blacks and John Brown,* Oxford University Press, 1974; (with Leslie H. Fishel, Jr.) *The Black American: A Documentary,* Scott, Foresman, 1976. Contributor to history journals. Member of editorial board, *Journal of Negro History.*

SIDELIGHTS: "I grew up in Boston, Mass., living in the inner city, as we would call it today. Upon completing elementary and high school, I worked for five years at unskilled jobs before deciding to resume my schooling. I went to Shaw University in Raleigh, North Carolina, where I found a number of dedicated teachers.

"One of these teachers aroused my interest in history, particularly black history. I sensed that this was a field in which one might find information that was new and fresh. I was not disappointed. Over the years I have found out and written about little known heroic black men and women who took part in one of the epic struggles for freedom in the United States."

RASKIN, Joseph 1897-

PERSONAL: Born April 14, 1897, in Russia; son of Naphthali (a merchant) and Lea (Vaniler) Raskin; married Edith Lefkowitz (a writer), October 30, 1936. *Education:* At-

BENJAMIN QUARLES

It was long ago when the first red men came to the shores of the Shatemuc, the mighty river now called the Hudson. ■ (From *Indian Tales* retold by Joseph & Ellen Raskin. Illustrated by Helen Siegl.)

JOSEPH RASKIN

tended National Academy of Design for seven years. *Politics:* Independent. *Home and office:* 59 West 71st St., New York, N.Y. 10023. *Agent:* Bertha Klausner, International Literary Agency, Inc., 71 Park Ave., New York, N.Y.

CAREER: Painter and etcher; work has been exhibited in Paris and Berlin and in galleries in the United States, including Carnegie Institute, Corcoran Gallery, and National Academy of Design. *Exhibitions:* One-man show of etchings of American Universities at the New York Historical Society, 1975. *Member:* Audubon Artists Association. *Awards, honors:* Chalon Prize for painting, 1921; Mooney European scholarship in art, 1922; Tiffany Foundation fellowship, 1922-1924.

WRITINGS: Portfolio of Harvard Etchings (self-illustrated), Rudge Publishing Co., 1935; (with wife, Edith Raskin) *Indian Tales,* Random House, 1969; (with Edith Raskin) *Tales Our Settlers Told,* Lothrop, 1971; (with Edith Raskin) *Ghosts and Witches Aplenty: More Tales Our Settlers Told,* Lothrop, 1973; (with Edith Raskin) *The Newcomers, Ten Tales of American Immigrants,* Lothrop, 1974; (with Edith Raskin) *Guilty or Not Guilty: Tales of Justice in Early America,* Lothrop, 1975; (with Edith Raskin) *Spies and Traitors: Tales of the Revolutionary and Civil Wars,* Lothrop, 1976; (with Edith Raskin) *Strange Shadows: Spirit Tales of Early America,* Lothrop, 1977. Contributor to anthologies, literature, mythology and folklore; two stories from *Tales Our Settlers Told,* Science Research Associates, 1973, 1974.

SIDELIGHTS: "Ever since I can remember I liked to draw and paint. When I was twelve years old, impressed by an event that occurred in my little town of Nogaisk, I wrote a tragedy in five acts with an epilogue, which has remained a secret to this day. Also, played the cornet in my high school band and tried to play any instrument I could lay my hands on.

"Believing that all the arts have basic principles in common, I tried to pursue them all. In time, however, painting and writing became my dominant interests.

"While studying abroad, I was impressed by the Rhine and the countryside along the Seine River. But returning home and seeing the Hudson River again, I was even more moved by the majesty of this waterway. Eventually its history prompted me, together with my wife, to write a group of tales about the Hudson which the Indians called the Shatemuc. Also, the legends of New England where my wife and I spent many a summer inspired us to continue writing about early American life.

"At present, my wife and I are engaged in writing still another book dealing with the same fascinating period."

HOBBIES AND OTHER INTERESTS: Travel, music, sports, cooking.

FOR MORE INFORMATION SEE: Library Journal, May 15, 1969.

REID, Eugenie Chazal   1924-

PERSONAL: Born December 21, 1924, in Woodbury, N.J.; daughter of Philip Maxwell and Mabel (Batten) Chazal; married George K. Reid (now a college professor), July 23, 1949; children: Louise, Philip. *Education:* Florida State University, A.B., 1945; University of North Carolina, B.S.

EUGENIE CHAZAL REID

It was a formidable crew that trudged along the almost deserted few blocks, trowels in hand...
■ (From *The Mystery of the Second Treasure* by Eugenie C. Reid. Illustrated by Reisie Lonette.)

in L.S., 1947; Stetson University College of Law, J.D., 1976. *Religion:* Presbyterian. *Home:* 2928 DeSoto Way South, St. Petersburg, Fla. 33712. *Agent:* Bertha Klausner, International Literary Agency, Inc., 130 East 40th St., New York, N.Y. 10016.

CAREER: Jacksonville (Fla.) public library, librarian, 1947; University of Florida Library, Gainesville, librarian, 1947-52; Commerce Clearing House, Tampa, Fla., law editor, 1976—.

WRITINGS: Mystery of the Carrowell Necklace (juvenile), Lothrop, 1965; *Mystery of the Second Treasure* (juvenile), Lothrop, 1967.

SIDELIGHTS: "Ever since I was quite young, I've enjoyed being a story teller. We were often called upon to do this in school, and my stories were more preposterous than most, apparently, for the students frequently persuaded the teacher to let me tell extra ones. It was a special kind of story telling, I realize now, which became a creative experience for the entire group. I used three main characters that everyone came to know, and involved them all in some ridiculous project. I generally had an idea of how it would end, but the twists and turns of the plot, along with the dialogue and humor (for it was, above all, comedy) were being suggested constantly by the audience and woven into the narrative. It was a marvelous experience for me, fun for the other pupils, I think, and surely a welcomed rest for the teacher.

"When my own children were small, they delighted in being able to nudge my bedtime tales in one direction or another. But when my daughter was in the fourth grade, she suddenly decided that I should write a book, and suggested horse stories or mysteries. I didn't know anything about horses, so mysteries are what I wrote. And because I was writing for my son, as well, I tried to write books that both boys and girls would like.

"My characters were based on people that I knew, and the places were actual places, with a few imaginative changes.

Then I thought up some unusual events to happen to these ordinary people in ordinary places. It was easier, I found, not to have to make up *everything*.

"After many years of staying at home, keeping the family and pets fed, playing the organ and doing a great deal of reading, I went back to college to get a law degree. My daughter enrolled a semester after I did, and in the course of the three years there, we often had classes together. We found this to be, at one time or another, helpful, annoying, embarrassing, or funny. Having your daughter (or mother) as a classmate can be a most unusual situation in itself. Perhaps one of us will put that in a book some day."

RINGI, Kjell Arne Sörensen 1939-
(Kjell Ringi, Kjell S-Ringi)

PERSONAL: Born February 3, 1939, in Gothenburg, Sweden; son of Arne (a sales director) and Ingrid (Adolfsson) Sörensen Ringi. *Education:* Attended Sloejdfoereningen, Gothenburg, Sweden, 1955-56 and Berghs Reklamskola, Stockholm, Sweden, 1957-58. *Religion:* Protestant. *Home:* Hvitfeldtsgatan 5, Gothenburg, Sweden.

CAREER: Gumaelius (advertising firm), Sweden, employee, 1960-62; author and illustrator of comic strip, "The Mirrors," for Swedish television and magazines, 1962—. Painter, 1962—, and illustrator-author, 1967—. Has had exhibitions in Stockholm, Gothenburg, Norrkoeping, Copenhagen, New York, Chicago, Seattle, San Francisco, Dallas, Trollhättan, New Jersey, Odense, Oslo, Amsterdam, Los Angeles, Houston, Palm Beach, San Diego among others. Represented in museums and collections in Europe and the United States. *Military service:* Swedish Army, 1959-60. *Awards, honors:* Sloejdfoereningen award, 1956; Berghs Reklamskola award, 1958; citation of merit, Society of Illustrators Annual National Exhibition, 1970, for *The Winner* and 1977.

KJELL RINGI

WRITINGS—All self-illustrated juveniles: under name Kjell Ringi: *The Magic Stick,* Harper, 1968; *The Stranger* (Junior Literary Guild selection), Random House, 1968; *The Winner,* Harper, 1969; *The Sun and the Cloud,* Harper, 1971; *The Parade,* Watts, 1975.

Illustrator: Adelaide Holl, *The Man Who Had No Dream,* Random House, 1969; Adelaide Holl, *My Father and I,* Watts, 1972; *The Parade,* Watts, 1975. Television films: "Pappa och Jag" (based on *My Father and I*), first produced on Swedish television, September, 1971, "Paraden" (based on *The Parade*), 1971, "Fisken," 1976, "Vännerna," 1976, "Hokus Pokus," 1976. Contributor of illustrations to magazines in the U.S. and Sweden.

WORK IN PROGRESS: Several exhibitions in Europe and the United States; various ideas for picture books and television films.

SIDELIGHTS: "My life as a child and teenager was somewhat a disaster. Mainly because I consistently refused to wear my glasses which I really needed because of my nearsightedness. Due to this stubborness, I seemed very absentminded and insecure which made my friends tease me. Being the tallest of my class, I was placed at the back of the room and, therefore, could hardly see the contours on the blackboard. Screened off from the world I often lost myself in fantasies writing grotesque figures on the desklid. Had I worn my glasses and passed college, I should probably have been

an average bank accountant or something similar today, instead of, as I see it, being in the lucky position of creating picture books and pictures.

"The turning point of my life took place in 1957 when I entered an advertising school in Stockholm and at the same time began to use my glasses. I acquired awards as well as self-confidence during this time. Employed at an advertising agency in Gothenburg during 1960 (after military service), I mostly made original drawings on the sketches of others.

"(This wasn't my way of life.) In order to get to know myself, I took an odd job on a cruise liner to New York, the West Indies and South America (1961). My first confrontation with New York ended very unfortunately. I was left astern without glasses and with only a toothbrush in my pocket. It was a terrible experience, but my visit six years later was to be more worthwhile. Perhaps I was given the igniting spark in the West Indies, because when I returned to Gothenburg three months later, I started painting (pictures) phrenetically day and night up to 1967 and had many successful art exhibitions in Sweden and abroad.

"People bought my pictures. The same fellows who had teased me, now, diffidently came up to me in the street and congratulated me on my latest successes. Very satisfying! During this time I, also, made two comic strips, 'The Mirror' and 'Comic Crew' which still are published on a small scale.

The next morning, bright and early,
Mr. Oliver hurried outdoors and,
for the first time in his life,
he began to work.
He spaded and raked
and planted and watered.
He built a beautiful park
all planted with leafy trees
and bright flowers.
People and laughing children
came there to romp and play
and picnic on grassy hills.

Something about the Author

■ (From *The Man Who Had No Dream* by Adelaide Holl. Ideas and pictures by Kjell Ringi.)

"In 1967, I went to New York trying to find a gallery for an art exhibition. The very first day, by coincidence, I visited Harper & Row and showed my pictures. I was asked to do an outline for a picture book. The same night at my hotel room I got the idea for *The Magic Stick* which was accepted the following day. The book didn't have any text, which to me was natural, as I so far had only been working with pictures. I was all excited and the following night I worked on a new idea. Then I visited Random House and *The Stranger* was accepted. I think the intensive atmosphere of New York had a good influence on my inspiration. Luckily enough this journey, also, gave me, not only a gallery in New York, but, also several illustrating assignments for major American magazines.

"After entering the exciting field of children's books, I sometimes find it hard whether to concentrate on painting pictures or to create picture books. I have found out that I get the inspiration to paint pictures after finishing a book and the other way around. The figures used in my books come from my paintings.

"I always show my books at the European and American art galleries where I have my exhibitions, and I'm glad to say, they seem to be appreciated even by the more sophisticated and grown-up audience. The picture book has one big advantage compared to the painting; it can be seen by many more people.

"I have worked for children in other fields, too. During the last few years I have produced several television scripts for children and I have, also, received orders for big paintings in different schools in Sweden. The pictures are placed in the refectories and entrances and I am very happy and proud that they have not yet been destroyed by sandwiches and balls!

"I think children's books can mean a lot in a person's life. The picture books I read as a child, I remember better than books I read two weeks ago. Now, at least, hours when I am working on a book, I am altogether back in a lost paradise. In order to get a good result, it's very important to me to enjoy myself while working on a book. I use in my picture books and television films just a few or no words to get the children to see as many things as possible in the pictures. If the parents who buy my books, also, are amused while looking through them with their children, I think I have succeeded. I am happy if I can give a human message through my books. I don't want to do it with grand airs or mastering manners—just with a discreet tap on the shoulder. As a matter of fact, I am a little bit bashful with children. And, therefore, I am glad and grateful to be able to speak to them through my books."

ROBERTSON, Barbara (Anne) 1931-

PERSONAL: Born July 20, 1931, in Toronto, Ontario, Canada; daughter of A. Ross (a chartered accountant) and Olive (Perrin) Browne; married Duncan Robertson (a university teacher), May 16, 1953; children: Elizabeth, Sarah, Katie. *Education:* University of Toronto, B.A., 1953; Queen's University at Kingston, M.A., 1957. *Home:* 52 Florence St., Kingston, Ontario, Canada.

CAREER: Queen's University at Kingston, Kingston, Ontario, tutor in Canadian history, 1955—.

BARBARA ROBERTSON

WRITINGS: (Compiler with Mary Alice Downie) *The Wind Has Wings* (anthology of Canadian poetry for children), Oxford University Press, 1968; *Wilfrid Laurier: The Great Conciliator,* Oxford University Press, 1971.

SIDELIGHTS: "I was born in Toronto, and brought up there, but my early years made no great impact on my imagination either then or later. The part that springs vividly to life were the summers, spent every year at my grandparent's farm outside Huntsville, on Fairy Lake, in the Muskoka district of Ontario. Muskoka has always been a summer playground; before us the Indians used to come and fish in the summers. That was quite a long time ago, of course, though they used to come to my grandmother for permission to cut sweetgrass for the baskets they wove.

"My grandparents died when I was little more than a baby, and the farm I remember was looked after by a cousin, while we continued to live in the old farmhouse by the lake. We swam and we fished, and lived in a mild way the life of Arthur Ransome children, though we had to get about as best we could in rowboats, lacking the amount of money necessary for sailboats. (Well, I got a small one when I was fifteen.)

"Here, among lakes with rocky shores and pine trees and birch trees, little farms and big forests, was born my affection for Canada.

"My parents, a little dissatisfied at the prospects offered by the neighborhood high school, sent me to a girls' school, Moulton College, and this was the second large formative experience of my life. Many of my teachers were women of character and distinction, and did manage to convey strongly that women could combine a career and marriage, with a little proper management. Indeed, several of them did. I am grateful to them both for their teaching and their example.

"As to writing, I suppose my interest began when I was about twelve. Then I wanted to be a foreign correspondent. In high school, I edited the school magazine for two years. And in university, I was editor of *The Varsity,* a daily newspaper for the undergraduates at the University of Toronto. That year, 1951-1952, was a very stormy one, and catapulted me back into academic life. I began to take a serious interest in my course of study, modern history; and after graduation (and marriage) started work on my M.A. in Canadian history here at Queen's University. Graduate work led to tutorial work—lots of essay marking—and to part time teaching.

"Academic life is certainly complicated by the accumulation of children—they are rather more time-consuming than is often acknowledged. But through the children, I began to develop a real interest in children's literature, and in the mid 1960's arrived a former acquaintance, Mary Alice Downie, to live in Kingston. We rapidly became friends. She, too, had children, and a more developed interest in children's literature. It was she who got in touch with the Toronto branch of Oxford University Press (where she had at one time worked) to see whether they would be interested in an anthology of children's poetry, something to carry on the enthusiasm children always have for nursery rhymes. The answer was that they would only be interested in an anthology of *Canadian* poetry. At first we felt rather bleak, for it seemed on the face of it impossible to find enough good Canadian poems suitable for children. How wrong we were! We persisted, and after a surprising amount of toil and effort came *The Wind Has Wings.*

"She has gone on to write many good stories for children. I have written a biography, *Wilfrid Laurier, the Great Conciliator* which is meant to be for high school students. Now I am engaged in doing research to help complete the history of Queen's University. Sometime, though, I would like to write more biographies of Canadians for young people, for our history is full of interesting people who should be brought alive for the present generation."

ROBERTSON, Dorothy Lewis   1912-

PERSONAL: Born August 31, 1912, in New York, N.Y.; daughter of Huber Berkley (a lawyer) and Anna (Stenson) Lewis; married Douglas Martin Robertson (mortgage appraiser for a bank), November 27, 1942. *Education:* Wells College, student, 1930-32; Columbia University, B.S., 1936; University of North Carolina, M.A., 1939. *Politics:* Republican. *Religion:* Congregationalist. *Home:* Brown's Hills Estates, Orient, N.Y. 11957.

CAREER: Instructor in speech and dramatics at Arlington Hall Junior College, Washington, D.C., 1939-42, American University, Washington, D.C., 1942, and Smith College, Northampton, Mass., 1944-46; remedial speech teacher in Orient, N.Y., and Shelter Island, N.Y., now retired. Teacher of creative dramatics and story-teller at Floyd

He called the place Hawili Falls, and from that time on, whenever he felt lonely or discouraged, he would sit by the running water and listen to the voice of the Fairy Goddess. ■ (From *Fairy Tales From the Philippines* retold by Dorothy Lewis Robertson. Illustrated by Howard M. Burns.)

Memorial Library, Greenport, Long Island; director of Orient Players and Orient Junior Players. *Member:* American Association of University Women, Long Island Speech and Hearing Association.

WRITINGS: Fairy Tales from Viet Nam (juvenile), Dodd, 1968; *Fairy Tales from the Phillipines,* Dodd, 1971.

SIDELIGHTS: "At the time I was doing a weekly story entitled 'Around the World with the Story-teller' at the Floyd Memorial Library in Greenport, I was continually combing through collections of foreign folk and fairy tales to find new ones to tell children. The more I read, the more interested I became in the field. I was amazed at the number of countries represented and at both the variety of stories and the many themes or characters that were common to them all.

"At this same time I was sponsoring a young Vietnamese boy in Saigon through Foster Parents' Plan, Inc. We wrote to each other every month and, among other things, exchanged information about our customs and holidays. A chance remark of his in one letter started the ball rolling.

DOROTHY LEWIS ROBERTSON

"In describing the Children's Lantern Festival in the fall, he told me that after the parade was over he went back home and had refreshments and then his grandmother told him his favorite story about the man on the moon.

"In all my reading I had not come across any Vietnamese stories and immediately I wondered if Kiem could tell it to me so that I could tell it to the children during the story hour. Since all of his letters had to be translated in Saigon from Vietnamese into English, I could not impose on the time of the translators at Foster Parents to do an entire story at once, so Kiem sent over the story in installments in his monthly letters. It was great, and the children loved it. Kiem said he had many more. The problem was how to get them without having to be translated. Fortunately his older brother, Thuan, was studying English in high school and was far enough advanced to be interested in a paying job of doing the translation for Kiem. Over a period of several years the stories came over to me and finally I had enough to rewrite and publish.

"The Public Relations Department at Foster Parent's was so delighted with the resulting book, they encouraged me to go on through a new child in a country of my choice. I picked the Philippines as one that might have an interesting blend of cultures and, therefore, a great variety of stories. I was not only helped by my own foster child, but several other children in the Manila area who were involved with a small

writing project at Foster Parent's office there. Since English is the second language for Filipinos, there was no need for translation so the collection progressed very rapidly.

"For both books I naturally had to do much research for the preface and for filling in the background on each story. At the time I was doing this, not much had been written about Viet Nam and most of it was in French and was located in New York City at Asia House library. Now there are hundreds of books about Viet Nam, but mostly about politics and the military. Each story had to be completely rewritten for better English, more detailed descriptions of people and places, clearer characterizations and less stilted dialogue. Dramatic conflict had to be heightened, unusual customs or traditions had to be explained so that a young American reader would understand them, and many other problems had to be worked out for acceptance over here. In doing so, I hope I have not gone too far astray from the original story, and have faithfully represented these wonderful people and their cultures through their folk and fairy tales.

"To get these two collections published was a great satisfaction to me as I feel I have added to the literature in the field, and by doing so, have shown our children that their foreign friends enjoy the same sort of stories that they themselves do. It was also a great personal satisfaction to break into a new field in my late fifties and with no connections to use in the beginning. A talk to children's librarians in Albany, N.Y. on the subject of 'Creative Dramatics in the Library' brought me to the attention of the head of the Suffolk County children's work, who in turn knew the circulation manager for Dodd, Mead, who in turn suggested I should send it in to their children's editor. This after a year and a half of fruitless effort and many rejection slips."

ROBERTSON, Jennifer (Sinclair) 1942-

PERSONAL: Born February 21, 1942, in Datchet, Buckinghamshire, England; daughter of William and Gertrude (Ball) Brown; married Stuart Lang Robertson (a theological student), February 19, 1966; children: Neil Sinclair, Aileen Margaret. *Education:* University of Glasgow, M.A., 1963, social sciences diploma, 1964; University of Warsaw, graduate study, 1964-65. *Politics:* "On the left." *Religion:* Christian. *Home:* 19 Netherton Rd. Bootle, Merseyside L20 6AB, England.

CAREER: School social worker in Glasgow, Scotland, 1965-68.

WRITINGS—Children's novels: *Fior,* Scripture Union, 1974; *Circle of Shadows,* Scripture Union, 1975. Also wrote *Encyclopedia of Bible Stories,* and contributed to newspapers and journals.

WORK IN PROGRESS: A book on an unmarried mother, *Linda;* research on Celtic Britain in prehistory and in the Christian era as a follow-up to *Circle of Shadows;* a retelling of the Christmas story called *King in a Stable,* for Scripture Union.

SIDELIGHTS: "I have always written stories. My twin sister was editor, reviewer and sole reader. Then, in my teens, after some searching for a life-style I came to a joyous acceptance of the Christian faith, and became involved in a dingy downtown church in an area where no one read books,

174   **Something about the Author**

JENNIFER ROBERTSON

and now I had an audience for my stories: the children of the district for whom I tried to weave golden cobwebs from the dull grey world of our everyday existence. I wanted to colour the workday with love. I was eighteen, a new piece of blotting paper, ready to soak up life and I read Donne's 'No Man is an Island. . . .'

"Within a year I was in Germany, working amongst displaced persons of all nationalities from Eastern Europe. I read the short stories of Borchert and Böll, and tried to put into prose the sufferings of the people I met. Faith had made me intensely aware of the world around me. The grey streets of Glasgow didn't change, but with all my heart I cried out 'Du,' and notebooks of poems resulted.

"I read for the first time, Simone Weil's, *Waiting on God.* There was real poverty in the city about me; the smell of it has never left me. Perhaps, because like Wormwood's victim my young faith still thought in terms of 'togas and sandals,' when I started on the third novel of my teen-age life, I chose a slave for my hero.

"Looking back, I can see that I was always on the side of the loser, the underdog, the persecuted and my cry was to identify, 'Here am I, Lord, send me.'

"On my return from Germany I met a student who had travelled widely in the countries behind the, then, newly-closed Berlin Wall. This student—who is now my husband—invited me to learn Polish. Polish is still 'our' language. For me, then, it was the opening into a new literature: works that had come out of centuries of suffering. As student days continued—greatly enriched by the friendship of overseas stu-

dents—I went out on placements, while still studying Polish. The placements were with various social work agencies. On one I met a young red-head, an unmarried mother of seventeen who discussed Pasternak with me while she nursed her baby in a poor tenement room. That girl became the subject of *Linda* which is still being worked over.

"Then came a year in Poland. My fiance's hostel was on the site of the Warsaw Ghetto. Emaciated ghosts whispered through the November mists. I listened to their whispers and started to read Polish translations of Yiddish songs. The story of the slave, forced from his homeland, grew and I carried the bundle of papers and cheap Polish school notebooks brought from newspaper kiosks, with me on my travels.

"On our return we married and I worked as a social worker. It was my good fortune to find a friend on the staff of the school where I worked. I was a school-based social worker, visiting the families of children with problems. Together we wrote songs and tried to communicate Christian truth to another generation of school children. 'Roddy' of *Fior* is one of these children, although I wrote *Fior* in the old walled city of York where we moved soon after my first baby was born. There were ghosts again, Roman ghosts, but my story of a slave had grown into an unwieldy one hundred thousand words and had been 'the best of the rejects' in a children's book competition. There were Jewish ghosts too—the church we attended was beside a street called Jewbury. I read the records of medieval York Jewry in the city library.

"Our second child was born. We kept an open home. Students keep late hours; babies demand round the clock attention, but I went on writing, sometimes all night, often with great joy. Yet it was later, in Nottingham, where my husband left language to become a student of theology that I began to publish my stories. Into *The Encyclopedia of Bible Stories* I tried to put the Jewish hopes and aspirations, history and thought, to communicate to today's child the feel of being alive in Bible times—and the tales I eagerly heard from friends from countries with simpler economies than our instant, pre-packed living, helped greatly. During our time in Nottingham, *Fior* was published and *Circle of Shadows,* the story of the slave changed almost out of recognition was sent off.

"Now we live in Merseyside. For over two months we were homeless ourselves as we waited for our house to be modernised. We shared our lives with a family of six and as I hung out washing each day for the ten of us the smells of the inner city, the sounds of its streets were about me, but the racing clouds and the squawks of the seagulls brought images from the Celtic world and the times of Dercc of *Circle of Shadows* whose tale is still to be completed in the love of a king which leads Dercc back to the blood twin who does know him. It is of this love that I write—no longer spinning golden cobwebs but kneading with words the dough of experience and adding the leaven of the Word that is Kingdom and Gospel and Ending, the wholesome, essential yeast that works and transforms."

ROBISON, Bonnie 1924-

PERSONAL: Born August 4, 1924, in Mound City, Kan.; daughter of Gilbert L. (a rancher) and Myrtle (Fouts) Bailey; married Richard Robison (an attorney), February 3, 1950; children: Rand, Leslee. *Education:* Attended Woodbury College, 1941-42. *Politics:* Conservative. *Religion:*

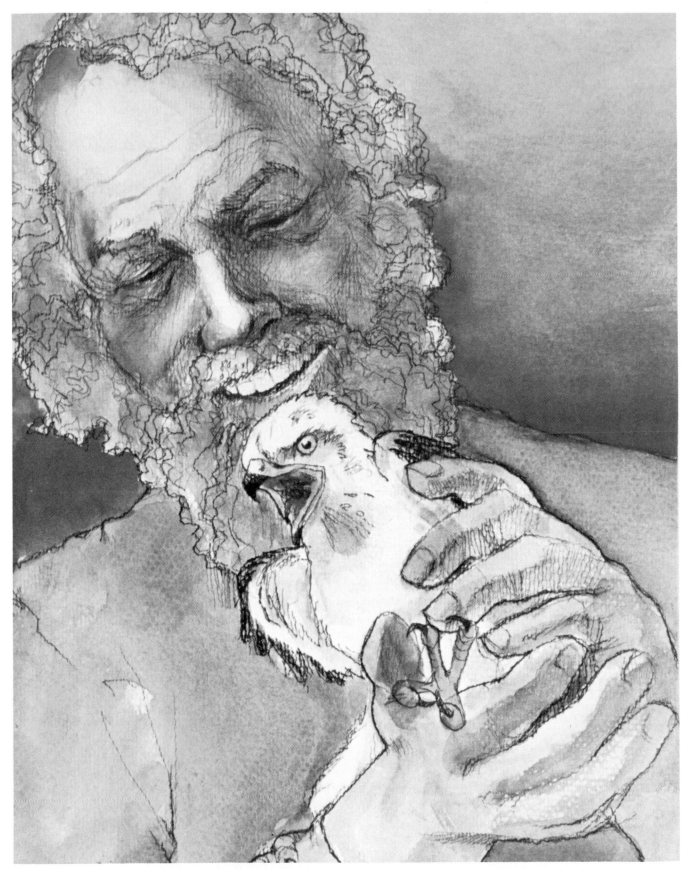

With gnarled fingers, the old man gently lifted Killer out of the box onto the table. ■ (From *Killer, the Outrageous Hawk* by Bonnie Robison. Illustrated by Rob Sprattler.)

BONNIE ROBISON

Protestant. *Home:* 2625 Allenton Ave., Hacienda Heights, Calif. 91745.

CAREER: Has worked as a secretary; licensed real estate agent. Board of directors, Reading is Fundamental (Los Angeles chapter). *Member:* Hacienda Golf Club, Atlantis Health Club, Reading Is Fundamental.

WRITINGS: (With others) *Volleyball,* Lippincott, 1972; *Killer: The Outrageous Hawk* (juvenile fiction), Childrens Press, 1974. Contributor to golfing journals, newspapers, and magazines.

WORK IN PROGRESS: A novel concerned with lobbying in Sacramento; research on overpopulation, abortion, and compulsive birth control; promoting reading in children.

SIDELIGHTS: "RIF, as you probably know, is concerned with motivating children to read. Our motto: If America is to grow up thinking, Reading is Fundamental. We give away books to children to stimulate their interest by pride of ownership (would you believe that some children have never owned a book?). Working through classrooms in deprived areas, Juvenile Hall and the Los Angeles County Museum, our program has produced remarkable results in improved reading skills in school, and increased book circulation in libraries.

"My hawk story is based on a true experience, and the characters are my own family. We actually raised a hawk, and

there is very little fiction added to the story. I am presently working on a children's book about bridges, illustrated with photos I have taken in my travels.

"In addition to the others, I have a consuming new hobby: photography. I am taking classes, and hope to do my own illustrating."

HOBBIES AND OTHER INTERESTS: Golf, volleyball, raquetball, bridge, gardening, and photography.

ROOD, Ronald (N.) 1920-

PERSONAL: Surname rhymes with "food"; born July 7, 1920, in Torrington, Conn.; son of Nellis Frost (a life underwriter) and Bessie (Chamberlain) Rood; married Margaret Bruce (a teacher), December 21, 1942; children: Janice, Thomas Elliot, Alison, Roger Warren. *Education:* University of Connecticut, B.S., 1941, M.S., 1949. *Home and office address:* RFD 1, Box 131, Lincoln (Bristol P.O.), Vt. 05443.

The vulture eliminates a potential source of disease and pollution, yes. But more than that: with splendid efficiency it quickly returns minerals and organic compounds to the world of the living. ■ (From *Animals Nobody Loves* by Ronald Rood. Illustrated by Russ W. Buzzell.)

RONALD ROOD and wife, Peg, with "Barney" Groundhog

CAREER: Long Island Agricultural and Technical Institute, Farmingdale, N.Y., instructor in biology, 1949-53; Grolier Enterprises, New York, N.Y., research editor, 1954-64; Middlebury College, Middlebury, Vt., instructor in biology, 1956-58; now full-time writer. Church choir director. *Military service:* U.S. Army Air Forces, fighter pilot, World War II; received Air Medal. *Member:* Forest and Field, League of Vermont Writers (president, 1965-67, 1974-75), American Forestry Association, National Wildlife Federation, Outdoor Writers Association of America, Vermont Natural Resources Council.

WRITINGS: *The How and Why Wonder Book of Insects.* Grosset, 1960; *The How and Why Wonder Book of Ants and Bees,* Grosset, 1962; *Land Alive: The World of Nature at One Family's Door,* Greene, 1962; *The How and Why Wonder Book of Butterflies and Moths,* Grosset, 1963; *The Loon in My Bathtub,* Greene, 1964; *The Sea and Its Wonderful Creatures,* Whitman Publishing, 1965; *Bees, Bugs and Beetles: The Arrow Book of Insects,* Four Winds, 1965; *Hundred Acre Welcome: The Story of a Chincoteague Pony,* Greene, 1967; *Vermont Life Book of Nature,* Greene, 1967; *How Do You Spank a Porcupine?,* Trident, 1969; *Animal Champions,* Grosset, 1969; *Answers About Insects,* Grosset, 1969; *Animals Nobody Loves,* Greene, 1971; *Who Wakes the Groundhog,* Norton, 1973; *May I Keep this Clam, Mother? It Followed Me Home,* Simon & Schuster, 1973; *Good Things are Happening,* Greene, 1975; *It's Going to Sting Me,* Simon & Schuster, 1976. Contributor to *Reader's Digest, Coronet, Audubon Magazine, Christian Herald, New York Times, Pageant, Vermont Life,* and others.

SIDELIGHTS: As a boy of seven, Ronald Rood wrote to Thornton Burgess with a question about a baby turtle; he received such a detailed and friendly answer that he decided he wanted to emulate the nature writer.

Primarily a naturalist, he has taken up writing as a livelihood. "A naturalist," he claims, "is a youngster who never grew up."

ROOKE, Daphne (Marie) 1914-
(Robert Pointon)

PERSONAL: Born March 6, 1914, in Boksburg, Transvaal, South Africa; daughter of Robert (a soldier) and Maria (a writer; maiden name Mare) Pizzey; married Irvin Rooke, June, 1937; children: Rosemary Elizabeth (Mrs. John Bower Hutchison). *Education:* Attended school in South Africa. *Home:* Bent St., Bardouroka, New South Wales 2315, Australia. *Agent:* Paul R. Reynolds, Inc., 12 East 41st St., New York, N.Y. 10017; and John Farquharson Ltd., Bell House, 8 Bell Yard, London WC2A 2JR, England.

CAREER: Writer. *Member:* P.E.N. South Africa. *Awards, honors:* Afrikaanse Pers Beperk novel prize, 1946, for *The Sea Hath Bounds.*

DAPHNE ROOKE

SIDELIGHTS: "Even if I tell a true story, it sounds like something I have made up. At school I was the despair of English teachers because my essays read like extracts from novels.

"The life I led as a child and young woman sparked off my desire to write. There was the exhilaration of the Rand where I was born; there was a cane plantation in Natal where I came in close contact with Zulus and Indians . . . my best friend was an Indian girl named Amoya . . . and then there was Zululand where we were next-door neighbours to Zulus who still held to the tribal ways. Lastly there was a fishing village on the East coast of Australia, a place that had been cut off from the mainland until a road was built by American soldiers in the second World War.

"Places have a profound effect on me, and I was fascinated by Port Stephens. I have written two children's books with this place as a setting (although, of course, I have renamed the landscape)—*Double Ex!* and *A Horse of His Own*. The district has changed now, but when I first came here, there were only about three-hundred people living on this peninsula, it was a world of its own.

"My stories deal with the differences in people. In my children's books as well as in novels I have singled out people who are in some sense handicapped, by race or other circumstances. For example, in *Double Ex!*, Herman is a displaced person who comes to Australia from Poland after the

WRITINGS—Novels: *The Sea Hath Bounds,* A.P.B. Bookstore (Johannesburg), 1946, published as *A Grove of Fever Trees,* Houghton, 1950; (under pseudonym Robert Pointon) *Apples in the Hold,* Museum Press, 1950; *Mittee,* Gollancz, 1951, Houghton, 1952; *Ratoons,* Houghton, 1953; *Wizards' Country,* Houghton, 1957; *Beti,* Houghton, 1959; *A Lover for Estelle,* Houghton, 1961; *The Greyling,* Gollancz, 1962, Reynal, 1963; *Diamond Jo,* Reynal, 1965; *Boy on the Mountain,* Gollancz, 1969; *Margaretha de la Porte* (first volume of a proposed trilogy), Gollancz, 1974.

Books for children: *The South African Twins,* J. Cape, 1953, published as *Twins in South Africa,* Houghton, 1955; *The Australian Twins,* J. Cape, 1954, published as *Twins in Australia,* Houghton, 1956; *New Zealand Twins,* J. Cape, 1957; *Double Ex!,* Gollancz, 1971; *A Horse of His Own,* Gollancz, 1976.

Short stories appear in anthologies, including *South African Stories,* edited by D. H. Wright, British Book Service, 1960; *Over the Horizon,* Duell, 1960. Author of short stories published in periodicals, including *John Bull* (London) and *Woman* (Sydney). Contributor of articles to periodicals, including *Optima* (Johannesburg).

WORK IN PROGRESS: The second volume in the trilogy begun with *Margaretha de la Porte.*

They were displaced persons, most of them from Europe. This was 1947 and in the aftermath of the Second World War many such people were migrating to Australia. ■ (From *Double Ex!* by Daphne Rooke. Jacket illustration by Richard Kennedy.)

second World War. This viewpoint applies to my African story *Fikizolo*. Fikizolo is an outcast, a cross between a donkey and a zebra!

"I think I write to establish contact with people. Although I write fiction, my search has always been for the truth. Each story has something of my own experience in it."

Daphne Rooke's manuscript collection is housed in the Boston University Library.

FOR MORE INFORMATION SEE: Forum (Johannesburg), April, 1952.

ROSE, Wendy 1948-
(Bronwen Elizabeth Edwards, Chiron Khanshendel)

PERSONAL: Born May 7, 1948, in Oakland, Calif. *Education:* Attended Cabrillo College and Contra Costa College; University of California, Berkeley, student, 1974—. *Home:* 1228-D Delaware St., Berkeley, Calif. 94702. *Agent:* Terry Garey, 820 Everett St., El Cerrito, Calif. 94530.

CAREER: Lowie Museum of Anthropology of University of California, Berkeley, manager of museum bookstore, 1974—. *Member:* American Museum of Natural History, Smithsonian Associates, Society for California Archaeology, Society for American Archaeology, Kroeber Anthro-

WENDY ROSE

pological Society, Poets and Writers, Inc., Society for Creative Anachronism, Elves, Gnomes and Little Mens' Marching and Chowder Society, Native American Community Council of Western Contra Costa County, (California; founder), Native American Student Association of the University of California, United Native Americans, Thursday Evening Cottage Industries Association of El Cerrito (Motto: "TOGETHER WE'RE A GENIUS!").

WRITINGS: Hopi Roadrunner Dancing (self-illustrated), Greenfield Review Press, 1973; *Long Division: A Tribal History,* Strawberry Press, 1976.

Illustrator: Duane Niatum, *Taos Pueblo* (poems), Greenfield Review Press, 1974; (contributor) Duane Niatum, editor, *Carriers of the Dream Wheel,* Harper, 1975; *Female Psychology,* Science Research Associates, 1975.

Contributor: Work appears under name Wendy Rose or pseudonym Chiron Khanshendel: *Speaking for Ourselves,* edited by Lillian Faderman and Barbara Bradshaw, Scott, Foresman, 1969, revised edition, in press; *From the Belly of the Shark,* edited by Walter Lowenfels, Random House, 1974; *Time to Greez,* edited by Roberto Vargas, Glide Press, in press. Contributor, occasionally under pseudonym Chiron Khanshendel, of articles and poems to literary magazines, including *Margins, Alcaeus Review, Greenfield Review,* and *Many Smokes.*

WORK IN PROGRESS: Four Worlds and Times of Light, a self-illustrated story-picture book of the Hopi creation story for pre-adolescents; *Lost Copper,* a book of poems; poems for *The Shadow of the Savage,* edited by Robert Alan McGill; several other poems for anthologies; illustrations for childrens' books.

SIDELIGHTS: "Before I learned how to write, I expressed myself through making up songs. It has always been a tradition of my people (the Hopi Indians from Arizona) to celebrate everything in life with song. For all occasions, both happy and sad, I sang my feelings. When I learned to write, my expression was written down as well as sung. Today I sing and write both (though my singing is more often so low no one can hear).

"I was alone most of the time as a child; I was in a neighborhood where there were many children, but they were all white and protestant. Because of the prejudices of their parents (perhaps more than themselves), they were not allowed to play with me and, eventually, they came to tease me so much when we did meet, that I chose, also, not to play with them. This kind of thing happens to many, many children and it's sad; but one way that such children can take advantage of this is to allow it to feed into them and fan the fires of creativity. When you feel alone, just talk to yourself—on paper, with your voice, with your body through dancing, with colors, whatever you like. And never throw away anything you create. Years later they will add to your sense of who you are.

"I was raised away from my own people; I am half-white and it was the white half of the family that raised me. Thus, I never learned to speak the Hopi language which is very beautiful to listen to and hear sung. But somehow I always felt more Hopi than white; perhaps that, too, is because of the loneliness created by the people around me. If my Indian-ness was so intense for them, then it was only natural

Something about the Author

that it should become intense for me. Today I am proud of my Indian heritage and I like to travel around and visit Indian people around the western part of this country; I like to work with them to help make conditions better. One way of doing this is through my writing; if I can make you feel better about the Indian people and arouse your sense of justice about what has happened to us, then I have succeeded in undoing years of watching what television has to say about us (mostly wrong) and that's what art is all about—Giving and receiving.

"The usual practice in bookstores upon receiving books of poems by American Indians is to classify them as 'Native Americana' rather than as poetry; the poets are seen as literate fossils more than as living, working artists. I have run into this kind of thing too often. Also, there is a great deal of stereotyping of Indian poetry (and Indian art in general); we may be seen as 'nature children' tapping some great earth-nerve and producing poems like pulses. But all art is that way; not just Indian art. There is also the concrete, the abstract, the analytical, the mystical—all components and levels of human understanding and expression. And those qualities stereotypically Indian also exist. The deferential treatment accorded to Indians in artistic and academic settings is just as destructive, ultimately, as out-and-out racism. It is startling to find your book of poems in an anthropology section of a bookstore instead of in the poetry section.... My songs are self-conscious when they have to dance alone. You know, I really just want to make people feel good."

RUTZ, Viola Larkin 1932-

PERSONAL: Born March 14, 1932, in New York, N.Y.; married Harold Rutz (now a professor), June 26, 1954. *Education:* Concordia College, River Forest, Ill., B.S. in Ed.; Montessori certificate (London), 1972.

CAREER: Elementary school teacher.

WRITINGS: Little Tree and His Wish, Concordia, 1966.

WORK IN PROGRESS: Children's books.

SIDELIGHTS: "Writing has always fascinated me even as a young child, and I did much writing throughout my school years. In college I majored in education, but took a minor in English. However, my college years were very busy as I worked my way through and writing was shelved.

"My interest returned as I read book after book to my own three children. The books made the children so happy and I wanted to produce something which would also make children happy and children laugh."

SACKETT, S(amuel) J(ohn) 1928-

PERSONAL: Born 1928, in Redlands, Calif.; son of Eben John and Jeannette (DeWolfe) Sackett; married Marjorie McGrath, 1950; children: Robert Eben, John Samuel. *Education:* University of Redlands, A.B., 1948; M.A., 1949; Stanford University, graduate study, 1950; University of California, Los Angeles, Ph.D., 1956. *Religion:* Unitarian-Universalist. *Address:* Box 386, Hays, Kans. 67601. *Office:* Fort Hays State University, Hays, Kans.

CAREER: Hastings College, Hastings, Neb., instructor, 1949-51; University of California, Los Angeles, teaching assistant, 1952-53; Fort Hays State University, Hays, Kan., professor of English, 1954—. *Member:* National Council of Teachers of English, American Folklore Society, Kansas Folklore Society (president, 1956-58; 1962-63, 1977-78).

WRITINGS: (Editor) Henry Fielding, *The Voyages of Mr. Job Vinegar,* Augustan Reprint Society, 1958; *Kansas Folklore,* University of Nebraska Press, 1961; *English Literary Criticism, 1726-1750,* Fort Hays Studies, 1962; (translator) Johan Daisne, *The Man Who Had His Hair Cut Short* (novel), Horizon, 1965; *Cowboys and the Songs They Sang,* W. R. Scott, 1967; *Edgar Watson Howe,* Twayne, 1972; (contributor) *American Government through Science Fiction,* Rand, 1974. Articles in folklore and literary journals; poems in *Paris Review, Kansas Magazine, Antioch Review* and other magazines; fiction in various periodicals; translations in *Michigan Quarterly Review.*

WORK IN PROGRESS: Two novels.

SIDELIGHTS: "I feel a little embarrassed about being included in a book of writers for young people, since only one of my books has been directed toward that audience. I have, however, completed a second and plan to do more later, and so, perhaps I qualify. Besides, my one book for young people, *Cowboys and the Songs They Sang,* was very well received and has been widely adopted by schools.

S. J. SACKETT

The cowboy who sings "Goodbye Old Paint" is leaving Cheyenne, Wyoming to go to Montana, leaving his best friend, a paint horse, behind him. The horse has grown old and can no longer keep up with the younger horses, although he still tries to do the best he can. ■ (From *Cowboys and the Songs They Sang* by S.J. Sackett. Photo by Charles J. Belden.)

"I wrote *Cowboys* because when my two sons were young, I used to read to them every night after dinner. They enjoyed cowboy shows on television, and I wanted to find a book about real cowboys, cowboys as they actually were in the Old West, which would include words and music to some of the great cowboy songs so that we could sing the songs together. I hunted for a book like that and couldn't find one. So I wrote it. Unfortunately, by the time the book was bought and published, my boys were too old to be read to; but I gave each of them copies, anyway.

"I had access to the material because I teach college classes in folklore, and at the time I worked on the book, I taught a class called American Folklore, which had a unit on cowboy songs. As I don't play the guitar myself, or sing in public, I played a lot of records in class. I put the songs I liked the best into my book.

"I enjoy writing. Even writing an interoffice memorandum at the college where I teach, or a section on 'Sidelights' for *Something About the Author,* gives me pleasure. To put a thought into words is difficult for me; I try out different ways of saying things in my mind, and when I find a way that really expresses what I have in mind, writing it down is ex-

citing and enjoyable. To write the sentence you have just read, for instance, I tried out many different patterns of words before I settled on the one that appears here, and when I found that one I felt very happy that I had overcome the difficulty.

"I have written many more things than I have been able to find publishers for, but I continue writing because of this element of challenge in it. And besides, who knows? Maybe the next thing I write will have an impact on a lot of readers. That, I think, is what I am really after in my writing—to touch people's lives in some way that will make a difference to them, perhaps interesting them in some information, perhaps making them happier, perhaps giving them some ideas to think about, perhaps simply letting them know that there are other people in the world who feel the same way they do.

"And because writing is for me a challenge, I want to do as many different kinds of it as I can. I have written both poetry and prose, both fiction and non-fiction. I have published in both magazines and books, I have written for both children and adults, I have addressed both popular and learned audiences. I have just finished writing two novels—one about life in the far future, when travel between the planets of different stars is a reality, and the other about life two thousand years in the past. When I have revised them and submitted them for publication, I plan next to write a musical play, which is a form I have never before attempted. As long as there is a kind of writing I haven't done, I'll be happy because that means there is a kind of writing I can still try to do."

HOBBIES AND OTHER INTERESTS: Gardening, bicycling.

SAGSOORIAN, Paul 1923-

PERSONAL: Born March 26, 1923, in New York, N.Y.; son of Aram (a grocer) and Elizabeth (Bozoian) Sagsoorian. *Education:* Attended Mechanic's Institute, Workshop School of Advertising Art. *Religion:* Armenian Apostolic Church. *Home:* 43 Aqueduct Avenue, Yonkers, N.Y. 10704. *Office:* c/o Viewpont Graphics, Inc., 303 Fifth Ave., New York, N.Y. 10016.

CAREER: Artist. *Exhibitions:* Mechanic's Institute, May, 1944; Agbu Gallery, June, 1976. *Military service:* U.S. Army, corporal, 1943-46.

ILLUSTRATOR: Donald Worcester and Wendell G. Schaeffer, *The Growth and Culture of Latin America,* Oxford University Press, 1956; C. P. Lee, *Athenian Adventure,* Knopf, 1957; Leon Surmelian, *Daredevils of Sassoun,* Swallow, 1964; Robert Newman, *The Boy Who Could Fly,* Atheneum, 1968; Jay Williams and Raymond Abrashkin, *Danny Dunn and the Smallifying Machine,* McGraw, 1969; Lou Hartman, *The Monstrous Leathern Man,* Atheneum, 1970; William Wise, *Charles A. Lindbergh,* Putnam, 1970; Meindert De Jong, *A Horse Came Running,* Macmillan, 1970; E. W. Hildick, *The Prisoners of Gridling Cap,* Doubleday,

Then, without turning, she said, "Dan! Leave those cookies alone." ■ (From *Danny Dunn, Invisible Boy* by Jay Williams and Raymond Abrashkin. Illustrated by Paul Sagsoorian.)

1971; Jay Williams and Raymond Abrashkin, *Danny Dunn and the Swamp Monster,* McGraw, 1971; Jay Williams and Raymond Abrashkin, *Danny Dunn Invisible Boy,* McGraw, 1974; Jay Williams and Raymond Abrashkin, *Danny Dunn Scientific Detective,* McGraw, 1975; Nubar Kupelian and Sylva der Stephanian, *Armenian History,* The Diocese of the Armenian Church, 1975; Alexandere Shirvanzade, *The Sake of Honor,* St. Martin's Press, 1976; Valarie Goekjian Zahirsky, *"All God's People,"* The Diocese of the Armenian Church, 1977.

SIDELIGHTS: "I am motivated in graphic forms, expressions I desire to convey. I like to work in watercolors and pen and ink. I also speak Armenian and besides art, I am very interested in history."

SAMUELS, Charles 1902-

PERSONAL: Born September 15, 1902; son of Samuel David and Bertha (Trum) Samuels; married Louise Bron-

PAUL SAGSOORIAN

augh; children: Joan Katherine, Robert. *Education:* Attended public schools, Brooklyn, N.Y. *Home:* Apdo. 1639, Cuernavaca Mor., Mex. *Agent:* Sterling Lord, 660 Madison Ave., New York, N.Y. 10021.

CAREER: Brooklyn Daily Eagle, Brooklyn, N.Y., feature and sports writer, 1923; *Brooklyn Times,* Brooklyn, police reporter, 1924-25; *Miami Tribune,* Miami, Fla., ship news reporter, 1926; Standard News Service, Brooklyn, police reporter; King Features Syndicate, New York, N.Y., associate editor, 1930-34; Hollywood screen writer, 1934-37; Coney Island press agent, 1938; Paramount News, city editor, 1943-45; also worked on newspaper columns of Ben Hecht and Billy Rose. Director of Rockland Foundation, 1954-56. *Member:* Authors League, Mystery Writers of America, Overseas Press Club, New York Reporters Association, Society of Magazine Writers. *Awards, honors:* Edgar Allan Poe award, Mystery Writers of America, for *Night Fell on Georgia.*

WRITINGS: The Frantic Young Man (novel), Coward, 1929; *A Rather Simple Fellow* (novel), Coward, 1931; *The Magnificent Rube* (biography of Tex Rickard), McGraw, 1957; *The King* (biography of Clark Gable), Coward, 1962; (author of text) *Only in New York* (photographs by Jan Yoor), Simon and Schuster, 1965; (with Louise Samuels) *Once Upon a Stage* (an informed history of vaudeville), Dodd, 1974.

As-told-to biographies: (With Ethel Waters) *His Eye Is on the Sparrow,* Doubleday, 1951 (Book-of-the Month Club selection); (with Norah Berg) *Lady on the Beach,* Prentice-Hall, 1952; (with William R. and Florence K. Simpson) *Hockshop,* Random, 1954; (with Boris Morros) *My Ten Years as a Counterspy,* Viking, 1959; (with Buster Keaton) *My Wonderful World of Slapstick,* Doubleday, 1960; (with Gerard Luisi) *How to Catch 5,000 Thieves,* Macmillan, 1962.

Accounts of famous trials: *The Girl in the Red Velvet Swing,* Gold Medal, 1953; (with Louise Samuels) *The Girl in the House of Hate,* Gold Medal, 1953; *Death Was the Bridegroom,* Gold Medal, 1953; (with Louise Samuels) *Night Fell on Georgia,* Dell, 1956. Has published more than one thousand signed magazine and newspaper stories.

SIDELIGHTS: "My father, his brothers and uncles were all employed in the circulation department of the old *New York World.* They talked of nothing but the newspaper and its writing and cartooning stars. As a small boy I was taken to the office often and in the dining room I saw such geniuses as Irvin S. Cobb, Lindsay Denison, Martin Green and Maurice Ketten.

"I dropped out of school at fifteen and worked at all kinds of jobs, unhappily and unsuccessfully. It was not until I was twenty and started to work on newspapers that I found myself in a world I enjoyed living in. At twenty-three I met Ben Hecht and became his protege. He taught me everything I know about writing, introduced me to editors, publishers and other famous writers.

"I never wanted to be anything but a writer, have talent for nothing else except fast, furious, and occasionally witty conversation. I wouldn't trade my memories for anyone's."

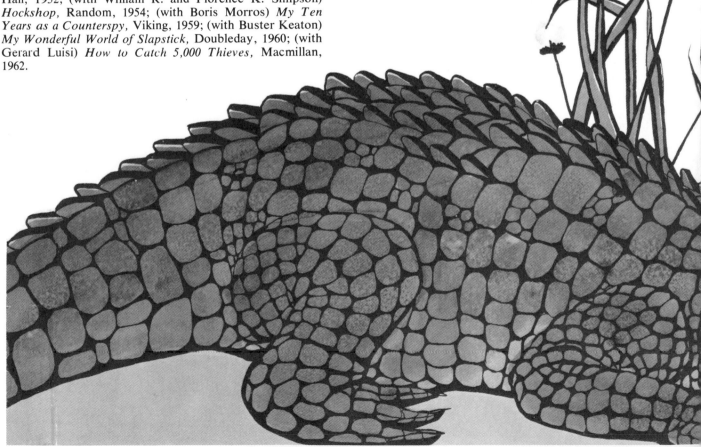

Something about the Author

Several of Samuels' books have been published in England, France, Germany, Australia and Italy. Others have been serialized and printed in part in magazines. *My Ten Years as a Counterspy* was made into the film "Man on a String" by Columbia Pictures Corp. *The Girl in the Red Velvet Swing* was made into a movie by Twentieth Century-Fox.

FOR MORE INFORMATION SEE: Seattle Times, May 13, 1951; *New York World, Telegram & Sun,* April 14, 1962.

SANDIN, Joan 1942-

PERSONAL: Born April 30, 1942, in Wisconsin; daughter of Robert L. (a teacher) and Frances K. (Somers; an interviewer) Sandin; married Sigfrid Leijonhufvud (a journalist), April 30, 1971; children: Jonas. *Education:* University of Arizona, B.F.A., 1964. *Home and office:* Torkel Knutssonsgatan 31, Stockholm, Sweden.

CAREER: Illustrator. *Awards, honors:* American Institute of Graphic Artists Best Childrens Books Award, *Crocodile and Hen,* 1970.

ILLUSTRATOR: Carol Beach York, *The Blue Umbrella,* Watts, 1968; Randolph Stow, *Midnite: The Story of a Wild Colonial Boy,* Prentice-Hall, 1968; Harold Felton, *True Tall*

Tales of Stormalong: Sailor of the Seven Seas, Prentice-Hall, 1968; Edith Brecht, *The Little Fox,* Lippincott, 1968; Eleanor Hull, *A Trainful of Strangers,* Atheneum, 1968; Ellen Pugh, *Tales From the Welsh Hills,* Dodd, 1968; Maia Wojciechowska, *"Hey, What's Wrong With This One?",* Harper, 1969; Joan Lexau, *Crocodile and Hen,* Harper, 1969; Jan M. Robinson, *The December Dog,* Lippincott, 1969.

Constantine Georgiou, *Rani, Queen of the Jungle,* Prentice-Hall, 1970; Joan Lexau, *It All Began with a Drip, Drip, Drip,* McCall/Dutton, 1970; Jean Little, *Look Through My Window,* Harper, 1970; Joanna Cole, *The Secret Box,* Morrow, 1971; Thomas P. Lewis, *Hill of Fire,* Harper, 1971; Barbara Brenner, *A Year in the Life of Rosie Bernard,* Harper, 1971; Ellen Pugh, *More Tales from the Welsh Hills,* Dodd, 1971; Jean Little, *From Anna,* Harper, 1972; Nathaniel Benchley, *Small Wolf,* Harper, 1972; Edna Mitchell Preston, *Ickle Bickle Robin,* Watts, 1973; Alison Morgan, *A Boy Called Fish,* Harper, 1973; Joan L. Nixon, *The Mysterious Red Tape Gang,* Putnam, 1974; Hans Eric Hellberg, translated by Patricia Crampton, *Grandpa's Maria,* Morrow, 1974; Faith McNulty, *Woodchuck,* Harper, 1974; Kathryn Ewing, *A Private Matter,* Harcourt, 1975; Liesel Skorpen, *Michael,* Harper, 1975; Liesel Skorpen, *Bird,* Harper, 1976; Sandra Love, *But What About Me?,* Harcourt, 1976; Alan Arkin, *The Lemming Condition,* Harper, 1976.

WORK IN PROGRESS: Completed a picture book for Swedish publisher, Rabén & Sjögren, title will be *Ida Och Dörren* (Ida and the Door); *Clipper,* for Harper.

SIDELIGHTS: "I most enjoy working with folk tales and books demanding research and/or travel. I've traveled quite a lot in Mexico, United States and Europe and have been living in Stockholm since April, 1972. I speak Swedish and Spanish."

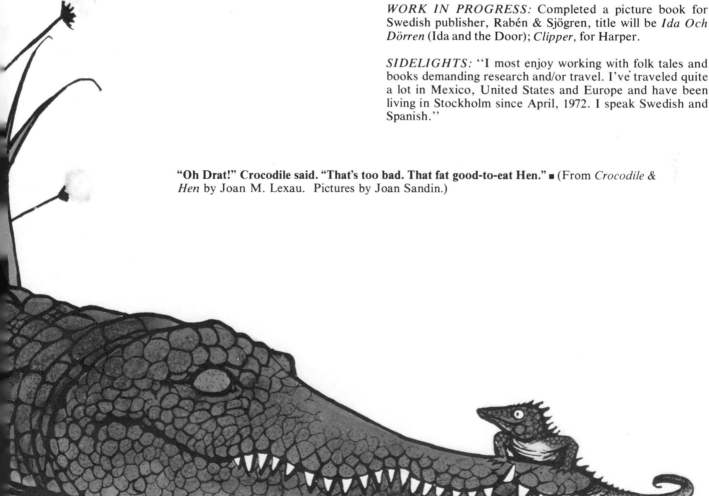

"Oh Drat!" Crocodile said. "That's too bad. That fat good-to-eat Hen." ■ (From *Crocodile & Hen* by Joan M. Lexau. Pictures by Joan Sandin.)

JOAN SANDIN

SAUNDERS, Keith 1910-

PERSONAL: Born February 21, 1910, in Elizabeth City, N.C.; son of W. O. (an editor) and Columbia (Ballance) Saunders; married Mary Newlin, October 5, 1940; children: Judith Anne Saunders Stephens. *Education:* Attended University of North Carolina, 1927-29. *Politics:* Independent. *Religion:* United Methodist. *Home and office:* 5120 Chevy Chase Pkwy. N.W., Washington, D.C., 20008.

CAREER: The Independent, Elizabeth City, N.C., staff member, 1929-38; *Raleigh Times,* Raleigh, N.C., staff member, 1939-41; *Norfolk Virginian Pilot,* Norfolk, Va., staff member, 1941-43; *Baltimore Evening Sun,* Baltimore, Md., staff member, 1943-46; American Aviation Publications, Washington, D.C., associate editor, 1947-52; *Aviation Daily,* Washington, D.C., managing editor, 1952-59; *Air Travel,* Washington, D.C., executive editor, 1959-68; *Airline Marketing Newsletter,* Washington, D.C., editor, 1968. *Member:* Society of American Travel Writers (national director and chapter chairman, 1963-65), First Flight Society, National Press Club, Sigma Delta Chi. *Awards, honors:* Trans World Airlines aviation writing award, 1951; man of the year award from Air Line Traffic Association, 1965.

WRITINGS: The Independent Man, privately printed, 1964; *So You Want to Be an Airline Stewardess,* Arco Pub-

lishing, 1968; *Guidebook to the Outer Banks of North Carolina,* privately printed, 1974. Contributor to *Encyclopedia Americana Annual* and to *American Way.* Editor of *National Aeronautics,* 1951-61, and *Air Cargo Newsletter,* 1958-68.

WORK IN PROGRESS: A book dealing with the criticisms and controversies surrounding the U.S. national anthem; an annual update of his *Guidebook to the Outer Banks of North Carolina;* another guidebook.

SIDELIGHTS: "I like to write and I like to travel; ergo, I like to write about travel. In fact, I like it so well that I came out of retirement in the fall of 1976 to accept a part-time position as travel editor for a leisure-time section that appears monthly in eleven trade journals. I calculate that in the past thirty years I have traveled to more than forty countries and islands and have made one-round-the-world trip. I somehow have missed traveling to Soviet Russia and China but hope to remedy these omissions in time.

"Over the years, I have written countless news stories and feature articles, hundreds of editorials and personal columns, and several books. And I expect to write many more travel articles and one or two more books before signing off. I have never had any desire to try fiction. I like to write about subjects I either know intimately or have had the desire and opportunity to observe closely and research extensively.

"I have had few regrets about my work, but I have one at present. After hundreds of hours of research, I put together what I consider to be an interesting and informative history/controversy book detailing the trials and tribulations, the vicissitudes and the victories, of our national anthem, 'The Star-Spangled Banner,' but the commercial publishers have no interest in such a book. Well, it's a timeless subject, so I'll put it on a shelf and try again in another year or two. Who knows? Lightning may strike the second time around.

KEITH SAUNDERS

186

"Although I have done it twice, I would advise other writers to shun the game of self-publishing. My first book was about my father and his crusading country newspaper and it drew a large number of favorable notices, but many of the newspapers and magazines, including *Time*, failed to print my name and address, and I was about the only person from whom the book could be purchased. Even so, I sold nearly 2,000 copies and recouped my cash outlay, but it wouldn't have been worth the time and effort had the book not been a labor of love.

"Arco published my second book, a how-to-become and what-it-takes book about the airline stewardess profession, and it sold nearly 10,000 copies in two hardcover editions. It was a serious book, but a fun book to write. Then came a guidebook to my native section of North Carolina and it, like my first book, was self-published. I printed two editions and more than broke even on it, but it would not have been worth doing had it not been another labor of love.

"My second and third guidebooks, dealing, respectively, with Tidewater Virginia (Colonial Williamsburg, Jamestown, Yorktown, etc.) and the Eastern Shore of Maryland and Virginia, are due to be published soon. I enjoyed researching and writing them because I am fond of both sections, although not quite so fond as of my beloved *Outer Banks* (Kitty Hawk, Nags Heads, Roanoke Island, Cape Hatteras and Ocracoke). I hope they sell well, not because that will mean money in my pocket, but because it will mean more people will learn about and want to visit these interesting areas.

"It will be seen that I am not a writer who is likely to get rich, but at least I am enjoying my research and writing and enjoying life. What more could a man who has had a full and interesting life and is now in the senior citizen category hope for?"

SCHISGALL, Oscar 1901-
(Jackson Cole, Stuart Hardy)

PERSONAL: Born February 23, 1901, in Belgium; son of Nathan (a merchant) and Helen (Blumenthal) Schisgall; married Lillian Gelberg (a writer), September 19, 1926; children: Richard, James. *Education:* Attended College of the City of New York (now City College of the City University of New York), 1919-21, and New York University, 1921-23. *Politics:* Independent. *Home:* 85 East End Ave., New York, N.Y. 10028.

**What animal can sleep for three or four years without eating or drinking?
The answer, of course, is that Remarkable Creature, the Snail.**
■ (From *That Remarkable Creature the Snail* by Oscar Schisgall. Photos by Alvin E. Staffan.)

CAREER: Author and speechwriter. *Member:* Authors League, Authors Guild, Society of Magazine Writers, American Society of Composers, Authors, and Publishers, Overseas Press Club. *Awards, honors:* Benjamin Franklin Award for magazine writing.

WRITINGS: Barron Ixell, Crime Breaker, Longmans, Green, 1929; *The Devil's Daughter,* Fiction League, 1932; *Swastika,* Knopf, 1939; *The Big Store,* Prentice-Hall, 1955; *Laura Jane Sees Everything at Hess's* (children's book), Public Service Syndicate, 1966; *The Magic of Mergers: The Saga of Meshulam Riklis,* Little, Brown, 1968; *That Remarkable Creature, the Snail* (children's book), Messner, 1970; *My Years with Xerox,* Doubleday, 1972; *Out of One Small Chest: The History of the Bowery Savings Bank,* American Management Association, 1975.

Novels; under pseudonym Jackson Cole: *The Ramblin' Kid,* G. H. Watt, 1933; *Gun Justice,* G. H. Watt, 1933; *The Outlaws of Caja Basin,* G. H. Watt, 1934; *The Cholla Kid,* G. H. Watt, 1935; *The Outlaw Trail,* G. H. Watt, 1935; *Black Gold: A Story of the Texas Rangers,* William Caslon Co., 1936; *Six-gun Stampede,* Dodge Publishing, 1937; *The Miracle at Gopher Creek,* Green Circle Books, 1938; *Lone Star Law,* M. S. Mill, 1939; *Lone Star Silver,* M. S. Mill, 1939; *Lone Star Legion,* M. S. Mill, 1940; *Lone Star Terror,* M. S. Mill, 1940; *Lone Star Treasure,* Arcadia House, 1944; *The Valley of Revenge,* Arcadia House, 1944; *Haunted Valley,* Arcadia House, 1945; *The Frontier Legion,* Arcadia House, 1945; *The Devil's Legion,* Arcadia House, 1946.

Novels; under pseudonym Stuart Hardy: *The Man from Nowhere,* Macaulay Co., 1935; *Arizona Justice,* Green Circle Books, 1936; *Montana Bound,* Green Circle Books, 1936; *The Mountains Are My Kingdom,* Green Circle Books, 1937; *Trouble from Texas,* Macaulay Co., 1938. Also author of five screenplays and twenty radio and television plays. Contributor to *Reader's Digest, Redbook, Saturday Evening Post, Woman's Day,* and other periodicals.

WORK IN PROGRESS: Several magazine articles and a corporate history to be published by Doubleday.

SCHMID, Eleonore 1939-

PERSONAL: Born March 15, 1939, in Lucerne, Switzerland; daughter of Josef and Elise (Wunderli) Schmid; divorced; children: Caspar Iskander. *Education:* School of Arts and Crafts, Lucerne, Switzerland, degree in graphics, 1961. *Home:* Wasserwerkstrasse 27, 8006 Zurich, Switzerland.

CAREER: Worked in graphics in Zurich, Switzerland, 1961-64, Paris, 1965, and in New York, N.Y., 1965-68; author and illustrator of children's books. *Awards, honors:* Awards of excellence from societies of illustrators in New York, Bolognia, and Bratislava.

WRITINGS—All self-illustrated: *The Tree,* Quist, 1966; *Horns Everywhere,* Quist, 1967; *Tonia,* Putnam, 1970; *Das Schwarze Schaf,* Nord-Sud Verlag, 1976.

Illustrator: Robert Louis Stevenson, *Treasure Island,* Verleger Reńe Simmen, 1963; Hans Baumann, *Fenny,* Pantheon, 1968; James Krüss, *Die Geschichte vom grossen A* (title means "The Story of Big A"), Thienemanns Verlag, 1973.

WORK IN PROGRESS: New illustrations and children's books.

SCOTT, John M(artin) 1913-

PERSONAL: Born April 8, 1913, in Omaha, Neb.; son of Patrick John (a civil engineer) and Nettie (a clerk; maiden name, Martin) Scott. *Education:* St. Louis University, M.A., 1935, S.T.L., 1945, M.S., 1948. *Politics:* "Not bound to one party." *Home:* 305 East Campion St., Prairie du Chien, Wis. 53821. *Office:* Campion High School, Prairie du Chien, Wis. 53821.

CAREER: Entered Society of Jesus (Jesuits), 1931, ordained Roman Catholic priest, June 21, 1944—, assigned to mission on Sioux Indian reservation in South Dakota, 1938-

"There they had all the best things by the bushel: smoked hams, bacon, sausages, fruit, grain, cheese, butter, cakes, chocolate, and candles. I was very rich and content." ■ (From *Tonia* by Eleanore Schmid. Illustrated by the author.)

JOHN M. SCOTT

1941; assigned to study theology, St. Louis University, 1941-45, assigned to study physics, 1945-48; Campion High School, Prairie du Chien, Wis., physics teacher, 1948-75. Conducted science workshops at Creighton University, summers, 1949-75; regional chairman of Wisconsin Junior Academy of Science. *Member:* National Science Teachers Association (field advisory board member for Future Scientists of America). *Awards, honors:* The Wisconsin Society of Professional Engineers chose John Scott as one of the two outstanding teachers in the state in 1959, and 1973; the National Catholic Educational Association conferred the title "Impact Teacher" along with thirty-nine other outstanding teachers throughout the nation in April, 1967; given an award as an "Outstanding Secondary Educator of America," 1974; *The Five Senses,* nominated one of the Outstanding Science Books for Children, 1976.

WRITINGS: Wonderland, Loyola University Press, 1958; *Adventures in Science* (high school text), Loyola University Press, 1963; *Rain: Man's Greatest Gift,* Culligan, 1967; *Our Romance with Sun and Rain,* Culligan, 1968; *Adventure Awaits You,* Culligan, 1968; *The Everyday Living Approach to Teaching Elementary Science,* Parker Publishing, 1970; *What Is Science?* (juvenile), Parents' Magazine Press, 1972; *What Is Sound?* (juvenile), Parents' Magazine Press, 1973; *Heat and Fire* (juvenile), Parents' Magazine Press, 1973; *The Senses* (juvenile), Parents' Magazine Press, 1975; *To Touch the Face of God,* Our Sunday Visitor, 1975; *Phenomena of Our Universe,* Our Sunday Visitor, 1976.

Author of "Talking It Over With Fr. John," a column in *Treasure Chest,* 1959-63. Author of about twenty pamphlets for adults and young people. Contributor to *Educators Guide.* Contributor of more than a hundred articles to magazines and newspapers. Science editor for *Queen's Work* and *Young Catholic Messenger,* 1949-63.

WORK IN PROGRESS: "Classroom Science Discovery Series," for Center for Applied Research in Education; *Fantastic You Are!*

SIDELIGHTS: "Take a young boy, turn him loose in the Land of Shining Mountains, alias Montana, and what can you expect?

"You can be sure of this—all his life will be filled with visions of beauty, his heart caught high in the branches of the golden aspen on the mountain slope, his dreams pinned tight to that distant star, and tangled in the boughs of the tallest pine.

"His favorite song will be that of the wind whispering its secrets to the tree tops. He will want to return to the mountain thunder, to the silence of the valley. He will hold untarnished through the years the radiant, molten glory of the light from distant stars white and topaz, and misty red. He will keep the breathlessness, the thrill, the heart's swift running out to meet surprise.

"Although Omaha, Nebraska is the city where I was born, I grew up in the mile-high, copper-city of Butte, Montana. I spent my summers with my grandparents in the lofty mountains to the south and west of Butte.

If I stood on top of a tall mountain and shouted your name, you would not hear me. The sound fades away, goes out, and is absorbed by the air. That is why you wouldn't hear the thunder if you had to count more than 20 between the lightning and thunder. ■ (From *What is Sound?* by John M. Scott. Illustrated by Lawrence DiFiori.)

"Under the magic spell of mountain beauty, I grew up in a land vividly conscious of the wind and the sky. The love of mountains spilled over into all of science, and it is this fascination with the universe around us that I try to relay to all who read my books.

HOBBIES AND OTHER INTERESTS: Hiking, travel ("from the Arctic Circle to Australia and New Zealand, and from Hong Kong to Egypt").

FOR MORE INFORMATION SEE: Blackrobe, March, 1973.

SEIGEL, Kalman   1917-

PERSONAL: Born October 17, 1917, in Brooklyn, N.Y.; son of Samuel and Ida (Levy) Seigel; married Lillian Turetsky, January 26, 1941; children: Ann Phyllis (Mrs. Melvin Goodman), Carolyn (Mrs. Barry Shanoff). *Education:* City College, New York, N.Y., Bachelor of Social Science, 1939. *Politics:* Independent. *Religion:* Jewish. *Home:* 1477 East 17th St., Brooklyn, N.Y. 11230.

CAREER: New York Times, New York, N.Y., general assignment reporter, 1939-53, assistant city editor, 1953-57, suburban editor, 1957-63, assistant metropolitan editor, 1963-67, editor, letters to the editor, 1968—. City College, New York, N.Y., lecturer and adjunct professor of English and journalism, 1942-67. Jewish Center of Kings Highway, member of board of directors, 1962-65. *Member:* Sigma Delta Chi, Society of the Silurians (chairman of awards committee). *Awards, honors:* George Polk Memorial Award for educational reporting, 1952.

WRITINGS: (With Lawrence Feigenbaum) *This Is a Newspaper* (juvenile), Follett, 1965; (with Feigenbaum) *Israel: Crossroads of Conflict* (juvenile), Rand McNally, 1968; *Talking Back to the New York Times,* Quadrangle, 1972.

WORK IN PROGRESS: Departmental editor (journalism) for *Encyclopedia Judaica.*

HOBBIES AND OTHER INTERESTS: "Opera and music lover, bad golfer, trying to become a good photographer."

FOR MORE INFORMATION SEE: New York Times, May 1, 1968.

SEROFF, Victor I(ilyitch)   1902-

PERSONAL: Born October 14, 1902, in Batoum, Russia; became U.S. citizen. *Education:* Studied law at University of Tiflis, then music with Moriz Rosenthal in Vienna and Theodore Szanto in Paris. *Home:* 122 East 92nd St., New York, N.Y. 10028.

CAREER: Pianist and biographer of musicians.

WRITINGS: Dmitri Shostakovich: The Life and Background of a Soviet Composer, Knopf, 1943; *The Mighty Five: The Cradle of Russian National Music,* Crown, 1948; *Rachmaninoff,* Simon & Schuster, 1950; *Debussy—A Musician of France,* Putnam, 1956; *Renata Tebaldi: The Woman and the Diva,* Appleton, 1961; *Maurice Ravel,* Holt, 1966; *Sergei Prokofiev—A Soviet Tragedy,* Funk, 1968; *Men Who Made Musical History* (juvenile), Funk, 1968; *Modeste Moussorgsky,* Funk, 1969; *Common Sense in Piano Study,* Funk, 1970; *The Real Isadora* (biography of Isadora Duncan), Dial, 1971.

Concise biographies of great composers: *Frederic Chopin,* 1964, *Wolfgang Amadeus Mozart,* 1965, *Franz Liszt,* 1966, *Hector Berlioz,* 1967 (all published by Macmillan).

VICTOR I. SEROFF

Did an adaptation of Sergei Prokofiev's "The Love for Three Oranges" for the libretto in English used by New York City Center Opera Company, and a new dramatic version of the libretto in English of Alexander Borodin's "Prince Igor." Contributor of more than sixty articles to *Saturday Review*, 1954-64; also contributor to *Collier's, Etude, New Republic, Vogue, Town and Country, This Week, Harper's Bazaar, New York Times Book Review, Opera News, Encyclopaedia Britannica*, and other periodicals.

SIDELIGHTS: Victor Seroff's biographies of Rachmaninoff and Debussy, were also published in London and Paris and in translation; in all, there have been nine translations of his books—into Portuguese, French, Spanish, Italian, and German. *The Real Isadora* has been published in London, also, translated and published in Italy.

SHARPE, Mitchell R(aymond)   1924-

PERSONAL: Born December 22, 1924, in Knoxville, Tenn.; son of Mitchell R. (a salesman) and Katie Grace (Hill) Sharpe; married Virginia Ruth Lowry, December 21, 1952; children: Rebecca, Rachel, David. *Education:* Auburn University, B.S., 1949, M.A., 1954; Emory University, graduate study, 1954-55. *Religion:* Unitarian-Universalist. *Home:* 7302 Chadwell Rd., Huntsville, Ala. 38502.

CAREER: U.S. Army Missile Command, Huntsville, Ala., technical writer, 1955-60; Marshall Space Flight Center, Huntsville, Ala., technical writer and historian, 1960-74. National Air and Space Museum, Washington, D.C., consultant, 1965—; Alabama Space and Rocket Center, historian, 1967—. *Military service:* U.S. Army, 1943-46, 1950-52. U.S. Army Reserve, 1952—; current rank, colonel. *Member:* National Association of Science Writers, American Institute of Aeronautics and Astronautics, Company of Military Historians, Society for the History of Technology, British Interplanetary Society (fellow). *Awards, honors:* Robert H. Goddard Essay Award in the history of rocketry, 1968 and 1975; Tsiolkovsky Gold Medal of U.S.S.R., 1973.

Valya leaned over and clinked her space helmet against that of Venera. It was the traditional farewell from the prime cosmonaut to the backup. ■ (From *It is I, Seagull* by Mitchell R. Sharpe. Photo courtesy of Novosti Press and Agency and Embassy of the USSR.)

MITCHELL R. SHARPE

WRITINGS: (With F. I. Ordway and J. P. Gardner) *Basic Astronautics: An Introduction to Space Science, Engineering, and Medicine*, Prentice-Hall, 1962; (with Ordway, Gardner, and R. C. Wakeford) *Applied Astronautics, and Introduction to Space Flight*, Prentice-Hall, 1963; (contributor) Ernst Stuhlinger and others, editors, *Astronautical Engineering and Science, from Peenemunde to Planetary Space*, McGraw, 1963; (contributor) Ordway, editor, *Advances in Space Science and Technology*, Academic Press, Volume 7, 1964, Volume 8, 1965; *Living in Space: The Astronaut and His Environment*, Doubleday, 1969; *Yuri Gagarin: First Man into Space*, Strode, 1969.

Satellites and Probes: The Development of Unmanned Space Flight, Doubleday, 1970; (with C. C. Adams and Ordway) *Dividends from Space*, Crowell, 1971; *"It is I, Seagull": Valentina Tereshkova, First Woman in Space*, 1975. Author of U.S. Army manuals. Contributor to *Encyclopaedia Britannica Year Book*, 1963-77, to *Compton's Encyclopedia, Encyclopedia of World Biography*, and to journals. Associate editor, *Space Journal*, 1957-59.

WORK IN PROGRESS: A history of rocketry from the thirteenth century through the late twentieth century; a book on the biological rhythms of life; a study of Wernher von Braun's team of German rocket engineers who put the first American satellite into orbit.

SIDELIGHTS: "As a boy in Knoxville, Tenn., I read every book I could get my hands on, at home, in school, or in the public library. As I grew older, I began collecting a library; and I now have almost 2,000 books of my own. To be a serious writer a person must be a serious reader.

"My paternal grandfather and his brothers were great talkers, especially when small children were around them. They spun tales only a little less tall than those of Davy Crockett, but they fascinated me by the hour. I suppose that oral literature and the ability to communicate with children are two of the things I learned early, long before I ever thought of becoming a writer.

"I was especially fortunate in having an imaginative and talented English teacher at Sidney Lanier High School, in Montgomery, Ala. Miss Laura Johnson encouraged me in every way to improve my themes in class by paying attention to the finer points of grammar. Then, she encouraged me to develop a style of my own, but always stressing precision and clarity. At Auburn University, then called Alabama Polytechnic Institute, I also had a really great English teacher in Dr. Charles Patterson. His standards were equally as strict as those of Miss Johnson. The final examination in freshman English was a set of three impromptu essays written under his demanding eye. The student had to pass two out of three to pass the course, no matter how good his grades were. Just one misspelled word or comma splice meant failure on an essay. In any profession one must have discipline, and I learned it from two of the best English teachers in the country as far as I am concerned."

HOBBIES AND OTHER INTERESTS: Photography (often illustrates his own work).

SHAW, Richard 1923-

PERSONAL: Born May 21, 1923, in Greensboro, N.C.; son of Charles B. and Dorothy (Joslyn) Shaw; married Benita Haines, June 8, 1950 (divorced, 1967); married Janet Noyes (a school nurse teacher), August 12, 1968; children: (first marriage) Karen, Jennifer; (stepchildren) Keith, Steven, Mark, Geoffrey. *Education:* Swarthmore College, student, 1941-44; George Washington University, student, 1944-45; Columbia University, A.B., 1946, M.L.S., 1951; graduate study at Harvard University, 1956, and University of California, Berkeley, 1960. *Home:* 40 Phyllis Dr., Pearl River, N.Y. 10965. *Office:* Department of English, Westchester Community College, Valhalla, N.Y. 10505.

CAREER: Columbia University, New York, N.Y., instructor in humanities, 1946-48; Brooklyn Public Library, Brooklyn, N.Y., librarian in language and literature, 1948-51; Friends Academy, Dartmouth, Mass., English teacher, 1951-52; English teacher and chairman of department in high school in Orleans, Mass., 1953-57; Bennett College, Millbrook, N.Y., professor of English, 1958-60; *New York Herald Tribune,* New York, N.Y., assistant editor of book section, 1961-62; *New York Times,* New York, N.Y., rewriter, 1962-63; Frederick Warne and Co., editor, 1965-75; Richard Shaw (editorial consultant), Pearl River, N.Y., owner, 1964—. Westchester Community College, associate professor of English, 1965—. *Member:* American Newspaper Guild, American Association of University Professors, United Federation of College Teachers.

WRITINGS—For children: *Budd's Noisy Wagon,* Warne, 1968; *Who Are You Today?,* Warne, 1970; (editor) *The Owl Book,* Warne, 1970; *Tree for Rent,* Albert Whitman, 1971; (editor) *The Fox Book,* Warne, 1971; (editor) *The Frog Book,* Warne, 1972; *The Kitten in the Pumpkin Patch,* Warne, 1972; (editor) *The Cat Book,* Warne, 1973; (editor)

RICHARD SHAW

The Bird Book, Warne, 1973; (editor) *Witch, Witch!,* Warne, 1975; (editor) *The Mouse Book,* Warne, 1975.

Young adult novels: *Call Me Al Raft,* Nelson, 1975; *Shape Up, Burke,* Nelson, 1976; *The Hard Way Home,* Nelson, 1977.

SIDELIGHTS: "Most of what I write is based either on a personal experience, an incident I've heard about or comes from the mind of one of my children or students. *Budd's Noisy Wagon* is about any number of small boys (myself included) who can't resist dragging home what other people throw away and treasuring it. Jeff, in *Who Are You Today?,* still lives with me, but is no longer a small boy desperately wanting to be someone else. The story of *Tree for Rent* is essentially true and was told me by the girl to whom it happened. Jenny, the small girl in *The Kitten in the Pumpkin Patch,* is my daughter. Until she grew out of it, she was an avid trick-or-treater who looked a great deal like the wistful little girl on page twelve of the book. The characters in *Call Me Al Raft,* a novel, are for the most part based on people I knew when I lived in California. Al's girl, Kit, has much in common with my daughter Karen. I did a lot of the things Al does in the book—hitch-hiked all over the place, body surfed at Old Mission Beach, ate hundreds of tacos—and I knew people like Al's mother and Pistol Ryder when I worked driving a truck in the Imperial Valley.

"Like Pat in *Shape Up, Burke,* some of my younger friends went to survival camps, ran away from home, learned a lot and came to terms with their fathers who thought they should be different kinds of boys. Because I have done a lot of teaching, I've known several boys like Gary in *The Hard*

. . . looking down he saw the wrinkled crone and the great pile of fish that she had cast on the bank, and his heart was grieved for two things—one that there was such a waste of good life, the other that he had left his spear hidden in the grass. ■ (From *Witch, Witch* edited by Richard Shaw. Illustrated by Clinton Arrowood.)

Way Home, boys who aren't as grown up as they should be for their ages and so have a hard time not only at home, but anywhere they go. Most of the Garys I've known grew up eventually. I've made use of some of the places I've lived and worked on newspapers and taught school—New England, California, the New York City area—as settings for my stories, particularly my novels. It doesn't matter to me so much where a story happens as to whom and why. So I try not to write too much description and instead, focus my attention on the characters and try to make them act and sound real.''

HOBBIES AND OTHER INTERESTS: Travel in Europe and Latin America, playing tennis, swimming, music, building with wood, living on a cat boat.

SHELDON, Aure   1917-1976

PERSONAL: Born October 12, 1917, in Peoria, Ill.; daughter of Irving Weir and Retha (Crumrine) Stevens; married George Andrew Sheldon, October 8, 1938 (died in January, 1956); children: Jeannine (Mrs. George V. Kallal), William George, James Allen. *Education:* Northern Illinois University, B.S.Ed., 1962. *Residence:* North Carolina.

CAREER: Elementary school teacher in Massachusetts, 1962-71; Pisgah Forest School, Pisgah Forest, N.C., elementary school teacher, 1971-76. *Member:* National Education Association, National Wildlife Federation, Wilderness Society, Audubon Society, Sierra Club, North Carolina Association of Educators.

The King of Upland had a problem. ■ (From *Fit for a King* by Aure Sheldon. Illustrated by Robert Sweetland.)

WRITINGS—For children: *Fit for a King,* Lerner, 1975; *Of Cobblers and Kings,* Parents' Magazine Press, 1976. Contributor of articles to adult magazines and stories to children's magazines.

WORK IN PROGRESS: Long Trail Winding; Into the Stubborn Wind; other fiction books for young teen-agers.

SIDELIGHTS: Aure Sheldon's son, William, wrote: ''Mother started writing to satisfy her natural creative urges, to put to use her many experiences, to provide additional income. She had hoped to develop writing into enough of an income source to retire to travel and gather new background.

''To tell about her 'interesting' life really would take a book because Mother was one to pack it all in and get something good out of every day.

Aure Sheldon actively participated in conservation, wildlife protection, and nature projects. ''A long time interest in children's literature led to a writing career, primarily for children.''

HOBBIES AND OTHER INTERESTS: Wilderness vacations, hiking, canoeing, rafting, horseback trips, camping, needlework, painting.

(Died March 23, 1976)

SHERMAN, Diane (Finn)   1928-

PERSONAL: Born December 6, 1928, in Boston, Mass.; daughter of Henry M. (a retailer) and Bess (Golding) Finn;

DIANE SHERMAN

Your Health Department works to keep the people in your city healthy in other ways. ■ (From *About the People Who Run Your City* by Shirlee Petkin Newman and Diane Finn Sherman. Illustrated by James David Johnson.)

married Matthew Sherman, June 26, 1949; children: Jane, Lisa, Adam. *Education:* Mount Holyoke College, B.A., 1950. *Home address:* 1915 S. Crescent Blvd., Yardley, Pa. 19067. *Agent:* Dorothy Markinko, McIntosh & Otis, 475 Fifth Ave., New York, N.Y. 10017.

CAREER: Free-lance writer, mainly for children.

WRITINGS: Little Skater, Rand McNally, 1959; *My Counting Book,* Rand McNally, 1960; *Myrtle Turtle,* Rand McNally, 1961; *Jumping Jack,* Rand McNally, 1962; (with Shirlee Newman) *About the People Who Run Your City,* Melmont, 1963; (with Newman) *About Canals,* Melmont, 1964; *You and the Oceans,* Childrens Press, 1965; *Nancy Plays Nurse,* Rand McNally, 1965; *All Around the City,* Rand McNally, 1967; *The Boy From Abilene,* Westminster, 1968; *My Oak Tree,* Rand McNally, 1973; *People Who Work at Night,* Rand McNally, 1973. Contributor of stories, articles, poems, and plays to *Child Life* and other children's magazines; contributor of science articles to adult magazines. Author of curriculum material for beginning readers.

WORK IN PROGRESS: Science writing; adult nonfiction on the occult.

SHOWALTER, Jean B(reckinridge)

PERSONAL: Born in Roanoke, Va.; daughter of English (an attorney) and Jean (Staples) Showalter; married John O. Strom-Olsen; children: Rolf, Anna. *Education:* Wellesley

College, B.A., 1963. *Religion:* Episcopalian. *Residence:* Montreal, Quebec, Canada.

CAREER: Doubleday & Co., Inc., New York, N.Y., associate editor of children's books, 1966-68.

WRITINGS: Around the Corner, Doubleday, 1966; *The Donkey Ride,* Doubleday, 1967.

SIDELIGHTS: "The Donkey Ride," adapted by Jean B. Showalter is included in "A Treasury of Modern Tales for Children," Miller-Brody Productions.

HOBBIES AND OTHER INTERESTS: History and historic preservation.

SIBLEY, Don 1922-

PERSONAL: Born March 16, 1922, in Hornell, N.Y.; son of Stanley D. (a civil engineer) and Mabel C. (Luce) Sibley; married Janet Augusta Maus, January 26, 1945; children: Linda (Potter), Diane (McCaffery), Mark D. *Education:* Pratt Institute, Brooklyn, N.Y., certificate, 1947. *Home and office:* R.D. 1 Headquarters Road, Litchfield, Conn. 06759.

CAREER: Free-lance illustrator. Philip E. Wilcox, Inc., New York, N.Y., bullpen artist, 1945-47; Western Electric Co., New York, N.Y., assistant art director, 1947-48; Lance Studios, New York, N.Y., partner-illustrator, 1948-55. *Military service:* U.S. Army Air Corps, first lieutenant, Euro-

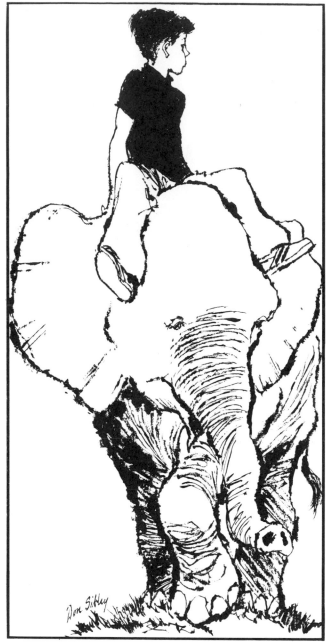

■ Drawing by Don Sibley for Cover of *Elephant for Hire*. Reprinted by permission of the illustrator.

pean theatre ribbon, air medal—three oak leaf clusters, 1942-45.

ILLUSTRATOR: Mary O'Hara, *My Friend Flicka* (Doubleday book club edition), Lippincott, 1941; Stephen Meader, *Sparkplug of the Hornets,* Harcourt, 1953; Nancy Hartwell, *A Blue for Illi,* Holt, 1954; Helen Fern Daringer, *Bigity Anne,* Harcourt, 1954; Evan Commager, *Tenth Birthday,* Bobbs, 1954; Jerrold Beim, *With Dad Alone,* Harcourt, 1954; Jerrold Beim, *A Vote for Dick,* Harcourt, 1955; Don Wilcox, *Basketball Star,* Little, Brown, 1955; Julia Montgomery Street, *Fiddler's Fancy,* Follett, 1955; Lillian Gardner, *Somebody Called Booie,* Watts, 1955; Elizabeth Kinsey, *This Cat Came to Stay,* Watts, 1955; Adele and Cateau DeLeeuw, *The Expandable Browns,* Little, Brown, 1955; Pauline Rush Evans, *A Family Treasury of Children's Sto-*

ries (two volumes), Doubleday, 1956; Adele and Cateau DeLeeuw, *The Caboose Club,* Little, Brown, 1957; Jerrold Beim, *Trouble After School,* Harcourt, 1957; Stephen Meader, *The Commodore's Cup,* Harcourt, 1958; Elizabeth Coatsworth, *The Dog From Nowhere,* Peterson, 1958; Lucille Chaplan, *Elephant for Rent,* Little, Brown, 1959; Miriam Young, *Marco's Chance,* Harcourt, 1959.

Stephen Meader, *Snow on Blueberry Mountain,* Harcourt, 1961; Anita Feagles, *The Genie & Joe Maloney,* W. R. Scott, 1962; Robert Burch, *Tyler, Wilkin & Skee,* Viking, 1963; Suzanne Martel, *The City Underground,* Viking, 1964; Robert Burch, *Skinny,* Viking, 1964; Madeline Robinson Stratton, *Negroes Who Helped Build America,* Ginn, 1965; Robert D. O'Neal and Marina Garcia Burdick, *Calidoscopio Español,* Ginn, 1967; Jan Farrington, *America Awakes,* Westover, 1971; Beth Tartan, *Good Old Days Cookbook,* Westover, 1971.

Has illustrated several textbooks; approximately seventy-five paperback volumes for the Doubleday "Around the World Program" and for their "Know Your America" program; eighty-five volumes for Doubleday's "Best-In-Books" series; eighteen volumes for Ginn & Co., "Today's World in Focus" series; also magazine illustrations for both children and adults.

WORK IN PROGRESS: Canals, Man-Made Waterways by Solveig Paulson Russell for Parents' Magazine Press.

DON SIBLEY

196

"I entered this world on March 16, 1922 at Hornell, then a railroading community in the southern tier of New York State. I was the first baby to arrive at the new wing of Hornell's Bethesda Hospital. To show how long ago that was, the 'new' wing, along with the rest of that building was razed for the construction of a fine modern structure to house the hospital on the same site about ten or fifteen years back.

"My primary recollections of childhood are three-fold—summers on my grandparents' farm; baseball, football and basketball, both in and out of seasons; and sitting at the radio on winter afternoons after school filling pages and pages of paper with drawings of Tom Mix, Bobby Benson, Jack Armstrong, Buck Rogers, Orphan Annie and the myriad others whose adventures filled the airways and my head.

"I graduated Hornell High School in 1939 and, after a post-graduate year there for a course in journalism, entered Pratt Institute to study illustration.

"Unfortunately, I was forced to leave Pratt a year prior to graduation for service with the Army Air Corps during World War II. I was a bomber pilot based in Italy.

"In 1945, returned from overseas, but still in service, I married, and lived in Laredo, Texas and Dothan, Alabama where I instructed aviation cadets in instrument flying during their advanced flight training.

"After my discharge from the service, Jan and I both worked so that I could finish my final year at Pratt.

"We have three children. The eldest, Linda, who has two children, Judson and Nathan, is now pursuing medical studies. Diane, our secondborn, also has a son, Damien and works in the field of education. Her husband, Peter, is an educator, counsellor and writer. Mark, our youngest, also graduated Pratt and now lives in the Teton Mountains of Wyoming where he climbs the pinnacles and paints the wildlife.

"We raised our children in the convenience of a contemporary house which Jan and I designed. When Mark graduated from college a few years ago to head west, I decided that I was tired of meeting deadlines and straining to earn the kind of income necessary to support a family and a rather luxurious home, so I abandoned the illustration field. We sold our house and went to work for a therapeutic center for emotionally disturbed people whose residents were largely young people recovering from drug addiction. Jan was a volunteer worker, in charge of the kitchen, directing the young residents in food preparation and serving meals, I was a paid employee, director of work projects, performed by the young residents, maintaining the mansion and estate which housed the center. I proved to be a sorry supervisor and lasted at the job for a year. My inadequacy stemmed from an inability to confront my charges when they bungled appointed tasks. Confrontation was the crux of the therapeutic program, but my bent was toward sympathetic instruction. We accomplished the maintenance work with reasonable efficiency, but I didn't contribute constructively to the residents' therapy.

"While employed at the center, Jan and I lived in a small farmhouse on the grounds, so when we left their employ we needed new housing. We acquired a badly neglected small colonial house whose interior had been stripped to the post-and-beam frame. We electrified, plumbed and restored the house, doing all the work ourselves to its present warm and comfortable condition.

"An interest in appointing our home in a manner appropriate to its colonial origins led us to libraries, museums and antique shops. Our research into colonial architecture, construction, implements and furniture spilled over into all phases of early Americana. We developed a deep respect for the vision and achievements of our forebears. This interest in our history has led me to more illustration of historical stories and books.

"My current hobby is carpentry and cabinetmaking—developed out of the needs for our new-old home. Our next project is, hopefully, a new barn which we'll try to make look old.

It's difficult for me to discuss my work and come up with any concrete conclusions. Each story is different and inspires an individual approach. But in most of the stories I find in some way a parallel in my own experience . . . ringing a bell that starts an identification process, so that I can relate to the story as a kid rather than as an adult. I suppose that happens with every adult who writes or illustrates a story for children. I don't see how it could be otherwise . . . and I don't mean that I assume a naivete or ignorance when I throw back to my childhood, but, rather, a sense of complete enthusiasm and eagerness for involvement in impending experiences of the character in the story. Also, there's an assumption that I can tackle the problems that loom and make them turn out okay. As an adult, I approach events and problems with caution. I consider the alternatives and consequences, then hedge as my intellect controls my instincts . . . so that seldom does anything that's very exciting occur. Things were livelier and a lot more fun in those days, it seems, so it would follow the story could best be illustrated from the child's point of view."

FOR MORE INFORMATION SEE: Illustrators of Children's Books: 1957-1966, Horn Book, 1968.

SICULAN, Daniel 1922-

PERSONAL: Surname is pronounced Si-kool-en; born December 30, 1922, in Martins Ferry, Ohio; son of George (a millworker) and Katherine (Petrila) Siculan; married Thelma Marsh, June 21, 1942; children: Dan L., Kenneth, Martha, Kathryn. *Education:* Attended Oglebay Institute, Wheeling, W.Va., 1937; American Academy of Art, Chicago, Ill., 1946. *Home and office:* 2523 Allison Court, Glenview, Ill. 60025.

CAREER: Illustrator; designs and produces silk screen prints for framing, 1969—. *Military service:* U.S. Army, corporal, 1943-45.

ILLUSTRATOR: Paul Bacon, *Luther Burbank,* Encyclopaedia Brittanica, 1961; E. F. Dolan, Jr., *Walter Reed,* Encyclopaedia Brittanica, 1962; Gorham Munson, *Robert Frost,* Encyclopaedia Brittanica, 1962; F. J. Cook, *P. T. Barnum,* Encyclopaedia Brittanica, 1962; John Logan, *Tom Savage,* Encyclopaedia Brittanica, 1962; (co-illustrator) *Braving the Elements, Childcraft Annual,* Field Enterprises

DANIEL SICULAN

Educational Corp., 1967; Harry Bricker, Yvonne Beckwith, *Words to Know,* Standard Education Corp., 1969; Virginia Holmgren, *War Lord,* Follett, 1969; (co-illustrator) *Questions Children Ask,* Standard Education Corp., 1969.

Stephen P. Sutton, editor, *Pat-A-Cake,* Rand, 1970; Emyl Jenkins, *Gregg Walker, News Photographer,* A. Whitman, 1970; Glennette Turner, *Surprise for Mrs. Burns,* A. Whitman, 1971; *Picturebook Dictionary,* Rand, 1971; A. B. Allen, *Fifth Down,* A. Whitman, 1974; K. Gezi, A. Bradford, *One Little White Shoe,* Child's World, 1976; K. Gezi, A. Bradford, *Beebi, the Little Blue Bell,* Child's World, 1976; Jane B. Moncure, *Where Things Belong,* Child's World, 1976; Jane B. Moncure, *A New Boy in Kindergarten,* Child's World, 1976; Sylvia Tester, *A World of Color,* Child's World, 1976; Mark Parker, *Horses, Airplanes & Frogs,* Child's World, 1976. Has done educational assignments for Laidlaw Brothers, Follett, Lyons & Carnahan, Scott Foresman & Co., Harper & Row and Rand McNally.

SIDELIGHTS: "I was five years of age when my interest in art was sparked. I watched one day while an older brother brought down from a well-hidden place, on an upper closet shelf, a loosely rolled sheet of paper held by a rubber band. He'd taken it down to show it to some friends of his and was greeted with a great deal of praise from each of them and I can still recall the high emotion I felt as his friends responded to the display.

"Except for a brief glimpse of the image on the paper, I couldn't see enough to satisfy my curiosity and was lightly rubuffed then and afterward when I asked to see his magical paper. I was determined to seek out this roll of paper and to see for myself what it was that caused such a reaction among my brothers friends. So with the help of a ladder-back chair I eventually found the roll, opened it up and beheld a pencil drawn image! It was the face of a man staring out at me with eyes so real that I was startled by it and my first reaction was to quickly roll it up and put it back. But, instead, I studied it carefully and again and again. In due time I had become so fascinated by the drawing (in later years I found it to be a rather ordinary schoolboy's attempt at copying a picture of William Shakespeare) that I finally produced my own pencil copy, one that I was assured by my mother was every bit as fine as the one my brother had drawn.

"A few years later while still in elementary grade level my activity in art had progressed. At this time I was an avid comic reader and being a newspaper carrier I had access to several different publications and enjoyed reading the comic strips in them all. Here my artistic expression manifested itself in the copying of every comic strip character that I cared about. I carried these around with me in the form of a rather substantial pack of cards with the images rendered on the blank sides, all held together with a rubber band. These would then be easily available to show to anyone who might be interested either in my drawing skills or who were simply comic buffs like myself.

"Ours was not a literary conscious family in those days. There were books, but none as I recall were readily available to me as a preschooler. At about this time I recall a large book, a well-worn historical volume that my father had brought home one day. I was allowed to look through it now and then, and again I found the pictures fascinating. These were battle scenes, both land and sea, most probably steel engravings because I can still recall the sharpness of the picture detail. My interests in books soon picked up however, for sometime soon after entering the first grade I was accompanied by an older brother on frequent trips to the public library. Here there were many books to read in a department set up for children, and there were also books that could be taken home to read. These were some of my happiest of early childhood memories.

"My career really began during my World War II army service in England where I served in some small capacity as artist in my unit. This was in 1944. After the war I left Martins Ferry, Ohio to begin a new life in Chicago with my wife and child.

"I started in the commercial art field as a package designer and aspiring illustrator. Later during the first year, I enrolled in an evening life class at the American Academy of Art and from that time I was determined to make illustration my life's work.

"After about five years of doing the usual commercial design work required of me, I gradually worked my way into general illustration. I received my first textbook assignment in 1958 from Laidlaw Brothers, a schoolbook publisher. It was a wonderful departure from the more restricting routine that I had been following. Eventually the volume of this type of work increased and after a few more years I was well on the way of establishing myself as a book illustrator.

"I had also a good deal of experience during this time of illustrating for calendars, greeting cards, posters and particularly magazine covers and articles. In 1969 I began to experiment with silk-screen printing during my slower periods and have by now become quite involved with it. A small part of this effort has gone into publishing, some textbook, posters and greeting cards; mostly the major effort is in my own production of limited edition series for framing purposes. These are silk-screen prints, or serigraphs that are displayed and sold through art galleries in a number of cities throughout the country.

"The economics of printed art work in the Chicago area plus a desire to contribute something, limited as it might be, to education, are the chief motivating factors in my career as an illustrator of children's books. I have executed my work in tempera, dyes, acrylics, ink and silk-screen printing.

"I believe that my earliest reading habits and movie viewing had a great deal to do with setting my general attitude to illustrating approach. I'm sure this has been so all my life, in spite of periodic attempts to alter or revitalize my style, I am referring to the reading of comics and the movie cartoons of the late 1920's."

SILCOCK, Sara Lesley 1947-

PERSONAL: Born January 30, 1947, in Leeds, Yorkshire, England; daughter of Leslie Edward (a clerk) and Joan (Louise) Silcock. *Education:* Hornsey College of Art, London, England, diploma, 1972. *Religion:* Church of England. *Home and office:* 46 Coombe Road, Croydon, Surrey, England. *Agent:* Linda Rogers Associates, 9 Halsey House, 13 Red Lion Square, London, W1, England.

CAREER: Illustrator.

ILLUSTRATOR: Geoffrey Trease, *A Voice in the Night,* Heinemann, 1973; *The Noel Streatfield Easter Holiday Book,* Dent, 1973; *The Noel Streatfield Summer Holiday Book,* Dent, 1973; *The Noel Streatfield Christmas Holiday Book,* Dent, 1973; John Fitzgerald, *Me and My Little Brain,* Dent, 1974; Pamela Davis, *Miss Mossop's Secret,* Nelson, 1974; Juliet Piggot, *Myth and Moonshine,* Muller, 1974; Ruth Thompson, *Clothes and Costume,* Macdonald, 1974; Frederick Hoare, *Gold,* Muller, 1975; Ruth Thompson, *North American Indians,* Macdonald, 1975; Ruth Thompson, *Joan of Arc,* Macdonald, 1975; Margaret Howell, *The Blue Fox,* Longmans, 1976. Has also illustrated numerous "Storychair" books published by Transworld, many pamphlets for BBC and ITV, radio school programmes, and numerous covers.

SIDELIGHTS: "I was born in Leeds, the west Riding of Yorkshire, England. My mother is English and my father, now dead, was Canadian. I spent the earliest part of my childhood there. I was an only child, but in spite of this I was never lonely, mainly due to the company of my 'imaginary friends.' I used to spend hours in the garden shed, entertaining them to tea, etc.

"Apart from being interested in drawing from my earliest recollections, I used to spend most of my time, when I was not at school, outside. There was a huge field behind the house where we used to live, and I spent most of my spare time there, with my dog, watching the animals, hedgehogs, mice, etc., going about their business, and making up little stories about them. I was often scolded for staying out there

SARA LESLEY SILCOCK

in the dark in one or another of the hiding holes I'd made for dog and me.

"I can still remember most clearly, the smells that used to be all around, the sweet smell of the wild lupins that grew there, with the pods that curled up and went pop! frightening the life out of me on hot summer days, and the smell of the privet flowers that grew everywhere. Some years ago I went back to the old house and was amazed to see how small and unexciting the whole place looked to my adult eyes. It had seemed so huge and mysterious when I was small.

"My father died when I was twelve. My mother and I moved to Southampton, and I spent most of my later school years there. I always knew what I wanted to do when I left school, go to college, so I did. I went to Southampton Art College for one year doing everything from textile design to life drawing when I had decided which aspect of art interested me most. I applied for a place at Hornsey College of Art in London to do a three year diploma course in graphic design and was delighted to be accepted after the interview. The first year was general, but for the last two I specialized in illustrative projects. We were fortunate in having excellent tutors there, the majority being practising artists as well as teachers—for example, Mr. Mel Calman the cartoonist whose advice was hilarious and invaluable. When I left college I started making the rounds of the various publishers here in London and J. M. Dent was kind enough to start my career off with my first published books, the three Noel Streatfield anthologies. The next couple of years were quite busy with illustration work.

"There has been a terrible lack of work available for my specific illustration talents. Just recently, I have had to turn my hand to other things such as motifs for children's clothes, etc. and I have just finished a t-shirt design for Marks & Spencer Clothing Company.

"I don't really know what the future holds for me now, I hope I shall be able to continue illustrating books for children, the thing I enjoy doing most; but I would also like to try my hand at writing stories as well."

SIMON, Martin P(aul William)   1903-1969

PERSONAL: Born February 16, 1903, in Angelica, Wis.; son of T. F. (a farmer) and Eleanor (Elbert) Simon; married Ruth Tolzmann, September 8, 1926; children: Paul, Arthur. *Education:* Concordia College, Milwaukee, Wis., graduate (with honors), 1922; Concordia Seminary, St. Louis, Mo., B.D., 1926; University of Oregon, M.A., 1931, D.Ed., 1953. *Politics:* Democrat.

CAREER: Lutheran minister. Missionary in China, 1926-28; pastor in Eugene, Ore., 1928-38; *Christian Parent,* editor and publisher in Eugene, Ore., 1938-46, in Highland, Ill., 1946-57; Scripture Press, Wheaton, Ill., editor of *Christian Parent,* 1957-61; writer, assistant pastor, pastor, 1962-69. *Member:* National Council of Family Relations.

MARTIN P. SIMON

WRITINGS: Bible Readings for the Family Hour, Moody, 1954; (with Allan H. Jahsmann) *Little Visits with God,* Concordia, 1957; (with Jahsmann) *More Little Visits with God,* Concordia, 1961; *Daily Family Devotions for the Whole Family,* Christian Life Publishing, 1963; *Points for Parents: A Book to Help Parents Understand and Guide Their Children,* Zondervan, 1963; *How to Know and Use Your Bible,* Zondervan, 1963; *Glad Moments with God,* Zondervan, 1964; *Meeting Current Family Problems,* edited by Oscar E. Feucht, Concordia, 1966. Contributor and consulting editor, *Lutheran Digest;* columnist, *Lutheran Layman.*

WORK IN PROGRESS: Bible Story Devotions, for Standard Press.

(Died September 23, 1969)

SLACKMAN, Charles B.   1934-

PERSONAL: Born June 10, 1934, in Brooklyn, N.Y.; married Betteanne Terrell (a ballet dancer), December 31, 1963.

CAREER: Illustrator. *Military service:* U.S. Army, SP4, 1957-59. *Member:* Illustrators Guild (secretary), American Institute of Graphic Artists.

ILLUSTRATOR: Elizabeth Janeway, *Angry Kate,* Harper, 1963; Gloria Steinem, *The Beach Book,* Viking, 1964; Shirley Jackson, *Famous Sally,* Harlin Quist, 1965; Leonard Todd, *Subsistence Toys & Games,* Viking, 1974; Judi Barrett, *I Hate to Take a Bath,* Four Winds, 1975.

FOR MORE INFORMATION SEE: Print Magazine, 1967; *Idea* Magazine, 1976.

In Rose City, the people planted roses in their gardens and in their parks, and all the buildings had roses growing along their tops.

His ancestors were fine domesticated animals. ■ (From *The Proudest Horse on the Prairie* by Beatrice S. Smith. Illustrated by Laurel Horvat.)

SMITH, Beatrice S(chillinger)

PERSONAL: Born in Madison, Wis.; daughter of Reynold J. and Jeanette (McGowan) Schillinger; married J. Robert Smith; children: Steven Robert, Peter Reynold. *Education:* University of Wisconsin, B.S. *Home address:* Box 116, Westfield, Wis. 53964. *Agent:* Ann Elmo, 52 Vanderbilt Ave., New York, N.Y. 10017.

■ (From *Famous Sally* by Shirley Jackson. Pictures by Charles B. Slackman.)

CAREER: High school teacher of English and art in the United States and South America. *Member:* Council for Wisconsin Writers. *Awards, honors:* Best juvenile by a Wisconsin writer award from Council for Wisconsin Writers, 1974, for *The Road to Galveston.*

WRITINGS—All juveniles: *Proudest Horse on the Prairie,* Lerner, 1972; *The Road to Galveston,* Lerner, 1973; *Don't Mention Moon to Me,* Thomas Nelson, 1974; *Six Mini-Mysteries,* Lerner, 1976. Contributor of articles and short stories to fifty magazines for children and adults.

WORK IN PROGRESS: Suspense fiction for both adults and children; researching the eighteenth century.

SMITH, Howard E(verett), Jr.   1927-

PERSONAL: Born November 18, 1927, in Gloucester, Mass.; son of Howard Everett (an artist) and Martha (Rondelle) Smith; married Louanne Norris, June 1, 1953; children: Carolyn Lavinia, Alexander Noel Howard. *Education:* Colorado College, B.A., 1952. *Religion:* Protestant. *Home:* 128 Willow St., Brooklyn, N.Y. 11201.

CAREER: Former surveyor for Independent Exploration Co., writer-editor, Science Materials Center, Basic Books; associate editor, Prism Productions, with "Mr. Wizard"; Foster Wheeler Corp., New York, N.Y., editor, 1964-65; McGraw-Hill Book Co., Junior Book Division, New York, N.Y., editor, handling science and art books, 1967—. *Awards, honors:* Wrote narration for "Collage," award winner at Venice Film Festival.

WRITINGS: (Self-illustrated) *From Under the Earth: America's Metals, Fuels, and Minerals* (for young people), Harcourt, 1967; *Play With the Wind,* McGraw, 1972; (with Louanne Norris) *Newsmakers: The Press and the Presi-*

**Here are other ways of telling
whether the wind is blowing or not.**
■ (From *Play with the Wind* by Howard E. Smith, Jr. Illustrated by Jacqueline Chwast.)

dents, Addison-Wesley, 1974; *Play With the Sun,* McGraw, 1975; *Dreams in Your Life,* Doubleday, 1975; *The Unexplored Earth,* Doubleday, 1976; *Giant Animals,* Doubleday, 1977; *The Complete Beginner's Guide to Mountain Climbing,* Doubleday, 1977. Writer of narration for "Collage," film produced at ACI Productions, New York, and script for "Ouija Board," Javien Productions, New York. With Thomas Aylesworth and Philip Baker wrote "The Juvenile Book Editor" for *Library Trends;* also, author of "The Art of Mary Bauermesiter" for *Arts & Artists,* London. Many of his poems have been published in *Epos, New Mexico Quarterly, University of Kansas City Review, Canadian Poetry Journal,* and other literary reviews; contributor of *Nature and Science,* publication of American Museum of Natural History and other magazines.

WORK IN PROGRESS: An adult book on sensory awareness for Putnam; an adult book on Western meditation for Regnery.

SIDELIGHTS: "I was fortunate enough to have had an exciting childhood. My family traveled frequently to new places. There was a succession of unexpected sights, seacoasts, deserts, rivers, wonderful old houses we rented, or unusual hotels where we lived. I had troubles in the numerous schools I attended as the curricula were so different, and I always had to adjust to different friends and learn how to manage strangers. Yet, it was always thrilling. As a child, I was far more interested in science, collecting animals, being active rather than studious. Eclipses, strange plants, weird rocks, the behavior, the lives of my many pets fascinated me. Occasionally I was forced to stay in bed for months on end because of severe illnesses. My parents were great readers and, luckily, they enjoyed reading aloud to me for hours. Both were artists and so were some of our ancestors. I thought of being a writer, but on the other hand, I thought of being a naturalist-explorer much more. At age fourteen, I prepared myself for it, learning how to navigate with a carefully built sextant which I made for myself. As it turned out, I was two centuries late. Unfortunate.

"During my high school years I began to realize some interest in writing. I wrote clever, audacious themes for my English teachers. I considered them mainly as a farce and a way 'to beat the system.' At the same time, we happened to be living in Lincoln Steffens house in Carmel, Calif. Needless to say, he owned a magical library. On long rainy nights I read his books which were actually way over my head. Yet, an amazing amount stuck with me.

"I liked college (Colorado College) because it was old, covered with ivy, peaceful and far removed from absolutely everything. Moreover, the Rockies were right next to it and I spent all of my spare time hiking and climbing in them. Academically, I received next to nothing from the professors, but much from the students. During my years there I had to leave to take care of my mother, who died. Family disasters followed. After that, for several years, the only thing which interested me were my difficult problems, my social life and my reading of books. Not until my third year of college did I switch from being an engineering major to an English major. In 1952, I received a B.A. degree.

"My first job was on an oil exploration crew in Wyoming and dangerous, thrilling work it was. The rough, out-door life and seemingly endless, sun-lit prairies left a deep impression on me.

"For three years my wife and I lived in an old adobe house in New Mexico. Our land bordered two Indian reservations, in Chupadero. We loved the hard work, taking care of our land and building an additional house. The loneliness of the place, the nearby desert and mountains in which we lived cast a spell on us. It afforded me a great opportunity to read and I devoured books. It was a major life experience for us.

"We moved to New York City for a constellation of reasons. Here I worked as an editor for Basic Books, Inc. and for McGraw-Hill Book Co., where I was an editor in charge of science books for children.

"At the present moment I am a full time free-lance writer. There are many projects which I desire to accomplish. I feel writers can and do help people, thus, in a way all writers are public servants. No matter what their personal life may be, or may have been, writers sell information, entertainment, or attempt to influence others. Writing is the hardest and most demanding work I've ever been in, but it is, also, the most challenging and at times exceptionally rewarding. Virtually all of my writings so far have originated from activities in which I have physically participated and gained personal experience. I write for people who want to get more of life and experience it. My attitudes toward my writings vary. At times it gives me tremendous joy, at times I still feel it is an amusing game, at other times it gives me excruciating problems. Hopefully my books have given people information, entertainment, insights and especially energy. My work makes me happy in as much as it benefits others.

"I have lived in many artist and writer's colonies, and have been around creative people all of my life. I love the outdoors, scientific instruments, painting, and because of my diverse interests I have tried in many ways to synthesize art and science."

SMITH, Imogene Henderson 1922-

PERSONAL: Born May 31, 1922, in Decatur, Ill.; daughter of Roy Edwin and June (Kirby) Henderson; married Dale Corwin Smith (deceased), June 30, 1945; children: Brooke Ellen. *Education:* Illinois State University, B.Ed., 1944; University of Colorado, M.A., 1952. *Religion:* Congregationalist. *Home:* 43 McKinley, St. Charles, Ill. *Agent:* Jacques Chambrun, 745 Fifth Ave., New York, N.Y. 10017.

CAREER: Teacher in Illinois high schools, 1946-56; Elgin Community College, Elgin, Ill., instructor in speech. *Member:* American Association of University Women, Kappa Delta Pi.

WRITINGS: Egg on Her Face (juvenile), Lippincott, 1963; *Time on Her Hands* (juvenile), Lippincott, 1965.

WORK IN PROGRESS: A juvenile book.

SIDELIGHTS: "I am a flatlander by birth and residence, although I have done all my graduate and postgraduate study at the University of Colorado within view of the majestic Rockies. I was educated in an Illinois high school, graduated from Illinois State University, and have lived in the Chicago suburbs most of my life.

"I am more of a professional teacher than writer, but I have managed to combine both careers. My first teaching love was high school students, but I am now teaching fulltime in college.

"My husband, Dale, a former athletic coach, was high school administrator in the suburbs, and my only child is a daughter, Brooke Ellen, who has shown such a marked interest in reading and writing that now we are battling for the use of the typewriter.

"In working with teenagers, I have appreciated especially their ebullience, effervescence, and humor and have tried to capitalize on these qualities in my writing. . . ."

SMITH, Marion Hagens   1913-

PERSONAL: Born December 13, 1913, in Grand Rapids, Mich.; daughter of William W. and Adah (Rogers) Hagens; married Benjamin F. Smith (now a mechanical engineer), February 19, 1937; children: Diana (Mrs. Arthur Curtis), Brian B. *Education:* Michigan State University, B.S., 1935. *Religion:* Protestant. *Home:* 8253 East Fulton Rd., Ada, Mich. 49301. *Office:* Fideler Co., 31 Ottawa Ave., Grand Rapids, Mich. 49503.

CAREER: Employed as laboratory chemist prior to World War II; Fideler Co. (publishers), Grand Rapids, Mich., staff writer. *Member:* Phi Kappa Phi.

WRITINGS: (With Jerry E. Jennings) *The South,* Fideler, 1965; (with Carol S. Prescott) *Families Around the World,* Fideler, 1970; (with Carol S. Prescott) *Our Needs,* Fideler, 1970; (with Carol S. Prescott) *Our Earth,* Fideler, 1970.

MARION HAGENS SMITH

NANCY COVERT SMITH

SMITH, Nancy Covert   1935-

PERSONAL: Born March 18, 1935, in Bascom, Ohio; daughter of Curtis C. (a machinist) and Mary (Forwalter) Covert; married James Smith, February 27, 1954 (divorced, 1973); married Larry Uno (an associate director of National Association for Mental Health), 1975; children: (first marriage) Mark, Leanne, Craig, Tammy. *Education:* Attended public schools in Ohio. *Residence:* Alexandria, Va. *Office:* National Association for Mental Health, 1800 Kent St., Arlington, Va. 22209.

CAREER: National Association for Mental Health, Arlington, Va., lecturer, 1973—. *Awards, honors:* Indiana University Writer's Conference non-fiction scholarship,·1970; National Association for Mental Health special award, 1973, for her contribution to public education about mental health through her writing.

WRITINGS: Journey Out of Nowhere (autobiography), Word, Inc., 1973; *Of Pebbles and Pearls* (nonfiction), Word, Inc., 1974; *Josie's Handful of Quietness* (novel), Abingdon, 1975. Contributor to *McCall's, Good Housekeeping, Modern Bride, Jack and Jill, Modern Maturity,* and other journals.

WORK IN PROGRESS: A book on human sexuality and attitudes of marriage for Word, Inc.; a juvenile fiction book about Hawaii; an adult fiction about World War II; and an adult book, *Apple Parings of My Mind,* for Word, Inc.

SIDELIGHTS: "A lecturer and workshop leader, I have traveled hundreds of miles each year throughout the United States in the interest of mental health. I speak to civic groups, students, churches, and clubs of all sorts.

"My most interesting fan was a seven-year-old girl from Venezuela living in Kansas. We had a long talk in the library about her saxophone lessons, dancing, and air traveling to and from South America. I've often thought of this little girl and wished I lived close enough to know her well enough to put her into a book.

"While taking a juvenile writing course from author Maia Wojciechowska, I asked her if she would help with the organization of my thoughts for a book, and told her the outline.

Josie knew that she had lost the race before they even started. While she was still getting her pedal up to push off, Lydia was already standing up, pumping down the road with such speed her red hair flew out behind. ■ (From *Josie's Handful of Quietness* by Nancy Covert Smith. Illustrated by Ati Forberg.)

" 'If you can tell me the most important part of your outline, I'll help you,' Ms. Wojciechowska said.

" 'The symbolism of the marigolds?'

" 'Right!' came the reply, 'Since you know that you can write the book.'

"When I was growing up in southern Ohio, tomato, pickle, and sugar beet fields lay on all sides of my family's small farm. The year I was born, my father planted an apple orchard such as Mr. Curtis has in *Josie's Handful of Quietness.*

"My four children, Mark, Leanne, Craig, Tamara, and several neighborhood children served as chapter by chapter critics.

"Whether I'm writing, or teaching writing, I consider one rule as most important, 'Show, don't tell.' The fun of writing is in creating word pictures using all five senses. Being able to teach classes of gifted children, as a visiting author, has taught me that children have active mental projectors, and it takes many vivid pictures to keep those projectors filled. I hope I can create interesting people and places for children to enjoy."

Nancy Covert Smith has herself made a successful recovery from mental illness. She has lectured in twenty-seven states and ninety cities, giving practical answers to the questions raised by such illness in oneself or a family member. She has appeared on "The Phil Donahue Show."

HOBBIES AND OTHER INTERESTS: Reading, music.

SMITH, Robert Kimmel 1930-
(Peter Marks)

PERSONAL: Born July 31, 1930, in Brooklyn, N.Y.; son of Theodore (in civil service) and Sally (Kimmel) Smith; married Claire Medney (a literary agent), September 4, 1954; children: Heidi, Roger. *Education:* Attended Brooklyn College (now of the City University of New York), 1947-48. *Residence:* Brooklyn, N.Y. *Agent:* (Literary) Harold Ober Associates, 40 E. 49th St., New York, N.Y. 10017; (Television/plays) Lois Berman, WB Agency, 156 E. 52nd St., New York, N.Y.

CAREER: Doyle, Dane, Bernbach (advertising), New York City, copywriter, 1957-61; Grey Advertising, New York City, copy chief, 1963-65; Smith & Toback (advertising), New York City, partner and writer, 1967-70; full-time writer, 1970—. *Military service:* U.S. Army, 1951-53. *Member:* Writer's Guild, Dramatists Guild, Leukemia Society of America, Eugene O'Neill Theatre Center, Eugene O'Neill Playwrights (co-chairman, 1974-75), Kayoodle Club (president, 1969), Knickerbocker Field Club. *Awards, honors:* Named Eugene O'Neill Playwright, 1971, for "A Little Singing, A Little Dancing."

WRITINGS: Ransom (novel), McKay, 1971; "A Little Singing, A Little Dancing" (play; produced at O'Neill Memorial Theatre, July, 1971; published as "A Little Dancing," in *Best Short Plays of 1975,* edited by Stanley Richards, Chilton, 1975); *Chocolate Fever* (juvenile), Coward, 1972; *Sadie Shapiro's Knitting Book* (novel), Simon &

In less time than it takes to tell it, Henry Green was covered with little brown lumps from the top of his head to the tip of his toes. ■ (From *Chocolate Fever* by Robert K. Smith. Illustrated by Gioia Fiammenghi.)

Something about the Author

Schuster, 1973; *Sadie Shapiro in Miami* (novel), Simon and Schuster, 1977.

Contributor of short fiction to periodicals, writing under pseudonym Peter Marks prior to 1970.

WORK IN PROGRESS: Another novel for Simon & Schuster.

SIDELIGHTS: "I wrote *Chocolate Fever* as a book on my daughter Heidi's suggestion. Before that, it was a go-to-bed story I used to tell her before she was tucked-in at night. I began the story with an idea: a boy who loved chocolate more than any other thing. (Actually, the boy was me—I have been a chocolate-lover since I was knee-high to a Hershey Bar.) And every night I would tell Heidi about five minute's more of the story. After a couple of weeks the story was done, but Heidi wanted to hear it again. The thing was, I had almost forgotten how it went. So, on Heidi's suggestion, I wrote it all out.

"Here is how I write: on yellow paper on a typewriter, from 9:30 a.m. to 2:00 p.m., five days a week. Weekends are for family fun and things. I treat writing as a job, going to my office in our house, and firmly closing the door against chil-

dren and other distractions. Actually, now that Roger and Heidi are grown, I really don't have to tell them to stay out.

"I learned to write in the advertising business. I wrote ads and commercials then. But I found that having a deadline, as you do in the advertising business, is a jolly good idea. It makes you stick-to-it and not dream your day away. So, that sort of discipline has stood me in good stead. You don't write a book in one day. In fact, the mere thought of writing a whole book is sort of staggering. But, if you can write five good pages a day (and you can), then pretty soon you have a book.

"When I write, I create my own special world. The people I make up—and my writing is all people—are mine. I tell them what to say, what to do, and no one else can do it. If the book or play I'm writing is really working well, then the people I've created start to speak and act for themselves. That's always the best part for me. But the world I create is my own, and it can be as crazy and weird as the characters want it to be. I have a saying I use: 'Don't be hemmed-in by reality.' Which means that characters are free to act as they wish, even illogically, as long as they tell me about it in advance.

"In 1970, at the age of forty, I decided to give full-time writing a shot and haven't looked back since. I have been pleased to discover a comic, human side of myself and I plan to keep writing in this vein. I feel that dialogue is my strength, and plan to concentrate on plays, film, and television scripts—with the occasional novel thrown in if I'm lucky enough to have a good idea."

SMITH, Susan Carlton 1923-

PERSONAL: Born June 30, 1923, in Athens, Ga.; daughter of Edward Inglis (an insurance agent and county treasurer) and Hart (Wylie) Smith. *Education:* University of Georgia, B.S., 1947, M.F.A., 1961; University of Virginia, summer study at Biological Station, 1947-49. *Religion:* Episcopalian. *Residence:* Durham, N.C. *Agent:* Paul R. Reynolds, Inc., 12 East 41st St., New York, N.Y. 10017. *Office:* Medical Center Library, Duke University, Durham, N.C. 27710.

CAREER: U.S. Public Health Communicable Disease Center, Atlanta, Ga., scientific illustrator in Medical Entomology Division, 1951-52; University of Georgia, Athens, costumer in speech and drama department, 1958-62, biological illustrator for Science Center, 1964-65, illustrated at times for archaeology department and Agriculture Extension Service; Duke University, Medical Center, Durham, N.C., staff of medical illustration department, 1966, assistant curator of Trent Collection, Medical Center Library, 1967—. Free-lance biological illustrator, 1953—, presently working as illustrator for botany department at Duke University. Had one-woman show, "From Nature, Interpretations," at Museum of Art, Duke University, 1971-72; watercolors of wildflowers and fungi also have been shown at International Exhibition of Botanical Art and Illustration at Hunt Botanical Library, Carnegie-Mellon University, 1968-69, North Carolina Wildlife Artist Show at State Museum of Natural History, 1969, International Botanical Congress, Seattle, 1969; International Exhibition of Botanical Art, Johannesburg, 1973. Painter of watercolor miniatures of nature subjects and creator of sculptures made of natural materials found in woods and fields.

SUSAN CARLTON SMITH

MEMBER: American Association for the History of Medicine, Phi Kappa Phi. *Awards, honors:* American Institute of Graphic Arts included *Ladybug, Ladybug* among fifty best children's books of 1969; Printing Industries of America Award for *Hey, Bug! And Other Poems About Little Things,* 1972.

ILLUSTRATOR: C. Ritchie Bell, *Plant Variation and Classification,* Wadsworth, 1967; (and compiler of appendix, Who's Who and What's What) Kathleen N. Daly, *Ladybug, Ladybug,* American Heritage Press, 1969; Elizabeth Itse, selector, *Hey Bug! And Other Poems About Little Things* (anthology, Child Study Association book list), American Heritage Press, 1972; Kathleen N. Daly, *A Child's Book of Flowers,* Doubleday, 1976. Illustrations appear in *Wild Flowers of North Carolina,* University of North Carolina Press, 1968, and in botanical texts and journals.

SIDELIGHTS: "For as far back as I can remember, I have always looked upon nature and forms of life as absolutely marvelous and incredible. I believe every form of life deserves attention, recognition, and acceptance.

"Everything must be looked at for all that it is and for all that it can be, just as every human being must be judged not only for what he appears to be, but for all that he is and can be. I believe when you recognize this, you are granting to each creature and form of life its own reason for being; you are recognizing and appreciating its many expressions.

"In return for the delight and surprises that forms of nature bring to me, I reciprocate by looking and listening carefully and giving my attention to the colors and shapes, to the simple and intricate forms of life about me.

"Every little thing, no matter how little, is worthy of keen observation and inquiry.

"Nothing is so little that it is not at the same time BIG. Consider the atom, its small size, its great power; from an acorn, the oak; from a seed, the flower.

"Everything is a world unto itself waiting for your observation and exploration. I say *exploration* because it is not enough just to look at things. You have to explore them by opening your eyes, ears, heart, and mind to them for all that they are and for all that they can be.

"I grew up in Athens, Georgia, with one foot in the woods and one foot in the biology building on the university campus. That is to say, I spent most of my time playing in the woods and making friends with the spring of each year. To me, spring was the most special of all things—*and it still is.* Each year I could hardly wait for it to come because it brought new things to play with and new things to see and hear, *and it still does.* I would pick up and collect butterfly wings, seedpods, rocks, moss, mushrooms, beetles, and bones—natural materials of all kinds that appealed to me from the standpoint of color, texture, shape and design, *and I still pick these things up.* In early childhood I had an intense curiosity about the wonders I saw—*and I still have this curiosity.*

"I am often asked what sculpture tools I use. I use my fingers so I can feel what's going on, and sometimes a straight pin to pick up and position minute seeds. I have been asked, 'Can you describe how these sculptures came about, how do you make them?' The answer is, I don't make them—not entirely anyway. They are already there. All I do is just pick them off the ground and give them to do what they want to do."

The Duke University Art Museum purchased Smith's collection of nature sculptures in 1972 to become a permanent exhibit.

She cried, "Look! who's that *handsome* man?"
They answered, "Mr. Toad."
■ (From *Hey Bug! and Other Poems About Little Things* selected by Elizabeth M. Itse. Illustrated by Susan Carlton Smith.)

BARBARA SOFTLY and "Tinkerbell"

SOFTLY, Barbara (Frewin) 1924-

PERSONAL: Born March 12, 1924, in Ewell, Surrey, England; daughter of Stanley Borders and Edith (Crouch) Frewin; married Alan Softly (now with Shell International Petroleum Co.), March 24, 1951. *Education:* Attended Clapham and Streatham Hill Froebel College, 1944. *Home:* 13 Windmill Lane, Ewell, Surrey, England.

CAREER: Manor House, Little Bookham, Surrey, England, teacher of history, English, geography, and art, 1944-57.

WRITINGS: *Plain Jane,* Macmillan, London, 1961; *Place Mill,* Macmillan, London, 1962; *A Stone in a Pool,* Macmillan, 1964; (contributor) *Miscellany Two,* edited by Edward Blishen, Oxford University Press, 1965; *Ponder and William,* Penguin, 1966; *Magic People,* Chatto & Windus, 1966, Holt, 1967; *Ponder and William on Holiday,* Penguin, 1968; *Hippo, Potta and Muss,* Chatto & Windus, 1969, Harvey House, 1970; *Magic People Around the World,* Chatto & Windus, 1969, Holt, 1970; *A Lemon Yellow Elephant Called Trunk,* Chatto & Windus, 1970, Harvey House, 1971; *Geranium,* Hutchinson, 1972; *Ponder and William at Home,* Penguin, 1972; *Ponder and William at the Weekend,* Penguin, 1974; *The Queens of England* (adult), Stein & Day, 1976. Contributor of short stories and articles to magazines and anthologies.

SIDELIGHTS: "I must have had some extraordinary ideas when a very small child! My earliest ambition was to pat a bull and my parents compromised tactfully by letting me meet a cow; my second ambition at the age of eight was to become a poet, but on being taken to see Poets' Corner in Westminster Abbey, London, I decided it was an extremely dull and uninteresting place in which to be buried and made up my mind then and there to become a writer instead; a fact which I did not divulge to anyone in case that was thought amusing, too.

"My first historical novel for children was written when I was thirteen, mainly because I had exhausted the supply of books in our well-stocked home and could find nothing else to read. Many years later that story formed the basis for *Plain Jane* which was published in 1961 and proved a popular tale of the English Civil War.

"Then came Ponder. Ponder was a panda pajama-bag who lived on my bed—he was given to me by my sister—and it was appropriate that I should make up stories about him for her small son. To him Ponder was so real that he used to ring me up and ask to talk to him. Needless to say, Ponder replied in suitably panda-ish tones and soon the stories were written down and new ones invented usually about little incidents which had really happened. Ponder has brought me friends from all over the world, but mostly from the United States of America. Children have written to me from as far apart as Oregon and Tennessee and the friendship started nine years ago with one small boy has resulted in two visits to him and his family. If it had not been for the *Ponder and William* series, I would not have the affection for America that I have now.

"My other interests besides writing are our own English cottage-style garden, the conservation of wildlife and photography. On summer days I may be seen like a praying mantis on my knees hopefully focusing my camera on bee or butterfly. My interest in folklore, started when I wrote *Magic People* for young children, has not diminished and I would still like to write about the folklore of trees.

"Cats, also, figure in my life and stories. I have never gone out of my way to possess a cat—they possess me and it

It was so hot that Cousin Winifred had made them both sun hats out of sheets of her newspaper. The hats looked like paper boats. ■ (From *Ponder and William on Holiday* by Barbara Softley. Illustrated by Diana John.)

seems I am to be the adopted parent of any stray. Tigger, Ginnie and Marmalade became part of the Ponder stories and gave me all the adventures I needed for *Geranium,* and now Blackie and Tinkerbell, whose antics will, no doubt, fill a few more pages.

"It was while I was teaching history that an outspoken ten year old said, 'I'm not interested in King John and Magna Carta. I want to know who his wife was and how many children she had.' It was a question I was unable to answer immediately and after having looked up the wives of the kings of England in all the volumes available, it seemed to me it would be more sensible if brief lives of these really interesting queens could all be housed in one book. It would have to be a small book for the ordinary reader and older children at college and include the consorts and reigning queens from the time of William I to our present Queen Elizabeth II. I hoped to call the book 'The Queen was in the Parlour' taking the title from the old nursery rhyme which implies that the queen enjoyed herself while the king worked, but history proved that many queens did not enjoy themselves and that some worked harder than their husbands and so the book became simply, *Queens of England.*

"Most authors have hidden away some manuscripts which cannot find a publisher and which, oddly enough, the author enjoyed writing immensely. I have two. One is about the summer adventures of some children in 1931 based on my own happy holidays by the sea, the other is a fantasy about a little man who works in a dull men's clothing shop and suddenly discovers that there is a great deal more in life if he stops to look around him. Possibly their fault is that they are too simple and happy and in our modern world it is usually only the harsh and the dramatic which make the headlines."

HOBBIES AND OTHER INTERESTS: Photography, gardening and gardens, wildlife conservation, and reading, particularly history.

MARY LYNN SOLOT

I wonder how I got fat. ■ (From *100 Hamburgers* by Mary Lynn Solot. Pictures by Paul Galdone.)

SOLOT, Mary Lynn   1939-

PERSONAL: Born May 7, 1939, in New York, N.Y.; daughter of Leonard M. and Virginia (Wise) Marx; married Edwin Lee Solot (a lawyer), June 24, 1962; children: Edwin Lee, Jr., Claire. *Education:* Sarah Lawrence College, B.A., 1962. *Home:* 45 East 89th St., New York, N.Y. 10028.

CAREER: Free-lance writer; composer of music for children's theatre, and song-writer.

WRITINGS—Juvenile: *100 Hamburgers,* Lothrop, 1972.

WORK IN PROGRESS: Several juvenile books.

SIDELIGHTS: "Writing *100 Hamburgers* was no great surprise. You see, I wrote exactly the story of myself. (Indeed, the editor changed the central character from a girl to a boy.)

"In many ways the story wrote itself. All I did was to close my eyes and think of those many times when I so wished I were thin. Happily, I am thin now. And from talking to many people, it seems that often if you are fat when you are growing up; you are likely to be thin as a grown-up.

"Now I am trying to write about other problems that children do face. Some of these include the death of someone close, parents separating and divorcing, being not exactly the most gorgeous kid in your class, and finding life just plain boring. Naturally I need lots of different ideas on these books. Have you time to send me a few of your best ideas? Please do."

SOMMER, Robert 1929-

PERSONAL: Born April 26, 1929, in New York, N.Y.; son of Robert M. and Margaret Sommer; married Dorothy Twente, 1957 (divorced); children: Ted, Kenneth, Margaret. *Education:* University of Kansas, Ph.D., 1956. *Office:* University of California, Davis, Calif. 95616.

CAREER: University of Alberta, Edmonton, assistant professor, 1961-63; University of California, Davis, 1963—, began as associate professor, became professor.

WRITINGS: Expertland, Doubleday, 1963; *Personal Space: The Behavioral Basis of Design,* Prentice-Hall, 1969; *Design Awareness,* Holt, 1972; *Tight Spaces,* Prentice-Hall, 1974; *Street Art,* Links Books, 1975; *The End of Imprisonment,* Oxford University Press, 1976; *Sidewalk Fossils* (juvenile), Walker & Co., 1976.

SIDELIGHTS: "I am a naturalist at heart. I enjoy looking closely at the everyday experiences people have. My children's book was about exploring sidewalks for the lessons they can tell about people, neighborhoods, dogs, and falling leaves. I do all my own photography and print my pictures in the bathroom while my wife and children grumble. I get up early in the morning to write when the house is very quiet. While I often get inspiration from talking to other people and being with them, writing for me requires detachment and isolation. The sight of another person or their conversation takes me away from that quiet place where writing begins.

"The best kind of writing is like singing, it just flows forth and it is hard to stop. After that comes the hard work of editing, revising, and putting it all together. I would compare this to slogging through the mud for six months or digging a trench a hundred miles long. I would suggest to anyone who wanted to do a book to begin with articles first. Then if you find that you enjoy regular focused writing, try a book.

"As writers go, I am unusual in that I write directly with a dictaphone. Basically, I talk the book rather than write it. However, once the first draft is written, then I work with the written manuscript. Using a dictaphone gives my books a conversational style. Some of my friends tell me that they can hear me talking as they read what I have written. I hope you can too."

In this way, many sidewalk fossils are being made every day. ■ (From *Sidewalk Fossils* by Robert Sommer and Harriet Becker.)

SORTOR, June Elizabeth 1939-
(Toni Sortor)

PERSONAL: Born June 4, 1939, in Utica, N.Y.; daughter of Ralph H. (a watchmaker) and Ada B. (an insurance clerk; maiden name, Lacey) Schneider; married John D. Blanchard, August 19, 1961 (died, October, 1962); married William G. Sortor (a fuel oil dealer), February 1, 1964; children: (second marriage) Laura Jean, James Henry, Steven Van Dyke. *Education:* Skidmore College, B.A., 1961. *Religion:* Episcopalian.

CAREER: High school teacher of English in public schools in Berne, N.Y., 1962-63. *Member:* Society of Childrens' Book Writers, Girl Scouts of the U.S.A.

WRITINGS: (Under name Toni Sortor) *Adventures of B.J.: The Amateur Detective* (juvenile novel), Abingdon, 1975. Contributor of short stories and poems to periodicals.

WORK IN PROGRESS: A second adventure of B. J.; an adult mystery.

SIDELIGHTS: "Although children's books seem to be in competition with television these days, I believe children still need and want to read. Television is, after all, a "two-sense" experience. Children know they smell things, touch

ROBERT SOMMER

At the rate they were loading that truck, we'd be on our way in a matter of minutes, and as far as I could see, there was no real reason to hope that help was on the way. ■ (From *Adventures of B.J., the Amateur Detective* by Toni Sortor   Drawings by Allan Eitzen.)

JUNE ELIZABETH SORTOR

things, experience heat and cold, etc. Books give them the opportunity to participate in these senses, to see others' reactions, to experience the world more fully than they can through television.''

SPOLLEN, Christopher 1952-

PERSONAL: Born August 12, 1952, in Staten Island, N.Y.; son of Christopher B. (a fireman) and Anna (Burns; a secretary) Spollen. *Education:* Parsons School of Design, B.F.A., 1974; The New School of Social Research, B.F.A., 1975. *Home and office:* 41 Groton Street, Staten Island, N.Y. 10312.

CAREER: Free-lance illustrator of children's books and magazines. *Exhibitions:* Society of Illustrators, three years; Bittersweet Gallery, Montauk, N.Y.; The Mauro Gallery, Staten Island, N.Y. *Member:* Philadelphia Print Club, Staten Island Museum Society, Federation of Staten Island Artists. *Awards, honors:* Society of Publication Designers, award of merit, 1975; Staten Island Museum, second place, 1975; Staten Island Conference House Award, second place.

ILLUSTRATOR: Cynthia Jameson, *Tales from the Steppes,* Coward, 1975; Eric A. Kimmel, *Mishka, Pishka & Fishka, and other Galician Tales,* Coward, 1976; Nancy Veglahn, *Coils, Magnets and Rings, Michael Faradays World,* Coward, 1976.

SIDELIGHTS: "Although I had been studying art since high school, it was not until my last year in college that I began to contemplate the possibility of making illustration my profession. Somehow I could never see this as a career.

"Today, as a free-lance illustrator, I enjoy a limited freedom. The demands of this field are such that I must constantly produce new ideas. Mediocrity, I have found, is not long hidden from one's fellow artists. I am constantly searching for innovations in both style and technique. Every story which I am called upon to illustrate presents a unique challenge. It is not unusual for me to reject half a dozen sketches and spend many hours at the drawing board before I'll hit upon the correct approach. It takes a great deal of self-discipline on my part to see that a piece moves through its initial stages as a rough sketch on to its final reproduction as a finished proof.

"Despite the rigors of my field—deadlines, disapproving editors, etc.—I find my work immensely satisfying and fulfilling.

"I am working in etchings, grease pencil and ink. These mediums provide me with a very rich palette.''

CHRISTOPHER SPOLLEN

His doughy fingers stroked his scraggly beard while he sniffed over the days agenda. ■ (From *Tales from the Steppes* by Cynthia Jameson. Illustrated by Christopher J. Spollen.)

STAMATY, Mark Alan 1947-

PERSONAL: Born August 1, 1947, in Brooklyn, N.Y.; son of Stanley (an artist) and Clara (Kastner; an artist) Stamaty. *Education:* The Cooper Union, New York, N.Y., B.F.A., 1969. *Home:* 118 MacDougal Street, Apartment 15, New York, N.Y. 10012. *Agent:* Sheldon Fogelman, 10 East 40th Street, New York, N.Y. 10016.

CAREER: Free-lance artist and author. Has held various part-time jobs including: taxi driver, camp counselor, file clerk and snack bar worker. *Exhibitions:* The New Jersey

Artists' Annual, State Museum of New Jersey, 1968, 1969, 1970; Boston Printmakers' Annual, 1970; National Academy of Design Annual Exhibit, 1970; Silvermine Print Show, 1970; "The New Jersey Artists (invitational) Composition," Jersey City Museum, 1970; Society of Illustrators Annual Exhibit, 1974, 1975. *Member:* Illustrators Guild.

AWARDS, HONORS: Hunterdon Art Center Annual Print Show, "Utopia," honorable mention, 1969; "Hallelujah" (an etching) has been awarded the following: honorable mention at the Audubon Artists' Annual in 1970, Museum Purchase Award, The State Museum of New Jersey at the New

But he wanted donuts, not just a few but hundreds and thousands and millions—more donuts than his mother and father could ever buy him. ■ (From *Who Needs Donuts?* by Mark Alan Stamaty. Pictures by the author.)

Jersey Artists' Annual in 1970 (now in their permanent collection), First Prize for Graphics at the "First Statewide Fall Art Show," Nutley Masonic Lodge, Nutley, N.J., 1971; *Yellow Yellow* received an "Art Books for Children Citation," Brooklyn Museum and Brooklyn Public Library, 1973, 1974, 1975 (now a permanent selection); *Who Needs Donuts?* was Child Study Association book of the year, 1973, and awarded Society of Illustrators Gold Medal for the title page in 1974, also received an "Art Books for Children Citation," Brooklyn Museum and Brooklyn Public Library, 1975; *Small in the Saddle* (cover) was selected for the American Institute of Graphic Arts cover of *Catch the Eye,* 1975.

WRITINGS—Self-illustrated: *Who Needs Donuts?,* Dial, 1973; *Small in the Saddle,* Windmill Books, 1975; *Minnie Maloney and Macaroni* (Junior Literary Guild selection), Dial, 1976; *Where's My Hippopotamus?,* Dial, 1977.

Illustrator: Frank Asch, *Yellow, Yellow,* McGraw, 1971.

SIDELIGHTS: "My basic motivation is to enjoy my life and live it as fully as I can. My work is central and essential to this. I have worked primarily in pen and ink, pencil and watercolor. I want to devote my life to creative self-expression.

MARK ALAN STAMATY

"I have a multitude of influences. None is really dominant. I had some great teachers at the Cooper Union. I usually say my favorite painter is Soutine. Lately I particularly enjoy and learn from Matisse. Also, the letters of the poet, R. M. Rilke, have had a strong influence on me philosophically.

"A few years back, I did a handful of etchings and met with a fair amount of success, but I have had to give it up for a while to develop a stable economic base and also because I love making books. Etching takes more time than I have for it right now. Someday I hope to do more etchings. I also hope to publish some books and other things which some people might consider less commercially feasible or more unusual than my children's books. I hope to find publishers for such projects eventually or publish them myself.

"Recently I took a trip across the United States. It was quite inspiring and awakened many new images in me which I hope to include in my pictures."

STEVENSON, Anna (M.) 1905-

PERSONAL: Born December 23, 1905, in Heber, Utah; daughter of Joseph White (a writer) and Rose (Borgquist) Musser; married Rulon E. Stevenson (a retired accountant), December 6, 1936; children: Ann. *Education:* University of Utah, B.A., 1926; University of California, M.A., 1930. *Religion:* Baha'i.

CAREER: Dixie College, St. George, Utah, art teacher, 1926-27; Wasatch High School, Heber, Utah, art teacher, 1927-28; Montana State College, Bozeman, Mont., art teacher, 1930-31; Department of Public Health, Berkeley, Calif., graphic artist, 1931-63.

ILLUSTRATOR: Baha' 'w' lláh, *Blessed is the Spot,* Baha'i Publishing Trust, 1958; Janet Lindstrom, *The Kingdoms of God,* Baha'i Publishing Trust, 1961; *Sing a New Song,* Baha'i Publishing Trust, 1968; *New Wind Blowing,* Baha'i Publishing Trust, 1970. *The Kingdoms of God* has been translated into French and German.

SIDELIGHTS: "Seventh in a family of eight, I grew up in a green valley walled in by blue mountains, huge and rocky to the east, low and dim to the west. When the Great War exploded on the other side of the earth, and red-winged airplanes droned over the east mountains (school was dismissed for the afternoon so that we might watch them better) my childhood ended. But until then, while the enchantment held, I lived in a lovely world.

"Father was away a lot on various enterprises. At intervals he breezed in, an exciting sun-king, with nickels or a bag of candy in his pockets for us. The older brothers and sisters left home one way and another, until only the family I knew best remained—four little girls and mother. We shared games and chores, stories and dreams, and we all drew. In time I drew best. I asked for pads of white thick paper at Christmas, and filled them carefully, privately, on both sides of each sheet. I drew children always, the *real* people: babies I saw at church, boys and girls I knew or read about. And I liked to show how older book heroes, even Greek gods, must have looked when little. I had my own apparent destiny. And I *never* confused the drawing exercises we did at school with the pictures that grew for me at home, alone. An understanding high school teacher, a productive painter himself, steered me toward the illustrations of Arthur Rackham and Edmund Dulac, and the magazines of the time were full of the cobalt skies and the sharply drawn palaces of Maxfield Parrish. I felt a deep kinship with these painters in

ANNA STEVENSON

their mysterious 'other worlds' of color and fantasy. I studied with Hans Hoffman and students of his.

"My own published work has been of a more everyday sort, executed in frugal ink drawings with only modest ventures into the luxury of color. In all of them I have stressed the fundamental relatedness of children everywhere, the world family. Now on my own, enjoying a sort of sabbatical from projects and orders, I explore more deeply into dreams and fantasy and mystery. I use a medium new to me, acrylics, a full color range. Perhaps I now paint more for children of my own present age group."

STEWART, Mary (Florence Elinor) 1916-

PERSONAL: Born September 17, 1916, in Sunderland, Durham, England; daughter of Frederick Albert (a clergyman) and Mary Edith (Matthews) Rainbow; married Frederick Henry Stewart, 1945. *Education:* University of Durham, B.A. (first class honours), 1938, diploma in theory and practice of teaching, 1939, M.A., 1941. *Address:* c/o William Morrow and Co., Inc., 1905 Madison Avenue, New York, N.Y. 10016.

CAREER: Abbey School, Malvern Wells, England, head of English and classics, 1940-41; University of Durham, Durham, England, lecturer, 1941-45. *Military service:* Royal Observer Corps, World War II. *Awards, honors:* Frederick Niven Award, 1973, for *The Crystal Cave;* Scottish Arts Council Award, 1974, for *Ludo and the Star Horse.*

*WRITINGS—*Adult fiction: *Madam, Will You Talk,* Morrow, 1956; *Wildfire at Midnight,* Appleton, 1956; *Thunder on the Right,* Morrow, 1958; *Nine Coaches Waiting,* Morrow, 1959; *My Brother Michael,* Morrow, 1960; *The Ivy Tree,* Morrow, 1961; *The Moon-Spinners,* Morrow, 1963;

This Rough Magic, Morrow, 1964; *Airs Above the Ground,* Morrow, 1965; *The Gabriel Hounds,* Morrow, 1966; *The Wind off the Small Isles,* Morrow, 1968; *The Crystal Cave* (ALA Best Young Adult book list), Morrow, 1970; *The Hollow Hills,* Morrow, 1973; *Touch Not the Cat,* Morrow, 1976.

Children's Fiction: *The Little Broomstick,* Morrow, 1972; *Ludo and the Star Horse,* Morrow, 1974.

WORK IN PROGRESS: A novel.

SIDELIGHTS: After her marriage to Frederick H. Stewart, a lecturer in geology whom she had met on V.E. Day, just two months before, Mary Stewart continued to lecture at Durham University and also at St. Hild's College, where she had been a student. She began writing in 1949 and soon found that "this I could do, this I must do. Story telling came as naturally as leaves to a tree, and it was a pity (I told myself) that I had wasted so much time. I started work immediately on a story called *Murder for Charity,* which later became *Madam, Will You Talk?*"

Madam, Will You Talk? was accepted for publication in 1953, and Mary Stewart's literary career was launched. *Wildfire at Midnight, Thunder on the Right,* and *Nine Coaches Waiting* were completed before she and her husband moved to Edinburgh, where Professor Stewart is regius professor in the department of geology at Edinburgh University, and chairman of the advisory board for the research councils in the United Kingdom. It was then, in 1956, that Mary Stewart decided to give up university work and devote all her time to writing.

It was a wise decision. Book followed book—*My Brother Michael, The Ivy Tree, The Moon-Spinners, This Rough*

Mary looked at Tib. Tib looked back with no expression whatever in his green, green eyes.
The women beckoned again.
Mary walked up the steps toward her.
■ (From *The Little Broomstick* by Mary Stewart. Illustrated by Shirley Hughes.)

■ (From the movie "The Moon Spinners," © 1963 by Walt Disney Productions, starring Joan Greenwood and Hayley Mills.)

MARY STEWART

Magic, Airs Above the Ground, The Gabriel Hounds, The Crystal Cave and *The Hollow Hills,* and the delightful children's stories *The Little Broomstick* and *Ludo and the Star Horse.* Every one has been a bestseller. The two Arthurian novels *The Crystal Cave* and *The Hollow Hills* grew out of Mary Stewart's interest in ancient history and the Roman period of her country's past, and it is proof of her narrative power that she has aroused her readers' interest in these areas as well. But as she has said, "If the writer is alive to the world around her and to what people are thinking and doing, if she is open all the time to new and living ideas, then, whatever the period or setting, the book is relevant to 'today.'" Mary Stewart's novels have been translated into sixteen languages, including Hebrew and Icelandic and Slovak. In 1974, her husband Frederick Stewart was knighted for his services to science.

HOBBIES AND OTHER INTERESTS: Music, painting and gardening.

FOR MORE INFORMATION SEE: New York Times Book Review, March 18, 1956, January 7, 1962; *Library Journal,* March 15, 1959, December 15, 1961; *Guardian,* February 26, 1960; *Kirkus Service,* November 1, 1961; *New York Herald Tribune Books,* March 4, 1962; Roy Newquist, *Counterpoint,* Rand McNally, 1964; *New Statesman,* November 5, 1965; *The Writer,* May, 1970.

STILLERMAN, Robbie   1947-

PERSONAL: Born May 12, 1947, in New York, N.Y.; daughter of Maxwell (a physician) and Carolyn (Rachlin; a medical technician) Stillerman. *Education:* Philadelphia College of Art, B.F.A.; University of Florence, Italy, certificate. *Home:* 20 Polo Road, Great Neck, N.Y. 11023. *Office:* 101 Lexington Avenue, New York, N.Y. 10016.

CAREER: Hallmark Cards, Inc., Kansas City, Mo., creative artist, 1970-72; free-lance artist, 1973—. *Exhibitions:* Master Eagle Gallery, New York, N.Y., 1976. *Member:* Arcphic Artist Guild.

ILLUSTRATOR: Richard Shaw, *The Cat Book,* Warne, 1973; Richard Shaw, *The Bird Book,* Warne, 1974; Richard Shaw, *The Mouse Book,* Warne, 1975; Martha and Charles Shapp, *Let's Find Out What's Light and What's Heavy,* Watts, 1975; Linda Berman, *Symetry,* Harcourt, 1977. Filmstrip: "The Little Black Fish."

SIDELIGHTS: "Children's books seems to be a natural media for me. It allows me to be the child and play. I love art, color and that certain whimsy. As I mature, my work keeps evolving and that I find exciting. I love color relationships. I enjoy placing different colors against one another and watch the way they bounce and react. That is how I discovered the wonderful media of paper. I never knew how to use color. I was afraid of it, primarily using pen and ink. I started placing one color next to another, and wow, what relationships, but I couldn't paint them, so I began cutting paper. It was a long tedious process, leaving wonderful color relationships and a very tired person. Then I discovered that those wonderful subtle colors just don't print and I had to throw out all those relationships and find new ones.

ROBBIE STILLERMAN

"Using collage, printed patterns, marbleized paper, dollies, etc., became my palette. Then one day I was assigned a job, 'The Little Black Fish,' a filmstrip. And somewhere deep inside me I felt I must rip the paper. I began. It had a movement, not the static of cut paper. The filmstrip flowed from my hands, I had a wonderful time. There is a wonderful reward in art when something you've done, you've done well. It feels good all over. And that is the reward from my work. I find my work difficult, frustrating, as I surge ahead to find new ways of expressing myself and yet I find it extremely satisfying."

TAIT, Douglas   1944-

PERSONAL: Born September 3, 1944, in Alberta, Canada; son of George W. C. (a physicist) and Gwen (Roxborough) Tait; married Elizabeth-Anne Kinnie (an artist), December 7, 1968; children: Amanda Ellen, Christopher Andrew. *Education:* Attended University of British Columbia, 1963; University of Chile (Faculty of Fine Arts), 1964; Vancouver School of Art, Canada, 1965-68. *Home:* 1652 E. 36th Avenue, Vancouver, British Columbia, V5P 1C4, Canada. *Office:* A/V Centre, Simon Fraser University, Burnaby, British Columbia, Canada.

DOUGLAS TAIT

A medicine rattle shook lightly in his right hand, while the white eagle tail in his left hand made graceful sweeps through the air. And the light in his eyes leaped like the fire that blazed in the center of the house. ■ (From *Once More Upon a Totem* by Christie Harris. Illustrated by Douglas Tait.)

CAREER: Free-lance artist. Coquitlam School Board, photography instructor, 1968, drawing instructor, 1969; Vancouver School Board, Vancouver, B.C., Canada, art instructor, 1968-71; Simon Fraser University, Burnaby, B.C., Canada, graphic designer, 1969—; co-director of Graphic Workshop Series conducted for: Department of Communications & Geography, Simon Fraser University, 1972, Industrial Audio Visual Association, 1973; consultant to Pacific Rim Conference on Children's Literature as a book illustrator, University of British Columbia, 1976; consultant to department of animal research ecology on media productions, University of British Columbia.

ILLUSTRATOR: Paul St. Pierre, *Chilcotin Holiday,* McLelland & Stewart, 1970; Christie Harris, *Secret in the Stlalakum Wild,* Atheneum, 1972; John B. Harrison, *Good*

Food Naturally, J. J. Douglas, 1972; Christie Harris, *Once More Upon a Totem*, Atheneum, 1973; Margaret Bemister, *Thirty Indian Legends*, J. J. Douglas, 1973; Robert Nicholson, *Colour in Your Winter Garden*, Douglas. David & Charles, 1973; Lois McConkey, *Sea and Cedar*, J. J. Douglas, 1973; Christie Harris, *Sky Man on the Totem Pole*, Atheneum, 1975; Christie Harris, *Mouse Woman and the Vanished Princesses'*, Atheneum, 1976; Maria Campbell, *People of the Buffalo*, J. J. Douglas, 1976; Christie Harris, *Mouse Woman and the Mischief Makers*, Atheneum, 1977. Illustrations have appeared in *Cricket*.

SIDELIGHTS: "The memories from my early life that come back to me as being important influences on my art are those based on simple day to day events. I am interested in the drama of the 'non event:' the tensions developed within a situation that are due primarily to secondary causes such as smell or sound. Although it is lightning that might kill us it is the thunder that terrifies us.

"Illustration should complement the writing. Far too often in the past the art work was considered as an after thought; visual syrup to mimic the action. Fortunately publishers are now beginning to realize the power that the two media have to affect each other and so enhance the total work.

"Although I illustrate mostly with pen and ink I enjoy the challenge of other media. My slide shows are produced with combinations of feltpens, coloured papers, and pen and ink. Several new books I have been commissioned to do will be in pencil and in full colour paint (acrylic).

"When I graduated from high school I had the good fortune to travel to Chile for a year. Although I was planning to study engineering at the University of British Columbia I made a last minute decision to enroll in the Faculty of Fine Arts at the University of Chile for the year that I was away. The decision to go to art school in Chile was, perhaps, one of the most important factors contributing to my present circumstance as an illustrator and artist. The rest of my development has basically been one of methodical work habits and conservative living."

TAMBURINE, Jean 1930-

PERSONAL: Born February 20, 1930, in Meriden, Conn.; daughter of Paul D. and Helen (Marks) Tamburine; married Eugene E. Bertolli (executive vice-president of design, Napier Co.), April 21, 1956; children: E. Robert, Lisa Marie. *Education:* Studied at Art Students League and Traphagen School of Fashion, New York, N.Y., 1948-50. *Religion:* Roman Catholic. *Home:* 73 Reynolds Dr., Meriden, Conn. 06450.

CAREER: Designer and publisher of greeting cards, 1945; Norcross, Inc., New York, N.Y., designer, 1948-50; Rust Craft, Boston, Mass., designer, 1954-55; free-lance artist, 1950—, illustrating more than thirty books. Paintings reproduced in annual Christmas card collection of American Artists Group. Lecturer. Member, Connecticut Commission on the Arts (founding member). *Member:* International Platform Association, Authors Guild, Allied Artists of America, Women's National Book Association, Society of Children's Book Writers, National Society for Literature and the Arts, North Shore Arts Association, Meriden Arts and Crafts Association.

WRITINGS—Self-illustrated: (With Jackie Peller) *The Three Little Pigs and Little Red Riding Hood*, Grosset, 1954; (editor with Jackie Peller) *Treasure Book of Favorite Nursery Tales*, Grosset, 1954; *Almost Big Enough*, Abingdon, 1963; *I Think I Will Go to the Hospital*, Abingdon, 1965; *How Now, Brown Cow*, Abingdon, 1967.

Illustrator: May Justus, *Peter Pocket and His Pickle Pup*, Holt, 1953; *Little Red Riding Hood*, Wonder Books, 1954; Helen Hilles, *Moving Day*, Lippincott, 1954; May Justus, *Surprise for Peter Pocket*, Holt, 1955; May Justus, *Use Your Head, Hildy*, Holt, 1956; May Justus, *Peddler's Pack*, Holt, 1957; May Justus, *Big Log Mountain*, Holt, 1958; May Justus, *Barney, Bring Your Banjo*, Holt, 1959; May Justus, *The Right House for Rowdy*, Holt, 1960; May Justus, *Winds a' Blowing*, Abingdon, 1961; May Justus, *Smoky Mountain Sampler: Stories*, Abingdon, 1962; Gina Bell, *Who Wants Willy Wells*, Abingdon, 1965; John Stanley, *It's Nice to Be Little*, Rand McNally, 1965; Mary Sue White, *See Me Grow*, Abindon, 1966; May Justus, *The Complete Peddler's Pack: Games, Songs, Rhymes, and Riddles From Mountain Folklore*, University of Tennessee Press, 1967; Helen Guittard, *Something Was Missing*, Follett, 1969; Marjorie Barrows, *Scamper*, Rand McNally, 1970. Contributor to *Woman's Day, Cricket*. For several years did original art for Pearl S. Buck and her foundation.

WORK IN PROGRESS: Illustrating two books for children; writing and illustrating a fourth book for Abingdon.

SIDELIGHTS: "Ever since I was a toddler I was happiest with pencil and paper. My mother remembers me at about three years of age busily scribbling away. Art, music, writing, reading have been part of my life for so long, and many times I prefer this work to eating or sleeping. As a child I loved children and animals and would, thus, be observer and recorder. This observation of people, animals, their behavior, are part of my work today. I relate to, or feel I am part of the subject I write about or paint. I liked being alone to think and wonder about everything. My extensive doll and animal collection were my make-believe family, and each one had a name and personality. I would make up stories with the dolls and animals 'acting,' and I'd write and draw. I follow a similar way today. I learned early the importance of knowing a subject and doing careful research.

"When I began kindergarten in a nearby one hundred-year-old brick school, I found an extension of home because the eight large rooms of Israel Putnam School had teachers who make learning and awareness stimulating, and they cared about the children. I loved going to school and almost every day was a discovery. In kindergarten Miss Immick called my mother and another mother who had a son named Bruce. She told them we were budding artists and to watch our development and to encourage us at home. Miss Simpson, and later, Mrs. Bowers, both art supervisors, were our guiding lights. Throughout grade school we were allowed, if our school work was done correctly, to go to the spare room used for programs, films, music, plays. Mr. Olland, the janitor, bought rolls of brown grocers' wrapping paper, and taped it on two long walls over blackboards. Bruce and I created murals for holidays, stories, parts of history. We naturally strove to have our regular school work done as quickly as possible because working on murals was like baseball is to good players. We were fortunate to have teachers who encouraged us in art and writing as well as other students in sports or music.

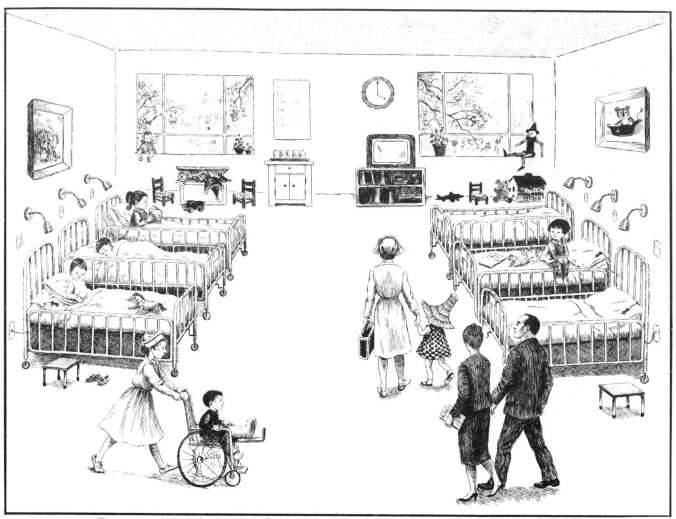

There were six beds in the room. Some of them already had children in them. A little girl smiled at Susy. ■ (From *I Think I Will Go to the Hospital* by Jean Tamburine. Illustrated by the author.)

"Leaving Israel Putnam ended a very special time where learning was a thing to seize hungrily, and there was time to think and dream and create. Junior high was too large with constant moving around. Mrs. Bowers had made Miss Higgins, the art teacher, aware of Bruce and me. We didn't like playground play and preferred to work during lunch hour. We were given permission to eat lunch and go to the art room to work on school posters, or work for contests, or just create. Bruce transferred to a private school. I really got through junior high and high school by adapting to the bigness, and I loved art, writing, music, ancient history and the library, where Miss Smith saved clippings from literary magazines and book catalogs for me.

"I always knew art, writing and books were my way of life. I wrote, illustrated and made books, sewing the gutter with a large embroidery needle. I went to New York after graduation to study at Traphagen and Art Student's League. I was offered a position as designer at Norcross, Inc., and so I happily began to design and study at Art Students League at night. From working at Norcross I learned the necessary steps in preparing art for the printer, and got my basics in color separation from which I developed my own technique. I wanted to begin free-lancing, my aim was working in the book field. Miss Norcross agreed to my working from home

in Meriden with salary. This left me time to write to editors and go to New York for interviews lugging my ungainly portfolio.

"I was a starry-eyed twenty when I got my first book commission. Virginie Fowler, the editor of children's books at Henry Holt, introduced me to May Justus, the noted author and Tennessee folklorist. I illustrated Miss Justus' book, *Surprise for Peter Pocket*. I did not know Tennessee and the ways of its mountain people, so I took a trip to observe and absorb. I illustrated eleven of May Justus' books and through her was introduced at Abingdon Press. Miss Katharine Fite, children's editor, was my wonderfully encouraging editor and *Almost Big Enough, I Think I Will Go To the Hospital, How Now, Brown Cow,* which I wrote, designed and illustrated resulted. In these books my study of children's behavior, living with my own children and realising how often we adults, in our busy adult lives, overlook the signs children give which show they need to be understood, comforted, enlightened; were an intricate part of telling the story.

"In April, 1956, I married Eugene E. Bertolli. He is a jeweler, sculptor, and enamellist. He is of Florentine background, Boston born and educated from Boston Latin

JEAN TAMBURINE

School, Boston College. When Gene returned from the service, he was offered a position as designer for the Napier Co., Meriden. He is now a director, vice-president; design, and designer of over eighty percent of the jewelry and giftware. Napier is one of the top three jewelry firms in the United States. In private life in our home-studio, Gene sculpts, makes exquisite enamels, and individual jewelry, religious appointments of precious metals, stones.

"Our son, Bob, and daughter, Lisa, are very creative. Bob hopes to make his life's work in the field of medicine and art. Lisa will work in art.

"When I married, I carefully thought out marriage and career and knew personally I wanted to be wife and mother and artist-writer so I had to accomplish this by being 'two people' in one. The needs of young children came first, and I worked in the studio at night. Many times I could work on art while the children did their own art work, but for writing, I needed quiet. Bob and Lisa have been brought up in a home with art material, books, exhibitions of all our work, so we never heard 'What will I do now?'

"I look at life as every decade being a time to accomplish certain things. I try to review as time passes to see if I've achieved at all. Now the time for raising children is over. Mother is a different role from the early years. Wife remains as strong as ever, and there is a rediscovery of each other almost like our earlier dating years.

"My husband has encouraged me throughout our marriage so we are close, our family life is close, and we all share in thriving on a creative existence. I paint portraits, and other subjects, write, illustrate, sculpt. It's a good life, and there never is enough time, but that's what makes tomorrow something to look forward to. There are trials in between that fall into focus because time helps one to accept, adapt or compromise.

"We consider being parents the most creative, challenging happening in life. We also consider what we, as individuals, create to be challenging, and one doesn't know if the fruits of labor are successful until the work is completed.

"From finite to infinite we are but a small particle wondering a lifetime about those words and all that is in between."

FOR MORE INFORMATION SEE: Meriden Record, July 10, 1963, July 23, 1963; *Hartford Courant,* August 11, 1963; *Elementary English,* November, 1966; Anne Altshuler, *Books That Help Children Deal with a Hospital Experience,* U.S. Dept. of Health, 1974.

THISTLETHWAITE, Miles 1945-

PERSONAL: Born September 23, 1945, in Cambridge, England; son of Frank and Jane (Hosford) Thistlethwaite; married Philippa Lewis (a picture researcher), January 2, 1975. *Education:* Attended Westminster School, England, 1964; Saint John's College, Cambridge, England, M.A., 1969. *Home:* 81 Charlotte Street, London, W.1, England. *Agent:* Laura Cecil, 10 Exeter Mansions, 106 Shaftsbury Avenue, London W.1, England.

CAREER: International Computers Ltd., London, England, computer consultant, 1970-76.

MILES THISTLETHWAITE

■ (From *Storm and Other English Riddles* translated by Kevin Crossley-Holland. Illustrated by Miles Thistlethwaite.)

ILLUSTRATOR: Translated by Kevin Crossley-Holland, *Storm and Other Old English Riddles*, Macmillan, 1970; Ruth Marris, *The Singing Swans and Other Stories*, Heinemann, 1975.

SIDELIGHTS: "Basically interested in printmaking. Not having been to art school, thought that illustrating would help me to learn to draw, which it has."

TINKELMAN, Murray 1933-

PERSONAL: Born April 2, 1933, in Brooklyn, N.Y.; son of Nathen and Sylvia (Tisman) Tinkelman; married Carol Greenstein, April 7, 1957; children: Ronni, Susan. *Education:* Attended Brooklyn Museum Art School, Brooklyn, N.Y., two years; Cooper Union, New York, N.Y., two years. *Politics:* Independent. *Religion:* Independent Jewish. *Home:* 75 Lakeview Avenue, West, Peekskill, N.Y. 10566. *Office:* Parsons School of Design, 2 West 13th St., New York, N.Y.

CAREER: Parsons School of Design, New York, N.Y., associate chairman, department of illustration, 1962—. Guest lecturer at various art schools. *Military service:* U.S. Army, 1951-53. *Member:* Society of Illustrators. *Awards, honors:* "Artist of the Year" awarded by the Artists Guild of New York; Society of Illustrators, gold medal, 1965; New York Art Directors Club, gold medal, 1970, silver medal, 1974; Society of Publication Designers, gold and silver medal, 1973.

ILLUSTRATOR: Pigeon Flight, Harper, 1962; *"Me,"* Crowell-Collier, 1964; *The Love for Three Oranges,* Putnam, 1966; *Prehistoric Man,* St. Martin's, 1971; *At the Center of the World,* Macmillan, 1973; *The Arctic and the Antarctic: What Lives There,* Coward, 1975; *Outer Space: What's Out There,* Coward, 1975; *Sharks,* Four Winds, 1976; *What's in the Names of Wild Animals,* Coward, 1976; *The Coral Reef: What Lives There,* Coward, 1977.

SIDELIGHTS: "Illustration is my passion. It is my career and hobby as well. I collect original illustrations (American) and have an extensive collection. I also initiated a new course at Parsons dealing with the history of illustration. I have been influenced by everybody from A. Durer to Walt Disney."

FOR MORE INFORMATION SEE: American Artist, October, 1970; *Idea,* #90, 1968, #129, 1975; *Art Direction* Magazine, May, 1974.

MURRAY TINKELMAN

The great bird rose to the sky, swooped and rose again, his wing tips cutting mountains and rivers, canyons and mesas. ■ (From *At the Center of the World* by Betty Baker. Illustrated by Murray Tinkleman.)

LUCILLE WOOD TROST

TROST, Lucille Wood 1938-

PERSONAL: Born November 4, 1938, in Candor, New York; daughter of Stiles Wood and Alice (an office manager; maiden name, Keim) Wood; married Charles H. Trost (a biologist), June 18, 1960; children: Scott A. *Education:* Pennsylvania State University, B.S., 1960; University of Florida, M.S., 1963; Union Graduate School, Ph.D., 1975. *Home:* 225 North Lincoln, Pocatello, Idaho 83201.

CAREER: Free-lance writer, 1964—. Westminster College, Salt Lake City, Utah, assistant professor of behavioral science and director of human relations program. *Member:* National Organization for Women (president of the Pocatello chapter). *Awards, honors:* Graduate Fellowship, University of Florida Medical School, 1961; Grand Prize in Pomona Valley (Cal.) writers contest for the article "A Grain of Sand," 1965; Children's Book Council and National Science Teachers Association selected *Lives and Deaths of a Meadow* as an outstanding science book for children, 1973.

WRITINGS—Juvenile books, except as noted: *Coping with Crib-Size Campers* (adult), Stackpole, 1968; *Biography of a Cottontail*, Putnam, 1971; *A Cycle of Seasons: Little Brown Bat*, Addison-Wesley, 1971; *A Cycle of Seasons: The Fence Lizard*, Addison-Wesley, 1972; *Lives and Deaths of a Meadow*, Putnam, 1973; *The Amazing World of American Birds*, Putnam, 1975; *Broken Ashes* (adult), Branden Press, 1977. Poetry and articles published in a variety of magazines.

WORK IN PROGRESS: "Owl Research Book," for Messner.

SIDELIGHTS: "I consider working for the rights of children in general and humanizing education, of vital concern. I also am concerned with increasing awareness and responsibility of all humans to/for the welfare of others and for themselves. I want to understand and transmit understandings of ways all people may develop to their highest potentials of intellectual/emotional development."

UNSTEAD, R(obert) J(ohn) 1915-

PERSONAL: Born November 21, 1915, in Deal, Kent, England; son of Charles Edmond and Elizabeth (Nightingale) Unstead; married Florence Margaret Thomas (her husband's secretary), March 15, 1917; children: Judith, Mary, Susan. *Education:* Goldsmiths' College, University of London, student, 1934-36. *Religion:* Church of England. *Home:* "Reedlands," Lakeside, Thorpeness, Suffolk, England.

CAREER: Schoolmaster in St. Albans, England, 1936-46; headmaster in Letchworth, England, 1947-57; self-employed author, 1957—. Director, R. J. Unstead Publications Ltd. *Military service:* Royal Air Force, 1940-46; became flight lieutenant. *Member:* Society of Authors and National Book League (both London).

WRITINGS—All published by A. & C. Black, except as indicated: *Cavemen to Vikings*, 1953; *The Middle Ages*,

Let us spend a summer's day at Wentworth Castle. ■ (From *Living in a Castle* by R.J. Unstead. Illustrated by Victor Ambrus.)

1953; *Tudors and Stuarts*, 1954; "English for Every Day" series, three books, 1954; *Queen Anne to Elizabeth II*, 1955; *Looking at History: Britain from Cavemen to the Present Day* (contains *Cavemen to Vikings*, *The Middle Ages*, *Tudors and Stuarts*, and *Queen Anne to Elizabeth II*), 1955, Macmillan (New York), 1956, 3rd edition, A. & C. Black, 1966, new edition, 1975; *People in History*, Book I: *From Caractacus to Alfred*, 1955, Book II: *From William the Conqueror to William Caxton*, 1955, Book III: *Great Tudors and Stuarts*, 1956, Book IV: *Great People of Modern Times*, 1956, published in America in one volume as *People in History: From Caractacus to Alexander Fleming*, Macmillan, 1957; *Teaching History in the Junior School*, 1956, 3rd edition, 1963; *A History of Houses*, 1958; *Travel by Road Through the Ages*, 1958, 2nd edition, 1969; *Looking at Ancient History*, 1959, Macmillan (New York), 1960.

(Editor with William Worthy, and contributor) *Black's Children's Encyclopaedia*, 1961; *Monasteries*, Dufour, 1961, 2nd edition, A. & C. Black, 1970; *Some Kings and Queens*, Odhams, 1962, Follett, 1967; *England: A History*, Book I: *The Medieval Scene, 787-1485*, 1962, Book II: *Crown and Parliament, 1485-1688*, 1962, Book III: *The Rise of Great Britain: 1688-1837*, 1963, Book IV: *The Century of Change, 1837-Today*, 1963; *Royal Adventurers*, Odhams, 1963, Follett, 1967; *Men and Women in History*, Book I: *Heroes and Saints*, 1964, Book II: *Princes and Rebels*, 1964, Book III: *Discoverers and Adventurers*, 1965, Book IV: *Great Leaders*, 1966; *Early Times: A First History from Cavemen to the Middle Ages*, 1965; *Britain in the Twentieth Century*, 1966;

Kings and Queens in World History (contains *Some Kings and Queens* and *Royal Adventurers*), Odhams, 1966; *The Story of Britain*, 1969, Thomas Nelson (New York), 1970; (with W. F. Henderson) *Homes in Australia*, 1969.

British Castles, Crowell, 1970 (published in England as *Castles*, A. & C. Black, 1970); *My World*, Herder, 1970; *Transport in Australia*, 1970; *Pioneer Home Life in Australia*, 1971; *Living in a Medieval City*, 1971; *Living in a Castle*, 1971; *Living in a Medieval Village*, 1971; *Living in a Crusader Land*, Addison-Wesley, 1971; *A History of the English-Speaking Peoples*, eight books, Macdonald & Co., 1971-74; (editor) *World War One, World War Two*, R. J. Hoare, 1973; *Invaded Island*, Addison-Wesley, 1974; *Kings, Barons and Serfs*, Addison-Wesley, 1974; *Years of the Sword*, Addison-Wesley, 1974; *Struggle for Power*, Addison-Wesley, 1974; *Emerging Empire*, Addison-Wesley, 1974; *Freedom and Revolution*, Addison-Wesley, 1974; *Age of Machines*, Addison-Wesley, 1974; *Incredible Century*, Addison-Wesley, 1974; *Living in Aztec Times*, Addison-Wesley, 1974; *Living in the Elizabethan Court*, Addison-Wesley, 1974; *Living in Samuel Pepys' London*, Addison-Wesley, 1974; *Living in the Time of the Pilgrim Fathers*, Addison-Wesley, 1974; *Living in Pompeii*, Addison-Wesley, 1976; *Dictionary of History*, Ward Lock, 1976; *Living in Ancient Egypt*, Addison-Wesley, 1977. General editor, "Looking at Geography" series, five books, A. & C. Black, 1957-60, and "Black's Junior Reference Books," thirty titles, A. & C. Black, 1958-63.

R. J. UNSTEAD

SIDELIGHTS: "As a small boy, I owned exactly three books—*Robinson Crusoe, Tales of Robin Hood* and *Stories of King Arthur and the Knights of the Round Table.* There was, also, a fat book called *World of Adventure* which had belonged to my grandfather; it contained 'eye-witness' accounts of such events as 'The Charge of the Light Brigade,' 'Crossing the Rockies,' 'How We Sacked Panama,' 'The Destruction of Pompeii' and 'Captured by North American Indians.' From these stories, I got my passion for history, a passion that was nearly killed stone dead by the sort of history we learned at grammar school—dates, statutes, Navigation Acts, Habeas Corpus—such fascinating topics. So, when I grew up, having tried my hand at short stories, articles, literary criticism and a novel (the two latter rightly rejected), I thought I would like to write books that made history come alive about how people lived their everyday lives, built homes, played games, worked, fought, travelled and enjoyed themselves.

"Luckily for me, my first series for primary children, 'Looking at History,' became a best-seller and has now sold over five million copies. So I was able to give up schoolmastering and go to live by a lake in Suffolk, near the sea, where I have gone on writing history books for the past fifteen years—is it fifty or fifty-five books so far?

"One of the best rewards to a children's writer is the arrival of 'fan' letters from all over the world, from Kenya and New Zealand to Manchester and New Mexico. One of my favourites came from Johnny H. of Long Beach, California, who wrote, 'I want to ask you three questions: how come you write all these history books? Where do you get the information from? How do you know it's true?' "

FOR MORE INFORMATION SEE: *Best Sellers,* February 15, 1971.

WALKER, Stephen J. 1951-

PERSONAL: Born May 5, 1951, in Seattle, Wash.; son of William H. (a designer-engineer) and Jean (Wilson; an accountant) Walker; married Jennifer Leila Carroll (a ballet dancer), May 23, 1976. *Education:* Attended University of Washington, 1968-72. *Mailing address:* 2210 104th Southeast, Bellevue, Wash. 98004.

CAREER: City of Seattle, Wash., resident artist, 1975. Mayflower Van Lines, Seattle, Wash., truckdriver, 1970-72; Hopkins Engineering, Seattle, Wash., designer, 1972-73. *Exhibitions:* Main Street Gallery, Seattle, Wash., 1971-72; Panaca Gallery, Bellevue, Wash., 1973; Penryn Gallery, Seattle, Wash., 1975-76; Domed Stadium Show, Farris Gallery, Seattle, Wash., 1976; Artist in the City Show, Seattle Art Museum Modern Art Pavilion, Seattle, Wash., 1976.

ILLUSTRATOR: Nanine Valen, *The Drac: French Tales of Dragons and Demons,* Scribner, 1975. Contributing artist to United Nations *Interdependent, National Lampoon,* and *Head.*

WORK IN PROGRESS: *Concise History of Dragons* (possible title).

SIDELIGHTS: "I have studied the arts most of my life, and valued its pursuit and peculiar rewards above other interests. It is experimental communication and as such has the capacity to deal with concepts not yet defined in standardized terminologies and to explore them in greater latitude than would otherwise be possible.

STEPHEN J. WALKER

Finally he went mad and ran about the moor yelling, "What do you want of me, damned spirit?"
And that is how they found him next morning, running round and round, screaming at the
Lady, who was not to be seen nor heard by then. ■ (From *The Drac French Tales of Dragons*
and Demons by Felice Holman and Nanine Valen. Drawings by Stephen Walker.)

"I have worried about inane things such as how to sign a painting without altering the composition and have experimented with random qualities such as edibility, but ultimately I think it is the artist's intensity of concentration and positive communication that matter more than the particular technique or medium.

"By positive communication I mean effectiveness as well as karma. In reality galleries and museums draw a fairly narrow audience, so I have directed my energies toward billboard murals and mobile sculptures, publishing and broadcasting mediums.

"Children's books is one of the finest of existing art forms and one of the most generous and sympathetic with its audience. Ernest Shepard was one of the first artists whose work I admired and sought to learn from, having been inspired by his genuinely charming drawings which I encountered in children's books. Later I discovered H. Ford and Arthur Rackham.

"I have long wanted to illustrate a children's book myself; outlined ideas, wrote sections, improved my illustrations and was never quite satisfied with any of them, but I have one in progress, a picture history of dragons and how through negligent management they have become extinct.

"Extraneously, I have done a lot of set and costume design; rowed with the University of Washington and now compete with club crew teams. Raced a seven-litre hydroplane with my father and brother, third national was best season; later Formula F with Hopkins."

WHITE, T(erence) H(anbury) 1906-1964 (James Aston)

PERSONAL: Born May 29, 1906, in Bombay, India; died January 17, 1964, in Piraeus, Greece; son of Garrick Hanbury and Constance Edith Southcote (Aston) White. *Education:* Queens' College, Cambridge, B.A. (first class honors), 1928.

CAREER: Teacher at Stowe School in England, resigning at the age of thirty to devote his time to writing. *Member:* British Falconers' Club.

WRITINGS—Fiction, except as noted: *Loved Helen, and Other Poems,* Chatto & Windus, 1929; *The Green Bay Tree; or, The Wicked Man Touches Wood,* Heffer, 1929; (with Ronald M. Scott) *Dead Mr. Nixon,* Cassell, 1931; (under pseudonym James Aston) *First Lesson: A Novel,* Chatto & Windus, 1932, Knopf, 1933; (under pseudonym James Aston) *They Winter Abroad: A Novel,* Viking, 1932, reissued under author's real name, Chatto & Windus, 1969; *Darkness at Pemberley,* Gollancz, 1932, Century, 1933; *Farewell Victoria,* Collins, 1933, H. Smith & R. Haas, 1934, new edition, Putnam, 1960; *Earth Stopped; or, Mr. Marx's Sporting Tour,* Collins, 1934; *Gone to Ground: A Novel,*

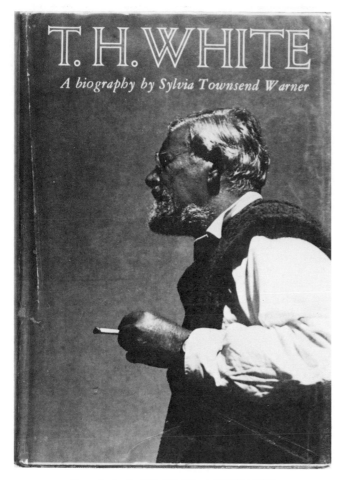

From the book: T.H. WHITE: A BIOGRAPHY

Collins, 1935; *Song through Space, and Other Poems,* Lincoln Williams, 1935.

The Sword in the Stone (Book-of-the-Month Club selection), Collins, 1938, Putnam, 1939, reissued, Collins, 1972; *The Witch in the Wood,* Putnam, 1939; *The Ill-Made Knight,* Putnam, 1940; *Mistress Masham's Repose* (Book-of-the-Month Club selection; illustrated by Fritz Eichenberg), Putnam, 1946, reissued, Heinemann, 1968; *The Elephant and the Kangaroo,* Putnam, 1947, reissued, J. Cape, 1966; *The Master: An Adventure Story,* Putnam, 1957 [adaptations for children by Vincent Whitcombe, Blackie & Son, 1967; Arthur J. Arkley (illustrated by Robert Micklewright), Nelson, 1969]; *The Once and Future King,* Putnam, 1958, reissued, Berkley Publishing, 1969 (contains *The Sword in the Stone, The Queen of Air and Darkness, The Ill-Made Knight,* and *The Candle in the Wind*); *Verses,* Alderney, 1962.

Nonfiction: *England Have My Bones,* Macmillan, 1936; *Burke's Steerage; or, The Amateur Gentleman's Introduction to Noble Sports and Pastimes,* Collins, 1938; *The Age of Scandal: An Excursion through a Minor Period,* Putnam, 1950, reissued, Penguin, 1964; *The Goshawk,* J. Cape, 1951, Putnam, 1952, new edition, Longmans, Green, 1973; *The Scandalmonger,* Putnam, 1952; (editor and translator) *The Book of Beasts: A Translation from a Latin Bestiary of the 12th Century,* Putnam, 1954, reissued, 1960; *The Godstone and the Blackymor* (illustrated by Edward Ardizzone), Put-

nam, 1959; *America at Last: The American Journal of T. H. White,* Putnam, 1965; *The White/Garnett Letters,* edited by David Garnett, Viking, 1968.

Author of the periodical publication, *Terence White's Verse-Reel,* 1939.

ADAPTATIONS—Movies and filmstrips: "The Sword in the Stone" (motion picture), Walt Disney Productions, 1963; "The Sword in the Stone" (filmstrips; both captioned and sound versions, each with teacher's guide), Walt Disney Educational Materials, 1973; "Camelot" (motion picture), adaptation of *The Once and Future King,* starring Richard Harris, Vanessa Redgrave, and Franco Nero, Warner Brothers, 1967; "Camelot" (filmstrip), Educational Audio Visual, 1968.

Plays: Alan Jay Lerner, librettist, "Camelot" (music by Frederick Loewe; first produced in New York at the Majestic Theater, December 3, 1960; directed by Moss Hart; starring Richard Burton, Julie Andrews, Robert Goulet, and Roddy McDowell), Random House, 1961.

SIDELIGHTS: **May 29, 1906.** Born Terence Hanbury White in Bombay, India, an only child. Goaded into marriage near age thirty, his mother threatened to marry the next man who offered, and did. The marriage was a catastrophe. "My parents loathed each other and were separated; divorced, when I was about fourteen or so.

"[When I was a child] father made me a wooden castle big enough to get into, and he fixed real pistol barrels beneath its battlements to fire a salute on my birthday, but made me sit in front the first night—that deep Indian night—to receive the salute, and I, believing I was to be shot, cried. . . .

"There was a great deal of shooting in the air in those days. I am told that my father and mother were to be found wrestling with a pistol, one on either side of my cot, each claiming that he or she was going to shoot the other and himself or herself, but in any case, beginning with me. If I woke up during these scenes, the censor of my mind has obliterated them as too terrible, but I believe they happened. It was not a safe kind of childhood." [Sylvia Townsend Warner, *T. H. White,* Viking, 1967.[1]]

His aunt recalled: "My husband and I stayed with my brother-in-law and his wife in Karachi when Terence was about two years old. Even at that time things were not very happy in the marital line. My sister-in-law was of an extremely jealous nature and if the little boy showed affection for his father, climbing on his lap or asking if he could go out with him, she at once tried to provide some counter-action. She dismissed the ayah [a servant] of whom he was extremely fond simply (she admitted this) because children 'must not prefer to go out with the ayah to staying with their parents.' The same insane jealousy prompted her to reprimand Terence when he wanted to play with Chota, a little native boy attendant, instead of listening to some music which she was playing.

"I don't want you to think that the fault was all with my sister-in-law. There were many things to put up with on either side."[1]

Of his mother he wrote: "She was clever and intelligent and wildly imaginative. You never knew who she was being—Joan of Arc on Monday, Cleopatra on Tuesday, Florence Nightingale on Wednesday. I adored her passionately until I was about eighteen, except for the time when I forgot all about her because she was in India and I was with my grandparents. I didn't get much security out of her. Either there were the dreadful parental quarrels and spankings of me when I was tiny or there were excessive scenes of affection during which she wooed me to love her—not her to love me. It was my love that she extracted, not hers that she gave. I've always thought she was sexually frigid, which was maybe why she thrashed it out of me. Anyway, she managed to bitch up my loving women. She made me dote on her when I was at school.

"She had a way of grinding her teeth."[1]

1912. About this time he was left in the charge of his maternal grandparents. "For six years I grew straight and rampaged and was protected.

"I was brought up with three cousins, two girls and a boy, grandchildren, also. Oh, the Christmas trees in the conservatory, and the antlers and weapons in the hall (each weapon had done a murder, or so I was given to understand, since the weapon of a murderer used to become the Judge's perquisite in India), and oh, the dining-room lift which we worked perpetually, and my own lovely playroom on the top floor (chock-full of soldiers, guns, forts, and zeppelins on strings) and my tortoise in the garden.

"Contemporary photographs show a fat little boy in an Eton suit too tight for him, with rather thick lips. It was taken to send to my mother in India, and she wrote back that my lips were growing *sensual*. I was to hold them in, with my teeth if necessary. Since then I have been ashamed of my lips and now wear them concealed by moustache and beard."[1]

1920. His parents were divorced. "This meant that my home and education collapsed about my ears; and ever since I have been arming myself against disaster. This is why I learn. Now, believe it or not, I can shoot with a bow and arrow, so when the next atomic bomb is dropped, poor old White will be hopping about in a suit of skins shooting caribou or something with a bow and arrow. I have made a list of some of the things which my compulsive sense of disaster has made me excel at. I won a prize for flying aeroplanes about thirty years ago. I can plough with horses. I used to ride show jumpers; I have taught myself to be a falconer. One of the odder things I have done is to learn to go down in diving suits—the old brass hat diving suit. I have had to learn to sail. I swim fairly well. I was a good shot before I took to spectacles—clay pigeons and geese and things of that sort. Fishing, I was a very good fisherman. I used to drive fast cars—God knows why. I had to be good at games, I had to be able to win at darts (in English public houses you throw darts against a board for drinks). I had to teach myself not to be clumsy.

"Compensating for my sense of inferiority, my sense of danger, my sense of disaster, I had to learn to paint even, and not only to paint—oils, art, and all that sort of thing—but to build and mix concrete and to be a carpenter and to saw and screw and put in a nail without bending it. Not only did I have to be physically good at things, I had to excel with my head as well as with my body and hands. I had to get first-class honours with distinction at the University. I had to be a

WHITE, age about thirteen

scholar. I had to learn medieval Latin shorthand so as to translate bestiaries."[1]

September, 1920. Entered Cheltenham College, a public school with a military side for training prospective army entrants. "The housemaster put on a thing called 'Satis.' This meant that you got a card which had to be signed by all your teachers each week. For three signatures of Non Satis you were caned—and even for one you wasted time in writing a large number of 'lines.' Once you were on Satis you had to do too much work, to save yourself, and this diminished your infinitesimal freedom. Then the prefect would put into the house platoon of the O.T.C. He would give you a punishment called Defaulters for each parade. This cut down the spare time to nothing. On top of these sorrows, there were a hundred pettiflogging exactions of time. A prefect would call out 'Orderly,' and all we little creatures had to run to do whatever shopping, etc., he wanted. Then we had to clean our O.T.C. equipment to Guards' standard. Between the upper and nether millstones they were able to crush us into crime.

"My housemaster was a sadistic middle-aged bachelor with a gloomy suffused face. His prefects were lither and brighter copies of himself. He used to walk in front of one up the long corridor, trailing his cane behind him. The prefects used to beat us after evening prayers. I used to pray madly every night (or it seemed like every night): 'Please God, don't let me be beaten tonight.' I knew in a dumb way it was a sexual

greenhouses and
my chair has got flu.
    There, I feel *slightly* better.
I will draw a picture and
feel better still

love from Tim.

T. H. WHITE, self-portrait

outrage, though I could not have phrased that charge. You had to go down a long passage to the gymnasium, where you took off your trousers and put on thin white rugger shorts. Then they came down, rattling their canes. All this was done with a kind of deaf-ear turned, a kind of surreptitiousness. It had the effect—unless something earlier had that effect—of turning myself into a flagellant. . . .

"There was just one master who praised and encouraged me to be a writer. His name was C. F. Scott, and I shall be grateful to him till I die."[1]

1925. Entered Queens' College at Cambridge.

February 28, 1932. Was appointed head of the English Department at Stowe. He wrote to a friend: "The only problem is how to support myself when they chuck me out of Stowe. The ideal job is farm labourer, but I am too stupid. I want to leave the upper classes.

"Everybody at Stowe hates and fears me, or everybody that is bound for hell anyway. Unfortunately this includes the headmaster, so that I shan't have that job for long. If I can hang on till I'm thirty, I'll try for the headmastership of a rural grammar school. I think I could bear that. But if only I could plough and sharpen a scythe and so forth. One feels so insecure without possessing any of the basic arts. . . .

"You are quite right in saying I shall never be a failure. Neither of us, now, will ever fail so far as to be successful. But

the real success is to accomplish the first death effectively and early. I am getting on well with it. For me it will mean (1) no more writing (2) no more luxuries like cars and hunting and the upper classes. My motives for writing were never good and life has cured my snobbery. Well, it may not be an advance. One can't tell what it's like to be dead in this way any more than in the other.

"I am not coming to Cambridge just now. Why this is, I can't quite say. It is probably something to do with the fundamental lethargy which I share with Dr. Johnson. When I make plans it costs me such an effort that I can't summon the energy to unmake them. Imagine the agony it must have given Johnson to go to the Hebrides. However, I suppose Boswell bought all the tickets. I wish I had a Boswell."[1]

He was presented with a gift: a red setter female dog he called "Brownie." "I felt vain about this, and accepted the dog graciously. Yes, I can distinctly remember thinking of her as 'the dog,' rather as one thinks of 'the chair' or 'the umbrella.' Setters are beautiful to look at. I had a beautiful motor car and sometimes I wore a beautiful top hat. I felt that 'the dog' would suit me nearly as nicely as the hat did. In this cheap, brutish and insensitive spirit, I embarked upon her great romance."[1]

1934. *Earth Stopped* published.

1935. *Gone to Ground* published.

March, 1935. Ran his car, a Bentley, into a cottage containing two old people sleeping in bed. "Several pleasant legends have begun to grow up about the accident. The first legend says that the Bentley had to be jacked up in order to extricate the old man's beard: the second that he slowly got up, put on his trousers, called his daughter and said, 'I think there is somebody trying to get in.'"[1]

October, 1935. He wrote a friend that he was anxious to leave his post at Stowe: "The advantages are that it would rescue me from here, and give me a chance of seeing a bit of the world while I am still young.

."The disadvantages are that I am not sure whether I want to see the world. I get on very well in England.

"I am doing exactly three full-time jobs at the moment (a) being psychoanalysed (b) being an author (c) being a schoolmaster. As a relaxation I am learning to be a farmer."[1]

"Brownie," his sole companion, became ill with distemper. "She had decided to die.

"She had had it for a day before I noticed, but when I did notice, the miracle happened all at once in my heart. Something in her dying look at last penetrated my thick skull. I wrapped her up in the best eiderdown; I bought bottles of brandy and port and stuff to make junket. I had a veterinary surgeon every day and even a human doctor twice, and I sat up beside her, day and night, with hot water bottles, for a week. She got rennet every two hours with a teaspoon of brandy, and I told her over and over again that if she would not die I would not keep hawks any more, or go to cinemas or to dances or to any place where she could not go as well.

"But I couldn't stop her. She got weaker and weaker, and it was awful to hear her breathe, and the doctor and the vet were useless, and you could hardly feel her heart. At last came a minute when I said:

" 'In a quarter of an hour she will be dead.'

"Then I said: 'Well, there is nobody left in it but me and Death! We will fight it out. I can't possibly make her any worse, so I will at least do something to see if I can make her better. . . .'

"I gave her half a human dose, which burned her weak throat, but she was too feeble to cough it up. When the quarter of an hour was up, she stood up on her shaky legs and was sick. The next time the whey came round she actually drank it, instead of having to have it poured down her throat.

"That night she suddenly ran out into the darkness, or rather tottered out, and vanished. It was pitch dark. I stayed for hours calling her and walking about the wood with candles, but I could not find her and she did not come back. At last I knew she had died in a ditch, so I went back to the house and cried myself to sleep, but I got up again at dawn, and went to look for her body. I was calling and looking when she staggered out of the wood, not quite sure who she was or who I was, and I carried her home in floods of tears, but they were quite needless. She was cured."

January 14, 1938. He wrote to a friend: "I have £41 in the bank. No book has been published since the last you heard of—England H.M.B.—but there is one in the press. I think it is one of my better books, so probably nobody else will. It is a preface to Malory. Do you remember I once wrote a thesis on the Morte d'Arthur? Naturally I did not read Malory when writing the thesis on him, but one night last autumn I got desperate among my books and picked him up in lack of anything else. Then I was thrilled and astonished to find (a) that the thing was a perfect tragedy, with a beginning, a middle and an end implicit in the beginning, and (b) that the characters were real people with recognizable reactions which could be forecast. Anyway, I somehow started writing a book. It is not a satire. Indeed, I am afraid it is rather warm-hearted—mainly about birds and beasts. It seems impossible to determine whether it is for grown-ups or children. It is more or less a kind of wish-ful-filment of the things I should like to have happened to me when I was a boy.

"I have also written a book called *Burke's Steerage* or the *Amateur Gentleman's Introduction to Noble Sports and Pastimes*. It is a short, cheap thing, doing for sports what Cornford's *Microcosmographia Academica* did for your damned university. But it is not good.

"Writing books is a heartbreaking job. When I write a good one it is too good for the public and I starve, when a bad one, you and Mary are rude about it. This *Sword in the Stone* (forgive my reverting to it—I have nobody to tell things to) *may* fail financially through being too good for the swine. It has (I fear) its swinish Milne-ish parts (but, my God, I'd gladly be a Milne for the Milne money) but it is packed with accurate historical knowledge and good allusive criticism of chivalry (I made the fox-hunting comparison with some glee) which nobody but you will notice."[1]

June 13, 1938. His diary entry:

WHITE, with his bust of Hadrian

"CREDIT

"I have a cottage at 5/- a week, and it is a very beautiful one, but I don't own it and can't lease it.

"I have credit until July 1st at the White Horse in Silverstone, at the Tingewick Co-operative Society, at Harrison's Stores Buckingham, at Markhams (iron-mongers), Busby (Market gardener), Smith's (Bookseller), Boots (Chemists), and I could probably get credit at some more.

"I have had enough to eat.

"I have a mother living, but apparently imbecile through what seems to be paranoia, a father, judicially separated from that mother, whom I have not seen for sixteen years, a red setter bitch that I love more than anything, a little owl (athene noctua) whose life I have saved if she lives, a tawny owl (strix aluco) about six weeks old called Silvia Daisy Pouncer, and a dozen set traps to feed them with.

"My cottage is furnished with several thousand books. I know one great man, David Garnett.

"In the garden I have a dozen delphiniums, two dozen hollyhocks, some dahlias, golden rod, Michaelmas daisies, chrysanthemums, nasturtiums, eight guineas worth of flowering shrubs, two peach trees, two fig trees, six sumacs, four cherries, two apples, two plums, some redhot pokers, lilies, spring bulbs, irises and geraniums and salvia, two rockeries in good trim and twenty pole of lawn mainly just sown and doing well. There is also a dovecot without any doves in it.

"I have my faculties.

"DEBIT

"I can see, feel, smell, touch and hear: but there is no wife or child to see, etc.

"I owe the bank £67, and they will not let me owe them more. There is no capital at all.

"I have consumption, or was once locked in a consumptive home for six months, and I drink much too much.

"Nevertheless, I look healthy enough to be conscripted or shamed into volunteering for the next massacre of innocents.

"My gum boots make my feet sweat."[1]

December 1, 1938. A diary entry at the age of thirty-two:

> "Of hapless father hapless son
> My birth was brutally begun,
> And all my childhood o'er the pram
> The father and the maniac dam
> Struggled and leaned to pierce the knife
> Into each other's bitter life.
> Thus bred without security
> Whom dared I love, whom did not flee?"[1]

February 22, 1939. Traveled to Ireland, where he lived for the next six years in the house of a family called McDonagh. "Meath and Louth are what you might get if you brought Norfolk to the boil—only all the fields are much smaller. A country of bubbles: you can see sixteen small hills wherever you stand. Mrs. McDonagh says that fairies are so high, holding her hand two or three feet from the ground. Quite possibly, for the country is on that scale also. Mrs. McDonagh has twice heard the banshee. Mrs. McDonagh's house: a beautiful 18th-century structure now painted pink, standing in seventy acres of land. The mattress is of straw; outside sanitation; oil lamps; hundreds of cheap religious pictures. Yet, the chairs and sideboard are Chippendale, the spoons solid silver, early Victorian; I drink from Bristol glass. Mrs. McDonagh says every day: 'You will get a fish today, *please God*.' This is a prayer, passionately genuine and spoken with intensity. . . .

"We spend endless pains in painting our houses and iron-works with gay colours—no houses are so clean and often painted as the Irish, and in no country are the iron railings so often and so defiantly coated with the wildest shades—but they all fall down quite soon. My own love of vermilions and frightful clashes is evidently inherited from my father's side. It is from him that I got the fierce enthusiasm for painting all the woodwork in my cottage an unsuitable shade of blue. Then I abandon the cottage to mildew and corruption, and all the blue peels off, and no doubt, the whole thing will burn to the ground."[1]

1939. *The Sword in the Stone* chosen as a Book-of-the-Month publication in the United States.

May 5, 1939. "I have very little news. I have finished the second volume of my Arthur series. It is called *The Witch in the Wood,* and I am bringing it over to England next week. I shall only spend a couple of days there, invest a little money, get rid of the book, and fetch my car. Then it will be back to Erin. My father was a Gael.

"I have made up my mind about this war at last. I am not going to fight in it. You Anglo-Normans can do as you please, but I am a Bard, and, according to the convention of Druim Ceat (A.D. 590) my person is inviolable. (Also I ought to be immune from taxes, but the Inland Revenue have overlooked this.)

"Seriously, I shall refuse to fight or run. My most important business is to finish my version of Malory, and so I shall tell any tribunal which sits on me. I cannot finish it if dead; I am the only person who can finish it. I have been at it unconsciously ever since I was at Cambridge, when I wrote a thesis on Malory; anybody can throw bombs."[1]

He decided to leave "Brownie" behind during this trip. "I think it may be good for her to be gently introduced to abandonment in case European war or some other act of God may make such an abandonment necessary and final in the future. . . .

"My mother was (is) a woman for whom all love had to be dependent. She chases away from her her husband, her lover and her only son. All these fled from her possessive selfishness, and she was left to extract her need of affection from more slavish minds. She became a lover of dogs. This meant that the dogs had to love her. I have inherited this vice."[1]

June 25, 1939. He drew up another one of his balance sheets:

"CREDIT

"1. I have written offering £45 a month for Sheskin Lodge, Co. Mayo, in September. This has two or three miles of the Owenmore and 10,000 bad acres of grouse, one livingroom, three double bedrooms, two single bedrooms, bathroom, lavatory and kitchens, etc. We might get between six and sixty salmon, and between twenty and fifty brace of grouse, according to the weather and season.

"2. I have written offering £4 for a pair of eyass peregrines, a falcon and a tiercel, and arranging for them to be sent by air to Baldonnel Airport.

"3. I have been offered the mastership of the Kill Harriers and accepted them provisionally.

"4. I go to the Trim schoolmaster every week for an evening, and do an hour's prep every morning, at my Irish.

"5. I have not drunk anything for a week, and hope to stay teetotal for three months, by which time I may have learned to drink in moderation.

"[Added in pencil], 'NOTE: I did not.'

"DEBIT

"The quenchless fear of war, which would smash all these innocent eccentricities and which, also, robs profits in the bookselling world even when it hasn't broken out.

"I had thought that as I was a Book-of-the-Month choice, and the author of the next Walt Disney full-length, and was earning £2,000 a year in America (which is high pay for a writer), and as I had also taken First Class Honours in Cambridge, I could do better for the 'war effort' than run about with a bayonet."[1]

■ (From the movie "Camelot," copyright © 1973 by Warner Bros., starring Franco Nero, Richard Harris, and Vanessa Redgrave.)

July 22, 1939. In a letter he wrote: "This drink business. Like most humourous writers (I suppose I am a humorous writer, even if I can't spell it) my life is in fact a melancholy one. I suppose nearly everybody thinks their lives are especially unhappy, so I am no exception to the rule. I used to drink because of my troubles, until the drink became an added trouble. Then I thought I had quite enough without it, so I stopped. After the first month I tried one Sunday to see if I could drink in moderation like any normal person, but I found I couldn't, so I had to stop altogether. If I ever find that I can take a normal sup I shall go back to it out of politeness to other people, but it seems an illogical thing to me to take intoxicants unless you want to be intoxicated. There has been a good deal of drink going on in my family for some generations. Well, there it is, anyway. The one bright spot in the whole melancholy business is that I can honestly say I don't feel any better for giving it up, and now I never go to sleep before 4 a.m.

"What a comfort to think that Tolstoy wrote *War and Peace* seven times. I bet he re-wrote the last chapters most of all, and that is why they are quite unreadable. *The Witch in the Wood* is nearly sending me mad."[1]

September 1, 1939. "In Ballina, at the Imperial Hotel, we heard at 10:30 this morning that war had broken out between Germany and Poland. We got a wireless, which doesn't work much, and came out to Sheskin, where I spent one of the most miserable days of my life. . . . 'I only wanted to keep quiet and be alone and behave as if I were already dead.'

"In Poland, living souls are being blown to atoms. The English wireless has fled from London to Scotland: it talks and talks about regulations for calling people up and hiding lights and buying food. On it Chamberlain talks of war. Meanwhile we, in our outpost of the spirit with nothing but heather to see, have no longer the heart to fly the hawks at all. They get fed listlessly at the block once more, and the wireless finally packs up. Why mention the hawks, or ourselves, or anything, or trouble to make these marks with ink? . . .

"It is only in the most highly organized or political creatures (ants, men, microbes) that genuine war is found.

"Why?

"To most other animals our warfare would seem much more deplorable than civil war seems to us."[1]

November 26, 1944. "Brownie is dead. 25.xi.xliv.

"She had a happy life, probably happier than most setters, except that the happier you are the more you want to be happy, so it evens out. Her major troubles were only being allowed to sit in my lap for six hours a day, and things like that.

"She lived fairly long for a working setter. I can't be sure if she was twelve or fourteen, but could make a good guess if I had a copy of *England Have My Bones*.

"She could have lived longer, but for the filthy piece of work that I was on one of my bi-annual trips (for nine hours) to Dublin at the time she had one of her annual attacks. I could have saved her, perhaps. The people here didn't understand her. But it was impossible not to go to Dublin sometimes, since I had our living to earn. This trip was about getting *The Elephant and the Kangaroo* to America. I had to leave her for a few hours every year, or we shouldn't have earned a living at all.

"All the same, I let her down in the end: she had trusted her whole life to me always, and I was not there to save it.

"I had saved it at least twice before, which is something.

"The dead body by my side is not Brownie. But what is? She was a sprite who danced before me through twelve perfect years of love. But she is not that now. It is gone. And the poor dead face is not it either. I have an actual physical feeling in my heart—muscular, not emotional—as if it were going to burst.

"It means that I died last night. All that me is dead, because it was half her.

"It is useless and ignoble to repine about one's lot. Is it any use repining about hers? Whose? The dead body's? The sprite's?

"Might-have-beens are too agonizing, and not practical.

"She was the central fact of my life.

"It is only me who has lost anything. Brownie has lost nothing. For when the self itself is lost, that self cannot lose anything."

"Now I am to begin a new life and it is important to begin it right, but I find it difficult to think straight. It is about whether I am to get another dog or not. I am good to dogs, so from their point of view I suppose I ought. But I might not survive another bereavement like this in twelve years' time, and dread to put myself in the way of it. Or I could get two dogs and breed up vast families of puppies, but what would be the good of that? It would only be an occupation. Brownie was my life and I am lonely for just such another reservoir for my love—not for an occupation. But if I did get such a reservoir it would die in about twelve years and at present I feel I couldn't face that. Do people get used to being bereaved? This is my first time . . .

"The whole and single unnaturalness of the position is that dogs and men have incompatible longevities. Everything else is perfectly natural and I would not have it altered in any respect. I regret nothing about Brownie, except the bitter difference of age. . . .

"I stayed with the grave for a week, so that I could go out twice a day and say, 'Good girl: sleepy girl: go to sleep, Brownie.' It was a saying she understood. I said it steadily. I suppose the chance of consciousness persisting for a week is several million to one, but that was the kind of chance I had to provide for. Then I went to Dublin, against my will, and kept myself as drunk as possible for nine days, and came back feeling more alive than dead.

". . . I bought a puppy bitch. Brownie had taught me so much about setters that it seemed silly to waste the education, so I stuck to them. No setter could ever remind me of her any more than one woman would remind you of another, except in general terms.

"The new arrangement looks like the foetus of a rat, but she has a pedigree rather longer than the Emperor of Japan's. She nibbles for fleas in my whiskers."[1]

March 12, 1945. Sent off the typescripts of *The Elephant and the Kangaroo* and *Mistress Masham's Repose*.

October 9, 1945. "Here I am on the top of an alp in Yorkshire, living alone in a stone haybarn with two dogs and having to carry our rations over stone walls up 1,000 feet in ¼ mile, because there is no road. I am really a sort of Quasimodo, a gargoyle brooding over Swaledale, and the freedom and altitude are giving me delusions of grandeur. I do all the housework and cooking and washing myself, which only leaves me four hours a day for writing. It is lovely. My only neighbours are grouse, of which there are some 2,400. I speak once a day for ten minutes to the woman who supplies me with milk from a farmhouse several hundred feet lower down, but have to go a four-mile walk down the precipice twice a week for shopping, which I carry back in a sack on my back. . . .

"So far I am simply ravished with joy at being Robinson Crusoe at last. It takes eighty minutes to walk to the village and back. On Saturday I carried home, in one load on my back, two gallons paraffin, three lb. paint, five loaves bread, one cauliflower, one box groceries and one chamberpot. . . .

"In the afternoon I walked down to the post-office, then some devil led me to the local pub, the Punch Bowl. They were hospitable, invited me to tea, tried to give me one pound of filleted plaice, one lb. Swaledale cheese, two grapefruit, one lb. dripping. I insisted on paying for these. Drank two double gins. Arranged to have lunch there on Mondays and Thursdays, as it is more convenient to shop in the morning. But I must, must, must regard this as opportunity for food only. If I start boozing, I shall never get any writing done.

"I consider this has been a wasted day. I hate pubs, I hate fiction, I hate gin, I hate people and I hate myself.

"No, I don't hate myself. The fact is that when I am alone with my books and dogs we are the best company in the world, and, if it were not for shopping, I would stay up here all day and every day and be content."[1]

June, 1947. Bought a house in Alderney. "I have bought, but solely as an investment, for about £800, a delicious little Frenchified house in the main *place* of Alderney. I would date it about 1850, but of course, fashions took longer to reach these outposts: consequently it is of a better and (then) old-fashioned period. Say, 1790. It has two immense greenhouses (broken) but with the vines in them. Also orchard, garage space, main drain, cobbled square—almost everything the heart could desire. . . .

"I spend my time like this—half the day mixing concrete, half the day writing books, half the day abusing plumbers, half the day writing to people in Italy or Sweden, half the day taking Killie for walks and half the day getting drunk. You may think there are not so many halves, but in my day there are."[1]

April 17, 1957. "Today, the seventeenth of April, 1957, I finished what I hope is my final revision of *The Once and Future King,* about twenty years after I started it, and I believe and hope it is a great book. It sounds presumptuous to say so, but on a great subject, which is the epic of Britain, you have to write downright badly to make a mess of it.

"It must be twenty years since I started off with Arthur, because I began writing the summer after I left Stowe, at the gamekeeper's cottage in the Ridings, which must have been 1937. Or could it have been 1936? It was a very happy summer, and I was a happy man. I had escaped from being a schoolmaster with £100 in the bank and a promise of something like £300 a year for two years. I was free, like a loose hawk at last, *ferae naturae*. I was training a goshawk.

"I have been a free man for twenty years. People don't realize this when they see me in the streets. They don't know what a rarity they are meeting. I have been free to get up when I want to and eat when I like and live where I like. I could at this moment get into an aeroplane and set up house tomorrow in Timbuctoo. In theory, in theory, in theory. In fact, I am bound hand and foot like everybody else by taxes and passports and sterling areas and immigration quotas and God knows what other filthy bureaucracies. But so is the Archbishop of Canterbury, and than him, who must breakfast at such a time to open that bazaar and be at such another place to attend this or that diocesan conference, I am at least more free."[1]

October, 1958. Hospitalized for a kidney ailment.

1958. *The Once and Future King* acclaimed on both sides of the Atlantic, reached the "Ten Bestsellers List."

1959. The musical "Camelot" based on *The Once and Future King* was announced as a projected Broadway venture in the United States.

October, 1959. "My leg is beginning to pack up, as it does in autumn and spring. I begin to regard myself as a sort of old bore I live with. He has handicaps and hobbies. . . .

"As I get older myself, bits keep falling off, like an old car, but one can't do much about it. In some ways it will be a relief to be dead—no more spare parts to fuss about, and think what a rest too!. . .

"My trouble is that my intelligence is materialistic, agnostic, pessimistic and solitary, while my heart is incurably tender, romantic, loving and gregarious."[1]

December 10, 1960. During the out-of-town previews of "Camelot": "The reviews of the musical have been mixed, but it will survive under its own power. I have pretended to

T. H. WHITE

everybody that I am perfectly satisfied with this new version of my book, as it is a corporate effort which involves many people, some of whom I love, and it is up to me to put a shoulder to the wheel. Financially, I am indifferent to the profits, as I have no kith or kin to spend them on and no ambitions for myself. But I do have a sort of obstinacy come Taxers.

"Julie [Andrews] is as always enchanting beyond words and Richard Burton, who plays Arthur, is a great Shakespearian actor from the Old Vic. I have been totally accepted by every member of the cast and every stage hand—even by Lerner and Loewe themselves—and spend every performance crawling over every corner of the theatre to find out how the wheels go round. If I were less miserable in my private life, I would be a very happy man."[1]

1963-1964. Lecture tour through the United States. "The students of La Salle College gave me, for the last time I shall get it, the stunning applause and affection which makes my heart turn over, and I am miserable that the tour is finished, and I don't want to stop ever ever ever. How will I do now, without the generosity and enthusiasm of youth, and the hospitality of my beloved continent, and the excitement of aeroplanes and trains and cabs and automobiles and even ferry boats? We have not missed a single connection, except through being in hospital, and we have gathered a sort of momentum of travel which does not know how to stop, and all the mountains, deserts, rivers, forests, homes, people, kindnesses, warmth, love . . . yes, love, novelty, discovery, beauty, grandeur, simplicity, seriousness, youth, vigour, enormousness of the United States combine to look over our shoulders and say, Don't go. In spite of the killing struggle, perhaps because of it, I have never been happier in my life."[1]

January, 1964. Sailed for Europe. Visited Spain, Italy, Egypt, and Lebanon, then on to Greece.

January 17, 1964. Died on board the *S.S. Exeter* of an acute coronary disease at the age of fifty-seven. He was buried in Athens, Greece. Two years earlier he had written to a friend: "I think I will go on to Venice and Naples and perhaps do a Byron and never come back any more. I expect to make rather a good death. The essence of death is loneliness, and I have had plenty of practice at this."[1]

His epitaph reads:

> T. H. WHITE
> 1906-1964
> AUTHOR
> WHO
> FROM A TROUBLED HEART
> DELIGHTED OTHERS
> LOVING AND PRAISING
> THIS LIFE

FOR MORE INFORMATION SEE: T. H. White, *America at Last: The American Journal of T. H. White,* Putnam, 1965; Sylvia Townsend Warner, *T. H. White: A Biography,* Viking, 1967; T. H. White, *The White/Garnett Letters,* edited by David Garnett, Viking, 1968; John K. Crane, *T. H. White,* Twayne, 1974; Obituaries—*New York Times,* January 18, 1964; *Illustrated London News,* January 25, 1964; *Newsweek,* January 27, 1964; *Publishers Weekly,* January 27, 1964.

WILLIAMS, Maureen 1951-

PERSONAL: Born August 12, 1951, in Kent, England; daughter of Herbert William (retired) and Eva (Foster; a secretary) Eves; married Gary Williams (a media resources officer), September 4, 1971; children: Thomas Sean. *Education:* Folkestone School of Art, England, 1968-71. *Home and office:* 51 Lansdowne Road, Purley, Surrey, England.

CAREER: Illustrator. Various full and part time office work, 1971-73.

WRITINGS—Self-illustrated: *Bd-Dd,* Macmillan, 1975; *On Safari,* Macmillan, 1975.

Illustrator: *Storytime from Playschool,* Piccalo/BBC, 1974; Southgate St. James, *The Ghost of Beestley Zoo,* Macmillan, 1974; Geranne Leonard, *The Mandarin's Daughter,* Abelard, 1975; *Beginner's Spanish,* Hodder & Stoughton, 1975; Diana Webster, *Pillbeam's Circus,* Macmillan, 1975; *Child's Talk,* Heinneman, in press; *The Blue Book,* Macmillan, in press.

SIDELIGHTS: "It was not my ambition to be an illustrator and although I enjoyed painting and drawing as a small child, I did not develop a major interest. I was, therefore, surprised to find myself being pushed into art school by an enthusiastic art teacher, whose lessons I had always found rather boring.

"I decided to take a three-year vocational graphic design course, which happened to be the first thing suggested. Towards the end of the three years, I specialised in illustration as did most students in that year, mostly due to the influence of an illustration tutor, John Dyke. I was quite convinced that, with a bit of effort, I could become a full-time illustrator. Although I trooped from one publisher to another, nothing was forthcoming. I took a job to fill in time and earn some money.

"When my husband and I moved to London, I received my first commission from Pan Books, *Storytime from Playschool.* After the book was published, other publishers became interested and more commissions followed.

"Out of all the books that I have read as a child, there is only one that has really influenced me as an illustrator. It was a book that I purchased for three pence in a school book sale. I think that I was eight years of age at the time. The title was *Eloise* and it was a large book with plenty of line illustra-

Pilb. You two are very funny, and you look like clowns. Now, am I going to find a policeman? Or are you going to be clowns. ■ (From *Pillbeam's Circus* by Diana Webster. Illustrated by Maureen Williams.)

tions, published in America. The book superbly related the exploits of a noisey little girl who lived at the Plaza Hotel with her nanny. The illustrations were quite unique in that they were totally unlike any I had experienced. They portrayed the more unpolite side of life; the side that was not normally considered suitable material for children's books.

"Humour transcends age and nationality. When observing life, it is possible to see humour in even the most mundane situation. I find a sketch book inhibiting and prefer to make mental notes, as individual situations can then be linked with others and synthesized.

"When I receive the script and brief for a book, I have no trouble in translating words into a mental image which usually is the basis for the start of an illustration. Alternatively, something emerges on paper. Although this latter method is an intuitive process, I can see that my training in design is a great asset, if it is necessary to build up an image.

"My husband has a B.A. in design and is, fortunately or unfortunately, my greatest critic. I hate criticism. I usually go along with his suggestions after a battle.

"I like to work straight onto the artboard and try to avoid doing sheets of roughs. Tracing and retracing reduces the freshness and sparkle of an illustration. I find that redrawing for a previously published book can be difficult if I have seen the original illustrations or if the art editor draws a little rough sketch to show an idea. My creative processes are inhibited.

"I prefer to use a mixed-media approach to give my work more depth. The media I use include pencil, inks, crayons, guache and felt-tip pens. For black and white line drawings, I use a technique of cross hatching and open line.

"A great amount of my work to date has been for the education market. I find this work more rewarding as the books reach and hopefully are enjoyed by, a larger number of children, than if they were only on sale in the book shops. My other interest in the education field is as a part-time teacher."

YANG, Jay 1941-

PERSONAL: Born January 15, 1941, in Taiwan; married Myra Hines (a sales director), May 25, 1973. *Education:* University of Pennsylvania, M.F.A., 1970. *Home:* Box 319, Springglen, New York. *Office:* P. Kaufman, Inc., 261 Fifth Avenue, New York, N.Y. 10016.

CAREER: Designer, illustrator. P. Kaufmann, Inc., New York, N.Y., head designer, 1973—. *Awards, honors:* J. D. Rockefeller III grant.

ILLUSTRATOR: Joy Anderson, *The Pai-Pai Pig*, Harcourt, 1967; Joy Anderson and Jay Yang, *Hai Yin, the Dragon Girl*, Harcourt, 1970; Robert Wyndham, *Tales the People Tell in China*, Messner, 1971; Sid Fleischman, *The Wooden Cat Man*, Little, Brown, 1972.

WORK IN PROGRESS: Chinese anecdotes in the form of a children's book; book on the humor of Chinese superstitions.

SIDELIGHTS: An around-the-world trip for research in 1976.

The Parade! It was the best one Su-Ling had ever seen. There was a band, with cymbals and big brass gongs and bamboo flutes. Lion dancers with red manes danced in and out of the crowd. ■ (From *The Pai Pai Pig* by Joy Anderson. Illustrated by Jay Yang.)

CHARLES ZURHORST

ZURHORST, Charles (Stewart, Jr.) 1913-
(Charles Stewart)

PERSONAL: Surname is pronounced *Zur*-hurst; born December 3, 1913, in Washington, D.C.; son of Charles S. and Edwinetta (Schroeder) Zurhorst; married Esther May McGinnis, August 19, 1936 (divorced, 1950); married Susan Mylroie, June 3, 1951; children: (first marriage) Charles S. III; (second marriage) Craig G. *Education:* St. John's College, Annapolis, Md., student, 1932-33; *Politics:* Independent. *Religion:* Christian. *Home address:* Roque Bluffs, Machias, Me. 04654.

CAREER: Guide and general deputy forest fire warden in Maine woods, 1933-40; press agent for Fulton Lewis Jr.

(radio commentator), 1940-48; producer of "American Forum of the Air" (radio program), 1941-43; public relations consultant to industry, 1948-56; free-lance writer, 1956—. Corporator, Springfield College. *Member:* National Press Club, Overseas Press Club, National Cowboy Hall of Fame.

WRITINGS: Conservation Is a Dirty Word, Books for Business, 1968; *The Conservation Fraud,* Cowles, 1970; *The First Cowboys,* Abelard-Schuman, 1973; *The First Cowboy and Those Who Followed,* Cassell, 1974. Contributor to *Grolier Encyclopedia.* Contributor, sometimes under pseudonym Charles Stewart, to magazines and newspapers, including *Better Camping, Pageant, Continental,* and *New York Times.*

WORK IN PROGRESS: Research for another conservation book and a book on pirates; magazine articles and newspaper features.

SIDELIGHTS: "To me, writing is a business. Some people are automobile mechanics, some are hairdressers, some are clerks or secretaries. I am a writer.

"True, I find my work most enjoyable, but the so-called glamor of being a writer has never impressed me. I have no desire to become a giant in the field of literature. I have no desire to write the great American novel. I have no desire to do a nonfiction exposé that would stun the nation. I want only to be a successful writer who makes his living by writing. The benefits from that alone are ample.

"Perhaps this attitude is due to the fact that, in one sense or another, I have always been a writer, but one who has applied his efforts in many different areas. I have, indeed, written books. I have written short stories. I have written magazine articles. But, I, also, have been a newspaper reporter, a columnist, a radio continuity writer, a ghost writer of sales catalogs and company histories for corporations. Even as a public relations consultant, it was necessary to write, rewrite, or edit publicity releases.

"This has been my writing world, and it is a world I wish more young people would consider entering. They would find it, as I have found it, a very pleasant way to make a living."

SOMETHING ABOUT THE AUTHOR

CUMULATIVE INDEXES, VOLUMES 1-12
Illustrations and Authors

ILLUSTRATIONS INDEX

(In the following index, the number of the volume in which an illustrator's work appears is given *before* the colon, and the page on which it appears is given *after* the colon. For example, a drawing by Adams, Adrienne appears in Volume 2 on page 6, another drawing by her appears in Volume 3 on page 80, and another drawing in Volume 8 on page 1.)

AUTHORS INDEX

(In the following index, the number of the volume in which an author's sketch appears is given *before* the colon, and the page on which it appears is given *after* the colon. For example, the sketch of Aardema, Verna, appears in Volume 4 on page 1).